https://doi.org/10.1142/9789811296000_fmatter

Reviews

"Democracy is under attack. Governments are not fulfilling the expectation of their constituents. The only way for governments to become impactful again and validate their roles as builders of the future, is if they embrace Anticipatory Governance. A government is not an isolated entity, in fact it must embed itself in the business ecosystem, evolving technologies and the international geo-political space. This book of curated chapters is a great starting point to understand skills and practices required for a public sector to embark on that journey. We must review the past, acknowledge the present and move forward shaping a better world for the benefit of all."

H.E. José María Figueres Olsen,
President of Costa Rica: 1994–1998

"It is impossible to overstate the scope and breadth of *Anticipatory Governance: Shaping a Responsible Future*. The book's topics and tools, ranging from foresight, to anticipatory analysis, backcasting, agility, design thinking, and systems thinking, give us means and methods for achieving the goal of the book, 'shaping the future for the intergenerational inclusive benefit of humanity and the planet'. Each of the authors adds insight and perspective that will be extremely valuable to policymakers and global leaders for generations to come."

G. Edward DeSeve, *The Coordinator of the Agile Government Center at the National Academy of Public Administration and The Executive Fellow at the IBM Center for the Business of Government*

"Future governments have two choices for future risks – navigate the future reactively or proactively shape the future. If the latter choice is where you wish to go, this book presents a starting point to understand how governments can begin their journey to transform their public sector. To shape the future, you need anticipatory governance, and the skills transformation for the next generation of leaders needs to be rapid. It is a must-read for all government officials who want to shape a better future for their people and the world we live in."

Mohammed Al Sharhan,
Managing Director, World Government Summit

"The complexity of the highly-connected environments in which governments must act; the acceleration of technological change, with LLM's already employing trillions of parameters, and gene-editing and neurological programming becoming commonplace; the increasing scale of social, economic and political disruption evident nationally, regionally, and globally; the inflection point in the global rules-based order apparent as the 'global South' diverges from the 'West'; and the dislocation of the earth system – climate, oceans and marine and terrestrial biodiversity; all make it clear that industrial-age strategic planning and derivative risk management are no longer fit for purpose.

"Anticipatory governance is a phrase that reflects the need to engage with future uncertainty with an open, enquiring mind; to do the [exceptionally] hard work needed to identify trends, areas of likely conflation and potential inflection; to discern the strategic consequences of these often fractal interactions, and their implications for leadership, systems and skills; and to build into one's government, through collective understanding, a quality of organic resilience that will enable it to survive, and emerge stronger from, the inevitable turbulence to which a complex [partially-]adaptive system will expose it.

"This book, with the laudable aim of 'shaping a responsible future', offers case studies, research and reflections by experienced policymakers and government officials on means to prepare for, and thrive in, these conditions."

Séan Cleary, *Executive Vice-Chair*
Futureworld Foundation, Switzerland

"Today's headlines are replete with terms like 'poly-crisis' or 'perma-crisis' and 'collapsology'. A global pandemic has underscored the fragility and brittleness of current institutions and relationships. The lack of awareness or interest in shared needs and interdependencies relegates challenges like climate change to the margins. Wars rage. No wonder for so many, despair seems to be winning out over hope. And no wonder we are also responding with new ideas, like those in *Anticipatory Governance*. Bravo to the authors for exploring with rigor and courage the need to break with the reductionist, command and control approaches of the past. Experimenting with new foundations for governance, daring to change the conditions of change, is exactly what is needed today. This book is an important contribution to finding ways to govern with humility, creativity, and openness. Preconditions for living in harmony with nature and each other."

Riel Miller, *Senior Fellow, J. Herbert Smith Centre for Technology Management and Entrepreneurship, Deep Change Initiative, Faculty of Engineering, University of New Brunswick (Canada) & former Head of Foresight and Futures Literacy at UNESCO*

Anticipatory Governance

Shaping a Responsible Future

Anticipatory Governance

Shaping a Responsible Future

Edited by

Melodena Stephens
Mohammed Bin Rashid School of Government, UAE

Raed Awamleh
École des Ponts Business School, France

Frederic Sicre
Tardis Advisors, UAE

World Scientific

NEW JERSEY • LONDON • SINGAPORE • BEIJING • SHANGHAI • HONG KONG • TAIPEI • CHENNAI • TOKYO

Published by

World Scientific Publishing Co. Pte. Ltd.

5 Toh Tuck Link, Singapore 596224

USA office: 27 Warren Street, Suite 401-402, Hackensack, NJ 07601

UK office: 57 Shelton Street, Covent Garden, London WC2H 9HE

Library of Congress Cataloging-in-Publication Data

Names: Stephens, Melodena, editor. | Awamleh, Raed, editor. | Sicre, Frederic, editor.

Title: Anticipatory governance: shaping a responsible future / edited Melodena Stephens, Mohammed Bin Rashid School of Government, UAE, Raed Awamleh, École des Ponts Business School, France, Frederic Sicre, Tardis Advisors, UAE.

Description: New Jersey : World Scientific, [2025] | Includes index.

Identifiers: LCCN 2024038428 | ISBN 9789811295997 (hardcover) | ISBN 9789811296000 (ebook) | ISBN 9789811296017 (ebook other)

Subjects: LCSH: Corporate governance.

Classification: LCC HD2741 .A6475 2025 | DDC 320.6--dc23/eng/20241102

LC record available at https://lccn.loc.gov/2024038428

British Library Cataloguing-in-Publication Data

A catalogue record for this book is available from the British Library.

The front cover design was illustrated by Paul Korfhage (https://paulkorfhage.com/).

For any available supplementary material, please visit
https://www.worldscientific.com/worldscibooks/10.1142/13924#t=suppl

Desk Editors: Aanand Jayaraman/Yulin Jiang

Typeset by Stallion Press
Email: enquiries@stallionpress.com

https://doi.org/10.1142/9789811296000_fmatter

Foreword

The role of Anticipatory Governance has increased in importance since the pandemic. In 2022, when most countries struggled, UAE's GDP grew by 7.6 percent, the highest in 11 years, driven by significant improvements in the non-oil sector with a record-breaking 17 percent growth, reaching more than AED 2.2 trillion for the first time in the history of our country. This positive outlook has continued into 2023, with UAE achieving a record high non-oil trade volume of US$952.93 billion in 2023 (a 12.6 percent increase from the previous year). This is the result of our country's leadership focus on growth, diversification, and good government.

The UAE has systematically embedded foresight at all levels in the governance architecture to build a sustainable economy with a strong focus on creating a society of talent. The road to diversifying the economy and focusing on high-tech sectors has been where dialogue, communities, and the marketplace are brought together. Shaping the future for shared prosperity can only be achieved through the connections of trade and mutual benefit. In the UAE, we are committed to creating a better future for generations to come. We cannot conquer the challenges of today or tomorrow without multilateralism.

As this book illustrates, the work is hard. Governments must be prepared to challenge assumptions and be agile in their approach to future opportunities and, inevitably, crises. We require a skilled public sector where governance is the default, especially as the world embraces unknown challenges at a scope we have never seen before.

This book should be a staple in every library. It is a rich repository of knowledge from authors from around the world who have reflected on critical public sector experiences, so we can take it to the next level. As we go into the future, Anticipatory Governance is a necessity, not an option.

H.E. Abdullah bin Touq Al Marri
Cabinet Member and UAE Minister of Economy

https://doi.org/10.1142/9789811296000_fmatter

Preface

Anticipatory Governance is the systemic process of future shaping built on the understanding that the future is not a continuation of the past or present, thus making foresight a complex task requiring the engagement of the whole of government with its constituents in a constructive and iterative manner to achieve collective intelligence and deliver long-term intergenerational public value for humanity and its planet. Effective anticipatory governance amplifies fundamental properties of agile government and uses its mechanisms to build trust, challenge assumptions, and reach consensus. Moreover, anticipatory governance prepares the ground to absorb and utilize exponential changes, making them more transformative as opposed to merely disruptive. This seismic shift should lead to an urgent rethinking of the ways and means governments and large corporate players formulate strategies, design processes, develop human capital, and shape institutional culture.

From a long-term multigenerational perspective, anticipatory governance is a key component in managing change. Systems thinking is needed to harness our collective intelligence, by tapping into knowledge trapped within nations, organizations, and people. Many of the wicked problems governments and corporations are grappling with, like AI applications and ethics, climate change, refugee migration, education for future skills, or healthcare for all, require a "system of systems" or anticipatory governance.

Yet, no matter how much we invest in foresight and shaping the future, we still need an agile government approach to manage unintended outcomes and people's expectations. Crisis management, which begins with listening to weak signals, sensemaking, intelligence management, reputation enhancement, and public value alignment and delivery, is critical. This book dives into the theory and practice of anticipatory governance and sets the agenda for future research.

https://doi.org/10.1142/9789811296000_fmatter

About the Editors

Prof. Dr. Melodena Stephens is Professor of Innovation and Technology Governance at the Mohammed Bin Rashid School of Government (MBRSG) in Dubai, UAE. She has over three decades of senior management experience in corporate, academic, and government sectors across Asia, Europe, the Americas, and Africa. She consults and trains in strategy, focusing on themes like agile government, Science, Technology, and Innovation (STI), brand-building, and crisis management. Melodena is the founder and executive board member of the Academy of International Business Middle East North Africa (AIBMENA), which fosters teaching and research capacity. AIBMENA was recognized by the Dubai government for its outreach, which has captured organizational memories through 100+ cases. On tech governance, she focuses on AI decision making, metaverse, and synthetic biology, often working with entities like the IEEE SA, the Council of Europe, Agile Nations, and the UAE government. She is passionate about human-centered design thinking and uses it to help clients build better services. Some of her most recent books are *AI Enabled Business: A Smart Decision Kit*, *Agile Government*, and *Business With Purpose: Advancing Social Enterprise*. Melodena is a 2024–25 Senior Fellow and Co-Chair of the Policy Group of The Digital Economist. Melodena loves to write and blogs at www.melodena.com.

Professor Raed Awamleh is a Distinguished Research Fellow at the Center for Policy and Competitiveness (École de Ponts Business School, Paris). Between 2015 and 2024, Professor Awamleh led the Mohammed Bin Rashid School of Government as Dean. He introduced Master programs in Innovation, Public Policy and Public Administration. Also, he developed leadership and executive education programs for government and corporate sectors. He launched the Global Economic Diversification Index and the Dubai Policy Review. Raed advises governments and corporations on strategy, governance, and policy. Amongst his many publications are coauthored books on *Agile Government: Emerging Perspectives in Public Management* (2023), and *Future Governments* (2021). Raed is a regular speaker and panelist at high profile events including the World Government Summit and the OECD's Network of Schools of Governments. He is also a leadership trainer. Formerly, Professor Awamleh was Pro-Vice Chancellor of Middlesex University's (UK) and Dubai Campus Director. Prior to that, he was Dean of Academic Affairs at the University of Wollongong (Australia) in Dubai. His industry experience includes serving as lead assessor for prestigious excellence awards such as King Abdullah II Excellence Award and Dubai Excellence Award. Raed holds a Ph.D. in Management from the University of Mississippi (USA).

Frederic Sicre is a Global Senior Executive with 30 years of experience in international relations and business development for public and private organizations. He spent 16 years at the World Economic Forum and as Managing Director was responsible for Global and Regional Strategies around the world. He subsequently spent over a decade in private equity focused on emerging markets and most recently was an Executive Advisor in the UAE Prime Minister's Office. Fred currently serves as Managing Partner of Tardis Advisors, offering advisory services to CEOs and government leaders in public and corporate affairs, business development, and strategic partnerships. Fred is from Geneva, Switzerland. He holds an MBA from IMD, a Fellowship from Stanford University, and a B.A. from Villanova University in Philadelphia.

https://doi.org/10.1142/9789811296000_fmatter

About the Contributors

Abhishek (Abhi) Balakrishnan has built his career at the intersection of culture and innovation to unlock technology's value at scale and power human ingenuity. He currently works with BCG's Business Model Innovation Team and BrightHouse, collaborating with Fortune 100 companies and government leaders on pivotal projects, from enabling a national digital transformation to setting strategic visions and deploying initiatives for AI transformations. Abhi's area of expertise leverages cutting-edge creativity rooted in human insights to ensure technological scale is purpose-driven. He started his career in entrepreneurship, as CEO of IDEA Venture Accelerator, where he spearheaded the global incubation of over 350 early-stage ventures, collectively raising over $800M in external funding. Now he is a Techstars Mentor. Abhi's has earned accolades – from being selected by BCG's leadership to be a CEO Ambassador, named one of BostInno's 25 under 25, and rewarded a spot on the Poets & Quants list of Best and Brightest business students at Northeastern University. His passion for how culture and innovation work together has been fueled by his experiences living and working in diverse innovation hubs such as Dubai, NYC, Atlanta, Boston, and now Washington D.C., USA.

Akshay Joshi is the Head of Industry and Partnerships for the World Economic Forum's Centre for Cybersecurity, where he is responsible for overseeing strategic priorities and day-to-day operations, developing key partnerships, and driving collaborative action to strengthen cyber resilience across industry ecosystems. Akshay joined the Forum as a Global Leadership Fellow in 2015 and was responsible for strengthening engagement with organizations based in South Asia before taking on operational leadership of the Centre for Cybersecurity upon its launch in 2018. Prior to joining the Forum, he had over a decade of experience in management roles in sectors including maritime transport and public relations. Akshay holds an Executive Master's degree in Global Leadership from the World Economic Forum, an MBA from the University of Manchester, and a Bachelor's degree from the University of Mumbai.

Andrejs Panteļējevs was born in 1961 in Riga in the Soviet-occupied Republic of Latvia. He studied physics at the University of Latvia after which he worked in the Theoretical Physics Department. In the second half of the 1980s, he was actively involved in the movement for restoration of the independence of Latvia. He was one of the founders of the People's Front of Latvia and headed its university wing. He was also a member of the People's Front Council. In 1990, he was elected as an MP to the Supreme Council of Latvia and voted for renewal of Latvian independence on May 4, 1990. After the restoration of the independence of Latvia, he stayed involved in politics and was elected three times in a row as MP to the parliament of the renewed Republic of Latvia. In parliament, he was chairman of the Human Rights and National Security Committee, and also a member of the National Security Council headed by the state president. For years, he was a member of the Latvian delegation to the Parliamentary Assembly of the Council of Europe. He was one the founders of the liberal conservative party — Latvia's Way (1993), chairman of the parliamentary faction of Latvia's Way (1993–1997) and later, its president (1997–2000). After 2002, he held various positions in the Latvian government, mainly as a counselor but also as parliamentary secretary in the Ministry of Defence (2014–2016). He has also worked as a political commentator for the Latvian daily newspaper *Diena*. Presently, he is working as a counselor to the Minister of Education and Sciences and is a teacher of political sciences at a high school.

Andy Redman is Managing Director at BCG BrightHouse, which is a team at Boston Consulting Group that focuses on articulating and activating purpose — why an organization exists. Andy is a core member of BCG's Public Sector practice and BCG Fed and his work focuses on three areas: Clarity (articulating and activating purpose, vision, mission, and values); Connection (bringing heart to communication and engagement efforts, including recruitment campaigns and strategic communications during major transformations); and Innovation (supporting leaders to step out of the day-to-day to reimagine what is possible). Prior to joining BCG BrightHouse, Andy spent a decade working in education where he led teams at Teach For America and OneGoal to dramatically grow and scale operations while consistently achieving ambitious results. Andy began his career in public sector consulting at Deloitte in the UK and US, focusing on business strategy and performance management. Andy is an honors graduate of Auburn University and holds master's degrees from the LBJ School at the University of Texas and the Judge Business School at the University of Cambridge. He lives with his wife and three daughters in Atlanta.

Angela M. Evans is the Dean Emerita at the University of Texas, Austin (LBJ School of Public Affairs), and former Deputy Director of the Congressional Research Service (CRS), the primary public policy agency of the U.S. Congress. She is a Fellow of the National Academy of Public Administration. Leading CRS, she oversaw all analytic research, development, and operations. She undertook the first agency reorganization in thirty years, developed the first agency-wide interdisciplinary research framework, and oversaw 700 professional staff. She led all analyses provided to Congress for 9/11, Katrina, the 2008 financial crisis, Y2K, and infrastructure disasters, among others. As dean, she recruited research faculty and professors of practice, increased research output and funding, and markedly increased student and faculty diversity. Evans improved the ranking of the LBJ School from #14 to #7 in 5 years, launched new research centers and labs, developed new interdisciplinary and joint degree programs, and dramatically expanded donor and alumni engagement.

Daniel Chenok is the Executive Director of the IBM Center for The Business of Government. Before joining IBM, Dan had several roles in senior leadership positions in industry, nonprofits, and government. He led consulting services for Public Sector Technology Strategy, working with IBM government, healthcare, and education clients. He began his government service as an analyst with the Congressional Office of Technology Assessment in 2003 and left as branch chief for Information Policy and Technology with the Office of Management and Budget. He served on President Barack Obama's transition team as the government lead for the Technology, Innovation, and Government Reform group and as a member of the OMB Agency Review Team. Dan has won numerous honors and awards, including a 2010 Federal 100 winner award for his work on the presidential transition, the 2016 Eagle Award for Industry Executive of the Year, and the 2002 Federal CIO Council Azimuth Award for Government Executive of the Year.

Donato Giorgi is the Space Counselor at the Embassy of France in the UAE and the Managing Director of the liaison office of the Centre National d'Études Spatiales — the French space agency — in the United Arab Emirates. Based in Abu Dhabi, he coordinates and promotes the development of space cooperation between France and the UAE and the Middle East region, in general. Before moving to the UAE, Donato served as Head of European and International Relations at CNES. Donato and his team's activities included coordinating the French delegation to the European Space Agency (ESA) and managing relations with European national space agencies, the European Commission, the UN, and a wide range of space agencies in the Americas, Africa, the Middle East, Asia, and Australia. Donato spent the previous ten years as a member of the French delegation to the ESA, then an expert at the European Commission, and finally as the space counsellor at the French Permanent Representation to the EU. Donato holds a Master's degree in aerospace engineering from Politecnico di Milano and a Master's degree in political science from Université Paris Panthéon-Assas.

Estela Alves de Medeiros has a Ph.D. in Administration by University of Brasília, Brazil. She is a Specialist in Public Policies and Government Management at the Brazilian Ministry of Management. She is currently Director of Corporate Management at the Agricultural Defense Secretariat of the Ministry of Agriculture, Livestock, and Supply. She develops projects and activities in the areas of international consultancy, strategic management, institutional development, people development, budget and financial management, process management, innovation in management, and information technology.

Giulia Moschetta is a Research and Analysis Specialist at the World Economic Forum's Centre for Cybersecurity, where she focuses on initiatives aimed at building cyber resilience across industry ecosystems and the quantum security initiative. Prior to joining the Forum, she was at the forefront of producing cutting-edge research and analysis on a wide range of security and geopolitical issues, including cyber defense at NATO and with the Italian government. Giulia holds a dual Master's degree in International Affairs from Sciences Po Paris and MGIMO, an M.A. in Diplomacy and International Cooperation from the University of Trieste, and a B.A. in International Relations from King's College London.

Immanuel A. Moonesar is Professor of Health Policy and Systems Research at the Mohammed Bin Rashid School of Government, Dubai, UAE. He holds dual citizenship of Trinidad and Tobago and France. He serves as Managing Director at "I AM Consulting" (Trinidad and Tobago) and President (Chapter Chair) and Executive Board member of the Academy of International Business Middle East North Africa (AIB-MENA). Throughout his career, he has worked in quality assurance and management, nutrition and dietetics, health and safety, teaching, and institutional research. His current research interests are IB policy, public policy, healthcare management and leadership, maternal and child health, health policy and innovation, nutrition, and quality management. He also has over 250 publications including articles in peer-reviewed journals, papers in peer-reviewed international conferences, co-authored books, and book chapters. His research grants and fundraising attainment amount to over 1,750,000 USD. More information on his publications can be found at the following: https://orcid.org/0000-0003-4027-3508

Ivana Milojević is Director of Metafuture.org and a researcher, writer, and educator with a transdisciplinary professional background spanning sociology, education, gender studies, peace and conflict studies, and futures studies. Since the mid-1990s, Ivana has been actively engaged in delivering speeches, facilitating workshops, and conducting research for various governmental institutions, international associations, and non-governmental organizations across Asia-Pacific, Africa, and Europe. She previously held academic positions at several universities, including the University of the Sunshine Coast (Adjunct Professor), the University of Novi Sad, and Tamkang University (Visiting Professor). Dr. Milojević is the author or editor of some 150 publications (e.g., academic books, book chapters, journal articles, and magazine articles). In 2016–2017, she led the foresight unit at the Centre for Strategic and Policy Studies in Brunei Darussalam. In 2022–2023, Ivana was a senior futures thinking and foresight specialist/consultant with the Asian Development Bank.

John Griffiths is a highly experienced Executive Director and Managing Consultant with over 30 years of international experience in the management and IT consulting sector in the UK, Europe, and the Middle East. He is a systems thinker who can provide meaningful insights into complex and interrelated networks of issues, crises, and critical situations in a holistic context. John has diverse experience in multiple verticals, which has enabled him to develop significant capabilities, competence, and knowledge across disciplines. He has provided strategic advice and acted as a guide and mentor to CXO-level executives over his many years of experience. John was a leader in bringing teams to the Middle East to deliver predictive analytics (AI) in 2005, many years before AI gained renown. John is currently undertaking a Ph.D. in Systems Science at the University of Hull, a significant climax to a wildly varied career.

Joshua Park is Professor and Dean of SolBridge International School of Business, Woosong University, Daejeon, South Korea. A graduate of Harvard Law School, he has extensive experience in conflict resolution and management, negotiation, communication, debating strategies, and practices. As Dean, he has designed and implemented strategic plans, largely utilizing agile anticipatory governance through information-based foresight for his highly internationalized and successful business school. In addition, he has participated in over 300 consultations and workshops for governments, businesses, and educational institutions domestically and internationally. His clients have included leaders and administrators from the Ministry of Education, Metropolitan Offices of Education, National Election Commission, Korea Electric Power Corporation (KEPCO), regional governments (cities and provinces), trade unions, start-ups and small to medium-sized businesses, global non-governmental organizations, and domestic and international academic institutions. His areas of academic research cover entrepreneurship, internationalization strategies, communication, fiscal policies, and industrial production.

Kamal Al Awamleh (PhD), is an Associate Professor of Commercial Law. He has a demonstrated history of working in the education industry and is an experienced legal counsel. He is skilled in banking law, European law, contract law, legal writing, commercial law, labor law, insurance law, litigation, arbitration, and corporate law. Dr. Kamal is a distinguished education professional with a Doctor of Philosophy (Ph.D.) focused on International Business, Trade, and Banking Law from the University of

Central Lancashire. Dr. Kamal has written many research papers that address different issues related to his research interests.

Keertana Subramani is Associate Researcher at the Mohammed Bin Rashid School of Government (MBRSG), focusing on economic policy and diversification, circular and green economy, digital economy, and education. She holds an M.Sc. in Econometrics and Mathematical Economics from the London School of Economics (LSE) and a B.Sc. in Industrial and Systems Engineering with a minor in Economics from Georgia Institute of Technology. Keertana has co-authored several reports at MBRSG. She previously served as a research assistant at Georgia Tech focusing on environmental economics and was a visiting scholar at UNU Macau. Her master's thesis focused on analyzing consumption poverty traps and the impacts of targeted subsidized grain distribution in India. She has also worked as an educator, a technology consultant, and an engineer.

Kesevan Sampanthar is a globally recognized thought leader at the intersection of business, human experience, and technology. Currently he is a Partner at Valize. He was Managing Director at BCG BrightHouse where he led Innovation + Purpose, helping companies make the world a better place through innovation. He is an award-winning innovator, technologist, and game designer, and is recognized as a strategic thinker and consultant to some of the biggest Fortune 500 companies. Over the last two decades, his research into neuroscience, game design, behavioral economics, and paleoanthropology has resulted in a new approach to creating engaging experiences — through motivational design and a reinvention of design thinking for business model innovation.

Maddalena Campioni is a foresight expert, practitioner, and capacity-building professional. Currently, she is a future foresight and strategy expert at Early Childhood Authority (ECA), Government of Abu Dhabi, setting up the Foresight function at ECA and developing future perspectives in the early childhood sector. She is also part of the Abu Dhabi foresight practitioner network. She was a senior faculty member at the Dubai Future Academy. Maddalena held various senior advisory roles including as a senior advisor to the Executive Director at the United Nations and a foresight advisor for the UK Government in foresight, science, and technology. She worked for multiple departments since 2005: the Department of

International Development, the Department of Health, and the Department of International Trade. She was also a former advisor to the WHO Representative to the EU and Executive-in-Residence Fellow at the Geneva Centre for Security Policy (2014–2015). In that period, she also chaired the Board of Global Future, promoting future dialogue among key stakeholders in Geneva. Maddalena is a neuroscientist with 24 years of experience in future scenarios and foresight.

Mark Esposito is recognized internationally as a top global thought leader in matters relating to the Fourth Industrial Revolution. He is a global expert at the World Economic Forum and an advisor to national governments. He serves as Professor of Economics, Strategy, and Foresights at Hult International Business School (where he directs the Futures Impact Lab) as well as at Harvard University's Division of Continuing Education where he teaches an award-winning executive course on Artificial Intelligence. He is also Full Professor of Public Policy at the Mohammed Bin Rashid School of Government in the UAE and holds visiting professorships around the world. He served from 2015 to 2019 as Institutes Council co-leader at the Microeconomics of Competitiveness (MOC) program at the Institute of Strategy and Competitiveness, Harvard Business School, under the mentorship of Professor Michael E. Porter and from 2016 to 2020 was a Founding Research Fellow of the Circular Economy Center at the Judge Business School at University of Cambridge.

Noah Frank is a strategic thinker with a passion for institutional change. Currently he is a Senior Consultant at Valize. As a former Strategist with BCG BrightHouse, he draws on a unique perspective at the intersection of policy and social impact to catalyze action. Throughout his career, his insights have supported the work of activists, policymakers, and Fortune 50+ leaders from around the world. He is a former UN Millennium Fellow, TEDx speaker, and alumnus of the University of Connecticut, from which he graduated with honors in 2022. He currently lives in Boston.

Patrick Noack is Executive Director of Future, Foresight and Imagination at the Dubai Future Foundation, where he manages the Dubai Future Institute which includes a research team, the Academy, the WEF C4IR, and the Dubai Future Forum. He is a Policy Fellow at the Centre for Science and Policy, University of Cambridge, and is a member of the WHO's Eastern Mediterranean Region's Technical Advisory Committee.

Time permitting, he writes an opinion column in *The National* on foresight topics. Patrick holds a Master's degree in Social Policy from the LSE and a Doctorate from the University of Aberdeen. He has been engaged in scenarios and foresight for the past 20 years.

Ricardo Gomes Dr. Ricardo Gomes is Director of the Research Degree Program in Public Administration and Government at Escola de Administração de Empresas de São Paulo FGV and Adjunct Professor in Public Management at the same school. He has a Ph.D. in Public Management issued by Aston University, UK. He is Associate Editor for the Public Management Review and a member of the editorial board of *JPART, Public Administration, International Journal of Public Sector Management*, and *Financial Accountability & Management*.

H.E. Rolands Lappuķe was born in 1956 in Paris into a family of political refugees from Latvia. He earned a Ph.D. in Neurosciences in 1982 from L'université Louis-Pasteur de Strasbourg (France). He conducted research work in Australia from 1982–1986, and then worked as a biology teacher at the Latvian High School in Munster (Germany) (1986–1993). Later he worked as a Latvian government diplomat from 1993 to 2016, with postings in Bonn as Head of Protocol; Ambassador to Portugal; Ambassador to France and to the UNESCO, non-resident Ambassador to Morocco and to Andorra; Ambassador to Spain; and Representative to the Council of Europe. He was appointed as Advisor on Smart Technologies to the State President of Latvia (2019–2023). Presently, he is involved in projects dealing with medical data, new technologies and innovation in the medical field particularly in EU cancer screening projects and on a Health Advancement Centre at the Children's Clinical University hospital of Latvia. He has published various articles on politics, history and culture.

Roger Spitz (M.Sc., FCA, APF) is an international bestselling author, President of Techistential (Climate & Foresight Strategy), and Chair of the Disruptive Futures Institute in San Francisco. As former Global Head of Technology M&A with BNP Paribas, Spitz advised on over 50 transactions with a deal value of $25bn. He has two decades of leading investment banking and venture capital businesses. Spitz advises CEOs, founders, boards, and shareholders on their most strategic decisions, evaluating their organizations' competitiveness and anticipating disruptions ahead. He sits on several boards, artificial intelligence and climate councils,

VC funds & academic institutions worldwide. A world-leading authority on foresight, sustainability, and transformative change, Spitz teaches strategic foresight and system innovation, and has written the influential book collection *The Definitive Guide to Thriving on Disruption*. Spitz publishes extensively on anticipatory leadership, change, uncertainty, and decision-making in complex unpredictable environments, with bestselling books in future studies, green business, strategic management, and forecasting.

Sara Al Ghalayini has a Bachelor's degree in Law and a Master's degree in Innovation Management. She specializes in Intellectual Property Laws. She has five years of experience as a litigation lawyer in the UAE, representing clients before Dubai Courts, covering commercial, civil, employment, and intellectual property litigation cases. She is currently working in corporate law as a legal advisor at Equus, providing advisory for corporate governance and compliance, business incorporation, governance, and corporate structuring and restructuring. She is also a legal associate at the Legal Boutique with a focus on drafting commercial contracts involving international transactions, IP licensing, copyrights and trademarks, and software licensing agreements.

Sohail Inayatullah is the UNESCO Chair in Futures Studies at Sejahtera Centre for Sustainability and Humanity, IIUM. He is a political scientist/futurist at Tamkang University, Taipei, and an Associate at Melbourne Business School, the University of Melbourne. In 2021, he was Futurist-in-Residence (virtual) for the Government of Abu Dhabi. From 2011–2014, he was an adjunct professor at the Centre for Policing, Counterterrorism, and Intelligence, Macquarie University, Sydney. In 1999, he was the UNESCO Chair in European Studies at the University of Trier, Germany. He is listed in the top 2 percent of the world's scientists as measured by the highest impact of citations. Inayatullah has authored and co-edited twenty-eight books, including *CLA 3.0: Thirty Years of Transformative Research* (2022); *From Anticipation to Emancipation* (2022); *The End of the Cow and other Emerging issues* (2022); and *Futures Thinking in Asia and the Pacific* (2020).

Susann Roth (PhD) is an Advisor at the Department of Communication and Knowledge Management at the Asian Development Bank (ADB) where she drives the reform agenda for the Knowledge Management program. With expertise in medicine, public health, gender and development, and futures studies, she fosters innovation via interdisciplinary collaboration. With 15+ years of experience, Susann led knowledge-sharing initiatives across 20 countries in the Asia-Pacific. Since 2018, she played a pivotal role in ADB's transformation, leading the innovation task force, ADB's futures thinking and foresight program and supporting culture and digital transformation. Susann was an adjunct professor at LKY School of Public Policy in Singapore and she speaks regularly as guest speaker at Columbia Universities, School of Professional Studies She holds a Medical and Doctoral degree from the University of Heidelberg, Germany, and a master's degree in public health from the University of the Philippines. She practiced medicine in the USA, Germany, and the Philippines before making a career shift to development. As a prolific author, she contributes to publications on development and innovation in Asia and the Pacific region.

Tal Goldstein is Head of Strategy and Policy for the World Economic Forum's Centre for Cybersecurity. He leads the Centre's relationships with the public sector and academia and oversees key strategic initiatives, including the Partnership against Cybercrime and the Global Cybersecurity Outlook report. Before joining the Forum, Tal helped establish the Israel National Cyber Directorate and led the development of Israel's national cybersecurity strategy. Prior to that, he served as an officer in the Israeli Military Intelligence Directorate. Tal holds a B.Sc. in Physics and Mathematics from the Hebrew University of Jerusalem as a graduate of the elite IDF Talpiot program and has received an M.A. in Economics from Tel-Aviv University. Tal is also Adjunct Professor at the University of Tel Aviv.

Yousif El-Ghalayini is Associate Professor in Public Administration at the Mohammed Bin Rashid School of Government, Executive MPA Program Coordinator, and Research Affiliate at the Centre on Governance at the University of Ottawa. His areas of teaching focus on public sector management and governance, HRM and PM, public policy development, and organizational behavior and development. Before joining the Mohammed Bin Rashid School of Government, Dr. El-Ghalayini was the program manager of the HRM Program at the School of Business affiliated to the Australian College of Kuwait. He spent a few years working with the United Nations as a specialist in civil society development and capacity-building in post-conflict zones. Yousif served as a consular services officer with Global Affairs Canada. He has a Ph.D. in Public Administration from the University of Ottawa, Canada, and a Master's degree in Project Management from Université du Québec en Outaouais (Gatineau).

https://doi.org/10.1142/9789811296000_fmatter

Contents

Reviews i

Foreword ix

Preface xi

About the Editors xiii

About the Contributors xv

Section 1 Anticipatory Governance **1**

Chapter 1 Anticipatory — The Next Form of Governance 3
Melodena Stephens, Raed Awamleh, and Frederic Sicre

1.1 We Have No Choice But to Move Forward 3
1.2 Anticipatory Governance 6
1.3 Anticipatory Governance — Shaping a Responsible Future 9
1.4 Conclusion 16

Chapter 2 Adjacent Possible Mapping — Exploring the Unknown and VUCA Environment 19
Kesevan Sampanthar, Noah Frank, and Abhishek Balakrishnan

2.1 Governing in an Age of Disruption 20
2.2 Connection and Unforeseen Consequences 23
2.3 The Present: The World of Exponential Change 27

	2.4 The Future: The World of Adjacent Possibilities	29
	2.5 Policy Recommendations: Building the Anticipatory Government of the Future	34
	2.6 Final Considerations	36
Chapter 3	Anticipatory Capacity through Foresight *Mark Esposito and Joshua Park*	39
	3.1 The Expanding Role of Foresight in Public Policy	40
	3.2 Building Resilience and Adaptability through Foresight	42
	3.3 Agency for Progress?	44
	3.4 The If and When of Real-Life Examples	45
Chapter 4	Elevating Anticipatory Analysis in Policymaking *Angela Evans*	49
	4.1 State of Affairs	49
	4.2 Power of Anticipatory Analysis	57
	4.3 Lessons Learned	64
	4.4 Final Comments	67
Chapter 5	Backcasting: A Design Thinking Approach to Creating Transformative Futures *Melodena Stephens and Sohail Inayatullah*	69
	5.1 Introduction	70
	5.2 Backcasting Design Thinking Methodology	72
	5.3 Conclusion	83
Chapter 6	Navigating Pathways toward Anticipatory Governance within a Systems Thinking Ecosystem *John Griffiths*	85
	6.1 Overview	85
	6.2 Systems Thinking — A Definition?	86
	6.3 Perspectives	88
	6.4 Defining Boundaries	88
	6.5 Systems Thinking Methodologies	91
	6.6 SOD — Systems-Oriented Design	96
	6.7 Non-Human Aspects	97
	6.8 Way Forward for Governance	98

Section 2 **Leadership and Transformation** **101**

Chapter 7 The AAA Framework: Responsible Leadership for Sustainable Futures 103
Roger Spitz

7.1 Beyond VUCA: New UN-VICE for Systemic Disruption 104
7.2 AAA Framework for Sustainable Futures 110
7.3 Antifragile: Laying the Foundations 111
7.4 Anticipatory: Preparing the Futures 113
7.5 Agility: Emerging in the Present 117
7.6 Agency and Alignment to Become AAA+ 120

Chapter 8 Unlocking the Power of Public Purpose 121
Andy Redman, Abhishek Balakrishnan, and Noah Frank

8.1 Introduction 121
8.2 Background 122
8.3 Detailed Discussion: Public Purpose 125
8.4 Implications and Recommendations 130
8.5 Conclusion 134

Chapter 9 Frontier Leadership 135
Raed Awamleh

9.1 New Wild West 135
9.2 New Leadership for Public Value 137
9.3 Frontier Leadership 138
9.4 Conclusion 141

Chapter 10 How a Forgotten Nation Managed Uncertainty — The Restoration of Latvia's Independence 143
Rolands Lappuķe and Andrejs Panteļējevs

10.1 Latvia — An Unforgotten Nation 143
10.2 National Identity and Europeanness 145
10.3 Challenges 148
10.4 Strengths and Weaknesses of a Nation Undergoing Transformative Changes 151
10.5 Independence at Last! 162

Chapter 11 Early Warning Systems: Whispers in the Global Corridors 165
Melodena Stephens, Frederic Sicre, and Raed Awamleh

11.1 Middle East and North Africa — Backdrop 166
11.2 Tribes: The Corridors of Connections and Conduits for Anticipatory Governance 170
11.3 Early Warning Signals (EWSs) 174
11.4 To Hear the Whispers, You Need to Be Invited into the Corridors and Find the Right Room 177
11.5 Diplomacy Has a Cascading Effect and Can Be Used to Listen 184
11.6 Steps to Create an EWS in Global Corridors 187

Section 3 Governing Advanced Technology 189

Chapter 12 Technology Anticipation and Regulation 191
Patrick Noack

12.1 Degrees of Separation: Tech Anticipation and Regulations 191
12.2 Global Regulatory Responses to Advanced Tech 194
12.3 The Case of Dubai 195
12.4 Creating a Regulatory Capacity for *In Silico* Regulation 197

Chapter 13 Anticipatory Governance on Cybersecurity 203
Akshay Joshi, Tal Goldstein, and Giulia Moschetta

13.1 Introduction 204
13.2 The Dynamic Nature of Cybersecurity 206
13.3 The Data-Driven Forces of Cybersecurity 208
13.4 Exploring Anticipatory Governance in the Cyber Realm 210
13.5 Applying Anticipatory Governance to Emerging Technologies to Leverage Their Transformative Potential and Proactively Manage Security Risks 215
13.6 Conclusion 219

Chapter 14 Envisioning the Future of Government: How Emerging, Secure Technologies and Data Flows Can Enable Anticipation and Action that Improve Performance 221
Daniel Chenok

14.1 Background 222
14.2 Key Technologies: Cloud, AI, and Quantum 225
14.3 How Can Agencies Tap Emerging Technologies to Use Data for Greater Anticipation and Improved Performance? 233

Chapter 15 Digital Transformation: A Tool for Anticipatory Governance 235
Yousif El-Ghalayini

15.1 Introduction 236
15.2 From Government to Governance 236
15.3 Anticipatory Governance and Digital Transformation 238
15.4 Conclusion 244

Chapter 16 Generative AI and the Copyright Minefield: Creating Safeguards 247
Sara Al Ghalayini and Kamal Al Awalmeh

16.1 Introduction 248
16.2 Data Colonialism and Global AI Governance 249
16.3 Global AI Governance 252
16.4 Complexities of Copyright Infringement 254
16.5 The Eligibility of Generative AI Creations for Copyright Law Protection 255
16.6 Copyright Infringement and AI Generative Model Liability 256
16.7 Anticipatory Government for Legal Maneuvering and New Tech 258

Chapter 17 Transformative Change: Future Children 261
Maddalena Campioni

17.1 Overview 261
17.2 Where Are We? 263

	17.3 What Should We Do?	267
	17.4 Drivers of Change for Future Learning Research	269
Chapter 18	Future of Education and Work: Using Backcasting to Design Guardrails *Melodena Stephens and Sohail Inayatullah*	271
	18.1 Introduction	272
	18.2 Example Using Backcasting	272
	18.3 Conclusion	288
Section 4	**Learning from the Past: Guardrails and Opportunities**	**291**
Chapter 19	From OldSpace to NewSpace: Not Just an Evolution, Not Yet a Revolution *Donato Giorgi*	293
	19.1 The Birth of a Commercial Space Age Full of Promises	294
	19.2 A Race Toward the New Economic Frontier	297
	19.3 Taking a Perspective on the Mainstream Narrative	298
	19.4 Anticipating to Avoid and/or Mitigate Potentially Disrupting Consequences of NewSpace	300
	19.5 Conclusion	303
Chapter 20	Frameworks for Impact Measurement under Uncertainty *Keertana Subramani*	305
	20.1 Introduction	306
	20.2 The Importance of Impact Measurement Frameworks	308
	20.3 Choosing What Policies Are Needed: Various Approaches for Analyses	312
	20.4 Toward a Structured Impact Measurement Framework	318
	20.5 Conclusion	320

Chapter 21	Anticipatory Governance and Decision-Making: Prevention of the Entry of Absent Quarantine Pests (AQPs) in Brazil *Estela Alves de Medeiros and Ricardo C. Gomes*	323
	21.1 Introduction	324
	21.2 Nature of the Problem: What Are Quarantine Pests and Why Should They Be Addressed?	325
	21.3 Anticipatory Governance to Face the Entry of Pests that Do Not Exist in Brazil	326
	21.4 Results to Date	329
	21.5 Conclusion	332
Chapter 22	Building an Architectural Framework for Anticipatory Governance: A Case Study of the Asian Development Bank *Susann Roth and Ivana Milojević*	333
	22.1 Introduction	334
	22.2 Asian Development Bank and Anticipatory Governance	335
	22.3 Lessons Learned: Moving Forward in Creating an Architecture for Anticipatory Governance	338
	22.4 Conclusion: Governing for the Future	343
Chapter 23	Humanitarian Logistics and Health Response *Immanuel Azaad Moonesar*	345
	23.1 Introduction	346
	23.2 The 3Rs to Managing Health Logistics during Crises	347
	23.3 3R Framework in Action	349
	23.4 Concluding Remarks	360
Chapter 24	Synthetic Biology Governance and Advocacy *Melodena Stephens and Abhishek Balakrishnan*	361
	24.1 Advocacy	362
	24.2 Comics for Advocacy: Synthetic Biology Governance	363
	24.3 Science Advocacy Recommendations	371
Index		373

Section 1

Anticipatory Governance

https://doi.org/10.1142/9789811296000_0001

Chapter 1

Anticipatory — The Next Form of Governance

Melodena Stephens*, Raed Awamleh†, and Frederic Sicre‡

**Mohammed Bin Rashid School of Government, Dubai, UAE*
†Center for Policy and Competitiveness,
École de Ponts Business School, Paris, France
‡Tardis Advisors, Dubai, Paris and Geneva

Key Takeaways

- Anticipatory governance is more than foresight; it is the process responsible for shaping the future and creating intergenerational impact, both on humanity and the planet.
- It has a variety of meanings; it begins with purpose, is translated through values, and is forged with strategies to achieve the envisioned future.
- The skills required are imagination, the ability to listen, reflect on a diversity of experiences (past and present), and use technology as a tool wisely to chart a path to an intended future.
- The journey requires participation from government, the private sector, and the public — at both domestic and international levels.
- Anticipatory governance requires an agile government approach as the context will change; hence, measuring impact across the years is an integral part of oversight.

1.1 We Have No Choice But to Move Forward

Since the pandemic, calls have increased for agile government, agile governance, foresight, and anticipatory governance. In 2024, 64 countries and the EU (another 27 member states), or nearly 50% of the world's population, would have voted in elections.[1] In some critical cases, entrenched leaders and political dynasties are expected to win, moving the world from open globalized politics to more radical polarization. The IMF suggests that globalization has plateaued with increasing geopolitical tensions,[2] highlighted by the two ongoing wars — one in Europe and one in the Middle East.

Furthermore, the fast adoption of new consumer technologies, like Generative AI, illuminates the cracks in regulatory and governance frameworks. The 2024 Edelman Trust Barometer finds trust is higher in businesses than in governments.[3] The drive by governments toward the privatization of public value services through outsourcing adds to the increasing tensions between the purpose of public value and commercial profits. The expanding use of AI technologies, for example, contributes to war, water scarcity, and affects human employability at a scale we have not experienced before in the Industrial Revolution (see Exhibit 1.1 for the systemic thinking required for AI). The report also finds a decline in trust in traditional media, possibly due to social media's dominance and so-called citizen journalism.[4]

The future looks complex, uncertain, and crisis-prone. So, how can policymakers work together across borders to achieve intergenerational public value? Is this even possible? Given the present uncertainty, how can they build governance frameworks to protect their citizens, future generations, and the environment in which we must coexist? How do they preserve the peace that seems so fragile with misinformation, new warfare technologies, and the decline of global citizenship? What trade-offs must they make when balancing the present and the future? The reality is that the past may anchor the present, but we cannot control time; hence, the only certainty is that as we move forward, we must ensure that the steps we take tell a tale of a journey into a better future for us and our descendants.

---

[1] Ewe, K. (2023). The ultimate election year: All the elections around the world in 2024. *Time*, 28 December. Available: https://time.com/6550920/world-elections-2024/ (Accessed 14 February, 2024).

[2] Aiyar, S. & Ilyina, A. (2023). Charting globalization's turn to slowbalization after global financial crisis. *IMF*. Available: https://www.imf.org/en/Blogs/Articles/2023/02/08/charting-globalizations-turn-to-slowbalization-after-global-financial-crisis (Accessed 16 February, 2024).

[3] Edelman (2024). 2024 Edelman Trust Barometer. Available: https://www.edelman.com/sites/g/files/aatuss191/files/202402/2024%20Edelman%20Trust%20Barometer%20Global%20Report_FINAL.pdf (Accessed 16 February, 2024).

[4] Dangerfiled, M.B. (n.d.). Power to the people. Available: https://www.tate.org.uk/art/art-terms/p/photojournalism/power-people (Accessed 13 February 2024).

Exhibit 1.1. AI systemic thinking and planning needed (behind the scenes).

- One microchip fabrication needs approximately 2,200 gallons of Ultrapure Water.
- GPT-3 inference for 10–50 questions consumes 500 milliliters of water (but has 100 million monthly users asking multiple questions). In the city of The Dalles, Oregon, Google's data centers consume more than 25% of the city's water supply.
- By 2027, global AI demand will need water usage equivalent to the consumption of 4–6 Denmarks, or half of the United Kingdom.
- Microsoft's global data centers for AI consume 1.8–12 liters of water for each kWh of energy usage. There are about 9,000–11,000 cloud data centers worldwide.
- The energy consumption of data centers will be equivalent to that of the country of Japan (1,000 terawatts).
- AI has created much uncertainty in the job market — layoffs, more inequality (34% of the world still does not have access to the Internet), and tension between augmentation and automation (that leads to unemployment). Often, augmentation (creation of new jobs) leads to automation (no new jobs, which is a side effect of augmentation). The transition time for job recovery (new jobs) is easily 40+ years, which governments may not have been planning for.

Source: Compiled from Autur, Chin, Salomons, & Seegmiller (2022),[5] Berrreby (2024),[6] Ren (2023),[7] and Resume Builder (2023).[8]

[5]Autur, D., Chin, C., Salomons, A.M., & Seegmiller, B. (2022). New frontiers: The origins and content of new work, 1940–2018. *NBER Working Paper*. https://www.nber.org/papers/w30389 (Accessed 15 February, 2024).

[6]Berrreby, D. (2024). As use of A.I. soars, so does the energy and water it requires. *YaleEnvironement 360*, 6 February. Available: https://e360.yale.edu/features/artificial-intelligence-climate-energy-emissions (Accessed 10 February, 2024).

[7]Ren, S. (2023). How much water does AI consume? The public deserves to know. *OECD*, 30 November. Available: https://oecd.ai/en/wonk/how-much-water-does-ai-consume (Accessed 10 February, 2024).

[8]Resume Builder (2023). 1 in 3 companies will replace employees with AI in 2024. Available: https://www.resumebuilder.com/1-in-3-companies-will-replace-employees-with-ai-in-2024/ (Accessed 15 February, 2024).

1.2 Anticipatory Governance

Anticipatory governance has many interpretations. While it is often associated with the future, it is rooted in the present and held back by chains from the past (see Exhibit 1.2).[9] The urgency is how quickly we can learn from the past (the good, the bad, and the ugly) and pivot to meet an uncertain future. How nimble are we on this journey? Are we able to embed agile governance models?

The concept of agile governance, which overlaps with digital governance, evolved due to three forces that governments created[10]: (1) disaggregation — the splitting up of large public sector hierarchies; (2) competition — to increase public value by competitively allocating resources; and (3) incentivization — rewarding performance that coordinates thinking and actions (both horizontally and vertically across the organization and other entities), resulting in seamless services and processes rather fragmented ones. These were more internally created forces. However, there was a push from the outside for more transparency, accountability, and ethical use of technology. This was true in the international space where funds flowed across borders, and its impact was gray.

Large intergovernmental organizations like the IMF (1997), World Bank (2016), and WEF (2018) adopted the term agile governance. Some of these pilot experiments have not achieved what they wanted. If the business of the government is to steer, then agile governance can be defined as the overall principles and processes that a country is built on, taking into consideration its political, historical, and social aspects to deliver public good.[11] Hence, the past and present help the government steer for the future. However, the future is very uncertain, with technological advancements causing exponential change in many areas rather than the more familiar linear change we expect. We are moving into unknown territory — how can we do better? The answer could be in anticipatory governance.

---

[9] Often discussed in CLA Analysis.

[10] Dunleavy, P., Margetts, H., Bastow, S., & Tinkler, J. (2006). New public management is dead — long live digital-era governance. *Journal of Public Administration Research and Theory*, 16(3): 467–494; Pollitt, C. (2003). Public management reform: Reliable knowledge and international experience. *OECD Journal on Budgeting*, 3(3): 121–134.

[11] Stephens, M., Awamleh, R., & Salem, F. (Eds.). (2022). *Agile Government: Emerging Perspectives in Public Management*. Singapore: World Scientific Publishing: p. 8.

Exhibit 1.2. Anticipatory governance: Moving forwards.

Source: Created and adapted using AI imagine.art (21 February, 2024).

Anticipatory governance has multiple layers. First, there needs to be a deep understanding of the complexity of the past, the existing power dynamics, and more importantly, an understanding that the context of the past is not a precedent for the future — still, the past needs to be acknowledged and leveraged. As more governments outsource critical parts of their planning and execution roles to consultants and the private sector, this could be a challenge, especially with the current focus on efficiency and productivity that may not reward knowledge transfer, especially tacit knowledge.

Second, governments need to develop foresight capabilities beginning with the purpose of foresight (which should be governance), which is embedded in uncompromisable values as they plan the future. This planning requires governments that are skilled, imaginative, willing to challenge their assumptions, and also have a deep understanding of the trade-offs to be managed to achieve objectives.

Foresight activities help sharpen the ability to read and hear signals — they act like early warning signals. Hence, a government with anticipatory governance capabilities can measure course deviations using a collaborative approach that may include technology (as an agent) at national and international risk levels.

Anticipatory governance will help the government prepare for shocks that cause ripple effects across the ecosystem. This is why this type of governance can be referred to as a *System of Systems*.[12] The agile responsiveness of policy interventions helps governments manage unintended impacts or changes in a course for greater resilience, thus building and reinforcing trust. Hence, a government needs a resilient public sector that can manage uncertainty and pivot ideas, resources, and talent to where they are most needed.

Moreover, while this discussion centers on the future, most government constituents mainly focus on the here and now. Here, the cornerstone remains the trust in government. If transparency is questionable, then today's trade-offs and "sacrifices" for the sake of the future may seem unjustified. Accordingly, a government must equip itself using various tools of communication and dialogue to foster transparency and trust through constructive narratives.

The editors of this book offer the following definition of Anticipatory Governance: *Anticipatory Governance is the systemic process of future shaping built on the understanding that the future is not a continuation of the past or present, thus making foresight a complex task requiring the engagement of the whole of government with its constituents in a constructive and iterative manner to achieve collective intelligence and deliver long-term intergenerational public value for humanity and its planet.* Collective intelligence is the capacity of groups of people, organizations, and technology to use the power of many to learn, make decisions, use sensemaking, and solve problems.[13] Effective anticipatory

[12] Fuerth, L.S. (2009). Foresight and anticipatory governance. *Foresight*, 11(4): 14–32; Jackson, M.C. & Keys, P. (1984). Towards a system of systems methodologies. *Journal of the Operational Research Society*, 35: 473–486.

[13] Mulgan, G. (2018). *Big Mind: How Collective Intelligence Can Change the World*. NJ: Princeton University Press.

governance amplifies fundamental properties of agile government. It uses its mechanisms to build trust, challenge assumptions, and reach consensus. Moreover, anticipatory governance prepares the ground to absorb and utilize exponential changes, making them more transformative than merely disruptive (for the sake of disruption).

1.3 Anticipatory Governance — Shaping a Responsible Future

In an increasingly polarized world suffering from the long-term effects of post-colonization, disinformation, and crises, we must all be accountable to chart a journey for a more responsible future. Weapons manufactured from one side of the world find their way to the other and are often not used for the intended purpose of security and peace. Products sold to address a hunger challenge may not tackle the root of the problem due to policy incoherence and poor logistics. Education may not result in the intelligence needed to ensure personal fulfillment, a secured income, or even good decision-making. Since we know so little about charting a responsible future, we asked the experts. Across the 24 chapters of this book, 31 authors from over 11 countries contributed, looking at the critical aspects of anticipatory governance.

This book offers recommendations and policy responses for governments from many different perspectives. It puts together the views of practitioners, policymakers, and academics who have labored to scope and dissect anticipatory governance — to chart out ways to understand the new frameworks of the present and the future.

This book explores tools for anticipatory governance — foresight, backcasting, AI, data, technology regulatory sandboxing, systems thinking, and advocacy. It sheds light on nation-building, diplomacy, and multilateralism. The future of the child, education, work, and biodiversity are highlighted. The role of leadership and skills are unpicked. For anticipatory governance, many skills are highlighted across the chapters, and the public sector needs to do much work to recognize, nurture, and reward these skills.

In particular, this book examines learnings from several countries — Brazil, Latvia, the USA, the UAE, and the Asian and Arab regions. For example, it looks at the role of tribes with their early warning systems and forms of governance, the birth pangs of the Latvian nation, the challenge of the International Humanitarian City in Dubai, the roles the Asian

Development Bank has taken to help facilitate reforms, and the proactive approach adopted by Brazil for preserving biodiversity. Further, it supplements the text via diagrams, cases, and even a comic for better knowledge translation (much needed for policymaking and governance).

As editors, we aim to present our perspective on this critical topic and thread together different angles from our contributing authors. This chapter will provide the reader with a road map to navigate this edited book, which we believe offers unique and valuable lessons from around the world. This book is divided into four sections. Section 1 focuses on building a solid foundation from the perspective of *Anticipatory Governance*. In Chapter 1, authors Stephens *et al.*[14] recap the historical need for anticipatory governance and define the term. In Chapter 2, Sampanthar *et al.* explain how the journey toward the future requires pattern mapping.[15] This process will help identify possible worlds outside what is currently known and help the policymaker understand the cascading order of effects. In Chapter 3, Esposito and Park[16] stress that governments must build anticipatory capacity through foresight as a strategy-making foundation. The authors illustrate how policymakers can use foresight skills as a shield, beacon, lifesaver, or buffer for many purposes.

In Chapter 4, Evans describes in detail why sound policymaking is based on the power of anticipatory analysis. This analysis can help recognize the root causes of wicked problems and act as an alert system where policymakers could react with agility and feasible options because they anticipated potential consequences of unanticipated events.[17] In Chapter 5, Stephens and Inayatullah explore how the backcasting process can help shape a transformative preferred future. The authors reiterate that this is

---

[14] Stephens, M., Awamleh, R., & Sicre, F. (2025). Anticipatory — the next form of governance. In Stephens, M., Awamleh, R., & Sicre, F. (Eds.), *Anticipatory Governance — Shaping a Responsible Future*. Singapore: World Scientific Publishing.

[15] Sampanthar, K., Frank, N., & Balakrishnan, A. (2025). Adjacent possible mapping — exploring the unknown & VUCA environment. In Stephens, M., Awamleh, R., & Sicre, F. (Eds.), *Anticipatory Governance — Shaping a Responsible Future*. Singapore: World Scientific Publishing.

[16] Esposito, M. & Park, J. (2025). Anticipatory capacity through foresight. In Stephens, M., Awamleh, R., & Sicre, F. (Eds.), *Anticipatory Governance — Shaping a Responsible Future*. Singapore: World Scientific Publishing.

[17] Evans, A. (2025). Elevating anticipatory analysis in policy making. In Stephens, M., Awamleh, R., & Sicre, F. (Eds.), *Anticipatory Governance — Shaping a Responsible Future*. Singapore: World Scientific Publishing.

not an easy process or skill and requires participants to challenge their assumptions as the future is not set in stone.[18] Finally, in the last chapter of this section, Chapter 6, Griffiths defines systems thinking and consolidates the many tools that can benefit anticipatory governance.[19] For valuable insights, there is a need to understand the purpose and the role of the tool being used. He emphasizes that systems thinkers need to comprehend the *How* and *Where* of the system boundary to navigate the future.

Section 2 looks at how *Leadership and Transformation* are needed for anticipatory governance to create a responsible and beneficial future for all. The responsibility of anticipatory governance and its implementation is that of leadership — it requires top-down ownership or political will. In Chapter 7, Spitz identifies the necessary leadership skills to achieve anticipatory governance. They are antifragile (the capacity to not just be resilient but improve), anticipatory (looking at more than scenarios, at next-order implications), and agility (a cognitive activity that coherently bridges the future with the present).[20] In Chapter 8, Redman *et al.* underscore the fact that the future needs to be embedded with *purpose*, which provides a guardrail for anticipatory governance.[21] The purpose involves the *So-What* and the *Why* that help leaders navigate critical situations. Public purpose is not a statement adopted for marketing reasons but is a reflection of the intersection of a government's unique strengths and the public goods (current and future needs) it provides. This process of embracing purpose requires a rehaul of culture.

In Chapter 9, Awamleh describes the current global situation as similar to the Wild West, which needed frontier leadership to chart a safe course through uncertainty.[22] The leader's job is to harness collective

[18] Stephens, M. & Inayatullah, S. (2025). Backcasting: A design thinking approach to creating transformative futures. In Stephens, M., Awamleh, R., & Sicre, F. (Eds.), *Anticipatory Governance — Shaping a Responsible Future*. Singapore: World Scientific Publishing.

[19] Griffiths, J. (2025). Navigating pathways towards anticipatory governance within a systems thinking ecosystem. In Stephens, M., Awamleh, R. & Sicre, F. (Eds.), *Anticipatory Governance — Shaping a Responsible Future*. Singapore: World Scientific Publishing.

[20] Spitz, R. (2025). The AAA framework: Responsible leadership for sustainable futures. In Stephens, M., Awamleh, R., & Sicre, F. (Eds.), *Anticipatory Governance — Shaping a Responsible Future*. Singapore: World Scientific Publishing.

[21] Redman, A., Balakrishnan, A., & Frank, N. (2025). Unlocking the power of public purpose. In Stephens, M., Awamleh, R., & Sicre, F. (Eds.), *Anticipatory Governance — Shaping a Responsible Future*. Singapore: World Scientific Publishing.

[22] Awamleh, R. (2025). Frontier leadership. In Stephens, M., Awamleh, R., & Sicre, F. (Eds.), *Anticipatory Governance — Shaping a Responsible Future*. Singapore: World Scientific Publishing.

intelligence (through people and technology) and use the expertise to navigate the new future. In Chapter 10, Lappuke and Panteļējevs[23] retell the history of Latvia's independence. Specifically, they look at diplomatic tools like *lure diplomacy* in navigating difficult political situations. The authors reiterate that nation-building needs to be rooted in historical, economic, and cultural ties and awareness. Hence, you need to understand the past to move forward in the future. In the last chapter in this section, Chapter 11, Stephens *et al.* address the need for an early warning signal system for anticipatory governance. The example they use is that of the Middle East and its system of tribes. They highlight the role of trust in finding suitable corridors to navigate the terrain and cross-reference information. While this skill may resonate with diplomacy, the world is too interconnected for policymakers not to understand the global context in which they plan their future.

Section 3 is titled *Governing Advanced Technology*. Artificial intelligence, or AI, is a big part of our lives, whether we need to use it, embrace it, or regulate it. In Chapter 12, Noack[24] stresses that technology development and its effects are happening faster than regulators can prepare for. There is a need to reverse the process of managing technology regulations and anticipating governance requirements before the tech is deployed. One possibility he suggests is *in silico* regulations, i.e., optimizing regulations with AI before deployment to navigate the complexities of national and international policies, laws, and regulations. Of course, this requires an understanding of *how* and *when* AI can be useful and under *what* parameters.

In Chapter 13, Joshi *et al.* examine how AI deployment has resulted in cyber inequality and security challenges.[25] Anticipatory governance

---

[23] Lappuke, R. & Panteļējevs, A. (2025). How a forgotten nation managed uncertainty – the restoration of Latvia's independence. In Stephens, M., Awamleh, R., & Sicre, F. (Eds.), *Anticipatory Governance — Shaping a Responsible Future*. Singapore: World Scientific Publishing.

[24] Noack, P. (2025). Technology anticipation and regulation. In Stephens, M., Awamleh, R., & Sicre, F. (Eds.), *Anticipatory Governance — Shaping a Responsible Future*. Singapore: World Scientific Publishing.

[25] Joshi, A., Goldstein, T., & Moschetta, G. (2025). In Stephens, M., Awamleh, R., & Sicre, F. (Eds.), *Anticipatory Governance — Shaping a Responsible Future*. Anticipatory Governance on Cybersecurity. Singapore: World Scientific Publishing.

would be helpful in the early identification of threats and their effective management. A government can build a resilient and adaptable security cyber ecosystem through this process. In Chapter 14, Chenok[26] describes how government leadership can use a *security-by-design* method to manage new technologies like AI, cloud computing, and quantum computing. Governments first need to understand the problem to be solved and then the role that secure technologies and data flow management can play. The ecosystem in which governments operate should be able to leverage innovations responsibly for a better future.

In Chapter 15, El-Ghalayini[27] presents the background of the digital transformation of governments. In some ways, anticipatory governance is an evolution of digitalization. One of the questions he asks is as follows: What were the governance parameters for the digital era? This topic is reiterated with the example of copyright laws and Generative AI in the next chapter. In Chapter 16, Al Ghalayini and Al Awamleh[28] explore the complex legal space of this new technology. They conclude that the role of anticipatory governance is being able to stress test existing laws and frameworks for suitability rather than trying to force fit them to new technologies. They state that the process of foresight may buy policymakers more time to change regulations.

The next two chapters highlight the role of children and education in the context of these new technologies. In Chapter 17, Campioni[29] asks a critical question: How are we responding to research on the impact of these technologies on the human brain, and what kind of society do we want for the future? She brings up an important point — any technology

[26] Chenok, D. (2025). Envisioning the future of government: How emerging, secure technologies and data flows can enable anticipation and action that improves performance. In Stephens, M., Awamleh, R., & Sicre, F. (Eds.), *Anticipatory Governance — Shaping a Responsible Future*. Singapore: World Scientific Publishing.

[27] El-Ghalayini, Y. (2025). Digital transformation: A tool for anticipatory governance. In Stephens, M., Awamleh, R., & Sicre, F. (Eds.), *Anticipatory Governance — Shaping a Responsible Future*. Singapore: World Scientific Publishing.

[28] Al-Ghalayini, S. & Al Awamleh, K. (2025). Generative AI and the copyright minefield: Creating safeguards. In Stephens, M., Awamleh, R., & Sicre, F. (Eds.), *Anticipatory Governance — Shaping a Responsible Future*. Singapore: World Scientific Publishing.

[29] Campioni, M. (2025). Transformative change: Future children. In Stephens, M., Awamleh, R., & Sicre, F. (Eds.), *Anticipatory Governance — Shaping a Responsible Future*. Singapore: World Scientific Publishing.

should be used to protect our children and society. Incidentally, in Chapter 6, Griffiths[30] highlights the need to acknowledge non-human actors in our systems, like nature. In Chapter 18, Stephens and Inyatullah[31] illustrate the process of backcasting with an example of personalized education and the future of work, using AI and digital twins to explain how the futures process can be utilized to choose a preferred space, build guardrails, and seek early warning signals to ensure the least unintended effects. This skill of backcasting and being able to iteratively jump from multiple frames needs to be cultivated. Government officials need to develop systems thinking and boundary-spanning skills. Hence, backcasting is not a trendy course to tick a box but a deep, thoughtful, deliberate, and time-consuming exercise to govern the future better.

Finally, in Section 4, the various chapters address *Learning from the Past: Guardrails and Opportunities*. The first chapter in this section explores the evolution of OldSpace to NewSpace. In Chapter 19, Giorgi[32] highlights many misconceptions about what is needed for a successful space strategy. The reality is that the old lessons — the need for long-term planning, transparent budgets, high tolerance for failure and risks, and understanding the complexities of the competitiveness in this sector — are still required to reap the benefits of this industry and de-escalate risks. The space industry requires long-term strategic planning. In Chapter 20, Subramani[33] describes many examples of plans that go awry without an impact measurement framework. She recommends three approaches to minimize government failures: plausibility analysis, scenario analysis, and monitoring aggregate indices.

Predicting failures and vulnerabilities could also be the remit of anticipatory analysis. For example, in Chapter 21, de Medeiros and

---

[30] Griffiths (2005), *Op. cit.*

[31] Stephens, M. & Inyatullah, S. (2025). Future of education & work: Using backcasting to design guardrails. In Stephens, M., Awamleh, R., & Sicre, F. (Eds.), *Anticipatory Governance — Shaping a Responsible Future*. Singapore: World Scientific Publishing.

[32] Giorgi, D. (2025). From oldspace to newspace and beyond: Anticipating the effects of the (r)evolution of the space sector. In Stephens, M., Awamleh, R., & Sicre, F. (Eds.), *Anticipatory Governance — Shaping a Responsible Future*. Singapore: World Scientific Publishing.

[33] Subramani, K. (2025). Frameworks for impact measurement under uncertainty. In Stephens, M., Awamleh, R., & Sicre, F. (Eds.), *Anticipatory Governance — Shaping a Responsible Future*. Singapore: World Scientific Publishing.

Gomes[34] present the case of Brazil and how it successfully used anticipatory governance in plant health policy to monitor, prevent, and control absent quarantine pests from entering the country and damaging its biodiversity and cash crops. They present the Analytical Hierarchical Process methodology, which can be used for other types of policy analysis. In Chapter 22, Roth and Milojević[35] explain the case of the Asian Development Bank and its role in facilitating futures thinking in anticipatory governance. They highlight the need for more multilateral organizations to enhance awareness and capacity-building for better reform management. The roles that the Asian Development Bank took in this journey were capacity developer, instigator, and documenter. The latter role was crucial for knowledge sharing. Again, the chapter stresses the need to understand first-, second-, and third-order implications of policies and learn how to use anticipatory governance to reduce blind spots and future-proof strategies. In Chapter 23, Moonesar[36] focuses on the role of organizations like the International Humanitarian City (IHC) in Dubai and how it manages humanitarian logistics and health responses during crises. He recommends the 3R approach — readiness, rapid responses, and resilience and recovery. Specifically in time-sensitive contexts, anticipatory governance allows entities to find partners, speed up response times, and optimize resource movement efficiency. The chapter looks at how the IHC created a data-sharing platform and used its networks (government, intergovernmental, and other parties) to ensure the vulnerable were reached.

In the final chapter, Chapter 24, Stephens and Balakrishnan[37] focus on advocacy through educational awareness of the need for synthetic biology

[34]de Medeiros, E.A. & Gomes, R.C. (2025). Anticipatory governance to protect biodiversity prevent the entry of quarantine pests in Brazil. In Stephens, M., Awamleh, R., & Sicre, F. (Eds.), *Anticipatory Governance — Shaping a Responsible Future*. Singapore: World Scientific Publishing.

[35]Roth, S. & Milojević, I. (2025). Building an architectural framework for anticipatory governance: A case study of the Asian Development Bank. In Stephens, M., Awamleh, R., & Sicre, F. (Eds.), *Anticipatory Governance — Shaping a Responsible Future*. Singapore: World Scientific Publishing.

[36]Moonesar, I.A. (2025). Humanitarian logistics and health response. In Stephens, M., Awamleh, R., & Sicre, F. (Eds.), *Anticipatory Governance — Shaping a Responsible Future*. Singapore: World Scientific Publishing.

[37]Stephens, M. & Balakrishnan, A. (2025). Synthetic biology governance — advocacy. In Stephens, M., Awamleh, R., & Sicre, F. (Eds.), *Anticipatory Governance — Shaping a Responsible Future*. Singapore: World Scientific Publishing.

governance. A previous policy paper is converted into a comic using Generative AI to increase visibility of an important topic. Hence, as mentioned at the beginning of the chapter, to change and shape the future, there is a need to communicate and inspire partners on this long journey.

1.4 Conclusion

To conclude, the editors of this book put forth a proposition that the world is experiencing a seismic shift at multiple levels of governance, which should make us urgently rethink the ways and means governments and large corporate players formulate strategies, design processes, develop human capital, and shape institutional culture.

We further argue that effective anticipatory governance amplifies fundamental properties of agile government and uses its mechanisms to build trust, challenge assumptions, and reach consensus. Importantly, anticipatory governance prepares the ground to absorb and utilize exponential changes, making them more transformative than merely disruptive. Furthermore, anticipatory governance can offer an effective platform for managing change by harnessing collective intelligence when taking a long-term multigenerational perspective. We suggest that many wicked problems that governments and corporations grapple with can be scoped, analyzed, and resolved through anticipatory governance.

This book dives into the theory and practice of anticipatory governance and sets the agenda for future research. From a theoretical lens, there is a need to understand the discourse and evolution of new public management theories, digitalization, agile government, agile governance, and anticipatory government. Further, while it is clear that anticipatory government is NOT just foresight and requires courage to break a reactionary response, more research is needed on its conceptual boundaries. Governance is a multilayered construct, and the role of other parties, including technology and non-humans, should also be considered.

There are many research areas in this field: What have been the levers governments in the past have used to manage and control future journeys? What are vulnerabilities that make policy plans obsolete or detrimental? When should a government have the courage to abandon an idea, and how can we prevent the too-big-to-fail dilemma? What are learnings from failures, and how can this knowledge be captured and shared? At what point does too much agility become disruptive, and can a vital EWS help provide the guardrails for future shaping?

Today's policymakers do not have the luxury of waiting for the future to arrive. The transnational nature of complex and dynamic problems and their interconnectedness may make taking any action fraught with the challenge of unintentional adverse effects. Hence, policymakers need skills to reimagine the future, and this means working on the one hand with data, the logical, rational side of processes that needs transparency, and on the other hand with creativity, to break free of the present and past to explore new areas. This process is difficult. Tools are not a formula for success as policymakers need to understand problems before looking for solutions. Collective intelligence will be required since no person (or AI) can capture domain knowledge. In a world where trust is rare, policymakers and governments must focus on personal networks, organizational reputation, or country soft power.

While we know we are leaving you with more questions than answers, at least we have a starting point as we journey into the future — a better future that benefits people and the planet, for all humankind.

https://doi.org/10.1142/9789811296000_0002

Chapter 2

Adjacent Possible Mapping — Exploring the Unknown and VUCA Environment

Kesevan Sampanthar*, Noah Frank*, and Abhishek Balakrishnan†

**Valize, USA*
†BCG BrightHouse, Atlanta, USA

Key Takeaways

- Strategic inflection points are moments of enormous transformational change that we must be able to harness.
- The exponential growth of social platforms created disruptions we could not have anticipated, not just in how we see and interact with one another but also in how we market, package, and consume information.
- Past precedent alone does not enable us to chart a future course. In a VUCA world, we need to identify patterns to map a trajectory of signals.
- Leaning on the *adjacent possible* or promising worlds outside our current purview helps us contextualize the effects of our decisions and the subsequent cascading order of impacts.
- To build anticipatory governance through the *adjacent possible*, governments must develop "meta-leaders" who understand how to network institutional knowledge, build strategic advisory groups, and embrace new technologies.

2.1 Governing in an Age of Disruption

The late 1980s and early 1990s marked a significant shift in strategic thinking for much of the international business community. It was in this world that Andy Grove, former CEO of Intel Corporation, introduced his concept of "strategic inflection points" (see Exhibit 2.1). Though not necessarily single moments in time, strategic inflection points occur when organizations face pressure from environmental alterations that force strategic change.[1]

Every organization, institution, agency, business, government, or social collective experiences reasonable change. However, the 10x major change that occurs in strategic inflection points can exert enough pressure to make or break organizations. As Columbia University professor Rita McGrath explains, "[These moments] can create both new, entrepreneurial opportunities and result in potentially devastating consequences for those still working under old models and assumptions."[2] The challenge is being able to identify these points and their unintended consequences early enough to do something about it.

Exhibit 2.1. Strategic inflection points: Moments of transformational change.

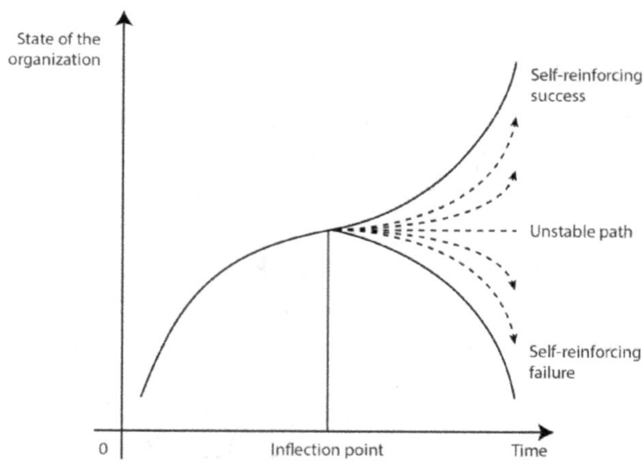

Source: Adapted from Deutsch (2016).[3]

[1]Grove, A. (1988). *Only the Paranoid Survive: How to Exploit the Crisis Points That Challenge Every Company*. London: Profile Book.

[2]McGrath, R.G. (2019). *Seeing Around Corners: How to Spot Inflection Points in Business before They Happen*. Boston: Houghton Mifflin Harcourt.

[3]Deutsch, R. (2016). The strategic inflection point is a time to wake up and listen. X @ randydeutsch, March, 2016. Available: https://twitter.com/randydeutsch/status/712290942594605057 (Accessed: 4 January 2024).

We are living through a strategic inflection point in human history. The international landscape today is fraught with a "perfect storm" of crises, each intersecting and amplifying others: climate change, ecological degradation, food and water insecurity, emergent pandemics, and demographic shifts.[4] Further compounding these challenges is the stark difference between today's world and past periods of structural change, such as the Industrial Revolution. This "Age of Disruption" is rapidly accelerating the speed and scope of new technologies that affect our daily lives.[5]

The following trajectory of data usage in recent years illustrates this exponential acceleration leading to *Informational Abundance*:

- In 2000, the publicly available World Wide Web taken in its entirety, contained about 6 terabytes (~6,000 gigabytes) of text data.[6]
- In 2018, the amount of data created, captured, copied, and consumed in the world was around 33 zettabytes (~33 trillion gigabytes).[7]
- In 2025, this number is projected to reach a mind-boggling 175 zettabytes (one zettabyte is 8,000,000,000,000,000,000,000 bits).[8]

The following are internet usage statistics:

- As of 2023, 5.3 billion people use the internet worldwide, which is approximately 65.7% of the world's population.[9]
- In 2023, about 92% of Americans use the internet, up from 75% in 2012.[10]

Extensive scholarship exists on the key role of government in responding to and creating the conditions for innovation. In their

---

[4]Kuecker, G. (2007). The perfect storm: Catastrophic collapse in the 21st century. *The International Journal of Environmental, Cultural, Economic & Social Sustainability,* 3(5): 1–10.

[5]Hartley, K., Kuecker, G., & Woo, J.J. (2019). Practicing public policy in an age of disruption. *Policy Design and Practice,* 2(2): 163–181.

[6]Lawrence, S. & Giles, C. (2000). Accessibility of information on the world wide web. *Intelligence*, 11: 32–39.

[7]Reinsel, D., Gantz, J., & Rynning, J. (2018). *The Digitization of the World — From Edge to Core*. Needham: IDC.

[8]*Ibid.*

[9]Petrosyan, A. (2023). Worldwide digital population 2023. *Statista.*

[10]*Ibid.*

1992 book, *Government's Role in Innovation*, researchers Patrick Leyden and Albert Link proposed that one of the government's chief roles is ensuring that society's general interests are represented in forthcoming innovations and private sector decision-making.[11] However, scholars often disagree on the methods for how a government promotes these interests. As evidenced by the contemporary struggle between neoliberals and statists, arguments like this about the proper role of government as an intervening force have existed since Adam Smith's *Wealth of Nations*. While there are advantages and disadvantages on each side, at least some government intervention and responses are generally required to promote outcomes that benefit the majority.[12]

In this context, governments around the world face challenges leveraging traditional approaches to governing with exponential technological change. As such, there is extensive evidence to suggest that the accelerating nature of disruptions today is outpacing a government's ability to respond in key sectors.[13] While it remains true that governments retain unique abilities, such as the capacity to convene diverse groups of experts and issue regulations, extended policy lag contributes to destabilized macroeconomic models.[14] As the speed and scale of technological adoption expand, so do the speed and scale of unintended consequences. Therefore, without addressing lags and gaps in policy, these will lengthen and proliferate, leading to exponentially worse outcomes.

Proactive public leaders have long sought tools to manage these types of social, economic, and technological shifts during strategic inflection points. One such concept that has gained considerable attention in recent years is called "strategic foresight." Defined by the OECD as the

[11] Leyden, D. & Albert, L. (1992). *Government's Role in Innovation*. Berlin: Springer Science & Business Media.

[12] Wang, J. (2018). Innovation and government intervention: A comparison of Singapore and Hong Kong. *Research Policy*, 47(2): 399–412.

[13] Marchant, G.E. (2011). The growing gap between emerging technologies and the law. In Marchant, G., Allenby, B., & Herkert, J. (Eds.), *The Growing Gap between Emerging Technologies and Legal-Ethical Oversight: The Pacing Problem*. Dordrecht, Germany: Springer: pp. 19–32; Costigan S. & Lindstrom, G. (2016). Policy and the internet of things. *Connections*, 15(2): 9–18.

[14] Asada, T. & Yoshida, H. (2000). Stability, instability and complex behavior in macrodynamic models with policy lag. *Discrete Dynamics in Nature and Society*, 5(4): 281–295.

"structured and explicit exploration of multiple futures in order to inform decision-making," effective foresight models necessitate that we have a rich understanding of the present to model the future.[15] Further scholarship on strategic foresight suggests that it has wide-reaching implications for businesses and relevant policymaking contexts.[16] We propose that, while novel on paper, many of these strategic foresight models are hampered by MECE thinking (Mutually Exclusive, Collectively Exhaustive)[17] in an exponential world and must be upgraded.

In this chapter, we will focus on how governments deploy this upgraded foresight — both to predict future worlds and model policy implications — as an essential component of anticipatory governance. But first, we will begin by examining a digital hotbed for unanticipated consequences: social media.

2.2 Connection and Unforeseen Consequences

At the time of writing this chapter, in the mid-2020s, we are living through the third decade of the social media revolution. Technology companies, responsible for the hosting and maintenance of these platforms, project an ideal picture of the world that their platforms create. One look at a few companies' missions, including Meta, X (formerly Twitter), and even newcomers like BeReal, reveals the philosophies that underpin these platforms:

- Meta's mission is to "give people the power to build community and bring the world closer together."[18]

---

[15]OECD (2021). Foresight and Anticipatory Governance: Lessons in Effective Foresight Institutionalization.

[16]Sarpong, D. & Maclean, M. (2014). Unpacking strategic foresight: A practice approach. *Scandinavian Journal of Management,* 30: 16–26; Weber, C., Sailer, K., & Katzy, B. (2015). Real-time foresight — preparedness for dynamic networks. *Technological Forecasting and Social Change*, 101: 299–313.

[17]Carey, M. (1981). On mutually exclusive and collectively exhaustive properties of demand functions. *Economica,* 48(192): 407–415.

[18]Meta (2024). About Meta. Available: https://about.meta.com/company-info/ (Accessed: January 2024).

- The "professional platform" LinkedIn has a mission to connect the world's professionals to make them more productive and successful.[19]
- A newer platform, "BeReal" claims that their model of instantaneous status updates from friends exists "to create an authentic world that keeps you connected with the people you really care about."[20]

In terms of sheer engagement, these platforms have a vast audience that is only growing. 4.95 billion people, or 61.4% of the world's population, are on social media.[21] With such influence, social media has transformed not only how we see and interact with one another but also how we market, package, and consume information. Within governments in particular, widespread access to social media has changed the landscape of agency-constituent relations, with rules being rewritten as we speak.[22]

Thanks to recent explorations into the influence of these platforms, such as Max Fisher's revelatory book *Chaos Machine*, the unforeseen consequences of mass social media usage are now finally being understood.[23] Related to political issues, media companies and scholars alike will be quick to point to examples where platform interconnectedness achieved seemingly great things. For instance, in 2010, the prevalence of internet usage and platforms like Twitter is credited with inspiring the pro-democracy "Jasmine Revolution" in Tunisia. The month-long struggle, including street demonstrations, ended with the ousting of longtime Tunisian president Zine El Abidine Ben Ali and set the country on a new path toward eventual reform.[24] Social media platforms offered a real-time window into the conflict for an audience of both Tunisian protesters and people around the world. It is

[19]LinkedIn (2024). About LinkedIn. Available: https://about.linkedin.com (Accessed: January 2024).

[20]BeReal (2024). Our mission and values. Available: https://help.bereal.com/hc/en-us/articles/10738198628637-Our-Mission-and-Values#:~:text=We%20innovate%2C%20experiment%20and%20disrupt,and%20keep%20each%20other%20accountable (Accessed: January 2024).

[21]Criado, J., Sandoval-Almazan, R., & Ramon Gil-Garcia, J. (2013). Government innovation through social media. *Government Information Quarterly,* 30(4): 319–326.

[22]DataReportal (2024). Digital around the world. *Kepios* (Accessed January 2024).

[23]Fisher, M. (2022). *The Chaos Machine: The Inside Story of How Social Media Rewired Our Minds and Our World*. New York: Little, Brown and Company.

[24]Miladi, N. (2015). Social media and social change. *Domes*, 25: 36–51; Breuer, A., Landman, T., & Farquhar, D. (2015). Social media and protest mobilization: Evidence from the Tunisian revolution. *Democratization*, 22(4): 764–792.

important to note that the actual path to change in governance is a long one and Tunisia, in 2024, is still struggling.

A more thorough analysis of these platforms' unforeseen consequences demonstrates their potential implications far beyond what most platform architects and politicians could have imagined. In one notable case, during the 2010 US congressional elections, Facebook (now Meta) conducted a randomized control study on 60 million users.[25] On the day of the election, a group of users was shown a message encouraging them to vote, along with an "I Voted" sticker, another group was shown six photos of Facebook friends who had already clicked the "I Voted" sticker (see Exhibit 2.2), and a third did not receive a message. Results of the study showed that this second group that was shown pictures of friends were more likely to vote by a factor of 0.4%. While this might not seem like much, the authors of the study claimed to have increased voter turnout by a factor of 340,000 votes.[26] To put this in perspective, this number is greater than the total 2020 presidential election margins of Georgia, Arizona, Wisconsin, Pennsylvania, North Carolina, and Nevada taken together (with around 100,000 votes to spare).

Exhibit 2.2. Voters on Facebook receive ads during the 2010 midterms.

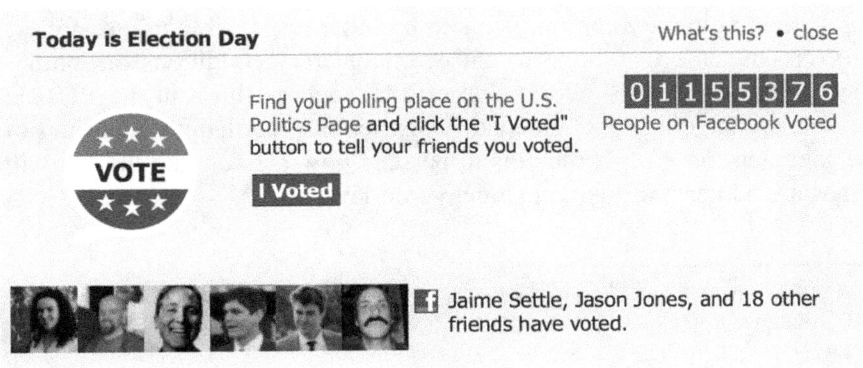

Source: Adapted from Bond *et al.*, (2012).[27]

[25] Bond, R., Fariss, C., Jones, J., *et al.* (2012). A 61-million-person experiment in social influence and political mobilization. *Nature,* 489: 295–298.

[26] Véliz, C. (2020). *Privacy Is Power.* London, UK: Bantam Press.

[27] Bond, R., Fariss, C., Jones, J., *et al.* (2012). A 61-million-person experiment in social influence and political mobilization. *Nature*, 489: 295–298. Reproduced under the Fair Use Policy.

There are still more depressing cases from Facebook and companies like it. In 2017, Facebook algorithms were credited to have directly contributed to the Myanmar security forces' ethnic cleansing of the minority Rohingya people. Coined the "Social Atrocity" by Amnesty International, their investigation revealed that the platform's ability to "incite violence, hatred, and discrimination" was at least partially responsible for the deaths of tens of thousands.[28] Clearly, the unforeseen consequences of widespread social media usage go much further than any bullish early proponent might have predicted. We now know that media platforms that optimize for engagement can over-index on heightened negative emotions like outrage and amplify tribalistic human tendencies to form groups.[29] They drive the exponential growth of information that makes it harder to discern truth and that contributes to the further proliferation of online misinformation and disinformation, which we expect to intensify with GenAI. These challenges are only further compounded by the fact that in places like the US, these companies enjoy a considerable degree of freedom and self-regulation.[30]

This problem of unanticipated outcomes is not unique to social media. The explosion of commercially viable LLMs and chatbots such as ChatGPT has elevated a new suite of players such as OpenAI and Anthropic to considerable recognition. While these companies have lined up behind voluntary commitments to promote responsible usage, policymakers are only beginning to enforce mandatory conditions of compliance with standards.[31] World-first efforts, such as those in the EU and China, are ongoing to set mandatory restrictions, regulations, and rules of engagement on AI.[32] It remains to be seen how nations like the US will translate AI harm mitigation strategy into law.

---

[28] Amnesty International (2022). The Social Atrocity: Meta and the Right to Remedy for the Rohingya. Report.

[29] Fisher, M. (2023). *The Chaos Machine: The Inside Story of How Social Media Rewired Our Minds and Our World*. New York: Little, Brown & Company.

[30] Susskind, J. (2022). *The Digital Republic: On Freedom and Democracy in the 21st Century*. New York: Pegasus Books.

[31] White House (2023, 12 September). Biden-Harris Administration secures voluntary commitments from leading artificial intelligence companies to manage the risks posed by AI. *White House Briefing Room*.

[32] Sheehan, M. (2023). China's AI regulations and how they get made. *Carnegie Endowment for International Peace*; Veale, M. & Zuiderveen Borgesius, F. (2021). Demystifying the draft EU artificial intelligence act. *Computer Law Review International*, 22(4): 97–112.

In forthcoming sections, we will explore how adjacent possible thinking enables us to make use of strategic foresight effectively to anticipate these distant, future worlds.

2.3 The Present: The World of Exponential Change

In March 2020, amidst the early days of the COVID-19 pandemic response in the US, Politico released a lengthy, bureaucratic, 69-page National Security Council document to the public. Titled the *Playbook for Early Response to High-Consequence Emerging Infectious Disease Threats and Biological Incidents*, the "pandemic playbook," its other more colloquial title, outlined a comprehensive strategy for the US government to follow in case of a major pandemic. The catch was that the document was created by the Obama administration four years prior, in 2016. When the Trump administration took over, the plan was shelved.[33] In this section, we will explore how key government functions are affected by decisions in the present and the strategies for which leaders can best view the present in service of future worlds.

There is considerable proof to confirm that, oftentimes, the "past predicts the future." We believe that, like Mark Twain, while history does not repeat, it often does rhyme. That will require some more sophisticated strategic foresight. In the US government, as in many legal systems around the world, precedent is a policy wherein present decision-makers have an obligation to review previous cases and, where appropriate, follow previous rule. In this way, the very "pastness" of previous decisions is what lends them their credibility.[34] However reverence for previous decisions has more of a psychological effect than many realize. Even legal scholars acknowledge that precedence has a role to play not only in law but also more broadly.[35] Perceptual studies suggest that direct experiences of past regularities are necessary for predicting the future.

Network theory and behavioral science research into disruption can shine much light on indicators of change in the public sector. Rita

---

[33]Diamond, D. & Toosi, N. (2020). Trump team failed to follow NSC's pandemic playbook. *Politico*, 25 March.

[34]Curt, C.L. & Zechmeister, E.B. (1984). Primacy, recency, and the availability heuristic. *Bulletin of the Psychonomic Society,* 22: 177–179.

[35]Schauer, F. (2012). Precedent. In *The Routledge Companion to Philosophy of Law*. Routledge: Oxfordshire, UK. pp. 123–136.

McGrath's theory of signal sensing is a valuable way of gauging proximity to an inflection point, in which leaders look to the edges of their organizations for signals of strengths and gaps.[36] Mapping the impacts of macro signals using a pattern library to explore the adjacent possible is a powerful technique to identify strategic inflection points and the future possible. Effective forecasting powered by pattern libraries can help organizations and governments provide easy access and a central repository to help teams anticipate the future.[37] In *Where Good Ideas Come From*, Steven Johnson writes that when patterns are "simple, but followed together, they make for a whole that is wiser than the sum of its parts."[38]

But how do you find these patterns and organize them in a meaningful, usable way? The Rumsfeld Matrix (see Exhibit 2.3) is one such way to model the future in a world of uncertainty. In a VUCA world,[39] one of the most important goals of any organization is to use pattern libraries to model and map the trajectory of signals across the four main categories:

- "Known-Knowns"
- "Known-Unknowns"
- "Unknown-Knowns"
- "Unknown-Unknowns"

In our rapidly changing world, the implications of every policy decision cannot possibly be charted or covered at once. In the next section, we will venture into this "black box" of the future and its worlds adjacent possible to our own.

---

[36] McGrath, R.G. (2019). *Seeing around Corners: How to Spot Inflection Points before They Happen.* Boston: Houghton Mifflin Harcourt.

[37] Vora, P. (2009). Chapter 13: Pattern libraries. *Web Application Design Patterns*, Elsevier, Amsterdam, NE. pp. 389–403.

[38] Johnson, S. (2011). *Where Good Ideas Come from: The Natural History of Innovation.* New York: Riverhead Books.

[39] Johansen, B. & Euchner, J. (2013). Navigating the VUCA world. *Research-Technology Management,* 56(1): 10–15.

Exhibit 2.3. The Rumsfeld matrix of modeling uncertainty.

Source: Adapted from Saravanan (2021).[40]

2.4 The Future: The World of Adjacent Possibilities

In the previous section, we explored the world of past and present "unknowns," both in their inability to be estimated and implications for policy. For the government to truly anticipate the future with strategic foresight, creativity is an essential element for public leaders to employ when envisioning a future state.[41] Unfortunately, creativity alone is not

---

[40]Saravanan, R. (2021). The Rumsfeld matrix: Degrees of knowledge. In *The Climate Demon: Past, Present, and Future of Climate Prediction*. Cambridge: Cambridge University Press: pp. 193–211.

[41]McGrath (2019), *Op cit.*

enough. Effective strategic foresight requires that we apply scientific rigor to inform creative techniques at all times. To illustrate the significance of these kinds of challenges, we can examine one such dilemma that has shaped the nature of computing for nearly six decades known as "Polanyi's Paradox."[42] In 1966, the philosopher Michael Polanyi observed that "We can know more than we can tell... The skill of a driver cannot be replaced by a thorough schooling in the theory of the motorcar; the knowledge I have of my own body differs altogether from the knowledge of its physiology." In this paradox, we will always know more than we can understand. Therein, our knowledge of a given subject (or lack thereof) will always exceed our comprehension of it.[43] Understanding the unknowns using a tool like the Rumsfeld Matrix is important to overcome the paradox and model the future.

In today's world, evidence of this paradox is coded in the fabric of the systems we are creating, from AI to much more. A new term for this is "capability overhang" or "tech overhang," for which the capabilities of a system already exist but we have not conceptualized how to make use of them.[44] Therefore, this suggests that the limits of technology have so surpassed our ability to comprehend them that we need more sophisticated techniques to model these new possibilities.

We believe that we can take this premise of our limited knowledge and understanding to push thinking about unintended consequences into theoretical, adjacent possible futures. In Steven Johnson's *Where Good Ideas Come From*, he defines "adjacent possible" in this context as "*... a kind of shadow future, hovering on the edges of the present state of things, a map of all the ways in which the present can reinvent itself.*"[45] Johnson got close, but missed a crucial point: These futures are intently shaped by our decisions.

We see an interesting use for this model rooted in economic principles and strategy, differing from the concept's early origins in structural

---

[42] McAfee, A. & Brynjolfsson, E. (2017). *Machine, Platform, Crowd: Harnessing Our Digital Future*. New York: W.W. Norton & Company.

[43] Autor, D. (2014). Polanyi's paradox and the shape of employment growth. *NBER Working Paper* No. 20485.

[44] Recke, M. (2023). Capability overhang, or the future of AI. *NEXT* (Accessed: January 2024).

[45] Johnson, S. (2011). *Where Good Ideas Come From: The Natural History of Innovation*. London: Penguin.

Exhibit 2.4. 1st-, 2nd-, and 3rd-order effects in the new adjacent possible.

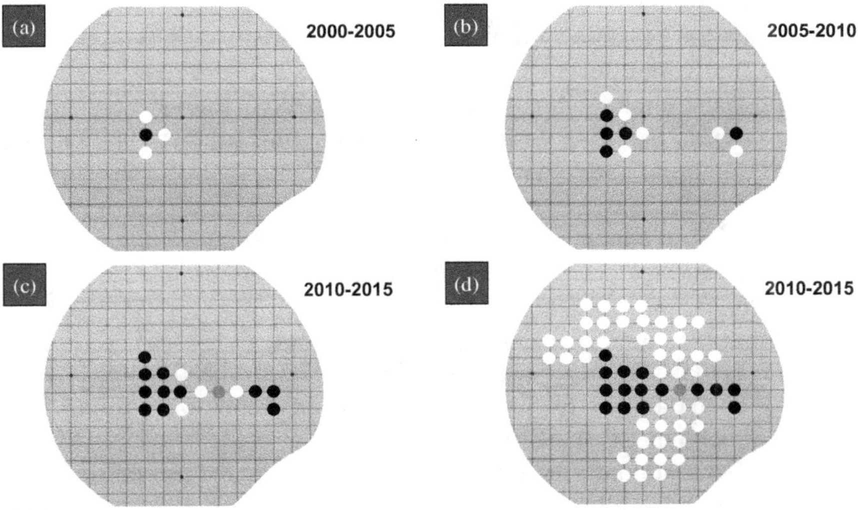

Source: Authors.

biology.[46] As such, there are degrees with which we can encounter adjacent possibilities. Our framework categorizing these possible worlds into 1st-, 2nd-, and 3rd-order effects can inform our decisions more effectively than using MECE models that ignore unknowns.

As such, the greater the degree order, the greater the "possibility surface area" (PSA) and opportunity for disruption. Exhibit 2.4 plays out the adjacent possible of social media through its 1st to 3rd Order. The diagram illustrates the adjacent possible patterns that took place during four stages of the evolution of social media.

A - *1st Order: New Technology Trend (Social Network)*

a. Adjacent Possible Patterns:

i. Network effects: Network effects occur when a product or service becomes more valuable as more people use it, creating a positive feedback loop that attracts even more users.

[46] Kauffman, S. (2000). *Investigations.* Oxford: Oxford University Press.

B - *2nd Order: Technology (Social Network) expands and 2nd New Social Trend (Millennials)*

b. Adjacent Possible Patterns:
   i. Network effects.
   ii. Generational effect: The Generational effect follows generations across their major life events — schooling, graduation, first job, marriage, kids, etc.

C - *3rd Order: Technology Trend hits exponential point (Social network becomes social media), Social Trend hits exponential point (Millennials start hitting the workforce),*

c. Adjacent Possible Patterns:
   i. Social media tipping point: The social media tipping point is characterized by the impact of social networks turning into social media publishers.
   ii. Generational life event: The Generational Life events map refers to key moments in the lifetime of a particular generation like when Millennials join the workforce.

D - *3rd Order: Both trends reach Inflection Point, leading to a self-reinforcing cycle and the explosion of social media news and advertising*

d. Adjacent possible patterns:
   i. Informational Abundance hits inflection point which is characterized by the impact of the social media tipping point (see above) driving an exponential rise in information.
   ii. Leading to scarcity of attention.

This method of adjacency is akin to John Conway's model for the famous *Game of Life*. In this simulation, rules governing a population can create unexpected and diverse adjacent structures given the relationship between different blocks on the board.[47] Population growth in the *Game of Life* occurs nearly instantaneously and simultaneously, as is the case

---

[47]Bak, P., Chen, K., & Creutz, M. (1989). Self-organized criticality in the 'game of life'. *Nature*, 342: 780–782.

with many prominent innovations today. Therefore, its use as a model for thinking through the changing nature of innovation cannot be overstated.

Similarly in our model, the further removed an adjacent possible future is from an event (ex: 3rd order impacts), the more abstract and unknown its effect will ultimately be. An illustrative example of this is the history of the FAA and airline deregulation:[48]

- **Event:** 1978 Airline Deregulation Act (ADA) partially shifts control over air travel from the political to the market sphere.
- **1st Order:** The Civil Aeronautics Board was phased out in 1984, limiting constraints on airline operations. Because the grid is still controlled by the government, this is only considered a "partial deregulation."
- **2nd Order:** After deregulation, airlines reconfigured their routes and equipment, making possible improvements in capacity utilization. These efficiency effects democratized air travel, making it more accessible to the public.
- **3rd Order:** Estimates suggest that when figures are adjusted for changes in quality and amenities, passengers save $19.4 billion dollars per year from airline deregulation.[49] This has further stimulated growth, creating an environment where LCCs (low-cost carriers) can unseat legacy players in the space. If you are looking at the 4th order, you might look at drones and privatization of space.

Therefore, the move to deregulate the space directly contributed to the rise of LCCs in the 3rd-order effects, decades after the initial provisions passed.

In the next section, we will look at existing foresight mechanisms that have had an impact on the world and offer some recommendations for all nations considering foresight initiatives in this disruptive age.

---

[48] Smith, F. & Cox, B. (2008). Airline deregulation. *The Concise Encyclopedia of Economics* (Accessed January 2024).

[49] Crandall, R. & Ellig, J. (1997). Economic deregulation and customer choice: Lessons for the electric industry. Center for Market Processes, Inc.

2.5 Policy Recommendations: Building the Anticipatory Government of the Future

Traditional strategic foresight is already a part of the international conversation on good governance. In fact, many nations have done remarkable things in the past couple of years:

- In Finland, the nation's National Foresight Network is co-run by the Prime Minister's Office in cooperation with Sitra, the national Innovation Fund. Sitra's mandate to "ensure the future well-being of Finland" enables it to support government ventures to build partnerships and internal coalitions across different groups.[50]
- In Singapore, the Centre for Strategic Futures, run out of the Prime Minister's Office, has developed frameworks to educate public decision-makers on emerging topics. One such framework and a core element of their instruction for leaders is their "SP+" curriculum, in which key decision-makers are educated on monitoring, sensemaking, and envisioning possible futures.[51]
- Estonia is an exceptional case, wherein the parliament operates a think tank called the Foresight Centre. The Centre not only envisions possible scenarios to "future-proof" policy outcomes but also post-assesses previous foresight work after a certain period to ensure compliance with new standards and scholarship.[52]

While the impact of these initiatives has been strong, traditional strategic foresight has still not been widely adopted, let alone leveraging an upgraded approach. The opportunities to create a more future-focused government apparatus are vast. As previous scholarship has explored, there are also many different forms in which this can take place.[53] Further, these

---

[50] Government of Finland (n.d.). National Foresight Network. Available: https://vnk.fi/en/foresight/national-foresight-network (Accessed January 2024).

[51] Centre for Strategic Futures (n.d.). Our approach. Available: https://www.csf.gov.sg/our-work/our-approach/ (Accessed January 2024).

[52] Foresight Centre (n.d.). About Foresight Centre. Available: https://arenguseire.ee/en/about/ (Accessed January 2024).

[53] Havas, A., Schartinger, D., & Weber, M. (2010). The impact of foresight on innovation policy-making: Recent experiences and future perspectives. *Research Evaluation,* 19: 91–104.

forces, however influential, have not stopped the geopolitical instability and regional conflicts that have marked the first half of the 2020s. We need a better system in a time of exponentially accelerating disruption.

We have a few strategies for policymakers to implement as they design new foresight programs and leverage their impact potential in this new age:

- **Network Institutional Knowledge:** Gather networks for institutional knowledge and decision-making and remove barriers to innovation. Institutions should take steps to reduce siloization and information gaps among key decision-makers. In a world of exponential information, we need to leverage the power of networks to understand the complex nature of systems. Frameworks like Team of Teams® are good starting places for this kind of thinking.[54]
- **Build Strategic Advisory Groups**: Organize resources for upgraded strategic foresight advisory groups within agencies and institutions. Today's strategies will not work tomorrow. Different levels and functions within governments should have bodies or leaders specifically responsible for superforecasting and leveraging the adjacent possible framework to map the second- and third-order impacts of policy decisions into the future.[55]
- **Embrace New Technologies:** Commit to integrating new technologies into functions performed and services offered. Taking a conscious approach to lean into technological change will help the government of the future go far, especially in the coming decades with ever-higher numbers of digital natives. Governments should open themselves to new opportunities as new technologies increasingly become free and instantaneously accessible.

We are already seeing some of these things play out in the real world. The UAE has established a "virtual ministry" dubbed the Ministry of Possibilities.[56] Launched in 2019, the stated goals of this effort are to "tackle impossible challenges effectively through new innovative models

[54]McChrystal, G.S.A., Silverman, D., Collins, T., & Fussell, C. (2015). *Team of Teams*. Portfolio Penguin. London, UK.

[55]Tetlock, P. & Gardner, D. (2015). *Superforecasting: The Art and Science of Prediction*. New York: Crown.

[56]UAE Government (2024). Ministry of Possibilities. Available: https://mop.gov.ae (Accessed January 2024).

and working methods aiming to improve people's quality of life." To date, the Ministry's first phase of work spanned four new departments: the Department of Anticipatory Services, the Department of Behavioral Rewards, the Department of UAE Talent, and the Department of Government Procurement.

2.6 Final Considerations

Klaus Schwab, the Executive Chairman and Founder of the WEF, calls the era we are living in the "Fourth Industrial Revolution."[57] Navigating this next period in human history successfully will be a pivotal point for our species and our world, and the step change nature of this transformation is represented in Exhibit 2.5.

Understanding the combination of past revolutions, present signals, and possible futures will be our best bet to help public leaders implement superforecasting and adjacent possible decision-making in an uncertain VUCA world. Some countries, like South Korea and Australia, are already beginning to contextualize their processes and innovations against this Fourth Industrial Revolution model.[58]

As our world reaches a critical inflection point, our focus should be on the training and development of "meta-leaders," a new leadership model for the 21st century. "Meta-leaders" overcome siloed thinking by intentionally connecting the purposes and work of different organizational units toward common goals, in recognition of both past successes/failures and new opportunities.[59] These leaders will be the beacons of light as we comprehend our darkness. With the right foresight mechanisms in place, they will have the "courage, curiosity, and imagination" to explore the exponentially growing unknown.

---

[57] Schwab, K. (2016). The Fourth Industrial Revolution: What It Means, How to Respond. World Economic Forum (Accessed January 2024).

[58] Yang, H., Kim, S.Y., & Yim, S. (2019). A case study of the Korean government's preparation for the fourth industrial revolution: Public program to support business model innovation. *Journal of Open Innovation: Technology, Market, and Complexity,* 5(2): 35; Government of Australia (2016). Australian Innovation System Report.

[59] Marcus, L.J., Dorn, B., & Henderson, J.M. (2006). Meta-leadership and national emergency preparedness: A model to build government connectivity. *Biosecurity and Bioterrorism: Biodefense Strategy, Practice, and Science,* 4(2): 128–134.

Exhibit 2.5. Navigating the pace of the Fourth Industrial Revolution.

Revolution		Year	Information
	1	1784	Steam, water, mechanical production equipment
	2	1870	Division of labor, electricity, mass production
	3	1969	Electronics, IT, automated production
	4	?	Cyber-physical systems

Source: Adapted from Schwab (2016).[60]

[60] Schwab, K. (2016). The Fourth Industrial Revolution: What It Means, How to Respond. Available: https://www.weforum.org/agenda/2016/01/the-fourth-industrial-revolution-what-it-means-and-how-to-respond/ (Accessed 16 January, 2024).

https://doi.org/10.1142/9789811296000_0003

Chapter 3

Anticipatory Capacity through Foresight

Mark Esposito[*,†] and Joshua Park[‡]

[*]*Mohammed Bin Rashid School of Government, Dubai, UAE*
[†]*Centre for International Development, Harvard Kennedy School, Cambridge, USA*
[‡]*Solbridge International School of Business, Daejeon, South Korea*

Key Takeaways

- Anticipatory governance needs foresight — a direct acknowledgment of the dynamic and ever-changing nature of the modern world.
- Foresight allows policymakers to peer into the complexities and uncertainties of the future, creating a roadmap that aligns the aspirations and objectives of society with the unpredictable contours of a world in flux.
- Foresight can take the role of many avatars: shield, beacon, lifesaver, and buffer.
- This adoption of foresight requires a transformative approach to shift governments from being merely reactive entities to proactive, forward-thinking institutions.
- Foresight helps governments prepare for a range of potential scenarios by developing policies and strategies that not only address immediate concerns but also lay the foundation for a sustainable and adaptable future.

3.1 The Expanding Role of Foresight in Public Policy

The landscape of public policy has undergone a profound transformation in the contemporary context, departing from the once straightforward and linear approach. The days of crafting policies based solely on historical data and past experiences have faded into obsolescence. The intricacies and rapid evolution of our world demand an approach rooted in anticipation and foresight.[1] Foresight planning, in this context, heralds a revolutionary paradigm shift that empowers policymakers to not merely look ahead but also engage in the proactive endeavor of gazing into the future, envisioning a spectrum of possible scenarios, and understanding the ramifications they may carry.

This anticipatory approach is a direct acknowledgment of the dynamic and ever-changing nature of the modern world.[2] It reverberates with the recognition that traditional, static policies are no longer sufficient to address the multifaceted challenges and opportunities that emerge in a global landscape characterized by unpredictability. Foresight planning does not merely react to events[3]; it anticipates, prepares, and shapes policies that are not just resilient but also forward-thinking. Such policies are not bound by the constraints of the present; they are designed to navigate the evolving terrain, offering solutions that align with the complex and ever-shifting demands of our times.

Foresight within the sphere of public policy serves as an invaluable tool for governments, allowing them to steer their decision-making processes away from reactive responses to proactive, anticipatory strategies. This new approach is instrumental in ensuring that public policies are not relics of the past but dynamic instruments[4] equipped to address the challenges and opportunities of the future. By integrating foresight into public policy, governments can transform governance into a proactive endeavor

---

[1] Stadler, C., Helfat, C.E., & Verona, G. (2013). The impact of dynamic capabilities on resource access and development. *Organization Science*, 24(6): 1782–1804.

[2] Felin, T. & Powell, T.C. (2016). Designing organizations for dynamic capabilities. *California Management Review*, 58(4): 78–96.

[3] Yoon, J., Kim, Y., Vonortas, N.S., & Won Han, S. (2018). Corporate foresight and innovation: The effects of integrative capabilities and organisational learning. *Technology Analysis & Strategic Management*, 30(6): 633–645.

[4] Hines, A. & Bishop, P. (2015). *Thinking about the Future: Guidelines for Strategic Foresight*. Houston, TX: Hinesight; Hines, A. & Gold, J. (2015). An organizational futurist role for foresight into corporations. *Technological Forecasting & Social Change*, 101: 99–111.

that empowers them to grapple with an ever-changing world in a more effective, resilient, and adaptable manner.

In this context, foresight does not exist in isolation. It is deeply intertwined with the foundations of public policy. Foresight allows policymakers to peer into the complexities and uncertainties of the future, creating a roadmap that aligns the aspirations and objectives of society with the unpredictable contours of a world in flux. It is a testament to the acknowledgment that today's policy decisions have profound and far-reaching implications for the future. Foresight bridges the gap between the immediate and the long-term, making it an indispensable component of public policy in the 21st century.

The integration of foresight into public policy reflects a profound commitment to fostering resilience, adaptability, and sustainability. Policies crafted with foresight are not rigid but flexible. They are not bound by the constraints of a single perspective but encompass a multitude of possible scenarios. By doing so, they offer the government and society the capacity to prepare for a wide range of potential challenges and opportunities. This capacity is the essence of anticipatory governance, providing the government with the tools to respond effectively to the uncertainties of a dynamic world.

In essence, the expanding role of foresight[5] in public policy transcends mere policy development. It is a transformative approach that redefines the very nature of governance in the 21st century. It champions the notion that governance should not merely be a response to the needs of the present but a visionary and anticipatory endeavor that actively shapes the future. Foresight within public policy is a powerful means to foster a more dynamic, adaptable, and forward-thinking approach to governance that aligns with the ever-evolving global landscape.

Foresight as a Tool for Informed Decision-Making: Foresight planning is not merely a theoretical exercise but a practical methodology that allows governments to make informed decisions in the realm of public policy. It equips policymakers with the necessary tools to understand the potential impacts of their choices. By considering the long-term implications of policies, governments can ensure that their decisions align with the broader objectives of promoting societal well-being, economic growth, and environmental sustainability.

[5]Chermack, T. (2018). An analysis and categorization of scenario planning scholarship. *Journal of Futures Studies*, 22(4): 45–60.

3.2 Building Resilience and Adaptability through Foresight

The capacity to navigate complexity and uncertainty is an invaluable asset in today's rapidly evolving world, where change is the only constant. Foresight stands out as a critical tool to enhance this capacity, equipping governments with the essential means to navigate through uncertainty with precision and effectiveness. It provides a strategic advantage by allowing governments to proactively prepare for a wide spectrum of potential scenarios, bolstering their resilience and adaptability to an ever-changing environment.

In an era where crises, both predictable and unforeseen, are intrinsic to the global landscape, foresight emerges as the linchpin of preparedness. It equips governments with the tools and insights necessary to confront these multifaceted challenges with greater efficiency and efficacy, ensuring that the adverse impacts are minimized and that the benefits of foresight are maximized.

There are indeed few circumstances where foresight in the regulatory approach[6] of any form of engagement and implementation may result in the most effective way to inform policy and consequent actions derived from it as shown in the following (Exhibit 3.1):

- *Environmental Crises: Foresight as the Shield*: The environment is perhaps one of the most dynamic and unpredictable facets of our world today. Climate change, natural disasters, and ecosystem disruptions have become ever-present challenges. Foresight, in this context, serves as a shield that safeguards societies against the vagaries of environmental crises. It allows governments to not just respond reactively to disasters but to also prepare for them proactively. By analyzing trends and patterns in environmental shifts, foresight can help governments identify regions prone to specific environmental challenges, enabling the development of targeted strategies for mitigation and resilience. It empowers governments to allocate resources and develop infrastructure that can withstand the impact of environmental crises. Furthermore,

[6] Yuan, B., Hsieh, C.H., & Chang, C.C. (2010). National technology foresight research: A literature review from 1984 to 2005. *International Journal of Foresight and Innovation Policy*, 6(1–3): 5–35.

Exhibit 3.1. Foresight avatars.

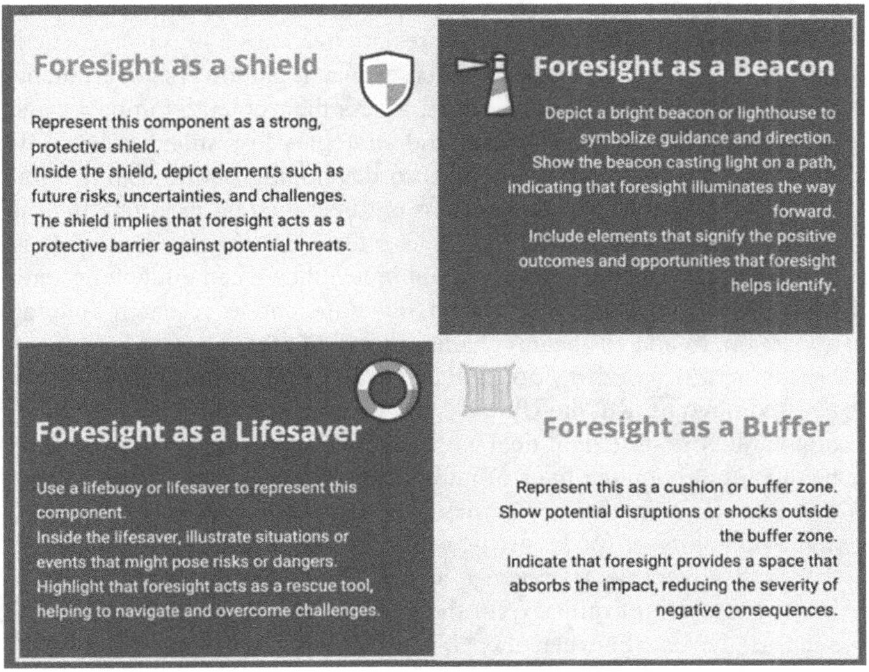

Source: Authors.

it encourages the promotion of sustainable practices that can help prevent or mitigate the onset of such crises in the first place.

- *Economic Challenges: Foresight as the Beacon*: The economic landscape is another arena where uncertainty and complexity reign supreme. Global market shifts, economic recessions, and technological disruptions can have far-reaching impacts. Foresight assumes the role of a guiding beacon in navigating these economic challenges. It enables governments to analyze economic trends and anticipate potential disruptions, providing them with the insights necessary to develop economic policies that can withstand the fluctuations of the global market. Moreover, foresight can identify emerging industries and technologies, helping governments position their economies strategically for future growth. This forward-looking approach ensures that governments are not merely reactive when economic challenges arise but also equipped to steer their economies toward sustainable prosperity.

- *Healthcare Emergencies: Foresight as the Lifesaver*: The recent COVID-19 pandemic serves as a poignant reminder of the critical role foresight can play in healthcare. Foresight becomes a lifesaver, particularly in the realm of healthcare emergencies. It empowers governments to anticipate potential health crises, assess their potential impacts, and prepare the necessary resources and strategies to respond effectively. From stockpiling medical supplies to developing public health infrastructure, foresight-driven decisions are instrumental in mitigating the spread of disease and minimizing its effects. In addition to its role in responding to emergencies, foresight in healthcare can guide long-term planning, from healthcare system development to research funding allocation, to address health challenges efficiently.
- *Geopolitical Conflicts: Foresight as the Buffer*: The Israel–Hamas war and the ongoing Russia–Ukraine war provide testimony to the uncertain nature of our geopolitical environment. Such events have wreaked havoc not only on the lives of individuals immediately on site but also on regional and global economies, with large-scale effects on the price and availability of food, energy, and other resources, impacting industries and government strategies alike. And such effects are not only limited to outright military conflicts. Politically motivated trade wars such as the one between the US and China or between East Asian nations (China, Japan, and Korea) may not have caused bloodshed, but have had a similarly devastating impact on entities that did not have a buffer to guard against such turns of events. Foresight could allow the building of an adequate buffer by calculating for such risks and building viable contingency plans in advance.

3.3 Agency for Progress?

In the rapidly evolving world we inhabit, the dynamic capabilities offered by foresight have the potential to catalyze progress across various domains. It is not limited to crisis management but extends to long-term planning and proactive decision-making. Foresight instills a culture of continuous improvement and adaptability in governance. It encourages the development of policies and strategies that not only respond to immediate needs[7]

---

[7]Fergnani, A. (2019). Mapping futures studies scholarship from 1968 to present: A bibliometric review of thematic clusters, research trends, and research gaps. *Futures*, 105: 104–123.

but are designed to anticipate future challenges and opportunities. It is also true that foresight when applied to the context of governance inherently adds agility to any form of contextualization,[8] given its intrinsic thrust into the future and its plethora of options. The agility ensues from the discretion that heralds from options nested into the interpretation of the future.

The integration of foresight into governance[9] signifies a transformative approach. It shifts governments from being merely reactive entities to proactive, forward-thinking institutions. This transformation is pivotal in addressing the inherent complexities and uncertainties of our times. Governments that employ foresight in their decision-making processes are better equipped to meet the challenges of a rapidly changing world. They develop the ability to anticipate, adapt, and respond effectively, ultimately leading to more efficient and resilient governance.[10]

The question that often arises from the study of capacity[11] built over foresight, and applied to the public policy application, is whether success depends mainly on isolated factors of contingency or whether a more systematic approach can be elicited from the experience of existing cases.

3.4 The If and When of Real-Life Examples

Real-life examples of foresight in public policy provide valuable insights into how governments can effectively anticipate challenges and seize opportunities. These instances highlight the benefits of proactive

---

[8] Wright, G. & Goodwin, P. (2009). Decision making and planning under low levels of predictability: Enhancing the scenario method. *International Journal of Forecasting*, 25: 813–825.

[9] Protogerou, A., Caloghirou, A., & Lioukas, S. (2011). Dynamic capabilities and their indirect impact on firm performance. *Industrial and Corporate Change*, 21(3): 615–647; Quinn, J.B. (1980). *Strategies for Change: Logical Incrementalism*. Homewood, IL: Dow-Jones- Irwin.

[10] Ramírez, R., Osterman, R., & Gronquist, D. (2013). Scenarios and early warnings as dynamic capabilities to frame managerial attention. *Technological Forecasting and Social Change*, 80: 825–838.

[11] Teece, D.J., Pisano, G., & Shuen, A. (1997). Dynamic capabilities and strategic management. *Strategic Management Journal*, 18(7): 509–533; Teece, D.J. (2007). Explicating dynamic capabilities: The nature and microfoundations of (sustainable) enterprise performance. *Strategic Management Journal*, 28: 1319–1350.

governance and underscore the importance of integrating foresight into policy-making processes. The following are some illustrative examples:

Singapore's Population Foresight: The government of Singapore has long been known for its strategic and forward-thinking approach to public policy. In the face of demographic challenges, such as an aging population and declining birth rates, the Singaporean government launched the "Our Singapore Conversation" initiative. This foresight-driven effort involved engaging citizens in a national conversation to anticipate future demographic trends, understand their implications, and develop policies that address issues related to healthcare, retirement, and workforce readiness. By involving the public in shaping policy, Singapore has embraced a more anticipatory approach to governance.

Norway's Pension Fund: Norway's Government Pension Fund Global, also known as the Norwegian Sovereign Wealth Fund, is a prime example of how foresight is integrated into economic policy. The fund is managed based on the premise of saving petroleum revenues for future generations. Its governance structure, investment strategy, and ethical guidelines reflect a commitment to long-term financial sustainability. By foresightedly investing petroleum wealth, Norway has secured financial resources for future generations and reduced the impact of resource depletion.[12]

Finland's Education Reform: Finland's transformation of its education system into one of the world's most successful models is a testament to the power of foresight in shaping public policy. In the 1970s, the Finnish government, with input from educators, implemented education reforms that emphasized student well-being, teacher training, and a holistic approach to learning. These decisions were based on a long-term vision for a knowledge-based economy and a recognition of the changing needs of the workforce. The success of Finland's education system is a result of its proactive stance in anticipating future demands.

Singapore's Smart Nation Initiative: Singapore's Smart Nation Initiative is a comprehensive effort that uses foresight and technology to anticipate and address urban challenges. By integrating data analytics, the Internet of Things, and digital innovation, Singapore is proactively preparing for

[12] Stokke, P.R., Raltson, W.K., Boyce, T.A., & Wilson, I.H. (1990). Scenario planning for Norwegian oil and gas. *Long Range Planning*, 23(2): 17–26.

future urbanization. This initiative includes smart traffic management, urban planning, and healthcare services, all aimed at enhancing the quality of life for residents and ensuring the city's resilience in the face of demographic changes and urbanization.

Estonia's E-Governance: Estonia's forward-thinking approach to e-governance is a prime example of using foresight to enhance public policy. The Estonian government has embraced digital innovation to streamline public services, making them more efficient, accessible, and secure. The X-Road, a decentralized data exchange platform, exemplifies how foresight has enabled Estonia to build a robust digital infrastructure, enhancing governance and service delivery.

United Arab Emirates (UAE): Vision 2021: The UAE's "Vision 2021" is an ambitious example of how foresight has been applied in public policy. This initiative aims to transform the UAE into a diversified and knowledge-based economy. It was launched in 2010 and involves seven key pillars, including education, healthcare, infrastructure, and a sustainable environment. The government utilized foresight and long-term planning to set specific targets for each of these pillars and establish a roadmap for achieving these goals.

South Korea: Green Growth: South Korea's "Green Growth" policy, launched in 2008, is a prime example of foresight-driven public policy in the context of environmental sustainability. The South Korean government recognized the long-term environmental challenges posed by climate change and the need to transition to a green economy. The Green Growth initiative aimed to promote sustainable development while simultaneously fostering economic growth.

Through this policy, South Korea invested in renewable energy, energy-efficient technologies, and sustainable urban development. The government anticipated that the global demand for clean and sustainable technologies would rise, and they positioned the country to become a leading exporter of green technologies. This foresight-driven approach has not only reduced South Korea's carbon footprint but has also enhanced its competitiveness in the global market for green technologies.

South Korea: Overcoming BKW (China's ban on the Korean Wave): When China implemented an unofficial ban in 2016 on Korean (especially Korean Wave) products as a retaliatory measure to the Korean government's decision to deploy THAAD (terminal high-altitude area defense) within its borders, Korean businesses faced a crisis as they had heavily invested in and relied upon the Chinese market. However, a measure of foresight had been employed by the Korean Wave industries to diversify their consumer base beyond the low-hanging fruits of the huge Chinese market, with consistent attempts to increase their reach not only to other East and Southeast Asian nations but also into Western markets.

This was done with the understanding that China could be more volatile and risky than other markets due to the close control exercised by its government. Such foresight allowed the industry to overcome the immediate dips in sales and stock prices to become even more successful globally, symbolized by the K-pop band BTS appearing for the first time on the Billboard Hot 100 Chart in 2017, before moving on to top the chart several times. Korean movie and drama industries followed similar pathways, with the movie "Parasite" in 2019 becoming the first foreign language film to win the Academy Award for Best Picture and "Squid Games" in 2021 becoming the most-watched Netflix series worldwide. While strategies employed by Korean Wave industries may not be strictly controlled by the Korean government, they were certainly in line with the government's diplomatic policy to walk the fine line of establishing close ties with neighboring economies while not putting all of their eggs in one basket.

These real-life examples underscore the transformative impact of foresight in public policy. They demonstrate how governments, by taking a proactive stance and anticipating future challenges, can develop policies and strategies that not only address immediate concerns but also lay the foundation for a sustainable and adaptable future.

In conclusion, the capacity to navigate complexity and uncertainty is an indispensable asset in the contemporary world, and foresight stands as a critical tool in this endeavor. It empowers governments to proactively prepare for a range of potential scenarios, making them more resilient and adaptable in the face of environmental crises, economic challenges, healthcare emergencies, and other multifaceted issues. Foresight is not merely a shield, a beacon, or a lifesaver; it is a catalyst for progress that transforms governance into a proactive and forward-thinking endeavor.

https://doi.org/10.1142/9789811296000_0004

Chapter 4

Elevating Anticipatory Analysis in Policymaking

Angela Evans

University of Texas, Austin, USA

Key Takeaways

- Shocks to management systems caused by unanticipated events can cripple operations and forestall consideration of promising actions.
- The absence of the ability to analyze the potential consequences of unanticipated events results in the assessment of public issues through parochial and static lenses and established institutional preferences.
- The power of anticipatory analysis rests in the promise of preparedness, the acceleration of innovative approaches, and the engagement of multidisciplinary expertise.
- Anticipatory analysis requires organizational agility to recognize a wide range of possible root causes of public problems and to ready feasible options to address them.
- Anticipatory analysis seeks alerts that are undetected when established organizational biases and institutional habits prevail.

4.1 State of Affairs

Are we surprised at the disruptive circumstances in which we find society today? If so, then we have not been paying attention. We have failed to heed recurring clues or signals[1] easily at our disposal. We have fallen victim to conventional thought, intellectual laziness, and the dulling of our curiosity. We appear overwhelmed by the complexity of societal challenges and unprepared to confront them.

The progressively complex, interconnected, and transnational nature of policy problems[2] punctuates the urgency of conducting research that results in timely, successful policies and managing these policies through agile governance structures. Transforming policy research methods and reimaging governance operations must be directed squarely on barriers potentially impeding change, like the ones mentioned in the following.

4.1.1 *Legitimacy of the problem*

We struggle to identify the essence of society's problems, distracted by extant policies whose relevancy to the real problem may be tangential at best and irrelevant at worst.[3] Focusing on primarily on potential solutions to implement remedial policies[4] assumes that a problem is clearly grasped, stable, and well defined. This confidence shifts focus away from ensuring the legitimacy of a problem[5] to evaluating policy remedies that may be attached to the wrong problem.

---

[1] Malmgren, P. (2017). *Signals: How Everyday Signs Can Help Us Navigate the World's Turbulent Economy*. UK: Weidenfeld & Nicolson.

[2] Stone, D. (2008). Global public policy, transnational policy communities, and their networks. *Policy Studies Journal*, 36(1): 19–38.

[3] For example, see: Hanberger, A. (2003). Public policy and legitimacy: A historical policy analysis of the interplay of public policy and legitimacy. *Policy Sciences*, 36(3–4): 257–278.

[4] Banerjee, A., Banerji, R., Berry, J., Duflo, E., Kannan, H., Mukerji, S., Shotland, M., & Walton, M. (2017). From proof of concept to scalable policies: Challenges and solutions, with an application. *Journal of Economic Perspectives*, 31(4): 73–102.

[5] For example, Parkinson looks at legitimacy as (1) legality or the rules of the game, (2) justifiability, which is the rightful source of authoritative decisions, and (3) procedures by which the people consent to decisions or regimes. (Reference: Parkinson, J. (2003). Legitimacy problems in deliberative democracy. *Political Studies*, 51(1): 180–196.)

4.1.2 *Timeliness*

The rapidly changing environments in which policy operates exacerbate the difficulty in ensuring that policy maintains its relevance and timeliness. Governments are facing uncertainties not seen before, and these are taxing governance capacities at all levels. Severe societal and political consequences are arising from disruptions caused by the largest displacement and migration of the human species: accelerated changes in the way the Earth renews and adjusts itself; proliferation of the most insidious viruses and microbes that can paralyze entire societies; unchecked potential and unintended consequences of the evolution of artificial intelligence, nano and biotechnologies, and other disruptive technologies; shifts in domestic and global political orders; democratization of space; growing strain between ensuring individual rights while preserving the public good; and rupture of confidence in, and devotion to, the rule of law. These issues, among others, will continue to cultivate problems, create challenges, and drive change at an unprecedented pace. These issues will test our relevance as public affairs professionals in coping with these changes and mitigating their implications for healthy societies.

4.1.3 *Sustainable actions*

Examining research in public affairs over decades reveals a steady recurrence of societal dilemmas and a string of unsuccessful attempts to offer sustainable actions to address them. While we have rich reservoirs of analytic research in so many public problem areas, we struggle to pose actions that can offer lasting remedies for these problems.

A study[6] of the US immigration system found that the Department of Homeland Security (the executive Agency responsible for the implementation of immigration policy in the US) and the agencies with whom it collaborates in other federal departments lack the assuredness and agility to effectively recalibrate and adjust to new circumstances.

[6]Messier, D. & Wasem, R. (2021). *Toward a Better Immigration System: Fixing Immigration Governance at the U.S. Department of Homeland Security.* Washington, D.C.: Migration Policy Institute.

Further, this study found that a sense of adapting to ever-changing migration dynamics, law enforcement cooperation and collaboration, and planning capabilities for implementing new strategies or mandates were absent.[7]

US immigration policies raise a plethora of issues arising from the desire to achieve a balance between securing its borders (see Exhibit 4.1) and allowing a steady flow of new immigrants into the country using legal constraints. How to determine who qualifies for entry, why they qualify, and how to handle emergency refugee needs has been a struggle for the US since its inception.[8] While scores of legislative and regulatory actions have been undertaken by the US government, these have not alleviated the tensions between securing borders and ensuring robust immigration policies.[9]

Exhibit 4.1. Securing USA borders.

Source: U.S. Customs and Border Patrol Protection.[10]

[7] *Ibid.*

[8] The Naturalization Act of 1790 (1 Stat 103, Chapter 3) is considered the first US immigration law defining access to the US and requirements for citizenship.

[9] For a discussion of the challenges faced by the US, see: Klobucista, C., Cheatham, A., & Roy, D. (2023). The US immigration policy debate, backgrounder. The Council on Foreign Relations Report: 2023. Available: https://www.cfr.org/backgrounder/us-immigration-debate-0 (Accessed 6 June, 2023).

[10] Image Source: https://www.cbp.gov/frontline/border-crisis-cbp-s-response (Accessed 30 January, 2024).

Exhibit 4.2. Dreamer demonstration.

Source: George W. Bush Presidential Center.[11]

This stalemate has serious consequences not only for those attempting to enter the US but also for those living in the US illegally — one such group has come to be known as the "Dreamers." These are children and youth brought to the US illegally by their parents when they were young and who have grown up in the US without legal status. They have contributed to the country both economically and socially — some have served in the US military. Their plight was predictable, and the means to address it were available.

Despite this knowledge, the US Congress has been unable to pass legislation clarifying their status or offering them paths to citizenship. While failure to act is based in part on political maneuvering, options that garner support across political lines have been missing. This speaks to the inability of the policy community to anticipate the outcome of illegal crossings of children who assimilate (albeit clandestinely) into US society, resulting in stale ideas, policy standoffs, and an uncertain future of over 500,000 "Dreamers" (see Exhibit 4.2).

---

[11] Image Source: https://www.bushcenter.org/publications/federal-judge-strikes-down-daca-again (Accessed 30 January, 2024).

4.1.4 *Repetitive issues*

It seems that we are doomed to engage in repetitive cycles of policy panic.[12] Policies fail at a high cost to society. When they do, we step in by evaluating already existing programs for why they failed, we offer ways to address the failure by often using recycled ideas, and we determine ways to assess and evaluate these "new" solutions until a new failure occurs. For example, in solving financial crises, one of the reasons for failure is the lack of new ideas for new paradigms that differ in context and demands.[13] There may be several reasons why we seem to be caught in this cycle. Research methods are entrenched in a narrow range of approaches. Generally, research tends to be confined to a single discipline community, which bolsters conventional thought. We promote the publication of relatively narrow, at times obscure, analyses covering technically specific topics. Most of the extensive policy research activities in which we engage are not controversial — they reflect conservative, incremental thinking. Perhaps the unintended consequence of this is that they also do not attract attention because they are too technical, esoteric, and irrelevant to the problems at hand. This is not a new phenomenon: We have been struggling with our relevance in critical policy debates for some time.

For example, the relationship between poverty and educational achievement has long been established (see Exhibit 4.3).[14] Years of research aimed to identify ways to alleviate the effects of poverty have focused on the same range of remedies: small class size, charter schools, school choice, teacher performance, after-school programming, etc. There is an uncanny déjà vu about this research. If one were to survey the research conducted 50 years ago on poverty and educational attainment, one would encounter similar if not identical concerns and ways to

---

[12] For example, see: Hoffmann, A. & Schnabl, G. (2011). A vicious cycle of manias, crises and asymmetric policy responses–an overinvestment view. *The World Economy*, 34(3): 382–403.

[13] For example, see: Peters, B.G., Pierre, J., & Randma-Liiv, T. (2011). Global financial crisis, public administration and governance: Do new problems require new solutions? *Public Organization Review*, 11: 13–27.

[14] For example, see: Paschall, K.W., Gershoff, E.T., & Kuhfeld, M.A. (2018). Two decade examination of historical race/ethnicity disparities in academic achievement by poverty status. *Journal of Youth Adolescence*, 47(6): 1164–1177; Nasrullah, A. & Greever, S. (2022). Poverty in education. *SSRN*. Available: https://ssrn.com/abstract=4277816 or http://dx.doi.org/10.2139/ssrn.4277816 (Accessed 15 November, 2023).

Exhibit 4.3. Student achievement gap.

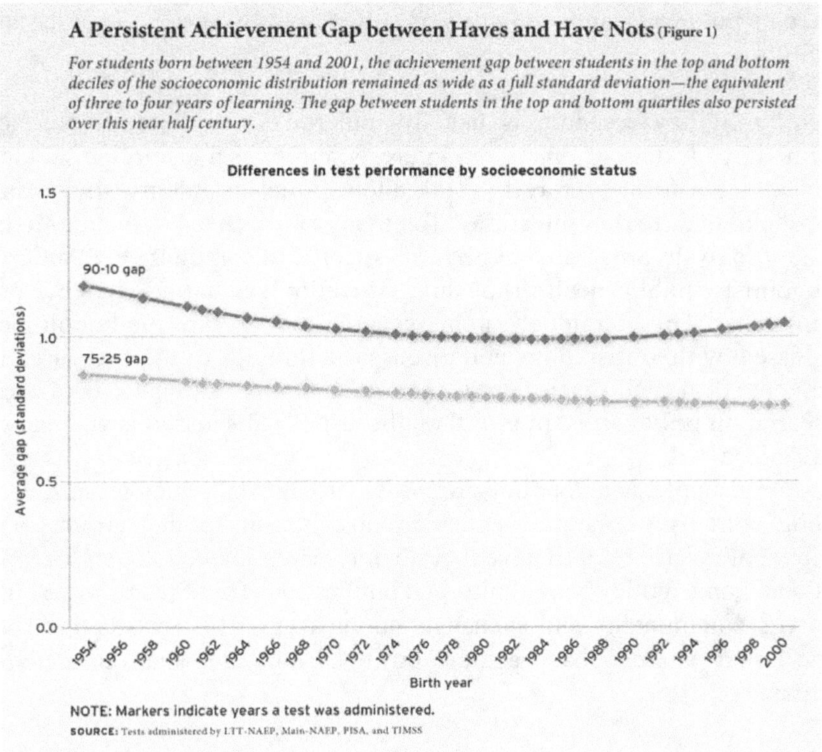

Source: Hanushek, Peterson, Talpey, & Woessman (2019).[15]

address them.[16] There have been virtually no new innovative, generally applicable ideas to alleviate the effects of poverty on educational attainment.

---

[15] Hanushek *et al.* (2019), *Op. cit.*

[16] For example, read Stevens, K.B. (2019). The socioeconomic achievement gap hasn't budged in half a century. Now what? *AEI*, 22 April; NAEP (2011). Achievement gaps. *National Center for Education Statistics*. Available: https://nces.ed.gov/nationsreportcard/studies/gaps/ (Accessed 13 January, 2024); Hanushek, E.A., Light, J.D., Peterson, P.E., Talpey, L.M., & Woessmann, L. (2019). Long-run trends in the U.S. SES-achievement gap. *Working Paper* 25648. Cambridge, Massachusetts: National Bureau of Economic Research (Revised 2022). Available: http://www.nber.org/papers/w25648 (Accessed 15 November, 2023).

4.1.5 *Identity and utility*

It seems policy research and analysis suffer from two crises: identity and utility.

Identity: Policy research is usually undertaken in diversified fields defined by clusters of functional interests, rarely as a discipline seeking to advance a form or way to think about policy problems, their solutions, and their real implications. Too many researchers who claim to be policy analysts are really experts in specific disciplines, e.g., microeconomists, public health, housing, education specialists, or environmentalists. They conduct their research using the methodologies endorsed by their discipline and discuss the findings of their research in the context of their discipline. If they refer to any implications of their research on policy, it is an afterthought, usually discussed at the end of their piece.

For example, health policy groups, environmental policy groups, education policy groups, trade policy groups, housing policy groups, and global policy groups each have their own research methodologies, organizational home, policy community, and publication. There seems to be little analytic commonality and exchange among them. This reveals that specific policy interests have a more powerful attraction than an analytic purpose.

Utility: The strong forces that govern the integrity of each discipline seem sufficiently overwhelming to create impenetrable constraints upon interdisciplinary integration, rendering policy analysis and research fractured and misaligned with the knowledge needs of policymakers.

The practice of policy analysis has become so broadly defined and executed that it has moved away from a core integrative approach to one on the periphery, touching other disciplines but not integrating them. At the very time when societal problems are growing more multidimensional, policy research and analysis remain siloed and confined. Policy research risks becoming indistinguishable from other individual disciplinary research. The unintended consequences of this are that the quality of research is judged against academic standards rather than its usefulness to policymakers, and it has become extremely difficult to undertake analyses that synthesize specific knowledge and expertise of relevant disciplines.

4.2 Power of Anticipatory Analysis

Overcoming these challenges by addressing separately the implications of each condition mentioned is Herculean and wrong-minded. The probability of successfully making headway on all of these is low and will not result in integrated problem-solving. But the implications of ignoring them are serious.

The steady recurrence of societal challenges, both man-made (wars, environment, governance models, crime, political rifts) and natural (weather disasters, resource availability, pandemics), provides opportunities for those interested in using anticipatory analysis to mitigate the consequences of these events.

4.2.1 *What is anticipatory analysis?*

Anticipatory analysis helps create analytic and governance mindsets that move the policy focus from the "as is" to the "what might be"[17] — from reacting to problems to anticipating them and preparing for their arrival. It can be the coin of the realm.[18]

Anticipatory analysis is a thought and action process used to determine root factors of recurring/emerging public problems, to identify the nature of these factors, to track changes and developments in these factors, and to regularly develop a range of action scenarios resulting from the effects of these changing factors. The purpose of this type of analysis is twofold: to avoid future public failures and to have available a variety of ways to address public challenges should they arise.[19]

Anticipatory analysis has the purpose of uncovering antecedents and causes of problems, speculating on their persistence, and designing

---

[17]Stephens, M. & Awamleh, R. (2022). The heart of an agile government: Future public value. *UAE Public Policy Forum*. Available: https://mbrsgcdn.azureedge.net/cmsstorage/mbrsg/files/ef/efc58c61-985b-4d6e-8d7b-3d598f601d60.pdf (Accessed 11 January, 2024).

[18]Havas, A., Schartinger, D., & Weber, M. (2010). The impact of foresight on innovation policy-making: Recent experiences and future perspectives. *Research Evaluation*, 19(2): 91–104; See longitudinal study on Wales: Rhisiart, M. & Jones-Evans, D. (2016). The impact of foresight on entrepreneurship: The wales 2010 case study. *Technological Forecasting and Social Change*, 102: 112–119.

[19]This definition is one created by the author and serves as the reference for discussions of anticipatory analysis in this chapter.

programs and policies that might solve them. It is iterative, interdisciplinary, and is used before decisions are considered and formulated.

There is objectivity, neutrality, and relevance to anticipatory analysis. By focusing on unknown, uncertain, and wicked[20] societal matters, it bypasses the pitfalls that exist in parochial, conventional methods and structures that deal with topical issues. There simply is no single discipline, level of government, or methodology robust enough to claim sole ownership of these societal matters. The complexities, mysteries, and consequences defining them warrant unique ways to think about, define, and address them.

While anticipatory analysis is premised on grappling with the unknown, anticipating problems is not new. Organizations work on persistent problems and recurring issues. There are several existing known and recurring events that offer frameworks to employ anticipatory analysis. The most obvious of these are the cycles used in legislative deliberations. Funding, reauthorization, and legislative sessions all operate on predictable and regular schedules. Preparing for each of these cycles involves asking questions like what pressures are likely to strain funding decisions; what programs need to be reauthorized; what are some of the issues facing those programs; are these programs still relevant; what are political leaders saying about their legislative priorities; and what proposals have been offered in the past, what was their fate, and what have we learned since. Anticipatory analysis can be applied to each of these questions.

Following the creation, deliberations, and reporting associated with ongoing commissions, agency studies, research grants, business reports, and investigative journalism also provide insights into new revelations that can make their way to policy settings. These offer opportunities to demonstrate the value of anticipating issues and their implications.

4.2.2 *Adopting anticipatory analysis*

Adopting anticipatory analysis requires establishing a comfort level that can be anathema to the ways policy research and practice have operated.

[20]The term "wicked" is used to discuss problems that evade solution. Its origins are embedded in building technological platforms to solve business needs but it has been adopted by policy researchers and practitioners to describe recurring, niggling problems that seem to evade solution. See: Peters, B.G. (2017). What is so wicked about wicked problems? A conceptual analysis and a research program. *Policy and Society*, 36(3): 385–396.

To embrace anticipatory analysis, one must accept the risks of being wrong, seek out and celebrate insights of those holding different expertise and opinions, and be willing to forego short-term success for long-term impact. To unleash the power of anticipatory analysis, its value as critical to the mission must be elevated — it is not simply something interesting or nice to do.

Traditional policy analysis has been at its strongest when used in the early phases of policy development: the intelligence phase and the recommendation phase of deliberations. It can be used to prescribe, innovate, appraise, and terminate policies and programs. Anticipatory analysis can escalate the role of policy research at critical junctures in deliberations and policy design and can result in timely and reasonable decision-making.

Acting upon underlying causes of recurring problems and using anticipatory analysis in developing policy agendas requires research frameworks and practice protocols grounded in facts and expectations and outcomes grounded in observation and imagination. Anticipatory analysis offers the potential to generate and synthesize reliable information and data required by policymakers as they choose to act — thus mitigating some of the effects of either making panic-driven decisions (reacting immediately to an urgent need without sufficient knowledge and information) or settling on decisions that are recycled from past events (lacking innovative new approaches).

4.2.3 *Conducting anticipatory analysis*

Discussing the value of anticipatory analysis and its potential as a game changer in public policy is relatively easy. Determining how and when to undertake anticipatory analysis and how to make it mainstream in policy research and practice, however, is not straightforward. The adoption of anticipatory techniques will likely vary across governing bodies and policies, thus rendering formulaic methodologies useless. Instead, it may be more useful to learn from past public failures to advance the acceptance and integration of anticipatory analysis. This section draws from my experience at the Congressional Research Service (CRS),[21] where I served as

[21] The Congressional Research Service (CRS) is a nonpartisan public policy agency within the Legislative Branch of the US Congress. Its purpose is to provide committees, Members, and their staff with objective, nonpartisan, and confidential research, information, and data they need while conducting their legislative, oversight, and budgetary duties.

the deputy director for 16 years. During those years, I had a bird's-eye view of how Members of Congress and their staff conducted their legislative and oversight duties. One of the responsibilities of CRS, as defined in its organic statute,[22] was to anticipate the needs of Congress as it carries out its duties. The organizational structure, responsibilities, and culture of CRS offered fertile ground for the practice of anticipatory analysis: The staff was interdisciplinary and practiced in undertaking interdisciplinary work; anticipating oversight and legislative issues was commonplace and expected, and the staff possessed both intellectual expertise and historical contexts, and tacit understandings of how Congress worked. Professional analysts knew law, regulations, program operations, and budgets well and were engaged with professional colleagues both in and outside of Congress.

During my years as deputy, I led the Service as it supported Congress's work during several major disasters, including 9/11, Hurricane Katrina, and the explosion of the Challenger Space Shuttle. The public failures in these events were catastrophic. While these events may have been anticipated, the analysis needed to either avoid them or to substantively address them when they occurred was missing. The type of anticipatory analyses discussed in this chapter simply was not available to Congress and, more importantly, to those responsible for managing a crisis. As Congress concluded in its work on Katrina, "there was no shortage of plans. There were plans, but there was not enough planning."[23]

Through this work, it became clear that not only was anticipatory analysis important but four conditions needed to exist for its successful

---

CRS employs professional degree-holding individuals from a wide variety of disciplines including the social and physical sciences, international diplomacy and security, administrative and constitutional law, and informational and technological sciences. The expertise, counsel, and advice of CRS staff is sought after and used by the Members of Congress and their staff in every aspect of their work.

[22] 2 USC 166. Statute establishing the Congressional Research Service.

[23] United States Congress. House. Select Bipartisan Committee to Investigate the Preparation for and Response to Hurricane Katrina (2006). A Failure of Initiative: Final Report of the Select Bipartisan Committee to Investigate the Preparation for and Response to Hurricane Katrina. Washington: U.S. G.P.O.: For sale by the Supt. of Docs., U.S. G.P.O. Web. https://lccn.loc.gov/2006360984.

adaptation into current environments where policies are deliberated and executed:

(1) an existing commitment to anticipatory intelligence in the regular order of operations (organizational readiness);
(2) established purposeful, longstanding activities aimed at preparing for future events (current protocols);
(3) an intellectual capacity to lead these efforts (the right people); and
(4) strong, ongoing communication between those who have conducted anticipatory analysis and those who convey this information to policymakers (strong communication networks).

Some or all of these conditions were missing in the most tragic, high-stakes, natural, and man-made disasters occurring in the US.[24] Using the findings and recommendations of various commissions and study groups from one of these disasters, Hurricane Katrina, may help illustrate the relevance of these four conditions and the consequences of their absence.

4.2.4 *Hurricane Katrina: Making the case for anticipatory analysis*

Hurricane Katrina (see Exhibit 4.4), a category-five hurricane that hit US Gulf Coast states in 2005, was the costliest hurricane in US history. The failure to anticipate this disaster and prepare for the potential outcomes of

---

[24]For example, see other commissioned studies: 9/11 Commission Report: National Commission on Terrorist Attacks. 2004. The 9/11 Commission Report: Final Report of the National Commission on Terrorist Attacks upon the United States. New York: Norton & Co. https://www.govinfo.gov/app/details/GPO-911REPORT/context; Space Shuttle Columbia Accident: United States National Aeronautics And Space Administration. Columbia Crew Survival Investigation Report. Houston, Tex.: National Aeronautics and Space Administration, Lyndon B. Johnson Space Center, 2008; British Petroleum–Deepwater Horizon well, oil spill: Deepwater Horizon Incident Unified Command, U.S. Deepwater Horizon Response. United States, 2010; Maui/Hawaii fires, ongoing US Congressional inquiry: https://energycommerce.house.gov/posts/recap-energy-and-commerce-committee-s-investigation-of-maui-fires.

a storm of this nature resulted in the deaths of over 1300 people and damages totaling US$160 billion.

Exhibit 4.4. Displaced people from Katrina in shelters.

Source: Federal Emergency Management Administration.[25]

Exhibit 4.5. Katrina hearings.

Source: C-Span (2006).[26]

[25]Federal Emergency Management Administration photo, included in U.S. Congress. Special Report. Senate (CRPT:109 SRPT322). Available: https://www.congress.gov/109/crpt/srpt322/CRPT-109srpt322.pdf (Accessed 30 January, 2024).

[26]Image Source: C-Span (2006). https://www.c-span.org/video/?191188-1/hurricane-katrina-response (Accessed 30 January, 2024).

Special congressional committee investigations established to study this disaster found failures that align with the conditions discussed previously (see Exhibit 4.5). Some of these are noted in the following:[27,28]

1. *Commitment to anticipatory analysis in current environments.*
   - Lessons from the past are relevant and should not be overlooked — they should be reviewed and become part of the anticipatory landscape.
   - In many respects, our report is a litany of mistakes, misjudgments, lapses, and absurdities, all cascading together, blinding us to what was coming and hobbling any collective effort to respond.

2. *Longstanding protocols to prepare for future events.*
   - The failure of initiative was also a failure of agility. "Response plans at all levels of government lacked flexibility and adaptability. … [o]fficials at all levels seemed to be waiting for the disaster that fit their plans rather than planning and building scalable capacities to meet whatever Mother Nature threw at them."[29]
   - The potentially devastating threat of a catastrophic hurricane to the Gulf Coast has been known for 40 years.
   - Before the storm, government planning was incomplete, and preparation was often ineffective, inadequate, or both. Afterward, government responses were often tentative, bureaucratic, or inert. These failures resulted in unnecessary suffering.
   - A failure on the part of all levels of government to plan and prepare for the consequences of Katrina.
   - Systems on which officials relied for support to their response efforts failed.

---

[27] United States Congress. House. Select Bipartisan Committee to Investigate the Preparation for and Response to Hurricane Katrina (2006), *Op. cit.*

[28] United States Congress. Senate. Committee on Homeland Security and Governmental Affairs (2006). Hurricane Katrina: a Nation Still Unprepared: Special Report of the Committee on Homeland Security and Governmental Affairs, United States Senate, Together with Additional Views. Washington: U.S. G.P.O.; For sale by the Supt. of Docs., U.S. G.P.O.

[29] Thompson, P. (2005). Executive summary of findings. Available: https://biotech.law.lsu.edu/katrina/govdocs/109-377/execsummary.pdf (Accessed 10 March, 2024).

3. *Intellectual capacity to lead anticipatory efforts.*
    - Many government officials continue to stubbornly resist recognizing that fundamental changes in disaster management are needed.
    - It remains difficult to understand how the government could respond so ineffectively to a disaster that was anticipated for years and for which specific dire warnings had been issued for days. This crisis was not only predictable, it was predicted.
    - We were horrified when the response to the Katrina catastrophe revealed — all too often, and for far too long — confusion, delay, misdirection, inactivity, poor coordination, and lack of leadership at all levels of government.
    - Government officials at all levels failed to provide effective leadership.
    - Top officials at every level of government — despite strongly worded advisories from the National Hurricane Center (NHC) and personal warnings from NHC Director Max Mayfield — did not appear to truly grasp the magnitude of the storm's potential for destruction before it made landfall.
    - There was a failure on the part of government leaders to think "big" before Katrina struck and to challenge existing planning assumptions in the face of what was known to be a "nightmare scenario."

4. *Strong ongoing communication.*
    - Massive communications damage and a failure to adequately plan for alternatives impaired response efforts, command and control, and situational awareness.
    - Warning is irrelevant unless it is brought to the attention of a policymaker — who understands that he has been warned.
    - Capturing the institutional memory and tacit understanding of those who have lived through a problem, dilemma, or catastrophe ensures anticipatory analysis heeds past experiences.

4.3 Lessons Learned

Lessons from the past are relevant and should not be overlooked — they should be reviewed and become part of the anticipatory landscape. It is clear that warning is irrelevant unless it is brought to the attention of policymakers who understand they have been warned. Capturing the institutional memory and tacit understanding of those who have lived through a problem, dilemma, or catastrophe ensures anticipatory analysis attends to past experiences. Failures can be avoided, and anticipatory analyses are employed in organizational settings that are ready for change and have the intellectual capacity to lead that change.

4.3.1 *Organizational/agency readiness*

An organization/agency that cultivates an awareness of new and emerging trends and seeks to question the wisdom of enduring assumptions is fertile ground for anticipatory analysis. This must be deeply rooted in the DNA of the organization. While the commitment of leadership is important, it is enrollment and dedication to these values[30] throughout the organization or community that fuel its success. This takes time during which anticipatory analysis can establish a proven track record affecting beneficial work outcomes. While it is unlikely that one organization or research group possesses all of the characteristics needed to successfully undertake anticipatory analysis, the following list offers indicators that can predict an organization's readiness:

- Allowing curiosity to dictate work direction.
- Seeking weak signals with high degrees of uncertainty and determining their value.
- Engaging fully and often with interdisciplinary experts to discuss events, identify emerging issues, and pursue unusual developments.
- Ensuring the representation of a variety of perspectives, reflecting a wide range of methods and practices.
- Regularly using design exercises/scenario planning to examine alternative futures — working through a wide range of scenarios.
- Developing ways to assess the viability of individual scenarios: Use methods to track these alternatives by observing events and actions, assessing risks, coping with gaps in knowledge and unknowns, and then assessing probabilities of occurrence and implications.

[30]Boxx, W.R., Odom, R.Y., & Dunn, M.G. (1991). Organizational values and value congruency and their impact on satisfaction, commitment, and cohesion: An empirical examination within the public sector. *Public Personnel Management*, 20(2): 195–205.

Risks to the successful continuation of these approaches, as well as to their adoption, exist within organizations and agencies. One of the most important risks is the lack of consistent financial support. The uncertainties of budget and appropriation determinations and their timing bring an extraordinary strain on organizational planning and risk-taking. These uncertainties often pit current operational needs against those required to undertake anticipatory work. A different approach to budget planning is needed — moving away from the assumption of an iterative, steady growth in funds to identifying ways to shift resources without diminishing or losing mission-critical activities.[31]

Other risks are those of recurring demands placed on agencies due to priorities imposed upon them by higher executive levels, coping with natural or man-made disasters, or public revelations of wrongdoing or failures. When any of these situations occur, an agency can be pulled away from regular business to focus on the immediate implications of the event. This distraction is often not confined to leadership but can engulf the entire agency and move it into reaction mode. In this state, anticipatory analysis can lose momentum and standing in the hierarchy of work priorities.

Anticipation requires a deep appreciation for history and a tenacity to stick with an issue after its immediate consequences have been addressed. Often, the strain of dealing with the immediacy of issues, especially those that have severe consequences, like terrorist attacks, weather-generated calamities, and infrastructure failures, leads to policy exhaustion. Because the policy process is iterative, policy problems often change shape in response to criticism, experience, and planning. It is under these circumstances that anticipatory analysis is most useful. However, oftentimes, little energy remains to tackle the implications of these consequential events: What if this happens again, and how to prepare? Thus, the cycle continues: React to a problem, evaluate solutions, and wait for the next problem to arrive.

Finally, staying current on the most recent technological developments essential to operations takes constant surveillance of new developments, determining relevance to the missions, and integrating new technologies into the work processes. Maintaining technological skills and systems are two of the most understated priorities when discussing the growth of expertise in anticipatory analysis.

[31] For example, see the concept of anticipatory public budgeting: Available: https://gic.mbrcgi.gov.ae/storage/post/4RDIYHad89Y93eamZd8eVAnfhRTRCdn6vNVJgdXS.pdf.

4.3.2 *Intellectual capacity*

Another critical risk to the adoption of anticipatory analysis is the ability to attract and maintain a steady flow of professional staff who have the appropriate expertise and skills to work in flexible, uncertain environments and who are skilled in anticipatory analyses. Recurring failures of public service, the lack of trust in governments, and the conventional training of potential public employees pose significant interruptions in the available pool of experts who can navigate and thrive in public settings. Choosing a career in public service is simply not attractive.

4.4 Final Comments

The group investigating the explosion of the air shuttle Columbia concluded, "*Complex systems almost always fail in complex ways*."[32]

Policymakers face issues that cannot be wished away — problems are real and situational — not abstract. If policy analysts and practitioners are to successfully intercede and mitigate problems given the complexities and range of existing issues, then they must deliberately and regularly provide insights with a high degree of fidelity, accuracy, relevance, and timeliness.

There is never a foolproof way of exploring unknowns and predicting future states, especially in a world exploding with issues and populations holding pluralistic and often polarized perspectives on the nature of problems and acceptable solutions. Understanding the value of anticipatory analysis, welcoming it, and normalizing it in policy deliberations offer hope that future challenges will be met with relevant, informed, and ready actions.

---

[32]The Columbia Accident Investigation Board (CAIB) was an internal commission convened by NASA to investigate the destruction of the Space Shuttle Columbia. Excerpt taken from the report on the space shuttle Columbia accident: NASA (2003). Columbia Accident Investigation Board. Available: https://history.nasa.gov/columbia/CAIB_reportindex.html (Accessed 13 January, 2024).

https://doi.org/10.1142/9789811296000_0005

Chapter 5

Backcasting: A Design Thinking Approach to Creating Transformative Futures

Melodena Stephens* **and Sohail Inayatullah**†,‡

**Mohammed Bin Rashid School of Government, Dubai, UAE*
†UNESCO Chair in Futures Studies, IIUM, Kuala Lumpur, Malaysia
‡Tamkang University, Taipei, Taiwan

Key Takeaways

- Backcasting is the process of shaping events to a preferred future. It has five stages: future horizon, present horizon, push-and-pull factors, anchor policies, and impact and early warning signals.
- It uses four iterative processes: imagination, scoping, boundary setting, and assessment, shifting frames from narrow to wide.
- Backcasting shapes the path toward a preferred future. In a continuous process, listing assumptions and reflecting on impact (using them as early warning flags) allow backcasters to track future trajectories.
- It is not a simple exercise; it challenges policymakers to confront their preconceived notions and hubris.
- This confrontation is critical as the future is not set in stone and also because the impacts of policy performance are often a perception of public value delivered over time.

5.1 Introduction

Backcasting is defined as the process of articulating trends, events, and metaphors (an overall narrative — from several alternative futures or a preferred future) with the intent to understand the details of various trajectories and enhance the plausibility of achieving a preferred future.[1] This horizon can be anything from 10 to 20 to 200 years ahead. However, by articulating what is desired and what is not desired, there is a stronger likelihood of having anticipatory policies in place as the team(s) will be able to recognize early warning signals. The preferred future (what should happen — see Exhibit 5.1) can change with time.

Exhibit 5.1. Future studies: Difference between three types of futures.[2]

Characteristics	Predicted Space	Possibility Space	Preferred Space
Ethos	What *will* happen	What *could* happen	What *should* happen
Focus	Assuming that the world moves on in the same trajectory.	Discovering the underlying structural features of the world.	Determining the freedom of action in a policy sense. Complements forecasting.
End Objective	Manage risk.	Leverage future world events to advantage.	Shape world events to ensure outcome.
Example	Trend extrapolations; business-as-usual scenarios. Backcasting is heavily quantitative based.	Forecasting, foresighting, strategic scenarios: Each scenario is backcasted with an event that needs to be enabled or avoided.	Normative scenarios, desirable futures, and future visions (used for backcasting). Backcasting is far more participatory here.

(*Continued*)

[1]Robinson. J. (1982). Energy backcasting: A proposed method of policy analysis. *Energy Policy*, December. Robinson credits the idea to Amory Lovins.

[2]Adapted from various sources like Vergragt & Quist (2011), *Ibid*; Robinson, J. (2003). Future subjunctive: Backcasting as social learning. *Futures*, 35(8): 839–856.

Exhibit 5.1. (*Continued*)

Data	Often relies on past data. Forecasting. Structure based.	Uses deep contextual knowledge. Focuses on the dialectics between structure and agency.	Uses imagination — thinking out of the box. Enhances agency.
Timeframe	Short term (1–5 years). Can be used for 5–50 years as well.	Midterm 5–60 years.	Intergenerational, more than 50+ years, but can also be used for 1–5 years. Indeed, can be utilized for personal futures from 6 months onward. In the preferred future, time is less critical than vision clarity.

Source: Authors.

Many governments use backcasting: Canada, Australia, Japan, Sweden, France, and Germany, for example.[3] However, since policies are designed to have a future impact, knowledge of the policies and strategies adopted (*the whys*) will give context for future policymakers when they plan other interventions. Too often, the context of why a policy was urgently formulated is lost, and hence, important early warning signals (EWSs) are missed.

There are two main types of backcasting. The first is more expert based, with participants suggesting events and trends to fill in the past. The second is far more participatory with group discussions and can use a variety of creative techniques to facilitate imagination. For example, the latter can be embodied when participants move to spaces, where spaces represent time to show the sequence of events that can lead to the creation of the preferred future. This method has been championed by Boulding

[3] Dreborg, K.-H. (1996). Essence of backcasting. *Futures*, *28*(9): 813–828; Vergragt, P.J. & Quist, J. (2011). Backcasting for sustainability: Introduction to the special issue. *Technological Forecasting and Social Change*, 78(5): 747–755.

and used extensively by Inayatullah. It is cognizant of the rational sequence of events. Participants initially stand in a line from the future to the past but then move to the perceived correct space where they think the events occurred or will occur. This backcasting process is done through conversation among participants mediated by a skilled facilitator.

We live in exponential times where change is experienced heterogeneously among different populations. This shift (technology, human decision-making, intentions, knowledge, and systems) means we cannot predict the future based on trends or a current problem alone (that may create a bias) or choose a scenario outcome based on probabilities (which may ignore possibilities). Rather than swaying to the changes of events, the purpose of backcasting is to help shape a more deterministic future under uncertainty, allowing for more deliberate implementation of choices to manage unintended impacts.[4,5] It is a sort of "*How to Get There*."[6] Backcasting uses imagination to ensure the future vision no longer seems far away. It enhances plausibility. It removes the distance to the future with intermediate steps. These steps can be events and actions, but they can also be new stories. Backcasting is a process where policymakers can "think out of the box"[7] and deal with wicked problems.[8] Hence, by following a particular process for backcasting, it gains legitimacy, thus facilitating the possibility of achieving a desired future. By clarifying the pathway to the future, it can significantly enhance agency.

5.2 Backcasting Design Thinking Methodology

There are five stages and four processes used in backcasting. The stages shift from a wide perspective to a narrow one in an iterative manner to force systemic thinking. This funnel approach allows the backcaster to challenge their beliefs. It helps them outline assumptions and identify future signals that can act as EWSs to inform future policymakers if the

---

[4] Dreborg (1996), *Op.cit.*

[5] Robinson, J.B. (1990). Futures under glass: A recipe for people who hate to predict. *Futures*, 22(8): 820–842.

[6] Dreborg (1996), *Op. cit.*

[7] Quist, J. (2007). *Backcasting for a Sustainable Future: The Impact after 10 Years*. Eburon Uitgeverij BV, Utrecht, Netherlands.

[8] Holmberg, J. & Robèrt, K.H. (2000). Backcasting — A framework for strategic planning. *International Journal of Sustainable Development & World Ecology*, 7(4): 291–308.

planned interventions are working or producing unintended side effects. EWSs are indicators along the future journey to help policymakers know if they are en route to the expected future or have detoured. This method allows them to judge if the destination can still be reached and if they can make up for lost time. In this sense, backcasting helps regulate the future — it is a soft road map that signals possible forks in the road.

Ideally, starting with a problem is unnecessary since the future is distant. The starting point is how life will evolve. Before beginning the backcasting process, it is essential to note that the diversity of thought (involving multiple ministries and diverse groups) will validate the process and help policymakers think through their dilemmas. The main principle used by the futurist is to ask, "*Who is not in the room*?" This question helps ensure that all parties are engaged. During the COVID-19 crisis, Singapore leaders had developed sophisticated scenarios but forgot to include migrant workers. COVID-19 spread through their cramped housing. Too often, the silo approach of the public sector acts as a straightjacket, preventing systemic thinking. As policies rarely operate independently but influence and interfere with each other at the local, national, and international levels, the ability to see these patterns by inviting many domain experts helps create robust future-shaping strategies.

5.2.1 *Five stages of backcasting*

The five stages of backcasting are sequential, though they are iterative in terms of reflection regarding the past, present, and future (see Exhibit 5.2). These stages are briefly explained in the following.

Stage 1: Future Horizon: This stage aims to get the participants in touch with their imagination — move from thinking outside the box from predicted and possible futures to an agreed-upon preferred future (narrowing this down to one or a few focus areas). In this phase, the vision is clarified. Imagination is used to evoke the preferred future.

Step 2: Present Horizon: This stage aims to have a reality check. Anchor the preferred future to the present by looking at assumptions, boundary conditions (spillovers across policy domains), and feasibility (of technology, resources, world affairs, or other conditions).

Exhibit 5.2. Design thinking approach to backcasting: Five stages.

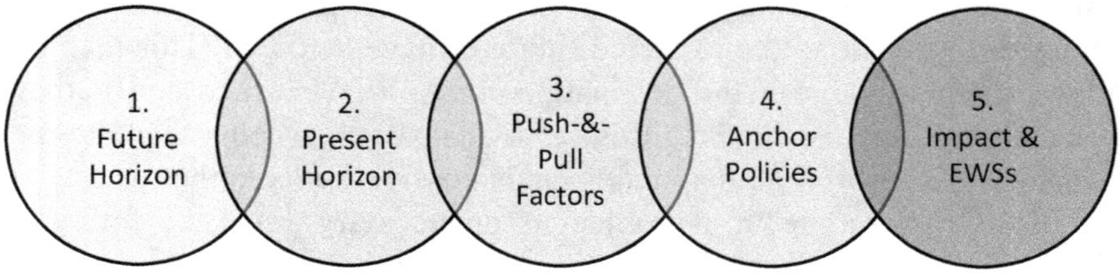

Source: Authors.

Stage 3: Push-and-Pull Factors: The purpose of this stage is to identify factors that will help or hinder the preferred future, revalidate the boundary conditions (other systems may need to be considered), and generate a list of signs or goalposts that act as EWSs if the strategy is on track to the preferred future with the norms agreed on.

Stage 4: Anchor Policies: This stage aims to understand the present, its policies, and long-term effects and decide which policies to use to anchor the preferred future. This stage will allow the identification of policy gaps (whether it is to ensure norms, leverage opportunities, or mitigate future risks).

Stage 5: Impact and EWSs: In the final stage, through a reflection on the policies, policy spillovers, and impact (planned and unintended), a finalization of metrics for EWSs can be created to chart future policy navigators.[9]

5.2.2 *The four processes used in backcasting stages*

The five stages have four major processes: imagination, scoping, boundary setting, and assessment.

Process 1 — Imagination: Imagination is linked to images and involves the dynamic processes of intuition, perception, thinking, and feeling.[10]

[9] A good tool is to reflect on the six basic futures questions here: See Inayatullah, S. (2008). Six pillars: Futures thinking for transforming. *Foresight*, 10(1): 4–21.

[10] Reichling, M.J. (1990). Images of imagination. *Journal of Research in Music Education*, 38(4): 282–293; Sepper, D.L. (2013). *Understanding Imagination. The Reason of Images.* Dordrecht: Springer.

The imagination process can result from a participatory process emerging from key project stakeholders.[11] This stage requires merging (1) experts' knowledge and the limits of what is known, (2) public perceptions and values (now and in the future), and (3) frontier knowledge or even knowledge of *adjacent possible* or what can be. Adjacent possible is "*a kind of shadow future, hovering on the edges of the present state of things, a map of all the ways in which the present can reinvent itself. The strange and beautiful truth about the adjacent possible is that its boundaries grow as you explore them. Each new combination opens up the possibility of other new combinations*."[12]

Across the five stages, imagination can take a broad or narrow scope. For example, in Stages 1 and 5, the scope is a broad funnel perspective, while in Stage 3, it is narrow. Mission-oriented innovation (as defined by OECD-OPSI[13]) may be too narrow for backcasting, as it focuses on a specific objective to be delivered within a specific timeframe.

In Stage 1, a broad scope can be illustrated with this example: The future of drones is limiting, but the future of mobility is broader. A future of flying cars cannot be considered in isolation without understanding how and why mobility will change in the future. Alternate competing futures like teleportation, space travel, or the metaverse may exist. This type of scoping should involve multiple ministries (and their stakeholders) to "see" the interferences of parallel policy futures. This visualization of the future will require many end-use cases. By choosing the broader scope, the future context shifts, i.e., it is no longer rooted in the present. This approach engages in forecasting but uses critical theory to challenge the assumptions behind the forecast.

The narrow scope (which is to be avoided at this stage) is often limited to a ministry (future of health) or even geography (country or political borders). It can focus on the positive and negative impacts of the decisions (in Stages 4 and 5). A very focused discussion can take place now as the knowledge base is broadened at both individual and collective levels compared to before. These observations will form part of the EWSs. Here, the participants need to be careful not to always define their impact in terms

[11] Robinson (2003), *Ibid.*

[12] Johnson, S. (2010). *Where Good Ideas Come From: The Natural History of Innovation.* New York: Riverhead Books.

[13] OECD-OPSI (2021). Public Sector Innovation Facets: Mission-Oriented Innovation. Available: https://oecd-opsi.org/wp-content/uploads/2021/10/OECD-Innovation-Facets-Brief-Mission-Oriented-Innovation-2021.pdf (Accessed 11 June, 2023).

of low-hanging fruits[14] or quick wins, which may lead to mission drift. Some observations may have already been recorded, but it is an affirmative process.

Process 2 — Scoping: Scoping aims to explore the *dialogue space*. These dialogues provide a scaffold[15] to shift or redefine the area of policy discussions by using the new insights generated. The funnel perspective can be broad or narrow. For example, in Stage 1, from a broad vision of the *possible* future, scoping narrows it to the *preferred* future (hence, the ministry or organization role). To understand the scope, backcasters must know the trade-offs (competing objectives) or complementary objectives (win-win).[16] These are decision choices — and they affect public perceptions. The trade-offs become prominent, especially if the future scope is very narrow (as we see decades later with the One China Policy, the globalization of silicon manufacturing,[17] and the COVID-19 pandemic response[18]).

From understanding trade-offs, the participants agree on norms for their preferred future, for example, human first, planet sustainability, and make not buy. Norms are different from values as they are rules for

[14]Holmberg & Dreberg (2000), *Op. cit.*

[15]Bamboo scaffolding is a term coined by Ambassador Lam from Singapore to refer to scenarios which are "adaptable and temporary (and often disposable) ..that reframe understanding": Normann, R. (2001). *Reframing Business: When the Map Changes the Landscape*. Chichester: John Wiley & Sons.

[16]The issue of trade-offs has been discussed in many scenarios: decarbonization policy instruments: environmental, technological, innovation, competitiveness, and distributional outcomes. For example, Peñasco, C., Anadón, L.D., & Verdolini, E. (2021). Systematic review of the outcomes and trade-offs of ten types of decarbonization policy instruments. *Nature Climate Change*, 11(3): 257–265. The authors look at trade-offs in the environmental, technological, innovation, competitiveness, and distributional outcomes; and with respect to time (short or medium term).

[17]Here, the issue was offshoring and the increased geopolitical threat, resulting in *friendshoring* or *nearshoring* strategies (moving sourcing or production to geographic or politically close markets) and focus on new regulations like the *CHIPS and Science Act* (USA) signed in 2022.

[18]Stephens, M., Berengueres, J., Venkatapuram, S., & Moonesar, I.A. (2020). Does the timing of government COVID-19 policy interventions matter? Policy analysis of an original database. *medRxiv preprint*. Referenced in https://doi.org/10.1101/2020.11.13.20194761.

decision-making.[19] In terms of meta-governance, values will help reflect norms and design principles that help choices in decision-making.[20]

A preferred future must address questions of time, space, and scope of analysis (for example, the policy domain may belong to a new ministry). These characteristics are articulated at each stage: assumptions underlying the preferred future (Stage 2), push-and-pull factors (Stage 3), policy analysis (stage 4), and consequences (or impacts of decisions — Stage 5)

Push factors are trends determined by the decisions and weights of the past, while pull factors are predicted trends for the preferred future.[21] For push factors, participants can look at issues within the boundary of the problem. The team decides what the critical factors are using tools like PESTLE (politics, economics, society, technology, legal, and environmental). These factors could be employability, demographics, technology (AI and genetics), national competitiveness, AI infrastructure, data, and policy. This activity is a brainstorming exercise within the boundary of the preferred future.

Broad scoping helps identify factors, some of which are exogenous (external and out of immediate control) and others endogenous, within the control of the entity doing the future study. A good way to start this exercise is to develop prompts that determine push-and-pull factors by asking a series of questions like the following:

1. What are possible crises, and what is their impact on our preferred future?
2. What global and national socio-political trends impact our preferred future?
3. What changes in technology development, adoption, and political stances impact our preferred future?
4. What planetary changes must we address to shape our future?

---

[19] Roobavannan, M., Van Emmerik, T.H., Elshafei, Y., Kandasamy, J., Sanderson, M.R., Vigneswaran, S., ... & Sivapalan, M. (2018). Norms and values in sociohydrological models. *Hydrology and Earth System Sciences*, 22(2): 1337–1349.

[20] Kooiman, J. & Jentoft, S. (2009). Meta-governance: Values, norms and principles, and the making of hard choices. *Public Administration*, 87(4): 818–836.

[21] Palmer, J. & Ellis, N. (2008). A layered approach to horizon scanning: Identifying future issues in military and veterans' health, *Journal of Future Studies*, 12(4): 77–92; Inayatullah, S. (2008). Six pillars: Futures thinking for transforming. *Foresight*, 10(1): 4–21.

5. What market and industry changes are occurring here and globally that impact our preferred future?
6. What monetary and financial market changes occurring here and globally impact our preferred future?
7. What behavioral and attitudinal changes occurring here at an individual, societal, and global levels impact our preferred future? What are the triggers for this? Demographic? Geographic? Tech Adoption? Economic? This analysis will help identify key stakeholders for shaping the intended future. These additional aggregated data points act as EWSs.

In another method like the Six Pillars method developed by Inayatullah and based on the Manoa school method,[22] backcasting emerges after the vision has been clarified. First, the future is mapped. Trends and weights are articulated. Then, the future is disrupted through the analysis of emerging issues. This is followed by the big picture or microhistory — the broader patterns. From there, we shift to Causal Layered Analysis. Once the future is deepened and assumptions challenged, then scenarios are developed. Finally, the last pillar is transformation — the vision of the preferred future is clarified and backcasted. Backcasting anchors the process, ensuring that visioning leads to strategic plans or, when possible, anticipatory action learning where the actional items are developed through prototypes.

Casual Layered Analysis (CLA)[23] can be used to understand the levels of the future, from litany to system to worldview to metaphor. It can also be utilized to ensure that the backcast has depth — that the events suggested have ontological depth to them, i.e., not just litany but suggested systemic changes and metaphor shifts over the time period being backcasted. This exercise aims to arrange the factors in order of importance and prioritize what the backcasters want to focus on (see Exhibit 5.3). The four layers can be used for better sensemaking (see Exhibit 5.4). CLA can be used with other methods as well. For example, the template below is linked to another method invented by Inayatullah, *The Futures Triangle*. In this method, the future is understood through three dimensions — the pull (the vision), the push (the measurable drivers), and the weight of the past (the worldviews that impede the desired future).

---

[22] Inayatullah (2008), *Op. cit.*

[23] Inayatullah, S., Mercer, R., Milojević, I., & Sweeney, J.A. (2022). *CLA 3.0 — Thirty Years of Transformative Research*. Malaysia: Tamkang University Press.

Exhibit 5.3. Push, pull, and weight factors (template).

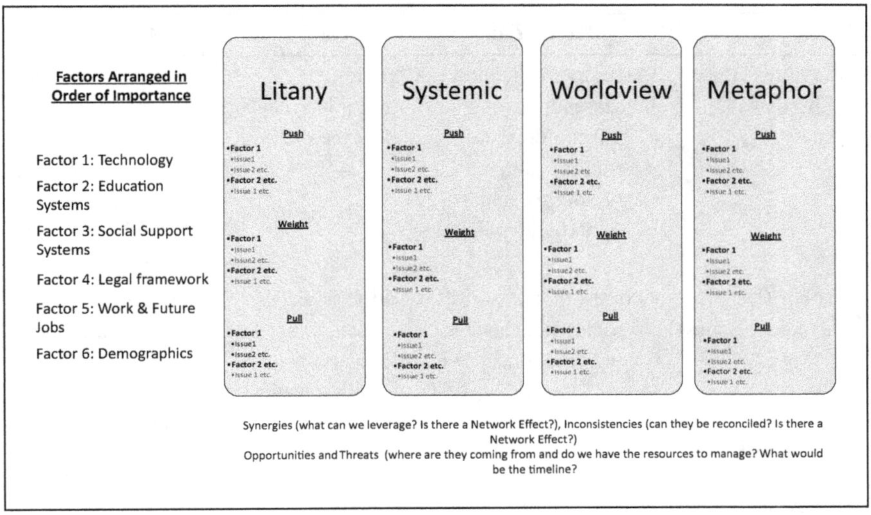

Source: Adapted from Palmer and Ellis (2008).[24]

Exhibit 5.4. Casual layered analysis levels.

CLA	Description	Problem-Solving	Challenge
Litany (visible problem)	The view of current reality (perceived facts), surface-level "talk" that captures public imagination: Official description of the issue.	Simple — captures the current narrative.	Between Litany and Systemic Perspective: Let's think about this. Is it too surface level?
Systemic perspective (Causes)	Causes for current reality: scientific, technical, historical, and policy facts.	Complicated — in this case, you may focus on one or a few systems.	

(*Continued*)

[24] Palmer & Ellis (2008), *Op. cit.*

Exhibit 5.4. (*Continued*)

CLA	Description	Problem-Solving	Challenge
Worldview (Frame of Analysis)	Assumptions behind causes of key stakeholders: culture, values, paradigms, and mental viewpoints.	Complex — multiple systems now interact.	Between Systemic Perspective and Worldview: Which opinion is the dominant view? Why? Can it be changed?
Metaphor (Deep, Unspoken Issues)	Stories: myths, archetypes, images, and emotions.	Chaotic — needs sensemaking. The focus is on intuition leading to deep change.	Between Worldview and Metaphor: Is there a clash of paradigms? Will it be significant?

Source: Adapted from various sources (Authors).

Process 3 — Boundary Setting: The domain edges for the preferred future are iteratively defined to understand the journey in the context of policy areas, norms, and no-go areas. At the beginning of the exercise, the purpose is to harness imagination and use blue-sky thinking, eventually narrowing the domain to one within some ministries to create policies that guide the country toward the preferred future. The process allows the definition of the system of focus, identification of its subsystems, and their interactions.

Process 4 — Assessment: The assessment stage involves deep reflections: bridges and chasms (gaps) in policies can be identified. An assessment of policies can be done to understand policy gaps and incongruencies. Some questions that can guide this analysis are as follows:

- What is the flexibility built into the current policies?
- What new policies may be needed?
- Who has the responsibility for the policy adaptation?
- What data do we need for evidence and baseline monitoring? Who and how should we capture them?
- What are the methods for rapid sharing of learnings?

Assumptions are outlined. For example, an assumption may be that GDP will grow at 1.5%. Identifying assumptions will help determine additional EWSs and impacts across the trajectory to inform future policymakers and policy custodians. There is a need to keep the process human-centered; as Karl-Henrik Dreborg, the Swedish futurist, said, "*To qualify as a backcasting study, the scenarios chosen in the project must reflect solutions to a specified societal problem.*"[25] The assumptions can be classified into layers: (1) local policies, (2) national policies, and (3) international policies.

5.2.3 *Other types of backcasting*

Backcasting can be used in different ways. In Exhibit 5.5, the expert focused on how the core metaphor of the brain would change through each time period. Thus, the actual parliamentary and national strategies were less important than the change in narrative. This activity was done for a large mental health organization. Over time, the strategy would become more complex, ecological, and far less technocratic — including different ways of knowing. In the first phase, change must happen; it is a no-brainer. Phase 2 identified the weaknesses and strengths, such as the lack of capability. Phase 3 was integrating left and right brains. Phase 4 was peer-to-peer sharing. Phase 5 was an ecology of strategies for mental health (see Exhibit 5.5).

In Exhibit 5.6, backcasting was embodied. This was done for the government of Cambodia.[26] The participants stood up and moved to the correct position on the timeline, where they used CLA to shape the vision with steps toward the future. Of course, after this process, there is the normal political process of negotiating with the various ministries, using the backcast to influence others.

Other practitioners use backcasting with far more detail and through various time horizons, as used by Australia for the Sunshine Coast Council in their City Futures report.[27] In another example, a backcast was done for the telecom industry for each of the four scenarios (see Exhibit 5.7). Backcasting is not always linear; it can meander as the organization tries different directions — the appearance of linearity is

[25] Dreborg (1996), *Op. cit.*, 816.

[26] Inayatullah, S., Durrani-Jamal, S., & Sandhu, S.C. (2020). Garment workers to women leaders and the wise E-Buddha: Cambodia 2050. *Journal of Futures Studies*. Available: https://jfsdigital.org/2020/05/12/garment-workers-to-women-leaders-and-the-wise-e-buddha-cambodia-2050/ (Accessed 12 May, 2020).

[27] Gould, S. (2012). Organisational Futures for the Sunshine Coast Council 2030. Report.

Exhibit 5.5. Change in narratives for mental health (example).

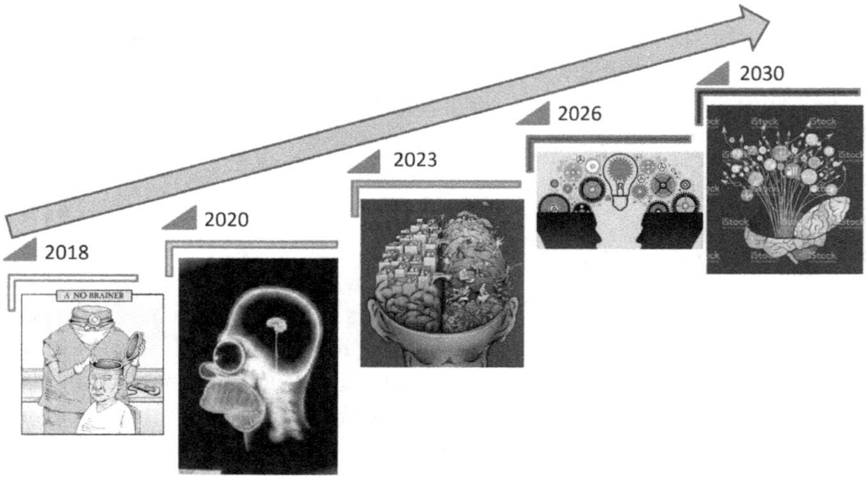

Source: Authors.

Exhibit 5.6. Embodied backcasting.

Backcasting using CLA

Litany description	Complicated	Simple and efficient
The System	Paper and C-drive	Paperless with an open platform
The Worldview	For the government department	For the Nation
Metaphor	E-Monk	E-Buddha

Events for Realization their Strategy

- By 2023, there is a Minister for ICT
- By 2025, near full literacy in the nation
- By 2025, a nationwide ICT infrastructure system
- By 2026, a system to evaluate what is working and not working in e-governance
- By 2027 a fully functioning agile cyber-security system
- By 2028, cost savings from the ICT revolution are visible
- By 2029, enhanced gender equity, possible as work ICTs are not gender-based
- By 2030, with a decade of data collection, the beginning of evidence-based policymaking.
- By 2030, Cambodia receives an award for e-government
- By 2035, women are visible leaders in Cambodia

Source: Authors.

comfortable, but the emergence of other geometrical shapes is important when designing backcasting.

Finally, backcasting can be done for personal futures. Once the vision of the preferred future is created, the steps needed to achieve that reality can be developed. This can be done in a solitary way, or friends and colleagues can be invited to present how they can support in the futures journey.

Exhibit 5.7. Backcasting for Telcom.

Theme	Year	Key milestones observed	2015-2020
Creating community agency (External transformations)	2015	Creating a Sunshine Coast with connected governance & community capacity to deliver local government services	Horizon 2
		New procurement strategy is developed to prove hubs of the future	
		Implement E vote & e-engagement tools and methods	
	2016	Develop learning strategies for creating new agency in our communities	
		New SCC identity emerges in line with 2030 scenario	
		Ros Cheales white paper on alternative local government workplaces	
	2017	Local Government Election	
	2018	Emergent community capability, governance & cooperatives	
		New industrial agreement that is flexible to match 2030 workplace	
		New Local Govt Act - Councillors responsible for whole region (no electorates)	
		Regional decision making	
		Green paper - recommendations adopted	
		State Government take over planning, roads, waste	
		Online plebiscites - major regional issues (should we sell the airport?)	
	2019	Equity of access to all to connect virtually	
Theme	**Year**	**Key milestones observed**	**2020-2030**
Virtual Local Workforce / Community Governance	2020	Local Government pilot program on alternative models of government	Horizon 3
		Local Government Election	
		LG & Community, anyone, anytime online	
		SCC is a small business	
		Community governance alleviates the burden	
	2021	Outdoor staff totally divested (create opportunity for staff to have local business)	
	2024	Referendum on major issues/election	
		Strong community partnerships with global learning communities to sustain our learning cultures	
		IR reforms implemented	
	2030	New voluntary participatory democracy evolved	
		Local Government Board - all major decisions by referendum	
		Autonomous, multi-skilled staff constantly moving between multiple employers for short to medium durations	
		Staff are confident of their broad skills and secure in knowing they will be valued in a range of contexts	
		A SCC culture and workplace that is like an amoeba or gazelle-flexible. Being efficient, innovative, IT savvy & mobile, quick to respond to challenging situations	

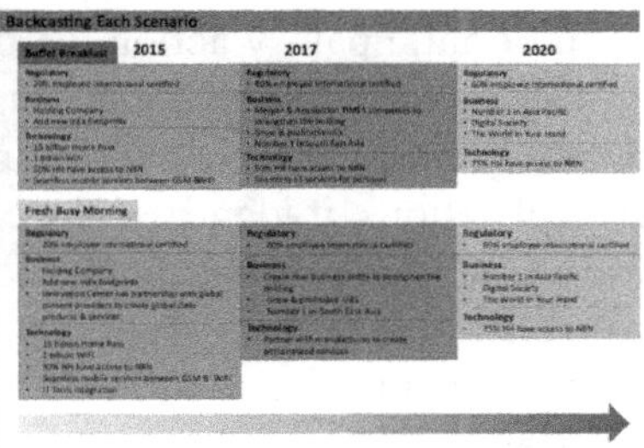

Source: Authors.

5.3 Conclusion

The backcasting techniques discussed are not simple but serve several key purposes. First and most importantly, backcasting makes the future more plausible. It links the preferred future with the present.

Second, it reduces risk by articulating what needs to happen to create a preferred future and, when linked with scenario planning, what needs to happen to avoid an undesired future.

Third, by positing different events and trends by populating the future, it challenges the policymakers to confront their preconceived notions and hubris. This is critical as the future is not set in stone and also because the impacts of policy performance are often a perception of public value delivered over time.

Fourth, the process acknowledges the uncertainty of the market and government shaping of strategies and allows for the identification of early warning signals. This helps future policy caretakers understand the purpose of the policy instrument and also helps them correct the course or purpose (if so needed).

Fifth, when done in a participatory style with numerous experts, the backcasting process helps get the agenda of the intended future accepted by more stakeholders, as they can now visualize their collective impact and understand the interference and resonance patterns.

Sixth, when done with experts and non-experts — i.e., when the question of who is not in the room is addressed — backcasting takes into account worldview blind spots, making futures planning, the strategic plan, or anticipatory action learning far more robust.

Seventh, ontological depth is brought to the process when linked with other methods, such as the Futures Triangle. Instead of merely events or critical actions, it identifies the changing pulls of the future, the pushes, as well as weights. When linked to CLA, the backcast would be populated with changing litanies, systems, worldviews, and, critically, the new metaphor in each horizon.

Eighth, applying CLA to backcasting itself challenges the worldview, which is often perceived as a linear development of actions, like a train going from one station to another until it reaches its final destination. This can be misleading — the real world has emergence. One event can cascade in another direction. The train can fly, become derailed, and lose passengers. We would prefer backcasting to be seen as a way to both enhance efficiency (in creating the next steps), reduce anxiety as to what is ahead (in terms of populating the future with steps), and provide agency. This is the critical aspect — the future can often seem like a mountain that cannot be climbed. Backcasting makes the steps attainable, and when the agency is a shared collective, we can jump over the mountain and create a new vision.

Backcasting develops skills like imagination, critical thinking, self-learning, patience, empathy, tolerance, boundary-spanning, and systems thinking. These are essential skills when our knowledge paradigms, skills, and expertise are constantly being challenged.

https://doi.org/10.1142/9789811296000_0006

Chapter 6

Navigating Pathways toward Anticipatory Governance within a Systems Thinking Ecosystem

John Griffiths

Centre for Systems Studies, University of Hull, Hull, UK

Key Takeaways

- Systems thinking has various tools, and there is a need to understand the tool's purpose in analysis.
- Systems thinking is about perspective; hence, it needs to be flexible and adaptable, and is also pluralistic.
- The boundary of the system will also limit the ability to anticipate navigable pathways to understand *how* and *where* these perspectives touch, interrelate, and interact.
- This type of thinking considers both living (animals, insects, etc.) and non-living (forests, rivers, etc.) aspects.
- Systems thinking needs a shift in organizational culture to be beneficial.

6.1 Overview

Systems Thinking (ST) has been diluted and corrupted over decades to a point where it can be confusing to know what it is and what it can provide leaders and organizations.[1] This chapter will provide a clarification on an approach to Systems Thinking, which will support readers in both understanding how the adoption of ST might be employed to navigate pathways toward Anticipatory Governance and which ST methodologies may be most appropriate in providing a framework for an effective ecosystem; this may include Viable Systems Model (VSM), Systems Dynamics (SD), Soft Systems Methodology, and Critical Systems Heuristics (CSH).

The chapter will provide insight into structural aspects and analytical linkages to predictive tools and methodologies (including AI/ML) that might be embedded and used within the ST ecosystem to support decision-making for identifying navigable pathways. Given the insights enabled by the ST ecosystem, the chapter will evolve to show how tangible, more effective, and inclusive policies might be defined and how robust engagement can be pursued with the stakeholder environment; this should include looking beyond human stakeholders. The prime aim of this aspect will be to enable navigable pathways that provide both anticipatory insight and adaptive capabilities.

6.2 Systems Thinking — A Definition?

A core issue of providing any definition of ST is that it depends on the individual's perspective, the problem situations one may engage with, one's biases (that's complex in itself!), and multiple other aspects that comprise an individual's "Self".

I do not intend to delve into the history of ST as there are many references to this in multiple academic articles and books. However, a helpful starting point is the work of Charles West Churchman and his defined principles of ST (see Exhibit 6.1).

The core of this foundation is understanding that ST needs to encompass multiple perspectives and surface *how* and *where* these perspectives touch, interrelate, and interact. There are no "experts" in ST; even facilitators become a part of the mess of perspectives, with frustration, conflict, and personal bias (amongst other things) impacting relationships while potentially marginalizing key stakeholders.

[1]Arnold, R.D. & Wade, J.P. (2015). A definition of systems thinking: A systems approach. *Procedia Computer Science*, 44: 669–678.

Exhibit 6.1. Principles of systems thinking.

1. The systems approach begins when you first see the world through the eyes of another.
2. The systems approach goes on to discover that every worldview is terribly restricted.
3. There are no experts in the systems approach.
4. The systems approach is not a bad idea.

Source: Adapted from Churchman, C.W. (1968). *The Systems Approach*. New York: Delta/Dell Publishing, p. 231.

Professor Russell L. Ackoff is a crucial formulator of ST and its development. His ideas expound the holistic nature of systems and their deployment into the organizational environment. The following are a couple of his famous quotes; they further underline the nature of systems:

> *"...the performance of the whole is never the sum of the performance of the parts taken separately, but it's the product of their interactions."*[2]
>
> *"A system is never the sum of its parts; it's the product of their interaction."*[3]

There are many definitions of ST, each providing a slightly different perspective based on the philosophical bias of the authors; however, the core remains the same: ST is about a holistic approach and the interrelationship between the constituent parts: interconnectedness, dynamic interactions, emergence, holism, and multiple perspectives.

ST is, by its very essence, both multidisciplinary and pluralistic. It is a way of "being" and a collection of tools and methods for understanding, intervention, synthesis, and design. It is a powerful means of establishing

[2]Discussion between Dr. Ackoff and Dr. Deming. Available: https://ackoffcenter.blogs.com/files/dr.-ackoff-dr.-deming.pdf (Accessed 3 January, 2024).

[3]YouTube (2003). Russell Ackoff Seminar. Available: https://www.youtube.com/watch?v=a0ooqJ-pOH4 (Accessed 3 January, 2024). There are many seminars by Professor Russell L. Ackoff on YouTube; you may wish to view them to get a more in-depth perspective.

a navigable pathway toward a desirable future, "desirable" being a contentious word in the messes ST seeks to address, as in whose desirable future! ST is a collective approach. It will involve a plurality of perspectives and values; ignoring even one perspective corrupts the model of the whole and discredits the resulting navigation efforts.

Around the world, there is an increasing interest in using ST in addressing issues that affect everyone. For example, the UN attempts to integrate ST with the Sustainable Development Goals (SDGs). Also, the UK Government and National Health Service (NHS) have begun a journey utilizing an approach that leans on ST.

In the words of Churchman, "*The systems approach is not a bad idea.*" Many are discovering, through its application, the many benefits of its adoption.

6.3 Perspectives

Perspectives are crucial for systems thinkers; everyone will have a different perspective of a system, what it does, how it works, and how internal/external events impact the parts. Even everyday objects we all take for granted can be affected by perspective. Take the simple example of a table (see Exhibit 6.2). What is it?

Each individual, embodied in these perspectives, sees an everyday object from their worldview. Each individual will have a defined perspective that comprises a mental model. ST seeks to surface these models, look at unfolding the complexity, and examine how we might exploit these perspectives to create understanding, dialogue, and the definition of a path to navigate toward a desired future.

6.4 Defining Boundaries

Let us begin to understand how ST can be applied. A key aspect of ST is defining the boundary of the system we are considering, often called *Boundary Judgments*. Who/What should we include/exclude? Who decides? How big/small should the area be within the boundary? Considering the elements shown in Exhibit 6.3, they offer a boundary that contains many values, judgments, perspectives, behaviors, needs, wants, etc.; this includes non-human elements too (more on that later). Some are

Exhibit 6.2. Perspective: What is this?

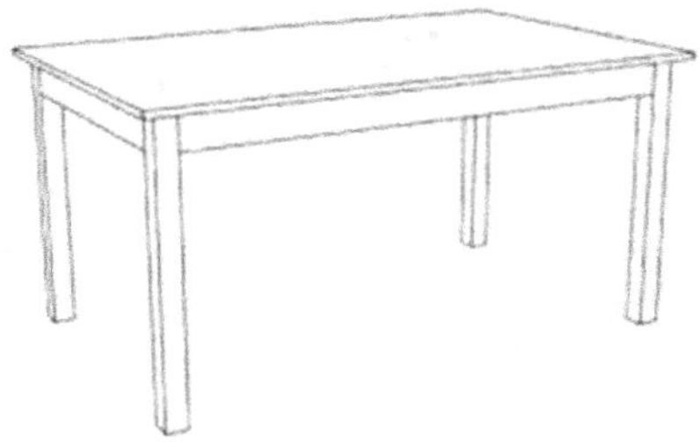

- Place of work.
- Meeting place.
- Something to dine at.
- A homeless person could see it as something to sleep on, to keep one off the floor.
- A table could be used as a platform to make a speech.
- For somebody cold, it could be used as firewood.
- Again, for the homeless, it is a frame for a shelter from rain and wind.
- And when the zombies attack, the legs can be used as clubs and the top could be a defensive shield.

Let us now add another layer of complexity. Consider the second example from the list — a meeting place. What emotional experience would unfold when summoned to the meeting place?

- Another hour of boredom.
- Developing our direction of travel.
- A place of abuse.
- A place of support.

Source: Author.

individuals, while others are in groups; diverse values and perceptions will exist even within the groups.

A focal issue will be addressed: climate change, pollution, and food security. This focal issue allows an initial boundary judgment to be defined. However, it is essential to understand that this will change as the

Exhibit 6.3. Boundary judgments.

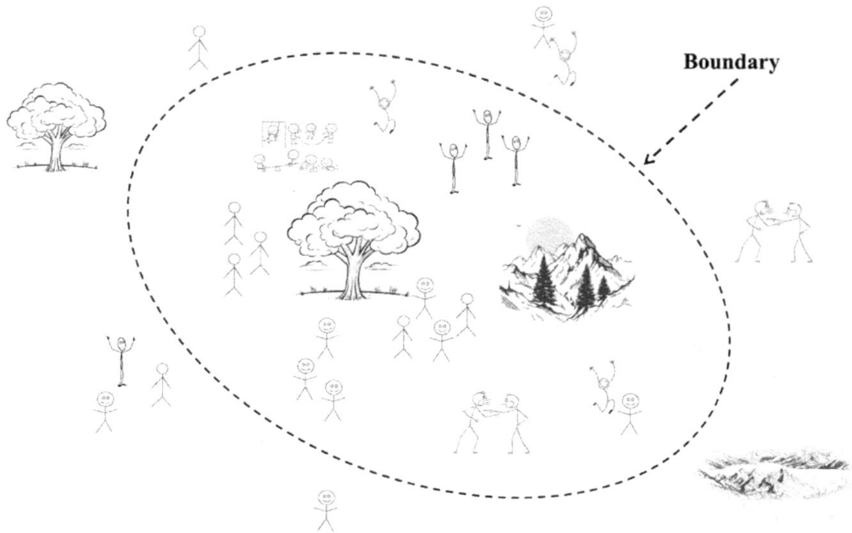

Source: Author.

intervention progresses; things will evolve and may include elements not even considered relevant at the outset. It is, therefore, vital to change boundary judgments to align with this evolution; ST embraces emergence and the evolution that materializes.

The following quote is something to always bear in mind when considering boundary judgments and the change inoculated into the core issue from emergence:

> *"No man ever steps in the same river twice, for it's not the same river, and he's not the same man." — Heraclitus*

I stated this earlier, but it is worth considering that ST is a collective approach. It will involve a plurality of perspectives and values; ignoring one corrupts the model of the whole and discredits any resulting navigation efforts.

Thankfully, we have a method to help and support the definition of boundary judgments. This method is Critical Systems Heuristics (CSH) from Werner Ulrich, to which I will provide an overview and links (see in Exhibit 6.4).

Exhibit 6.4. Systems thinking methodologies overview.

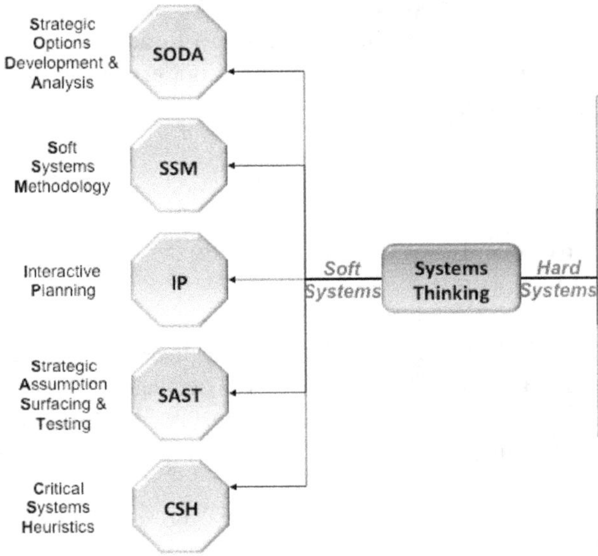

Source: Author.

6.5 Systems Thinking Methodologies

There are numerous ST methodologies and associated tools, each with a philosophical, empirical, and cognitive bias. The following is an introductory overview of some of these. How they are categorized can differ; however, I choose to reflect a well-founded path forged by leading ST practitioners and academics such as Michael C. Jackson and Robert L. Flood that categorizes ST as either "Hard" or "Soft." There are four hard systems and five soft systems, as shown in Exhibit 6.4.

Hard Systems are based around a more technical, engineering-biased ecosystem with a more scientific approach and, although they can include qualitative methods, they are more focused on a structured quantitative approach. The core bias is objective and aims to address a well-defined problem with a tendency toward an ideal solution as an outcome.

Soft Systems approaches evolved to address poorly structured (messy) issues; this includes what is termed *wicked problems*.[4]

[4]Rittel, H.W.J. & Webber, M.M. (1973). Dilemmas in a general theory of planning. *Policy Science,* 4: 155–169.

These problems deal with a plurality of perspectives and have a bias toward subjectivity. Soft Systems approaches embrace the human factor in problem situations. They revolve around learning and understanding, which is a never-ending inquiry. The focus is on gaining understanding as opposed to defining a clear solution.

6.5.1 *Hard systems*

There are four types of hard systems: systems engineering, systems analysis, systems dynamics, and the Viable Systems Model.

Systems Engineering (SE)[5]: It is firmly based in the engineering space, using logic and functional analysis to address a clearly defined problem. Traditionally, SE focused on physical systems; contemporary evolution seeks to take a more holistic stance by considering wider ST.

Systems Analysis (SA)[6]: This method evolved from the operational research conducted during the Second World War and was further developed by the RAND Corporation. It tends toward structured and quantitative analysis with a focus on finding alternatives. The term SA can be found throughout the IT industry. I am not wholly convinced there is a formative link to ST; however, it is clear that both SE and SA had and continue to have a strong influence.

Systems Dynamics (SD): It was developed by Professor Jay Forrester at MIT.[7] SD provides a powerful tool for analyzing dynamic, nonlinear complex systems employing stocks, flows, and feedback loops. Mapping uses "Influence Diagrams"; these provide potentially significant insights into a dynamic system and its inherent causality. Due to the complexity of interactions in a dynamic system, SD is usually undertaken with powerful

---

[5]The following document provides a deeper insight into ST and its linkage to SE learning and adoption of ST: See Camelia, F. & Ferris, T.L. (2016). Systems thinking in systems engineering. *INCOSE International Symposium*, 26.

[6]The following document provides a detailed account of SA (from a traditional perspective): Quade, E. (1972). *Systems Analysis: A Tool for Choice*. United States. Available: https://www.rand.org/pubs/papers/P4860.html (Accessed 3 January, 2023).

[7]For an introduction to SD by the creator, Forrester, J.W. (1961). *Industrial Dynamics*. Portland, Productivity Press.

software simulation packages. Embedded within SD models can be complicated formulas and algorithms. In my opinion, there is potential for the evolution of SD with new technologies like AI/ML within the simulations; this could provide richer insights to enable enhanced flexibility and adaptability for navigating the uncertainty of the future.

SD models have the potential for application in many areas:

- Economic modelling.
- Manpower planning.
- Policy creation.
- Scenario planning.
- Manufacturing and production planning.
- Climate change.

Viable Systems Model (VSM)[8]: Stafford Beer developed it within Organizational/Management Cybernetics. It concerns defining organizations that can survive in dynamic environments; a key to this is that the organization is adaptable and capable of autonomy. This is a compelling model for structuring and operationalizing organizations.

6.5.2 *Soft systems*

There are five types of soft systems: strategic options development and analysis, soft systems methodology, interactive planning, strategic assumption surfacing and testing, and critical systems heuristics.

Strategic Options Development and Analysis (SODA)[9]: It was developed by Colin Eden and Fran Ackermann. It is a robust approach based on

---

[8]For an in-depth appreciation of the VSM, the following books should be considered: Beer, S. (1979). *The Heart of Enterprise*. Chichester: Wiley; Beer, S. (1981). *Brain of the Firm*, 2nd edn. Chichester: Wiley; Beer, S. (1985). *Diagnosing the System for Organizations*. Chichester: Wiley.

[9]The following books provide a comprehensive insight into SODA: Eden, C. & Ackermann, F. (1998). *Making Strategy: The Journey of Strategic Management*. London: Sage; Bryson, J.M. (2004). *Visible Thinking: Unlocking Causal Mapping for Practical Business Results*. Chichester: Wiley; Hoboken, N.J., Ackermann, F. & Eden, C. (2010). *Strategic Options Development and Analysis*. DOI: 10.1007/978-1-84882-809-4_4.

cognitive/causal mapping. Individual maps reflect their perception. These are combined to produce a single map to reflect the issue. Following dialogue to enable agreement, goals and strategies are developed and allocated for delivery. The software has been created to deliver Causal Mapping (a network diagram that captures complex phenomena and their relationships), which supports SODA.

Soft Systems Methodology (SSM)[10]: It was developed by Peter Checkland. SSM evolved from the inadequacies of operational research and SE in dealing with ill-structured, messy problems. It is a rich collection of tools and techniques for surfacing understanding, which might provide improvement of a problematical situation. While there are seven stages to SSM, it is not a linear process; it is about continuous learning and understanding. SSM is a potent methodology applicable to unstructured, messy, problematical situations.

Interactive Planning (IP)[11]: Russell Ackoff, a significant figure in the evolution of ST, developed it. It is a model based on participation and collaboration between stakeholders, where power dynamics are seen as an obstacle to overcome. IP seeks to define a future based on what can be done now. It supports the collaborative view of a desirable future and how to design the steps to get there creatively. IP is a robust ST methodology worthy of inclusion in a comprehensive toolkit. The following are steps to deliver this:

1. Formulate the mess or problem.
2. Ends planning.
3. Means planning.
4. Resource planning.
5. Design of implementation and control.

[10]There are many references to SSM throughout ST literature; however, the definitive reference book remains: Checkland, P. (1981). *Systems Thinking, Systems Practice*. Chichester: Wiley.

[11]The following books will also provide a detailed description and deployment of IP: Ackoff, R.L. (1981). *Creating the Corporate Future*. New York: Wiley; Ackoff, R.L. (1994). *The Democratic Organisation*. New York: Wiley. As suggested earlier in this chapter, there are many videos on YouTube of lectures and seminars of Russell Ackoff detailing IP; it is suggested these provide not only some detail of IP but also about ST in general; viewing is recommended.

Strategic Assumption Surfacing and Testing (SAST)[12]: It was developed by Richard Mason and Ian Mitroff. The five-phase process seeks to surface assumptions in defining a policy or plan and then challenge them within a structured methodology. It is a dialectical approach to unfolding ill-structured, messy problem situations. SAST is another robust methodology in ST's toolkit. The five phases are as follows:

1. Group formation.
2. Assumption surfacing and rating.
3. Within group dialectic debate.
4. Between group dialectic debate.
5. Final synthesis.

Critical Systems Heuristics (CSH)[13]: It was developed by Werner Ulrich. As previously mentioned, the core concept of CSH is to support the understanding of boundary judgments; the intent is not to define boundaries but to provide a boundary critique. CSH utilizes a set of twelve questions to enable an uncovering of judgments; this offers a view of situations and garners an appreciation of the big picture. The questions allow the unfolding of essential insight into a plethora of issues aligned with the following:

- Values and motivations.
- Power structures.
- The knowledge basis.
- The moral basis.

While an independent methodology, with its use in evaluating an intervention, the power of CSH can provide for a powerful synergistic collaboration tool embedded within the delivery of other methodologies.

---

[12]The book reference for further reading: Mason, R.O. & Mitroff, I.I. (1981). *Challenging Strategic Planning Assumptions: Theory, Cases and Techniques*. New York: Wiley.

[13]Deeper insight into CSH can be found at the following references: Ulrich, W. & Reynolds, M. (2010). Critical systems heuristics. In: Reynolds, M. & Holwell, S. (Eds.), *Systems Approaches to Managing Change: A Practical Guide*. London: Springer: pp. 243–292.

The home page of Werner Ulrich is also a rich source of information: http://wulrich.com.

6.5.3 *Multi-methodologies*

As this chapter has evolved, I have shown multiple methodologies all under the ST banner; this plurality does, of course, provide for apparent tensions. Their creators would argue that their methodologies must be kept whole; this is their strength. CSH is distinct; it has been developed to be integrated within disparate methodologies.

Some have recognized genuine plurality as utilizing tools within the methodologies to create synergistic ST interventions that provide more excellent tangible value. For example, from my experience, the use of "Rich Pictures" (a tool from SSM) as a starting point in any intervention creates a strong foundation and anchor point. Then, we could use CSH to unfold boundary perspectives. If organizational structure is an agreed issue, we could bring in the VSM. ST is there to exploit positively; the methodologies are not set in concrete, and cross-pollination is the key to maximizing value and insight. An advocate of this has been Professor Michael Jackson with his Critical Systems Thinking (CST); his work is worth exploring, and his book relates the development of CST and its evolution from ST.[14]

6.6 SOD — Systems-Oriented Design

A criticism sometimes directed at ST is that no solution is generally provided; this criticism is primarily directed at Soft Systems methodologies. An area of interest that may provide a linkage to enabling tangible output is slowly garnering interest as it develops SOD. The key developer of SOD is Professor Birger Sevaldson at the Oslo School of Architecture and Design. A tool he created is Gigamapping, an evolution from Checklands SSM Rich Pictures. This is just one example of how design and ST can combine to provide tangible and powerful outcomes.[15]

---

[14] For more information on work by Professor Michael Jackson, look at: https://www.youtube.com/watch?v=zJZDIA5UCxw or his book: Jackson, M.C. (2019). *Critical Systems Thinking and the Management of Complexity*. John Wiley & Sons.

[15] Further insight, tools, and case studies can be found at the following website: https://systemsorienteddesign.net; Additional reading: Sevaldson, B. (2022). *Designing Complexity: The Methodology and Practice of Systems Oriented Design*. Common Ground Research Networks.

Another exciting set of tools under the SOD thread has been developed by Kristel Van Ael (a lecturer at the University of Antwerp) and Peter Jones (founder of the Systemic Design Association). The Systemic Design Toolkit (with templates) is freely available to download[16]; these are powerful tools to create collaborative interventions and designs for the future, utilizing ST to address complex organizational and societal issues.

6.7 Non-Human Aspects

ST is an approach that considers wholes and interrelationships; that being the case, an essential element that must be considered is the "Non-Human" aspect — this is both living (animals, insects, etc.) and non-living (forests, rivers, etc.). There are examples of several countries worldwide that are now giving legal "Personhood" to non-humans, New Zealand and Columbia being two countries.[17,18] For example, refer to The Treaty of Waitangi,[19] The Te Urewera Act,[20] and The Whanganui River[21] from New Zealand.

While this is extremely important, there are questions of how non-human aspects can be represented and by whom. It is also essential to understand how ST can support effective collaboration between humans and non-human elements in developing synergistic ecosystems and communities in delivering the future.

---

[16] Tools available here: https://www.systemicdesigntoolkit.org. Additional reading: Jones, P. & van Ael, K. (2022). *Design Journeys Through Complex Systems: Practice Tools for Systemic Design*. BIS Publishers.

[17] Gordon, G.J. (2018). Environmental personhood. *Columbia Journal of Environmental Law*, 43(1): 49–91.

[18] Clark, C., Emmanouil, N., Page, J. & Pelizzon, A. (2019). Can you hear the rivers sing? Legal personhood, ontology and the nitty gritty of governance. *Ecology Law Quarterly*, 45: 787–844.

[19] New Zealand History. (n.d.). The Treaty in Brief. Available: https://nzhistory.govt.nz/politics/treaty/the-treaty-in-brief (Accessed 9 March, 2024).

[20] New Zealand Legislation. (2021). Te Urewera Act 2014.

[21] This became the first river in the world under the Te Urewera Act to have legal personhood status. See https://natlib.govt.nz/he-tohu/learning/social-inquiry-resources/cultural-interaction/cultural-interaction-supporting-activities-and-resources/change-maker-whanganui-river#:~:text=When%20the%20Bill%20was%20passed,and%20its%20iwi%20and%20hapū.

An example SOD work (in which ST is embedded) is being undertaken by Dr. Marie Davidova at the University of Stuttgart in Germany. This work, CoLife,[22] is already providing tangible results using Artificial Intelligence (AI) in consideration of the performance of, for example, insects in collaboration efforts, say, in pollination, and the value this provides to the community.

ST can provide valuable insights in defining paths to be navigated by inclusive understanding and collaboration involving non-human aspects. Disregarding this inclusivity could lead to anthropogenic extinction. While there is much to be accepted and defined for future direction, ST can contribute positively.

6.8 Way Forward for Governance

The development of tangible and workable anticipatory governance must be holistic. It cannot be linear as the future is not linear nor a process. Governments are generally designed for stability and the management of situations. With the speed and complexity of change being experienced globally, hierarchical and bureaucratic structures are incapable of flexible adaption and governance; this is not only down to structure but also mindset.

The current reality of interaction and relationships with government stakeholders is biased toward a mechanistic perspective; considering the preponderance of digital feedback methods, it has infiltrated every aspect of our lives. The point to note is that this provides a true reflection of individual perspective; with intelligent software that provides analysis and reports, decision-makers are drowning in an ocean of data and information. The easy option is to squeeze it all into pre-formed templates. It is a drill-down and reductionist approach that aligns with hierarchical and bureaucratic structures; same and same again, it seems safe and is easy to manage, but in reality, it massages egos or provides a stick to berate someone (the blame culture!).

[22] Davidová, M. (2023). COLife — More-than-human community codesign: Cocreating synergetic post-anthropocene within systemic approach to architectural performance. In: Rubbo, A., Du, J., Thomsen, M.R. & Tamke, M. (Eds.), *Design for Resilient Communities*. Sustainable Development Goals Series. Cham: Springer. https://doi.org/10.1007/978-3-031-36640-6_26.

Utilizing ST to deliver *anticipatory governance* provides an approach that enables views of the future to be unfolded and provides a means of analysis and simulation (think Systems Dynamics); let's play with the future and anticipate paths of navigation. ST can also provide new structures that deliver anticipatory governance (Viable Systems Model). How can we create flexible adaptation strategies that help us design the future? Why not employ *interactive planning*; with all of this, we operate within a Viable Systems Model ecosystem that gives us constant feedback to enable adaptive monitoring and governance. Practical input from SSM will provide *rich pictures* to allow anchoring and communication with internal and external stakeholders. We must also ensure we understand boundary judgments/perspectives and the associated values these represent; it just so happens that ST can support this: Critical Systems Heuristics.

Systems Thinking provides a very effective approach for government organizations adopting anticipatory governance. However, it must be seen as something other than one more training course from which attendees get another certificate to display on their walls or add to their CVs. ST must be a practice fully embedded within an organization's culture and delivery.

Leon Fuerth and Evan Faber define *anticipatory governance* as a "system of systems." This effectively provides a significant relationship to ST. The plurality of methodologies available via ST can fully support the development and implementation (and continuing success) of anticipatory governance programs.

Section 2
Leadership and Transformation

https://doi.org/10.1142/9789811296000_0007

Chapter 7

The AAA Framework: Responsible Leadership for Sustainable Futures

Roger Spitz

Techistential (Foresight Strategy), San Francisco, USA
Disruptive Futures Institute, San Francisco, USA

Key Takeaways

- The letters "AAA" are used to represent the "Antifragile, Anticipatory, and Agility" framework that defines what leadership skills need to be developed because standard playbooks and legacy organizational models are becoming increasingly ineffective.
- "Antifragile" describes things that benefit and improve from shocks.[1] Developing antifragility means focusing on the amplitude and nature of potential consequences, not only the probability. Building antifragile foundations is like building an immune system.
- "Anticipatory" refers to thinking with which we imagine next-order implications, including unexpected consequences. The capacity to be anticipatory helps us better prepare for any futures ahead while creating our preferred future.

---

[1]Taleb, N.N. (2012). *Antifragile: Things That Gain from Disorder*. New York: Random House Inc.

- "Agility" is a strategic cognitive ability that allows us to simultaneously bridge our longer-term strategy with the present. Reconciling different time horizons with decisions today requires leveraging uncertainty through curiosity, creativity, and experimentation.

7.1 Beyond VUCA: New UN-VICE for Systemic Disruption

There is a broad consensus on the tensions and contradictions of our world, often referred to as VUCA (Volatility, Uncertainty, Complexity, and Ambiguity). Today, there are two additional features that define our world better, ignored by those who rely on VUCA.[2] The missing features are "Intersecting," which defines the interplay of cascading impacts, and "Exponential," a qualifier for the shape of change, which increasingly permeates every facet of our hyperconnected technological lives. With "*intersecting,*" cross-impacts more frequently determine outcomes (as combinatorial effects interact in our liminal world). With "*exponential,*" change is initially slow, but inflection points are rapid.[3] These *intersections* and *exponentiality* are not inherently good or bad; they are updated drivers for our increasingly changing operating environments.

In VUCA, "U" stands for uncertain and "A" for ambiguous. Together, these elements articulate that the field of behavior is confusing and that the agents lack "knowledge." This UNknown environment increases uncertainty. In recognizing our UNknown, Volatile, Intersecting, Complex, and Exponential (UN-VICE) world (see Exhibit 7.1),[4] we have the power to shape our own futures without having to rely on previous solutions (or *ad*-vice). Framing the dynamics of change as UN-VICE provides an empowering response beyond VUCA, as we are not helpless victims

---

[2]VUCA was formulated by the US Army in the context of the Cold War and the messy world of multilateralism. It grew in popularity after September 11, 2001. See: Lawrence, K. (2013). Developing leaders in a VUCA Environment. *UNC Executive Development*, 1–15.

[3]As with all complex systems, change is intermittent, oscillating between fast and slow variables, sometimes simultaneously. Lance H. Gunderson and C. S. Holling examine how systems function in their book *Panarchy Synopsis: Understanding Transformations in Human and Natural Systems*. Gunderson, L.H. & Holling, C.S. (2002). *Panarchy: Understanding Transformations in Human and Natural Systems*. Washington: Island Press.

[4]Spitz, R. & Zuin, L. (2022). *The Definitive Guide to Thriving on Disruption: Volume I. Reframing and Navigating Disruption*. Disruptive Futures Institute. San Francisco, USA.

Exhibit 7.1. Our best UN-VICE for systemic disruption.

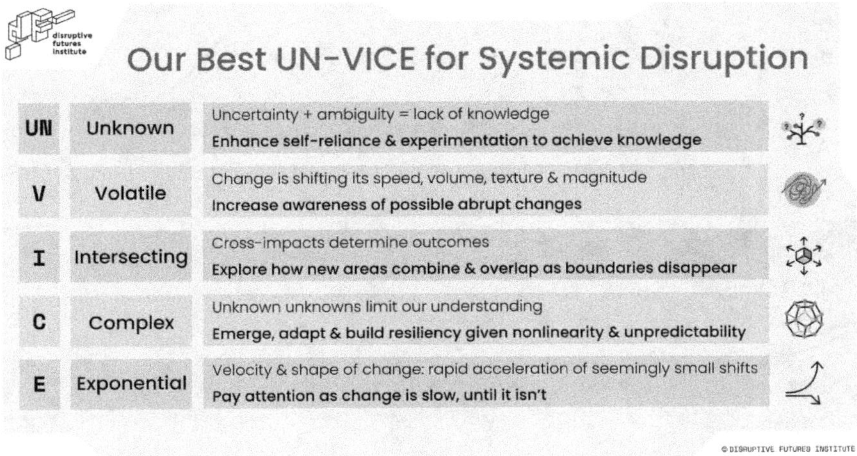

Source: Reproduced with permission from Disruptive Futures Institute.

buffeted by changes and unable to make decisions. Drawing on the Deleuzo–Sartrean philosophy for the emergent nature of being, UN-VICE reflects our existential condition for strategic decision-making in complex environments, requiring us to exercise our freedom, agency, and choice.[5]

In our increasingly UN-VICE world, leaders need to find effective and adaptive solutions rather than rely on decaying ones (*ad*-vice). Systemic disruption establishes new paradigms, which themselves evolve, compounding ripple effects that interact multiplicatively. Systemic change has diminished the value of *ad*-vice. Instead, we offer our best UN-VICE: Don't rely only on the advice of experts and existing models. Be empowered to learn and adapt to rapid change with your own tools and frameworks, with the agency to better prepare for any futures ahead, however unpredictable.

[5] Spitz, R. & Nykänen, R. (2021). An existential framework for the future of decision-making in leadership. In Mengel, T. (Ed.), *Leadership for the Future*. Cambridge: Cambridge Scholars Publishing: pp. 233–265.

Exhibit 7.2. Risk, uncertainty, and deep uncertainty.

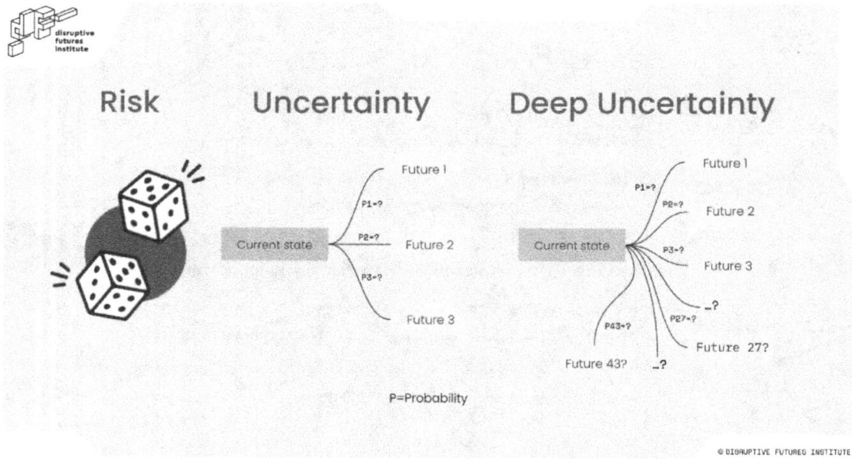

Source: Reproduced with permission from Disruptive Futures Institute.

7.1.1 *Deep uncertainty prevents prediction*

In the context of deep uncertainty, which goes far beyond risk (see Exhibit 7.2), prediction becomes more subjective, maybe even arbitrary. The central idea of uncertainty is that you cannot know the probability.[6] Three factors contribute to the loss of predictability in UN-VICE: compound parameters, unknowability, and complexity:

- **Compound parameters in highly uncertain environments:** The variables, occurrences, or possible outcomes are numerous and not known.
- **Unknowability**[7]**:** In deep (or radical) uncertainty, one may be able to enumerate many possible or plausible futures, but will not be able to rank them in terms of likelihood, importance, or possible occurrence. Stakeholders themselves do not know and cannot agree on the nature of the potential future states.

[6]Taleb, N.N. (2007). *The Black Swan: The Impact of the Highly Improbable.* New York: Random House.

[7]Kay, J. & King, M.A. (2020). *Radical Uncertainty: Decision-Making for an Unknowable Future*. New York: W. W. Norton & Company Inc.

Exhibit 7.3. Certainty is in the past.

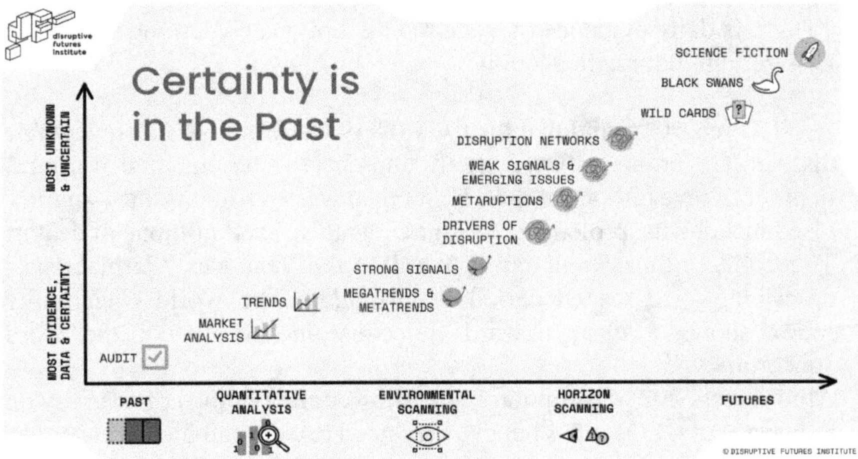

Source: Reproduced with permission from Disruptive Futures Institute.

- **Complicated vs. Complex:** *Complicated* situations allow predictability as they are ordered and linear: There is a range of right answers, and we can rely on experts given known unknowns. However, *complex* environments are unpredictable.[8] There is multidimensional causality, the outcomes cannot be predicted given unknown unknowns, and there may be no right answers. Complexity flies in the face of what is merely complicated.

7.1.2 *Certainty is in the past*

Using a timeline to illustrate the relative perspectives on uncertainty can be useful in understanding current and past situations (see Exhibit 7.3). Trends are based on the past, so these are visible in hindsight, while signals give us indications of possible futures.[9] As disruption is constant, we

[8]Snowden, D.J. & Boone, M.E. (2007). A leader's framework for decision making. *Harvard Business Review*. November.

[9]Malmgren, P. (2016). *Signals. How Everyday Signs Can Help Us Navigate The World's Turbulent Economy*. London: Weidenfeld & Nicolson.

should seek to understand the dynamics and paradoxes of underlying change to enhance our capacity to creatively imagine futures.

There is daily evidence of systemic disruptions coalescing where the stakes are high but resilience low:

- A WHO report[10] found that the COVID-19 pandemic was a preventable disaster. Governments were utterly unprepared; they ignored warnings in order to save billions of dollars, but then wasted trillions due to improvised lockdowns, prolonged economic paralysis, and millions of deaths.
- The 2022 Collins Dictionary's Word of the Year was "Permacrisis," describing an extended period of instability. The World Uncertainty Index shows a clear upward trajectory in the use of the word "uncertainty."[11]
- AlixPartners 2023 Disruption Index showed the findings of a survey on thousands of CEOs: 98% believe they need to overhaul their companies' business model within the next three years; 85% do not know where to start; and 72% say their executive teams lack the agility to deal with it.[12]

Across all aspects of society, we are now realizing that there are daily events that are presented as "historic," "unique," or "unprecedented." There are new parameters for "unprecedented," as unprecedented becomes the norm.

7.1.3 *Limitations of traditional planning*

Pursuing certainty through conventional planning often depends on techniques that rely on assumptions about the understandability of the world. Standard playbooks are becoming increasingly ineffective in our UN-VICE world. Hence, we need to differentiate between strategic planning and futures thinking (see Exhibit 7.4).

When parameters are known and specific questions are being asked, then seeking to predict an answer within a range of possibilities may be

[10]The Independent Panel for Pandemic Preparedness and Response (2021, May 12). COVID-19: Make It the Last Pandemic. Available: https://theindependentpanel.org/mainreport/ (Accessed 14 October, 2023).

[11]World Uncertainty Index (2023, September 30). Available: https://worlduncertaintyindex.com/ (Accessed 14 October, 2023).

[12]AlixPartners (2023). AlixPartners 2023 Disruption Index. Available: https://docs.alixpartners.com/view/397725974/ (Accessed 14 October, 2023).

Exhibit 7.4. Strategic plan vs. futures.

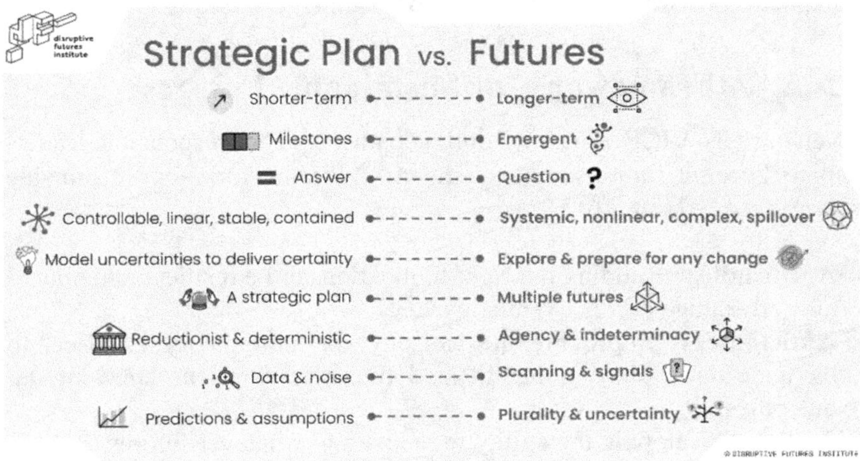

Source: Reproduced with permission from Disruptive Futures Institute.

Exhibit 7.5. Prediction/foresight.

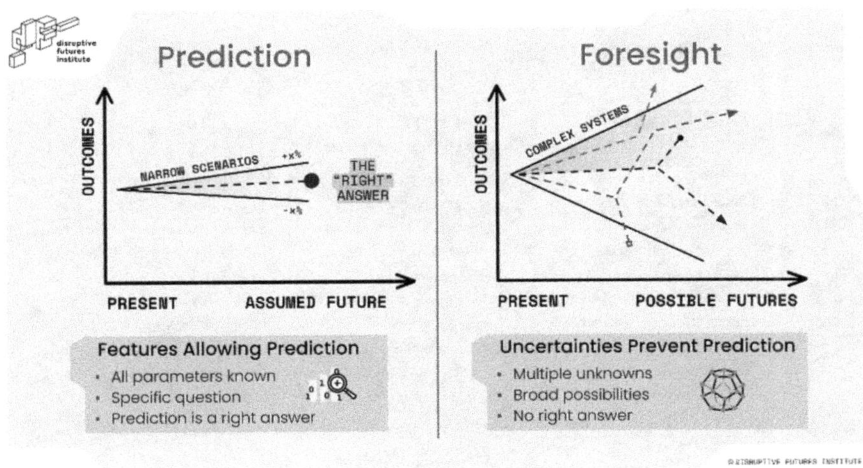

Source: Reproduced with permission from Disruptive Futures Institute.

reasonable. The challenges arise when we seek answers before questions, especially if there is deep uncertainty. In such environments, outright prediction can be at best futile — even dangerous — if decision-making relies on such assumptions. As the future is unmapped, you cannot rely on modeling uncertainties to deliver certainty. Therefore, there must also be a distinction between prediction and foresight (see Exhibit 7.5).

7.2 AAA Framework for Sustainable Futures

Given our UN-VICE world, we outline pathways[13] for responsible leadership to become future-savvy — the AAA Framework for Sustainable Futures (see Exhibit 7.6):

- **Antifragility**: Building the right foundations to be resilient and able to take advantage of any eventuality.
- **Anticipatory**: Improving the capacity for anticipatory mindsets to navigate uncertainty, going beyond linear assumptions and singular outcomes.
- **Agility**: Developing the agility to respond to whatever futures emerge, while reconciling our preferred vision of the futures with today's unpredictable reality.

Exhibit 7.6. AAA Framework.

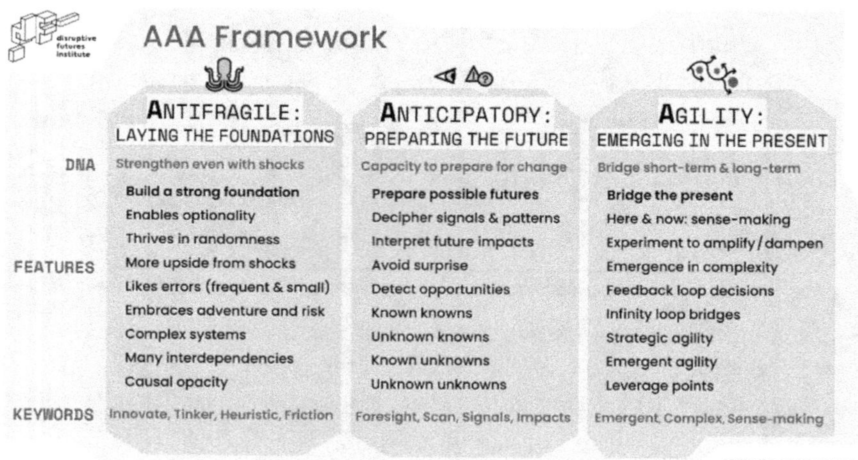

Source: Reproduced with permission from Disruptive Futures Institute.

[13] Spitz, R. (2020). The future of strategic decision-making. *Journal of Futures Studies*. Available: https://jfsdigital.org/2020/07/26/the-future-of-strategic-decision-making/ (Accessed 14 October, 2023).

7.3 Antifragile: Laying the Foundations

For our AAA taxonomy we borrow the term "antifragile" from Nassim Nicholas Taleb:[14] "*Antifragility is beyond resilience or robustness. The resilient resists shocks and stays the same; the antifragile gets better.*"

Developing antifragility means focusing on the amplitude and nature of potential consequences, not only the probability. Building antifragile foundations is like building an immune system.

Antifragile foundations enable constant optionality through innovation, adventure, and experimentation. This is in contrast to "fragile" environments, which are optimized for an apparently frictionless world — and are revealed to be fragile when shocks arise. Antifragile foundations provide an upside from random shocks, benefiting from frequent and small errors that provide helpful lessons to build upon. Thus, antifragility is best adapted to our complex world's dynamic interdependencies.

Exhibit 7.7. Fragile, resilient, and antifragile.

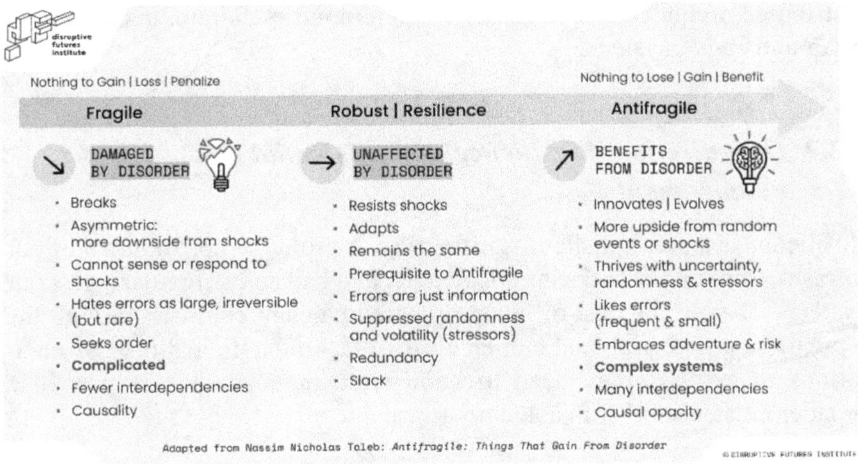

Source: Reproduced with permission from Disruptive Futures Institute.

Evaluating risk, uncertainty, and data is necessary to develop antifragility, as the focus shifts from probabilities to potential outcomes. The

[14]Taleb (2012), *Op. cit.*

insights derived from data can be invaluable as a feedback loop to decision-making, but should never be confused with being a proxy for the future, a predictor of the future, or the future itself. Furthermore, understanding the difference between reversible and irreversible decisions and embracing critical thinking and first principles to examine assumptions are also foundational to antifragility.

Organizations and individuals move along a continuum to reach antifragility, which is a higher objective than being merely resilient (see Exhibit 7.7).

7.3.1 *Example of antifragile communications*

At the onset of Russia's invasion of Ukraine, Moscow's cyberattacks knocked out infrastructure and satellite networks owned by US Viasat. Starlink's distributed network of low Earth orbit (LEO) satellites provided antifragility during this period. Starlink remained operational despite Russia's attacks, providing Ukrainians access to the world's internet.[15] Its distributed architecture eliminates a single point of failure, a key feature of an antifragile system.

7.3.2 *Organizational resilience and existential risk management*

Resilience is a prerequisite to antifragility. A prolonged breakdown of our infrastructure or networks is conceivable, and bad actors regularly test our systems' limits. The cost of being prepared pales in comparison with the reputational, financial, and human costs of lacking anticipation. For institutions to survive, they need to build strategic resilience as part of a broader existential risk management strategy.

[15] Miller, C., Scott, M., & Bender, B. (2022, June 8). UkraineX: How Elon Musk's space satellites changed the war on the ground. *Politico.* Available: https://www.politico.eu/article/elon-musk-ukraine-starlink/ (Accessed 14 October, 2023).

Exhibit 7.8. Chief Existential Officer (CEO²).

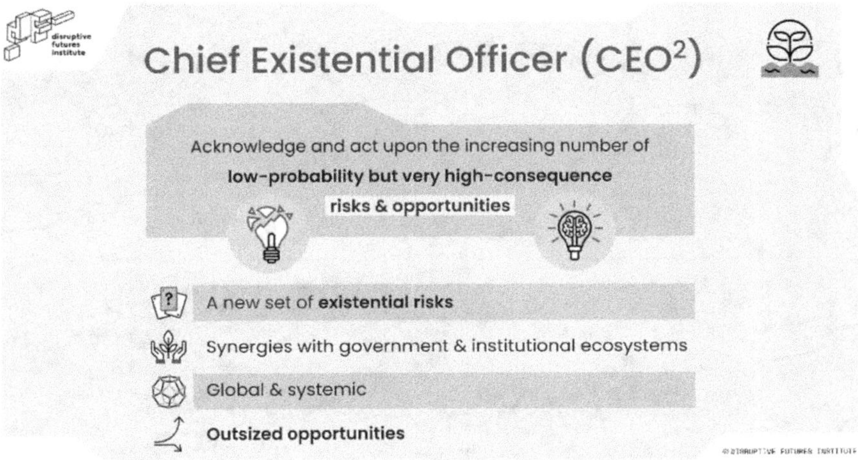

Source: Reproduced with permission from Disruptive Futures Institute.

With an increasing number of low-probability but very high-consequence risks and opportunities, organizations may need a Chief Existential Officer (CEO²) to complement the Chief Risk Officer (who focuses on operational, regulatory, or technology risks). The CEO² acknowledges and acts upon a new set of extreme considerations, including AI, climate, cybersecurity, pandemics, and societal and geopolitical paradigm shifts, beyond business-as-usual cycles. Exhibit 7.8 highlights the role of the Chief Existential Officer (CEO²).

7.4 Anticipatory: Preparing the Futures

The term "anticipatory" is intimately related to the foresight field. This second pillar of our AAA framework establishes how we can thoughtfully anticipate our futures to inform decision-making today. Anticipatory leadership is a form of futures intelligence, where we learn to qualify weak signals, imagine next-order impacts, and connect the shifting dots.

Exhibit 7.9. The Complex Five.

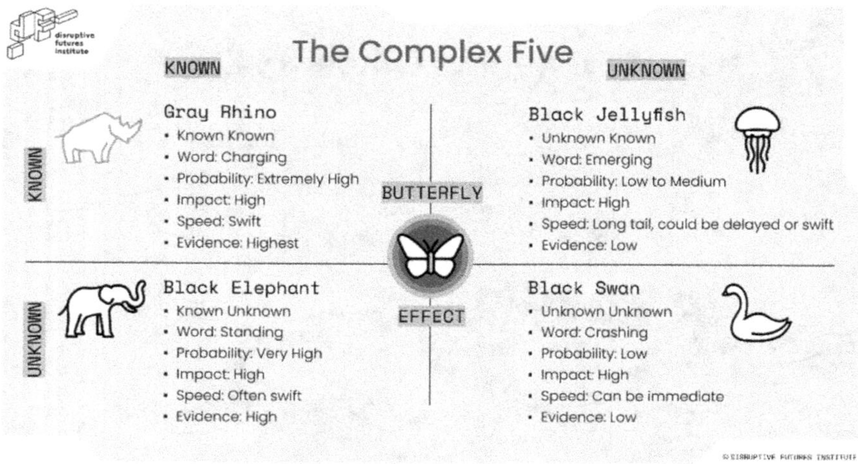

Source: Reproduced with permission from Disruptive Futures Institute.

7.4.1 *Know your unknown unknowns*

Anticipatory leaders need to develop the ability to better prepare for unknown futures by appreciating the different types of uncertainty (see Exhibit 7.9):

- **Known Knowns:** Things we know that we know, such as "the sun rises in the morning and sets at night." For these, we use author Michele Wucker's definition of "*Gray Rhino.*"
- **Unknown Knowns:** Things that we think we know, but it transpires that we may not actually understand them when they manifest. For example,[16] climate change's dramatic effect on increasing ocean temperatures and acidity levels prompted perfect conditions for jellyfish populations to rapidly increase. This forced shutdowns due to jellyfish clogs at coastal nuclear reactors around the world. To describe such unknown knowns, *Postnormal Times* uses the term "*Black Jellyfish.*"[17]

[16]Gershwin, L.-A. (2013). *Stung!: On Jellyfish Blooms and the Future of the Ocean.* Chicago: University of Chicago Press.

[17]The Centre for Postnormal Policy & Futures Studies (n.d.). Black Jellyfish. *Postnormal Times.* Available: https://postnormaltim.es/black-jellyfish (Accessed 14 October, 2023).

- **Known Unknowns:** Things we know we don't know, including flight cancellations, storms, new diseases, migration, or geopolitical conflict. These tend to be obvious impending threats — with few willing to acknowledge them. We call these known unknowns "*Black Elephants*," based on a term at times attributed to environmentalist Adam Sweidan and the Institute for Collapsonomics.[18]
- **Unknown Unknowns:** Things that we don't know that we don't know. For these, we use Taleb's "*Black Swans.*"
- **Ripple Effects:** While we might be tempted to look at events in isolation, one beautiful and brightly colored flying insect flaps its wings to bring them together. The term "Butterfly Effect" is related to the research of meteorologist Edward Lorenz who discovered how small initial changes can result in profoundly amplified and seemingly unrelated outcomes. In our dynamic complex world, there are a multitude of cause-and-effect relationships that cannot be identified or understood. A single trigger can generate an avalanche of disproportionate impacts. Together with our Gray Rhino, Black Jellyfish, Black Elephant, and Black Swan, our Butterfly brings together our Complex Five.

C-suites and policymakers incorrectly label many events as "Black Swans" as "go to" taxonomy to justify their surprise in the face of the assumptions they made about the world, signals they chose to ignore, and preparation they decided to skimp on. The difference in how we classify an event in terms of its "knowability" depends on our level of preparation, the broadness of our assumptions, and the extent of our imagination.

7.4.2 *Increasing cost of relying on business as usual*

The world's increasing lack of predictability permeates every aspect of life today. This deep uncertainty means that we lack visibility of the events that may happen, let alone their likelihood.

There is an inverse relationship between predictability and uncertainty, and an increasing cost of assuming a stable, linear, and predictable world. The greater the extent of unknown variables and wild cards, the

---

[18] The Institute for Collapsonomics (n.d.). Available: http://collapsonomics.org (Accessed 14 October, 2023).

Exhibit 7.10. The increasing cost of business as usual.

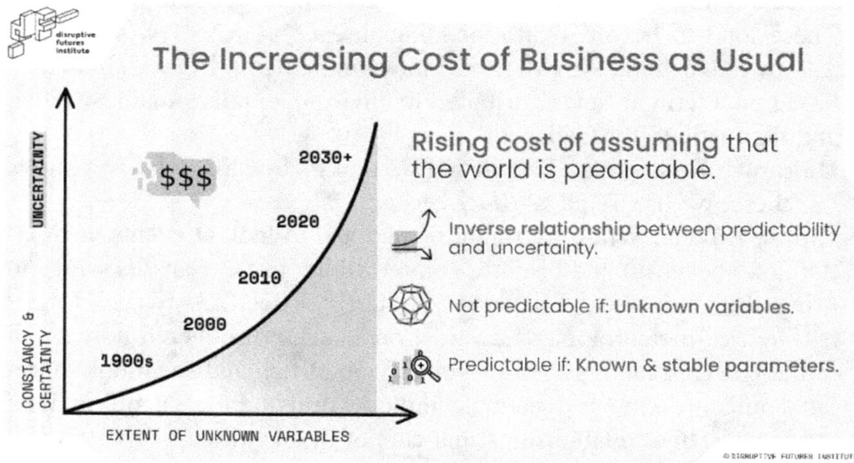

Source: Reproduced with permission from Disruptive Futures Institute.

less predictable the environment. For those intent on business as usual, the scope of value destruction is growing.

The world's consultants spend their time advising on optimizations and savings. At the same time, the greatest cost of all is ignored: the cost of relying on assumptions, which is going through the roof (as depicted in Exhibit 7.10).

Many of the perceived cost savings can actually make these organizations more fragile (e.g., optimizing supply chains). Think how much companies could save if they were more thoughtful about the assumptions they relied on. Ignorance, or absence of evidence, is not evidence of absence. In unknown situations, humility about one's knowledge is paramount.

Ineffective quantitative forecasts threw the world into the highest inflation in half a century. Even the US Treasury had to acknowledge that it was blindsided by what it qualified as the "unanticipated" shocks to the economy; it assumed inflation would take a specific and controllable path.[19]

[19]Liptak, K. & LeBlanc, P. (2022, June 1). Treasury secretary concedes she was wrong on 'path that inflation would take'. *CNN*. Available: https://www.cnn.com/2022/05/31/politics/treasury-secretary-janet-yellen-inflation-cnntv/index.html (Accessed 14 October, 2023).

7.4.3 *Futures and foresight: Alternatives to relying on assumptions*

Strategic foresight offers alternatives to relying on assumptions, which can be limiting and costly. Foresight is the capacity to explore possible futures systemically, as well as drivers of change, to inform short-term decision-making. This can be done through scenario planning, which builds on linear strategic planning but recognizes that futures are different from the past, that longer timeframes matter, and that next-order impacts need to be captured.

After the first atomic bomb was dropped during World War II, the world was confronted with the unprecedented possibility of nuclear annihilation. The idea of using scenarios for situations of high uncertainty was originally developed by Herman Kahn for military strategy in the 1950s (RAND Corporation) and by Pierre Wack (Royal Dutch Shell) for business in the 1970s.[20]

Scenario planning allows the exploration of many plausibilities without relying on fixed assumptions or an arbitrary outcome. There are no data on the future. Scenarios offer narratives for many alternative futures, some to create and others to prepare for. The purpose of scenario development is preparation, not prediction. This allows us to scrutinize potential consequences and build the capacity to sustain even serious outcomes. As longer-term thinking and complex problem-solving can be difficult to address with discrete linear strategic planning, foresight prepares us for the swerves.[21]

7.5 Agility: Emerging in the Present

The third pillar of our AAA framework explores agility through multiple perspectives (see Exhibit 7.11). A key concept is emergence, which is the process whereby the formation of novel collective behaviors, properties, or phenomena emerge when the parts of a system interact in a wider whole. As the separate parts would not have these properties on their own,

---

[20] Chermack, T.J., Lynham, S.A., & Ruona, W.E.A. (2001). A review of scenario planning literature. *Futures Research Quarterly,* 17(2): 7–32.

[21] Spitz, R. & Zuin, L. (2022). *The Definitive Guide to Thriving on Disruption: Volume II. Essential Frameworks for Disruption and Uncertainty*. Disruptive Futures Institute. San Francisco, USA.

Exhibit 7.11. Emergent and strategic agility.

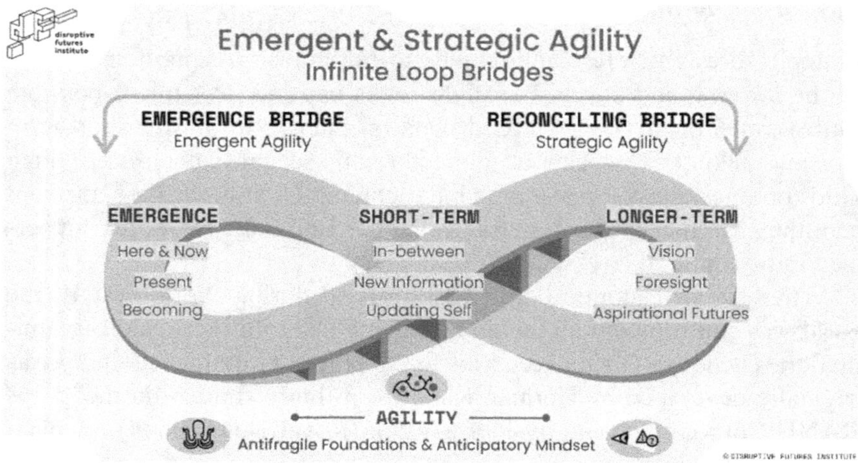

Source: Reproduced with permission from Disruptive Futures Institute.

emergence generates synergies between individual aspects that occur only thanks to their interactions.

We use two properties of "agility" to describe what is required for emergence in complex environments:

- **Emergent agility:** Our ability to emerge in the "here and now." It involves real-time trial and error as there may be no right answers to guide us.
- **Strategic agility:** Our agility in reconciling different time horizons. It involves the agility to reconcile the strategic long-term vision with short-term decision-making and problem-solving.

We want to amplify or dampen our evolving behaviors based on feedback, allowing instructive patterns to emerge. Lean and nimble cells that attack problems independently can influence leverage points to create attractors for emergence. These agile strategies have risen in all sorts of areas, from nature itself to lean start-ups.

In contrast, our uniform, centralized, and hierarchical organizations are not agile. Most move slowly, continuing with unchanged approaches. These fragile strategies do not respond well to constantly changing circumstances.

7.5.1 *Cognitive agility: Problem-solving for systemic risks*

Cognitive agility allows us to respond to change with an appreciation of the entire system, to experiment with emergent behaviors, and to bridge fields to move naturally between disciplines, creating new combinations in a world where patterns are hard to interpret.

In *The Collapse of Complex Societies*,[22] Joseph Tainter studies the collapse of civilizations (Maya, Chacoan, and Roman) and finds that as humans and institutions become less versatile in problem-solving, collapse ensues. Societies collapse as they reach a point of rapidly declining marginal returns on their investments in problem-solving capacity. Sustainable futures may be contingent on humanity's ability to problem-solve ourselves out of the most complex, systemic, and existential risks.[23]

7.5.2 *Chief Strategy Officer out, Chief Bridging Officer in*

Just as the changing environments require new decision-making and operating models, leadership roles should drastically evolve as we bridge to the futures. Disruption in the C-suite is underway, with the roles of Chief Strategy Officer (CSO) and Chief Innovation Officer (CIO) fading.[24] We imagine a role called Chief Bridging Officer (CBO) — defined by the agility to connect and bridge the organization's vision within constantly updating environments (see Exhibit 7.12).

The CBO's role is a journey of discovery, with the emergent, strategic, and cognitive agility to anticipate and constantly respond to changes in the external environment. The CBO initiates needed changes, consistent with long-term aspirations. This "outside-in" thinking requires anticipating the next-order implications, rather than reacting to them.

Emergencies are not equally distributed. The degree of anticipatory thinking influences our preparations, as well as the nature, responses, and impact of the many possible emergencies that might arise.

---

[22] Tainter, J. (1989). *The Collapse of Complex Societies.* Cambridge: Cambridge University Press.

[23] Spitz, R. & Zuin, L. (2023). *The Definitive Guide to Thriving on Disruption: Volume IV. Disruption as a Springboard to Value Creation.* Disruptive Futures Institute.

[24] IBM Corporation (2021, February). Find your essential: How to thrive in a post-pandemic reality. Available: https://www.ibm.com/downloads/cas/WVPWGPYE (Accessed 14 October, 2023).

Exhibit 7.12. Chief Bridging Officer.

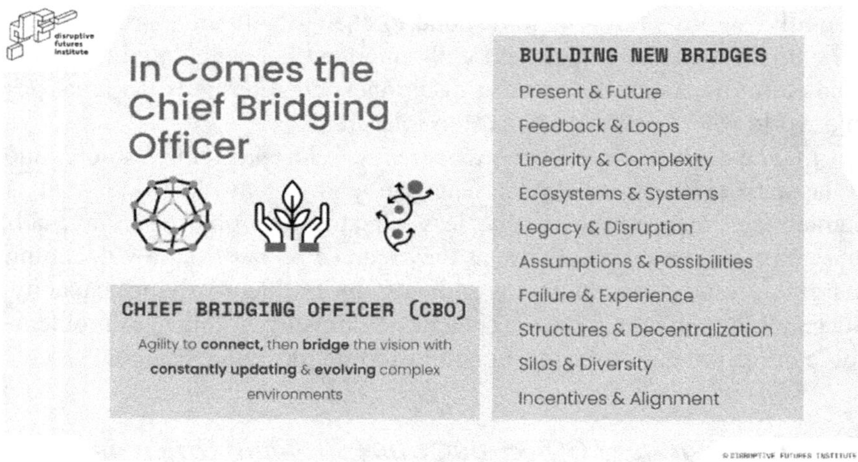

Source: Reproduced with permission from Disruptive Futures Institute.

7.6 Agency and Alignment to Become AAA+

No matter how antifragile, anticipatory, and agile we are, the AAA framework is ineffective unless one has the passion to exercise the *Agency* to act on choices with *Alignment*. One must be aligned internally and with our external environment. Only then do you become AAA+.

Being AAA+ enables responsible leadership for sustainable futures. It integrates longer timeframes within a broad scope — broader than looking at your business, activity, or region in isolation. As systemic disruption is multidisciplinary, multidimensional, and multilayered, resilient leadership requires antifragile foundations, agility, and a systems approach to drive effective change. Last but not least, trust is a prerequisite for effective leadership. Anticipatory thinking can restore trust, by honoring ethical commitments with multistakeholder alignment.

To operate in today's UN-VICE environment, we all need to be effective leaders. Reconciling short-term priorities and surprises with longer-term aspirations can be tricky in constantly evolving environments. This means being anticipatory, vision- and action-oriented, seeking resilient changes, accepting unknown conditions, and maneuvering with agility in novel circumstances.

https://doi.org/10.1142/9789811296000_0008

Chapter 8

Unlocking the Power of Public Purpose

Andy Redman[*], Abhishek Balakrishnan[*], and Noah Frank[†]

[*]*BCG BrightHouse, Atlanta, USA*
[†]*Senior Consultant, Valize, USA*

Key Takeaways

- Anticipatory governance, powered by purpose, gives us a lens with which public leaders can act with agility to confront issues head-on and at their source. In order to anticipate the future, leaders must first have a clear understanding of their purpose in the present.
- Purpose is often overlooked but is essential to national strategy. It is a rallying cry that supplies the "so-what" and "why" in critical situations. This is an organization's North Star — it should never change.
- Purpose lies at the intersection of a government's unique strengths, the needs of the world, and the common good that your work provides for the public.
- Purpose should be fully integrated in ways of working to guide decisions in culture, strategy, and branding.
- Purpose provides the guardrails for anticipatory governance.

8.1 Introduction

Since the times of Hegel, leading philosophers and thinkers have puzzled over whether there is a "goal" to history. Blockbuster movies regularly tell this story through world-ending asteroids, and today regular reports of AI takeovers circulate the news. Francis Fukuyama contemplated the end of history in 1989 as the Soviet Union fell, proclaiming that the moment brought the end of the "universalization of Western liberal democracy as the final form of human government."[1] More than three decades later, Fukuyama — now a fellow and professor at Stanford University — is still contemplating these questions. In a 2022 article for The Atlantic, titled *More Proof That This Really Is the End of History*, he further defends this theory in the context of modern conflict and global democratic backsliding over the 30 years since that first article was released.

But, for many, the opening half of the 2020s paints an entirely different picture. In several ways, the world of the 2020s feels perhaps the furthest from the "end of history" than we have been in decades. So, how might we know what is yet to come? Will we ever know? And more practically, how do governments continue to evolve to meet citizen needs and demands given both the unknown future and the rapid changes of today? Governments will need to know how to conceptualize the infinite possibilities that constitute today's systemic and existential challenges and develop priorities and plans to deliver value to citizens.

To anticipate the future, leaders must first have a clear understanding of their purpose in the present. *Public purpose provides a lens through which government leaders can act with agility to confront issues head-on and at their source.* In this chapter, we will first explore the challenges to achieving anticipatory governance. Then, we will introduce our framework for public purpose and its power to transform our comprehension of foresight. Finally, we will discuss a set of recommendations on some strategies to bring Public purpose and anticipatory governance practices to life.

8.2 Background

8.2.1 *A post-pandemic world that needs the public sector to tackle polycrises*

In January 2023, the World Economic Forum's Global Risks Report[2] presented an existential picture of the post-COVID landscape:

> *"The world is facing a set of risks that feel both wholly new and eerily familiar. We have seen a return of "older" risks — inflation,*

[1]Fukuyama, F. (1989). The end of history? *The National Interest*, 16 (Summer): 3–18.

[2]World Economic Forum (2023). Global Risks Report 2023. World Economic Forum. Available: https://www3.weforum.org/docs/WEF_Global_Risks_Report_2023.pdf (Accessed 25 January, 2024).

cost-of-living crises, trade wars, capital outflows from emerging markets, widespread social unrest, geopolitical confrontation, and the specter of nuclear warfare — which few of this generation's business leaders and public policymakers have experienced."[3]

These challenges culminate in what the WEF calls a "polycrisis." The Cascade Institute defines a polycrisis in the following manner: (1) Crises in multiple global systems become casually entangled in ways that significantly degrade humanity's prospects; (2) The interacting crises produce harms greater than those of the crises in isolation.[4]

Public leaders and policymakers are uniquely positioned to be in the driver's seat when it comes to limiting the effects of these existential challenges on our world, in part due to the sheer scale of government budgets and scope and in part due to their role in delivering public goods like defense, environmental protections, and education. Government action "creates value without which the private creation of value would be rare and difficult."[5]As an institution, it is qualified to implement and deliver solutions to issues at scale.

8.2.2 *Deploying long-term thinking to address polycrises*

The most challenging aspect of a polycrisis considers the constraints on time and resources that must be overcome in achieving its overall mitigation.[6] A 2022 report by the UNDP Regional Bureau for Asia and the Pacific on *Polycrisis and Long-term Thinking Reimagining Development in Asia and the Pacific Foresight Brief* highlights the following:

"*These are all major, complex challenges for which no quick fix is available. Addressing them will require more long-term thinking to reframe the decisions behind development processes. Long-term thinking can be*

---

[3] *Ibid.*

[4] Lawrence, M., Janzwood, S., & Homer-Dixon, T. (2022). What is a global polycrisis? And how is it different from a systemic risk? *Cascade Institute*. Available: https://cascadeinstitute.org/technical-paper/what-is-a-global-polycrisis/ (Accessed 25 January, 2024).

[5] Kirlin, J.J. (1996). What government must do well: Creating value for society. *Journal of Public Administration Research and Theory*, 6(1): 161–185. https://doi.org/10.1093/oxfordjournals.jpart.a024298.

[6] Janssen, M. & Van der Voort, H. (2016). Adaptive governance: Towards a stable, accountable and responsive government. *Government Information Quarterly*, 33(1): 1–5.

> *thought of as an intentional consideration of what might happen in the future, the choices for influencing it and the consequences of those choices."*[7]

The report highlights that governments can enhance long-term thinking through strategic foresight methods or anticipatory governance. It is crucial to get the following core pillars right for building anticipatory governance:

1. A foresight system (providing the means to generate and interpret knowledge about the future);
2. Pathways to integrate intelligence about the future into policies and implementation;
3. A feedback system to assess outcomes;
4. An overall shift in culture and structures.[8]

Given the immense stakes and efforts required to tackle polycrises — not to mention the day-to-day business of running government services — it can be challenging for leaders to employ long-term thinking and foresight. Anticipatory government is easier said than done, so where can government leaders start? Being able to effectively address the above-mentioned pillars requires a level of decision-making that provides clarity and alignment, guardrails for decision, and empowerment to act.

In recent years, the private sector has been deploying the concept of *Organizational Purpose* to help leaders transform their businesses, enact change, and be an effective tool for decision-making.[9] In 2019, BlackRock CEO, Larry Fink, titled his annual letter to CEOs *Purpose & Profit* and in it wrote the following mandate to share the significance of purpose:

> "*Purpose unifies management, employees, and communities. It drives ethical behavior and creates an essential check on actions that go against the best interests of stakeholders. Purpose guides culture, provides a framework for consistent decision-making, and, ultimately, helps*

[7] Baylon, C. & Robele, S. (2022). UNDP RBAP Foresight Brief: Polycrisis and Long-term Thinking. New York: UNDP.

[8] Janssen & der Voort (2016). *Op. cit.*

[9] Hurth, V., Ebert, C., & Prabhu, J. (2018). Organisational purpose: The construct and its antecedents and consequences. *Cambridge Judge Business School Working Paper* No. 02/2018. Available: https://www.jbs.cam.ac.uk/wp-content/uploads/2020/08/wp1802.pdf (Accessed 25 January, 2024).

sustain long-term financial returns for the shareholders of your company"[10]

In the next section, we further define purpose as it relates to the public sector and provide a framework for how to articulate it.

8.3 Detailed Discussion: Public Purpose

What is a purpose and how is it different from a mission and a vision? BCG BrightHouse creative consultancy, which has pioneered purpose in organization strategy for over 30 years and has worked with Fortune 50 clients and government leaders across the world, defines organizational purpose as why you exist (see Exhibit 8.1). It is the intersection of who you are and what need you fulfill in the world. It is the underlying reason your organization exists.[11] While mission and vision may change over time, your company's purpose will not.[12] The organizational purpose is timeless. Purpose is a company's reason for being, beyond what it does, makes, or sells. Vision is "where you are headed" and will change every 3–10 years, and Strategy involves the decisions that you make or "How you will achieve the vision." Mission is what you do every day and could change as organizations develop culturally, scale, and advance technologically or be focused depending on department.

The concept of purpose has been a key tool that the private sector has adopted.[13] In Exhibit 8.2 is an example from the Mercedes-Benz Group. A clear and authentic statement of purpose that addresses how and why the organization serves society. It can provide internal and external stakeholders with increased confidence and clarity that the organization can address key challenges and can take unique and actionable steps to solve them.[14]

---

[10]Fink, L. (2019). Larry Fink's 2019 letter to CEOs. *BlackRock*. Available: https://www.blackrock.com/corporate/investor-relations/2019-larry-fink-ceo-letter (Accessed 25 January, 2024).

[11]Boston Consulting Group (n.d.). Business & Organizational Purpose — Overview. Available: https://www.bcg.com/capabilities/business-organizational-purpose/overview (Accessed 2 January, 2024).

[12]University of Oxford (2020). Enacting Purpose Initiative — EU Report. Available: https://enactingpurpose.org/assets/enacting-purpose-initiative---eu-report-august-2020.pdf (Accessed 2 January, 2024).

[13]Fink (2019). *Op. cit.*

[14]Sandoghdar, A.L. & Bailey, C. (2023). Review of the practitioner literature on purpose. *King's College London*. Available: https://www.kcl.ac.uk/business/assets/research/review-of-the-practitioner-literature-on-purpose.pdf (Accessed 25 January, 2024).

Exhibit 8.1. Purpose framework.

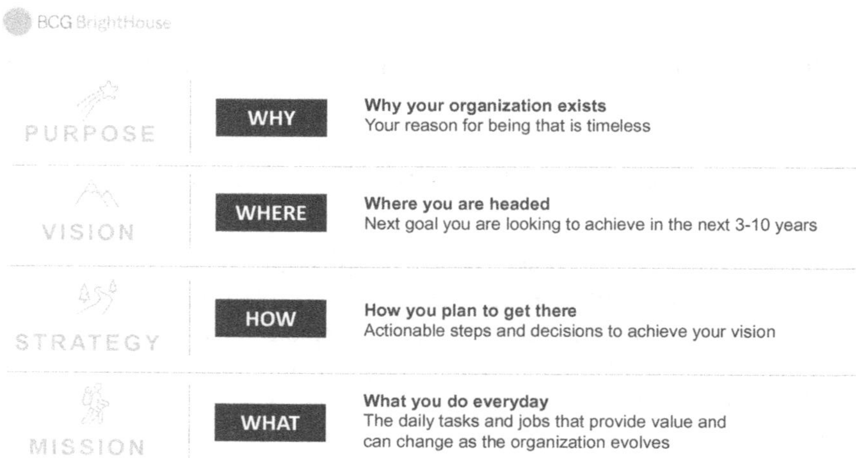

Source: Adapted from BCG BrightHouse.

Exhibit 8.2. Mercedes Benz purpose framework.

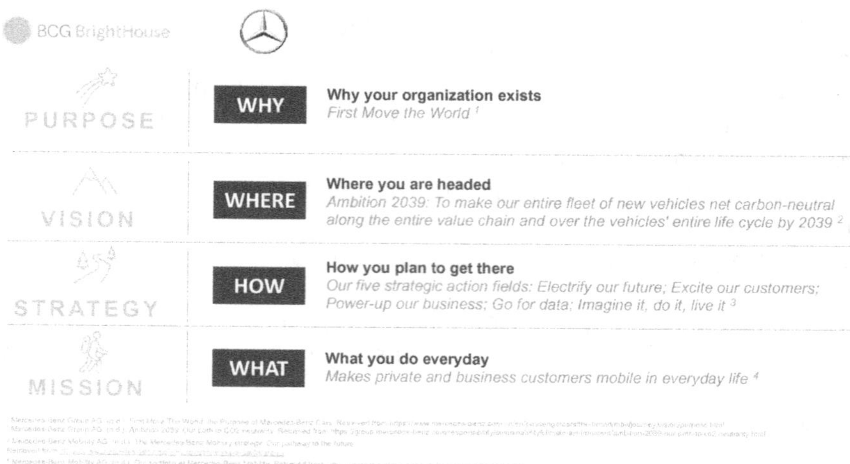

Source: Adapted from BCG BrightHouse.

The discovery, articulation, and embedding of purpose have yielded tremendous results across different dimensions of private organizations. A Northwestern study on the "Power of Purpose" suggests that employees increase engagement and alignment with organizational values when they experience a sense of meaningfulness at work.[15] Purpose can provide a clear context for decision-making[16] and organizations who have effectively embedded it have been able to see long-term value in terms of Total Shareholder Return (TSR).[17]

8.3.1 *Articulating public purpose*

As noted, purpose lies at the intersection of an **organization's unique strengths, the needs of the world that the organization fulfills, and the common good that your work provides for the public** (see Exhibit 8.3).[18] With an understanding of public purpose, public leaders can better solicit buy-in from citizens and achieve their goals, including preventing the next major disaster or finding the next greatest innovation.

8.3.2 *An example: Georgia State University*

Georgia State University (GSU) has transformed into a national model for higher education. The university's unofficial purpose is to drive social mobility in Georgia, offering equal educational opportunities that lead to improved life outcomes for graduates. In the past two decades, GSU increased its graduation rates from 32% to 55%, becoming a leading pipeline for African American graduates in the US. To achieve this, GSU implemented a strategic plan, leveraging predictive analytics, tailored academic support, micro-grants, and AI tools to enhance student success.

---

[15] Alexander, A. (2017). The power of purpose: How organizations are making work more meaningful. *Northwestern University School of Education & Social Policy*. Available: https://www.sesp.northwestern.edu/masters-learning-and-organizational-change/knowledge-lens/stories/2016/the-power-of-purpose-how-organizations-are-making-work-more-meaningful.html (Accessed 25 January, 2024).

[16] Hurth *et al.* (2018), *Op. cit.*

[17] Hemerling, J., White, B., Swan, J., Castellana Kreisman, C., & Reed, J.B. (2018). For corporate purpose to matter, you've got to measure it. *Boston Consulting Group*. Available: https://www.bcg.com/publications/2018/corporate-purpose-to-matter-measure-it (Accessed 11 November, 2023).

[18] Sampanthar, K., Redman, A., Hussain, A., Frank, N., & Balakrishnan, A. (2023). Shoot the Moon: Why our biggest ambitions need public purpose. *BCG BrightHouse*. Available: https://bcgbrighthouse.com/thinking/shoot-the-moon-how-public-purpose-can-help-unlock-the-impossible/ (Accessed 11 November, 2023).

Exhibit 8.3. Articulating purpose.

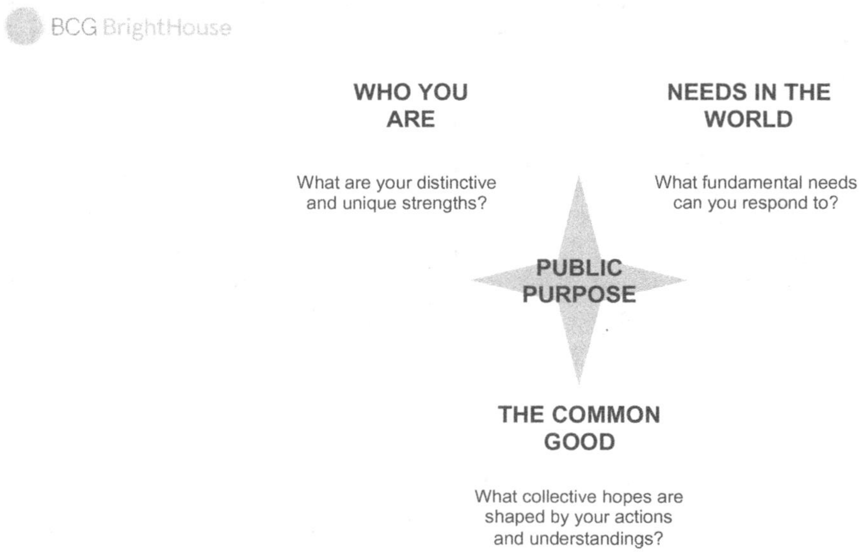

Source: Adapted from BCG BrightHouse.

Senior leadership's commitment to the purpose has been crucial. GSU's success underscores the importance of a clearly defined purpose for higher education institutions, inspiring authentic and impactful change.[19]

Connecting GSU's purpose to the previous framework in Exhibit 8.3, the following is an example of how GSU might have articulated its purpose (noting that it did not use this process):

Defining an organization's authentic strengths: These are who the organization is on its best day. It is not a definition that is articulated from outside perspectives; rather, it comes from inputs within to be truly authentic. These strengths or principles speak to a unique cornerstone of the organization — from its unique ability to innovate, having a culture of care, to solving the toughest problems. When applying this to Anticipatory Governance, the identified unique strengths can be guardrails for decision-making or a lens to activate the best resources to tackle a

[19]Redman, A. & Tejus, K. (2019). The power of purpose in higher education. Available: https://www.bcg.com/the-power-of-purpose-in-higher-education (Accessed 11 November, 2023).

challenge.[20] In GSU's case, serving the local population was its strength, with a history of being a key institution for atypical students (e.g., working professionals, and first-generation students) and a workforce that was committed to this ideal. At their best, GSU was also a data-driven organization — leveraging the power of quantitative and qualitative insights to drive performance.

Understanding the need in the world: Anticipating the future also necessitates that organizations understand their role in the world and the problem they are trying to solve. For many public institutions, there is a clearly stated need or mandate that intuition services. To ensure that the "need" collectively resonates and drives action within the organization, it is crucial to prospect into the "need" to get to the larger "why" behind it. The need should resonate as the reason for being for an organization and the aspirational solving of key societal problems.[21] It should answer questions such as the following: "Why is solving this need important?" and "What would the world lose if we did not solve this need?"[22] For GSU, there was a clear need for access to education, and the opportunities that access unlocks for individuals and communities.

Driving toward the common good: Finally, with public purpose, it is important for government organizations to have a clear idea of how their work will benefit the "common good." The "common good" refers "to those facilities — whether material, cultural or institutional — that the members of a community provide to all members in order to fulfill a relational obligation they all have to care for certain interests that they have in common."[23] It is a unifying element that enables people to resonate with a universal benefit of their work. Many organizations use Sustainable Development

---

[20] Fontán, C., Alloza, A., & Rey, C. (2019). (Re)discovering organizational purpose. In Rey, C., Bastons, M., & Sotok, P. (Eds.), *Purpose-Driven Organizations*. Cham: Palgrave Macmillan: pp. 107–118. https://doi.org/10.1007/978-3-030-17674-7_9.

[21] Van Ingen, R., Peters, P., De Ruiter, M., & Robben, H. (2021). Exploring the meaning of organizational purpose at a new dawn: The development of a conceptual model through expert interviews. *Frontiers in Psychology*, 12. https://doi.org/10.3389/fpsyg.2021.675543.

[22] Carlisi, C. (2022). How purpose drives success. *Forbes,* 17 January. Available: https://www.forbes.com/sites/karlmoore/2022/01/17/how-purpose-drives-success-with-cathy-carlisi-managing-director-of-brighthouse/?sh=4e5c9c344997.

[23] Heath, J. (2020). Common good. In Zalta, E.N. (Ed.), *The Stanford Encyclopedia of Philosophy.* Available: https://plato.stanford.edu/entries/common-good/ (Accessed 11 November, 2023).

Goals (SDGs) as a reference point. The *(Re) Discovering Organizational Purpose* paper highlights that people want organizations to have a positive impact on people's lives and to progress humankind (see footnote 20). When incorporating this type of communitarian thinking, public purpose helps place individuals within a larger system. It can unlock collective action and collaboration, and unite people around how the organization will benefit the public.[24] For GSU, there was a clear need to provide access to education and opportunity, and the common good is about being a channel for the community to improve wealth and well-being across generations — ultimately attacking the income inequality that exists in the state and country.

Purpose is an often overlooked but essential component to any successful business plan or national strategy. It is a great tool for decision-making and alignment when it comes to enacting change in anticipatory governance. In the next section, we provide further practical recommendations for how leaders can articulate and activate purpose.[25]

8.4 Implications and Recommendations

The public sector often lags in leveraging the power of purpose. Yet, given their public mandate, government organizations should shine when compared to the private sector. The lack of adoption is lost potential for agencies — and citizens — as purpose affects overall performance and employee engagement as well as the leadership's ability to anticipate "what's next." Purpose provides the guardrails for anticipatory governance.

However, knowing an organization's purpose is just the beginning of a multi-year journey, as Exhibit 8.4 shows. The ultimate goal — especially when considering purpose's role in anticipatory governance — is to have purpose become second nature. Purpose should be fully integrated in ways of working to guide decisions in culture, strategy, and branding.

Amidst constant change and pressures from a range of stakeholders, how does government leadership move toward a more purposeful organization? The following recommendations can serve as potential guidance.

First, create a plan to activate purpose throughout the organization, launching with leaders and then cascading purpose throughout the organization. This roadmap includes three stages:

---

[24] Hollensbe, E., Wookey, C., Hickey, L., George, G., & Nichols, C.V. (2014). Organizations with purpose. *Academy of Management Journal*, 57(5): 1227–1234.

[25] Sandoghdar & Bailey (2023), *Op. cit.*

Exhibit 8.4. Purpose journey.

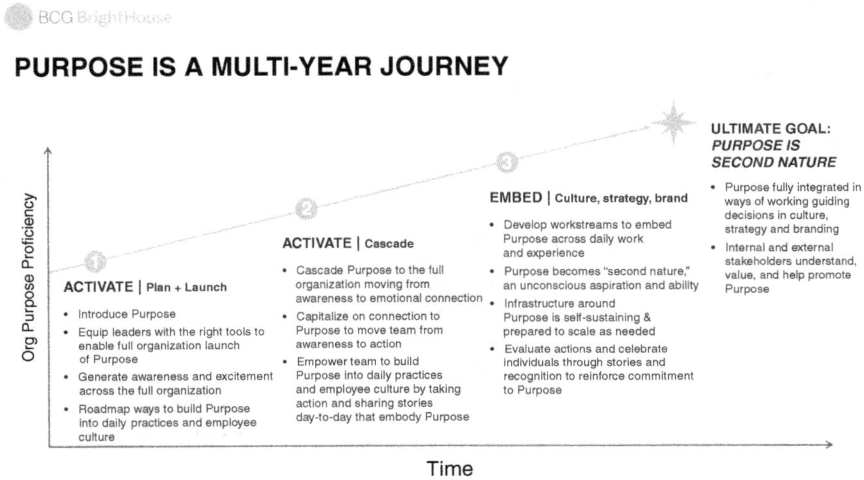

Source: Adapted from BCG BrightHouse.

1. *Planning*: Develop the strategy for launch and cascade, socialize purpose with leaders, assemble a team, and ideate ways to live purpose.
2. *Launching*: Launch purpose to the organization through custom content and experiences in order to build awareness and inspiration.
3. *Cascading*: Empower leaders to help employees personally connect to the purpose and generate grassroots ideas to bring the purpose to life.

Second, once activated, leaders can move to embed purpose within culture, strategy, and branding. Within culture, leaders can fully leverage the meaning behind the organization's purpose throughout the employee lifecycle — from recruiting to onboarding to rewards and recognitions. Within strategy, purpose can serve as a single edit point for decision-making, with its principles as guardrails. Within branding, purpose can guide how the organization shows up to the world — from citizens and communities to current and future employees.

Though not in the public sector, Microsoft is an excellent case study in understanding how purpose can transform an organization; its culture, strategy, and brand; and the role that leaders play in helping employees connect with what motivates them personally to their work. When Satya Nadella took over as CEO in 2014, he made the company's culture and purpose one of his top priorities.

Exhibit 8.5. Example of purpose in Microsoft.

Source: Adapted from BCG BrightHouse.

The entire leadership team began asking the following: "*Why do we exist, and what do we stand for?*" Leaders began to connect their personal mission to the work they do, coalescing around the shared purpose of empowering people. This created a shift in Microsoft's understanding of its role in the world and helped the company articulate a vision that speaks to a deeper meaning behind its work — a paradigm shift from selling products to solving problems for customers. This drove a wave of engagement among Microsoft employees — people began giving more of their discretionary time than ever before because they felt that Microsoft's role was also fulfilling their personal purpose. It also led to tangible changes across their culture, strategy, and brand — from recruiting and onboarding to organizational structure to office facilities (see Exhibit 8.5).[26]

Embedding purpose like Microsoft is easier said than done (see Exhibit 8.6). Exhibit 8.6 presents a flywheel for purpose movements within organizations. The center focuses on the organizational purpose and principles — the timeless "reason why" and the guide for employee behavior to achieve it. Moving out of the center are actions across four dimensions — interventions, inspiration, integration, and involvement.

[26]Gino, F., Ciechanover, A., & Huizinga, J. (2020). Culture transformation at Microsoft: From "know it all" to "learn it all." *Harvard Business School,* Case 921, 4.

Exhibit 8.6. Flywheel for purpose movements within organizations.

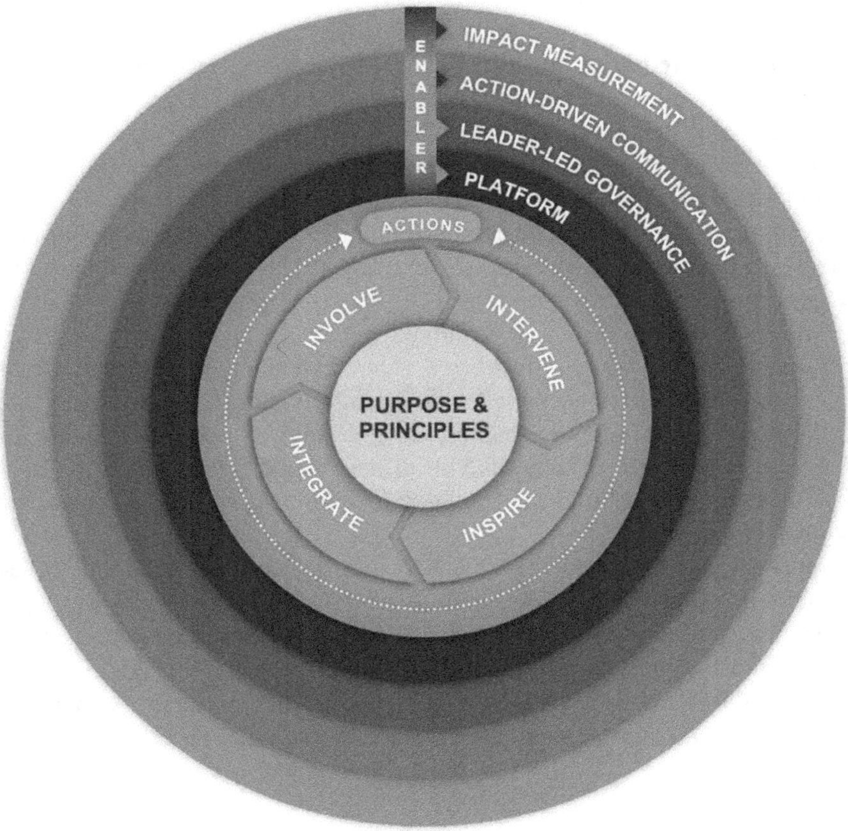

Source: Adapted from BCG BrightHouse.

Finally, the outer ring focuses on the enablers of purpose such as KPIs, communications, and governance.

There is, however, one trap: Many organizations focus too much effort on the communication and communal spirit of purpose and not the holistic change required to move from folklore to a truly epic story. To overcome this, leaders should roughly orient toward communication being 25% of the embed effort and action being 75%.[27] Returning to the flywheel, the actions are where government leaders might focus efforts in

[27]University of Oxford (2020), *Op. cit.*

order to drive purpose across all dimensions of the organization. The following, in particular, are important:

- *Inspiration:* Ignite enthusiasm and enable leaders to lead the movement within their area of responsibility. Much of this can happen in the activation phase (Exhibit 8.4) and ongoing communications.
- *Intervention:* Translate purpose and principles into bold central action and strategies that lead the way to bringing the purpose to life. An example of this could be meaningful, newsworthy, and measurable actions that are defined centrally and inspire the whole organization to pursue its timeless "reason why."
- *Integration:* Define tangible and impactful actions and processes to implement purpose within every division and function. An example of this is embed charters, which define tangible action to close the gaps between the current and aspired future state to become a purpose-driven organization. They take all divisions and functions on the purpose journey and build the roadmap to ingrain purpose in all areas of your organization.
- *Involvement:* Engage employees as committed co-creators in the implementation journey and shape daily behavior change. Involving employees as active co-creators through grassroots initiatives and daily behavioral nudges is a powerful strategy. These approaches not only make the purpose journey tangible but also encourage consistent behavioral changes, enhancing engagement at every level.

8.5 Conclusion

In confronting the complex polycrisis of our era, the integration of public purpose into anticipatory governance emerges as a crucial strategy. This chapter has emphasized the vital role of a clearly defined, enduring public purpose in guiding government actions toward their understood reason for being. As a strategic compass, public purpose enables governments to navigate contemporary uncertainties with clarity and coherence, aligning various initiatives toward a unified goal. In anticipatory governance, such a purpose aids in preparing for future challenges and ensures decisions are deeply resonant with public values and needs. Ultimately, the effective implementation of public purpose is key to creating responsive and forward-thinking governance committed to the organization's "why."

https://doi.org/10.1142/9789811296000_0009

Chapter 9

Frontier Leadership

Raed Awamleh

Center for Policy and Competitiveness,
École de Ponts Business School, Paris, France

Key Points

- Frontiers are like the Wild West, which government officials face when disruptive changes in the environment rupture established power structures.
- Global trends, the rapid rollout of new technologies, changes in generational lifestyles, political views, and consumption habits, and the impending climate crisis force leaders to reexamine their beliefs and methods.
- The need is urgent to redefine the role of public leadership in this new volatile world.
- The chapter will introduce some new ways to look at leadership and the adjustments leaders need to make to be more effective in the future.

9.1 New Wild West

The title of this chapter, *Frontier Leadership,* is undoubtedly ambitious and potentially problematic, especially within the context of anticipatory governance. Frontier assumes a world with no set rules, every person for himself, where collaboration is minimal, as a zero-sum game is the norm.[1]

---

[1]Larson. J. (2017). Why the West became wild: informal governance with incomplete networks. *World Politics: A Quarterly Journal of International Relations*, 69 (4): 713–749.

Frontier is generally associated with the concept of the "Wild West," where conditions of the environment necessitate certain styles of action that aim to test boundaries of behaviors and reactions in order to reach a shared understanding of the rules amongst all inhabitants and participants at some point in time. These rules are often implicit and become embedded in the norms and behaviors that are generally adhered to collectively. Sometimes, these norms and behaviors are "enforced". The governance of the Wild West, through formal and mostly informal structures, is based on accepting the notion that most terrains are new and unchartered. It is the process of discovery that occupies all participants. Trust in the "system" cannot be taken for granted, nor is trust between participants. Accordingly, the hypothesis here is that the world is in a state of flux representing a "wild west." Therefore, public officials must adopt a new frontier style of leadership to effectively navigate the environment and make policy decisions that create and maintain public value. The notion that current leadership styles are no longer sufficient is implicit but obvious.

From the outset of this century, it seemed to have been generally accepted that global and national affairs are in serious disarray.[2] This chaos was evident in wars, civil unrest, financial crises, funded propaganda, terrorism, massive immigration issues, climate change, pandemics, social change, and the rise of artificial intelligence. In a way, these events led to several trust crises between governments and the public and many unanswered questions about the appropriateness of the existing global governance systems. All of that and more, coupled with populism, is no doubt raising genuinely worrying concerns about the future of humanity in general. We are at another crossroads for the human condition. Where to from here? True, the world has always been in conflict and facing crises one after the other; however, what is happening now is that the speed of change is accelerated, and principal factors are conflicting and converging in a way that sensemaking is much less straightforward than it ever was.

With the massive social change at the global level, we are witnessing the rise of new generations that are espousing lifestyles and consumption

---

[2] World Economic Forum. (2024) Global Risk Report 2024. World Economic Forum. Available: https://www3.weforum.org/docs/WEF_The_Global_Risks_Report_2024.pdf (Accessed: February 17, 2024).

habits that widely deviate from the "rules" and norms of pre-2000.[3] Public leaders at all levels struggle to engage their people, make sensible policies with inter-generational impact, and ensure security for all (often focusing disproportionately on quick wins). More importantly, leaders are unable to build consensus on important issues. Instead, polarization and fragmentation seem to be the norm. Leaders are battling to make sense of this new world. Of course, it should not go unnoticed that some leaders around the world are, knowingly or unknowingly, contributing negatively to this new deteriorating state of affairs. At the same time, this current state of the new Wild West constitutes an opportunity for public value-driven leaders to contribute positively and help societies through the storm.

9.2 New Leadership for Public Value

The previous section argued that we live in a new state that requires a new style of leadership. Effective traditional leadership had its foundations in established governance systems and norms that were shared and understood by the majority of the population in a given society or region of the world. Rules were established and generally followed. Most people accepted decisions even if they did not agree with them in detail, as public value is reached through compromises, acceptance, and consensus. These fundamentals have changed over the last three decades, and people are subscribing to alternative governance models.

What are these emerging new models of governance? And how can they be scoped and articulated? In the most recent 2024 World Governments Summit[4] held in Dubai, UAE, it was "declared" that a new era of governments is ushered. Many of the keynote speakers listed some of the new forces shaping government thinking, including the youth's ambitions, climate change actions, and applications of artificial intelligence or other advanced technologies. One way to capture the challenges that public leaders face is to think about the existing/potential gaps at multiple levels

---

[3] Pew Research Center (2019). Millennial life: How young adulthood today compares with prior generations. Available: https://www.pewresearch.org/social-trends/2019/02/14/millennial-life-how-young-adulthood-today-compares-with-prior-generations-2/ (Accessed: 16 February, 2024).

[4] World Government Summit 2024. Dubai, UAE. Available: https://www.worldgovernmentsummit.org/events/2024/world-government-summit-2024 (Accessed: 17 February, 2024).

between leaders and their constituents. The following points can illustrate some of these gaps:[5]

- *Public value*: The gap exists between what leaders know is best and what people believe they need.
- *Communications*: This gap is between what public leaders say and what people actually hear.
- *Management*: There exists a gap between what gets planned and what finally gets implemented and between the cost of delivery and the value delivered. This further feeds distrust.
- *Governance*: A gap exists between governance and stewardship in terms of values and ultimate accountability, especially across intergenerational ideals and changing leadership.

These gaps and others have been exacerbated by global trends and crises over the last decades, where trust in public leaders has declined,[6] moving us into a "Wild West" type of environment where leaders now have to rethink leadership in this new "brave" era.

9.3 Frontier Leadership

In the search for an answer to the leadership dilemma, it would not be wise to suggest a wholesale departure from well-established leadership fundamentals. Leaders at all levels will still require an excellent understanding of human behavior, the ability to empathize, develop a positive vision, communicate that vision, empower people, and have the stamina to see it through. However, the question here is what adjustments, additional layers, and refocused lenses leaders need to tackle emerging problems in their new shapes and forms.

Our new Wild West described earlier, while plausible in terms of analogy, comes with a twist. First, in the original Wild West, information flow at the individual level was very limited, and scientific discovery and

[5] Stephens, M. (2023). Leading the Future. *Mohammed Bin Rashid School of Government Executive Education Course Day 2*. Slide 75 — Challenges for Government Leaders. Dubai.

[6] Edelman Trust Barometer (2024). Available: https://www.edelman.com/trust/trust-barometer (Accessed 20 February, 2024).

diffusion of technology were extremely slow. So, leaders did not only have an advantage of knowledge but also were able to develop foresight that many others lacked. So, when those leaders expressed their vision and described a path, they were generally followed. Essentially, those leaders *led from the front*. In this new Wild West, the situation is such that people have so much information (also misinformation and disinformation) that the leader's role has to be modified in order to address this crucial factor. Second, in the original Wild West, while individualism and self-reliance were key, having an individual voice was not a viable option in most cases. The situation is now reversed, and a critical leadership role is to properly inform that voice and channel it in the right direction. In effect, *leading from the back*.

According to the above analyses, effective public leadership in the new Wild West requires more delicate handling of vital issues that are more emotionally charged, given the individual's ability to broadcast their voice to the masses and influence public opinion. Crucially, leaders today must be able to address this phenomenon through effective policymaking and "good" science, developing the collective wisdom that will lead to effective foresight and, in the process, gaining credibility for their position. Importantly, given the rapid developments in science and technology, leaders need to adjust their course without losing legitimacy. A critical and tough task.

At the individual leader level, it is now more true than ever that foresight is at the forefront of required abilities, given the complexity of the current and future environment described above. This will require the activation of two parallel processes. One technical which will heavily rely on advanced technologies to mine a huge number of data points and summarize them into useful information form, which will be analyzed and tabulated to produce models of knowledge in certain areas of public affairs such as health or education. This knowledge is institutional. However, there is a caveat: institutional knowledge does not capture implicit knowledge, which may be made redundant before knowledge sharing happens.

In the second process, frontier leaders, as a result of that technical process and parallel to it, will gain ways to develop actionable insights from knowledge models gleaned through collective experiences. In turn, these insights over time will equip leaders with wisdom that they can use to develop foresight across sectors of activities. This foresight will inform and influence public opinion, which will subsequently allow for more sensible and effective ways forward.

In a 2017 report, the OECD[7] on future skills required by public sector professionals emphasized four categories and advised strong action on them by governments. Public sector professionals (future leaders) first need to acquire the ability to work effectively with citizens at the grassroots level. This will require skills in innovation management, crowdsourcing, co-creation, and co-managing. Second, as we move towards more dynamic and agile institutional structures, collaborating in networks becomes an essential competence. This means working with partners and developing platforms for joint projects. Third, with the rapid move towards more public-private partnerships in their various forms, the skill and experience in commissioning and contracting have become pivotal. Fourth, the skill to develop and implement public policy highly depends on expertise and foresight.

These four categories, along with the previously proposed leadership competencies, seem to go hand in hand with the literature on agile government that similarly stipulates the need for policy development, public-private partnership models, and future foresight in addition to youth empowerment.[8] In the same vein, earlier exploratory work on agile government skills summarized three broad categories. These are *policy entrepreneurship skills* which include policy development experience in addition to enterprising and achievement orientation. Next are *boundary spanning skills* that encompass facilitation, networking, and resourcefulness. Finally, we have *transformational skills*. This last category of skills seems to be at the heart of frontier leadership, as it underlines resiliency, vision development, advocacy, and a people-focused approach.[9]

Moreover, the emerging literature on agile government and agile leadership is moving in the right direction regarding skills required for the wild west and associated frontier leadership. However, the concept of frontier leadership has a wider scope since it focuses on global and macro

---

[7]OECD (2017). Skills for High Performing Civil Service. Available: https://read.oecd-ilibrary.org/governance/skills-for-a-high-performing-civil-service_9789264280724-en#page1 (Accessed: February 14, 2024).

[8]Awamleh, R. (2022). Post-COVID19 UAE Government restructuring: Reflections and future directions. In Stephens, M. Awamleh, R. & Salem, F. (Eds.). *Agile Government: Emerging Perspectives in Public Management* (pp. 53–68). Singapore: World Scientific Publishing.

[9]Stephens, M., Spraggon. M, & Vammalle, C. (2019). Agile government. A policy council paper. *Mohammed Bin Rashid School of Government*. Available: https://mbrsgcdn.azureedge.net/cmsstorage/mbrsg/files/75/75a9f893-19da-465a-8668-d04e19ed6cb2.pdf (Accessed: 17 February, 2024).

levels and is not limited to institutional levels. More importantly, in the context of anticipatory governance, frontier leadership constitutes a potentially effective response to the new environment that is even more unpredictable and complex. We live in a world of what seems to be so many moving pieces that are profoundly independent and interdependent at the same time. The difficulty of achieving remote consensus on climate action illustrates this last point. Here, it can be argued that adopting a frontier leadership style globally within anticipatory governance can better facilitate the desire for multilateral solutions.[10]

Building on all of the above and more, it would be prudent at this point to propose a working definition for "Frontier Leadership" as follows: *Frontier Leadership is a style of leadership that effectively meets the requirements of a complex and fast-moving environment where principal factors are known and tracked while their impact and direction are not known nor predicted. Frontier leadership arrives at foresight through collective intelligence.*[11] This process starts with data analyses, which lead to information being distilled into knowledge that yields wisdom and results in foresight. The ability to develop foresight in a turbulent environment will separate highly effective frontier leaders from others.

9.4 Conclusion

While it needs to be recognized that the above discussion about frontier leadership in the wider context of anticipatory governance is still in its infancy, the impact of the Wild West new era is clear and present. We live in a world that is experiencing profound changes in almost all spheres of life — a world full of many questions with few answers. The pace of change is leaving governments and institutions, public and private alike, yearning for the right path. This book argues in a way that attention to anticipatory governance will provide good direction for answering these questions. Within that, this chapter stipulates that serious scholarly work on frontier leadership is warranted as it constitutes a crucial piece of the constantly changing puzzle.

---

[10] The Summit of the Future in 2024 (UN). Multilateral solutions for a better tomorrow. Available: https://www.un.org/en/common-agenda/summit-of-the-future (Accessed: 17 February, 2024).

[11] The definition for collective intelligence is taken from this article: Leimeister, J.M. (2010). Collective Intelligence. *Business & Information Systems Engineering,* 2: 245–248.

https://doi.org/10.1142/9789811296000_0010

Chapter 10

How a Forgotten Nation Managed Uncertainty — The Restoration of Latvia's Independence

Rolands Lappuķe[*] and Andrejs Panteļējevs[†]

[*]Former Ambassador of Latvia
[†]Publicist, Former Politician, Latvia

Key Takeaways

- Nation-building is rooted in deep historical, cultural, and economic awareness and ties.
- National consciousness requires coalitions and awareness building.
- Cultural identity needs to be fostered for national consciousness.
- Family remains the strongest root for national awareness.
- The use of non-violence and lure diplomacy for national awakening is key to a successful peaceful transition.
- Anticipatory governance comes from an acknowledgment of the injustices of the past.

10.1 Latvia — An Unforgotten Nation

Latvia, as well as its Baltic neighbors Estonia and Lithuania, reappeared on the world stage of independent states in August 1991, playing a significant role in the breakdown of the Soviet Union in December of the same year. Until then, the so-called Baltic states had been widely forgotten in everyday world politics, but, as a matter of fact, they had never ceased to exist as international subjects.

In 1940, the Soviet Union invaded the Baltic states, an act of political aggression recognized as a clear violation of international law by most democracies. Occupied then by Nazi Germany and later by the Soviet Union, the three states preserved a *de jure existence* as the subject of international law since 1945, maintaining diplomatic representations in countries like the United States, the United Kingdom, and France. Therefore, in 1991, Latvia (along with Lithuania and Estonia) did not emerge as a new state — instead, its independence was fully restored.

When history brought the Baltic nations to the threshold of renewed independence, most people were probably not aware of the challenges in front of them. In the last fifty years, they had lived under an unwished domination — an occupation by a foreign state, a foreign regime, and a foreign mentality. Most inhabitants rejected this foreign power as deeply unfair. Therefore, they showed a peaceful but strong determination based on a few principles to overcome all yet unknown obstacles.

The 1990s and the process of leaving an integrated system like the Soviet Union — a *Baltexit*[1] — came indeed with many hard tests. It will be enough to say that Latvia lost half of its GDP and survived an inflation of 960% in 1992. Before describing the tremendous challenges the Latvian nation was to be confronted with, it is necessary to describe the shaping of the Latvian nation that led to the formation of a national state in 1918 and motivated it to renew its independence in 1991, taking the path toward a democratic state. Then, after explaining the challenges faced by the Latvian nation, the authors,[2] as active witnesses of this period, will describe some of the crucial decisions and actions taken by the people on the way to independence.

---

[1]"Baltexit" is a notion created by the authors to describe the process of the three countries deciding to leave a plurinational economic and political system. The Baltic nations chose to leave the Soviet Union similar to the Brexit, British citizens deciding to leave the European Union. Juridically, the situations are different as the Baltic states never joined the Soviet Union by their free will.

[2]Additional key sources for this article are Bergmane, U. (2023). *Politics of Uncertainty: The United States, the Baltic Question, and the Collapse of the Soviet Union*. UK: Oxford University Press; Muižnieks, N. (1993). The Baltic popular movements and the disintegration of the Soviet Union. PhD dissertation in Political Sciences at the University of California Berkeley. Various publications from Andrejs Plakāns — a Latvian American historian.

10.2 National Identity and Europeanness

In its struggle against the totalitarian Soviet regime, a major asset of the Latvian population was a strong national awareness and a sense of historically belonging to Western Europe. The Latvian state was founded at the end of the First World War when several European empires disappeared — the German, the Austrian-Hungarian, the Ottoman, and the Tsarist empires. In accordance with *The Fourteen Points* made by the US President W. Wilson, in 1918,[3] the Latvian population proclaimed its independence on 18th November 1918, with the creation of the Latvian state whose territory more or less followed the Latvian ethnographic borders.

It took several centuries for Latvians to be ready to form a nation state, a process closely linked to a degree of Western European integration. Baltic tribes, from which Latvians originated, used to live in the region for millenaries and are still now there. They were in contact with their Scandinavian and Slavic neighbors when German knights arrived in the 12th century. After having stopped their activities in the Middle East region, Pope Innocent III asked the German knights to Christianize the Eastern coast of the Baltic Sea in Northern Europe. The city of Riga was founded in 1201 by Bishop Albert, and soon an Order of Knights was created, which was to be affiliated with the Teutonic Order. These crusades lasted for the better part of the 13th century and resulted in the emergence of Terra Mariana — the Land of Mary (also referred to as Livonia) — a loose confederation of ecclesiastical principalities. Livonia encompassed present-day Latvia and Estonia. Its eastern border still marks a dividing line not only between the two states and the Russian Federation but also between Eastern and Western Christianity. It is worth noticing that it coincides with the Eastern border of the European Union with Russia.

The Christian Church, the German Order, and the ties with the Holy Roman Empire constituted the fundament of the first European network that politically and culturally integrated the territory of today's Latvia with Western Europe. Toward the end of the 13th century, a strong

[3] Wilson, W. (1918). The Fourteen Points. Available: https://www.theworldwar.org/learn/peace/fourteen-points (Accessed 1 January, 2024). While it does not specially mention Latvia, it mentions territorial integrity of Balkan states (point 11).

commercial network was built up — the Hanseatic League.[4] It was a merchant guild dedicated to promoting and defending free commerce in one hundred cities from Germany to Northern and Eastern Europe, of which eight cities were in Latvia, with Riga becoming an important town on the east coast of the Baltic. As a result, Roman law was introduced, and a citizenry appeared.

Power struggles among the clergy, the knights, and citizens led to a decisive historical split with the Catholic church and conversion to Protestantism. The first Lutheran parish was created in 1523 (the fourth one overall, but the first one outside the German empire) only six years after Martin Luther published his 95 theses in Wittenberg in 1517. An immediate consequence was the publication of the first book in the Latvian language in 1525 — a Catechism.

During these centuries, political domination over the territory of Latvia (under various denominations in those days: Courland, Livonia, and Latgale or Inflantia) passed from the Holy German Empire to an affiliation to the Polish–Lithuanian Commonwealth and then the Swedish kingdom during the 16th and 17th century. However, the German nobility always kept a firm hand on the local situation and the indigenous population.

When, in the course of the 18th century, Latvia's territory became the subject of the Tsarist Empire, the Russian authorities, in order to consolidate their positions, first expanded the rights of the Baltic German nobility to peasantry, strengthening serfdom on peasants. The status of the local population progressively became more precarious, and peasants lost most of their rights. Nevertheless, at the same time, the Latvian population's literacy reached about 70%, making ideas of the Enlightenment and the French Revolution more accessible to a wider public, paving the way to the first riots at the end of the 18th century.

Later on, the Tsarist regime aimed to weaken the rights and power of the German nobility. Serfdom was abolished in the Baltic provinces (roughly Estonia and Latvia) until 1819, during the reign of Alexander I, partially in the spirit of the Enlightenment and partially as a tactical measure. Latvians gained a certain freedom, even if precarious, and had the opportunity to move up on an economic and social scale. Industrious

[4]Britannica (2023). Hanseatic League. Available: https://www.britannica.com/money/topic/Hanseatic-League (Accessed 1 January, 2024).

people made a living, and credit opportunities developed in the course of the 19th century.

A Latvian cultural identity was also being fostered. Latvian teachers' seminars were founded, and newspapers in Latvian were published like Latviešu Avīzes (in 1822) (not without a certain involvement of the Baltic German clergy) and Pēterburgas Avīzes (in 1862).[5] As a central aspect of the expression of an authentic Latvian identity, some enthusiasts stepped up to gather Latvian folksongs, supposed to best express the real Latvian spirit. These folksongs belonged to a vastly preserved tradition of singing, and up to two million folksongs were gathered in a few decades. In fact, the *National Library of Latvia* has a Cabinet of Folk songs (see Exhibit 10.1) collected by Latvian folklorist Krišjānis Barons in the late 1860s.[6]

All in all, in the middle of the 19th century, the core of a Latvian political, cultural, and economic elite was launching a movement of *national awakening*,[7] similar to what was taking place in the rest of Europe, which would lead further toward the shaping a nation.

Toward the end of the 19th century, together with the tremendous economic growth in Latvia, whose capital city Riga had become a significant industrial center and the third port of the Tsarist Empire, social movements occurred like the development of a Latvian bourgeoisie and a growing working class. Some Marxist literature was easily available due to the geographic and cultural proximity to Germany.

The first political party — the Latvian Social-Democratic Party — was founded in 1904. The so-called Russian Revolution of 1905 was very fierce in Latvia and contributed to shaping social awareness with even

---

[5]Plakans, A. (1995). *The Latvians: A Short History*. USA: Hoover Institution Press; Plakans, A. (2011). *A Concise History of the Baltic States*. UK: Cambridge University Press.

[6]UNESCO (2010). The Cabinet of Dainas/Dainu Skapis. Available: https://web.archive.org/web/20200727072724/http://www.atmina.unesco.lv/page/98 (Accessed 6 January, 2024).

[7]National awakening is a phenomenon often associated with the early stages of historical phases of nationalism which may or may not lead to a birth of a nation; see, for example, Maxwell, A. (2020). Contingency and "National Awakening". *Nationalism and Ethnic Politics*, 26(2): 183–201; Lazda, M. (2009). Reconsidering nationalism: The Baltic case of Latvia in 1989. *International Journal of Politics, Culture, and Society*, 22: 517–536; Straumanis, A. (1972). Latvian theatre: A synthesis of ritual and national awakening. *Journal of Baltic Studies*, No: 3/4, 175–183; Plakans, A. (1995). *The Latvians: A Short History*. USA: Hoover Institution Press; Plakans, A. (2011). *A Concise History of the Baltic States*. Cambridge: Cambridge University Press.

Exhibit 10.1. Latvian Cabinet of Folk Songs.

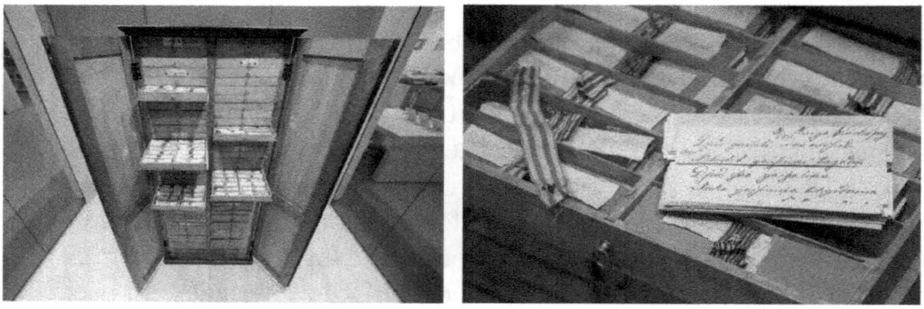

Source: Reproduced with permission from Didzis Grodzs.

some national dimension. Other parties would be created around the time of the 1917 revolution. A definite political awareness was in place — partly nationally oriented and partly internationally oriented. The latter would actively participate in the Bolshevik Revolution and mostly stayed in Russia. Tens of thousands of Latvians, mostly Bolsheviks, were shot in the Soviet Union during the purges in 1936–1938 when, under the impulsion of Stalin, the internationalism movement got Russified in its traditional imperialistic spirit.

The nationally oriented parties, including social-democrats, founded the Latvian state in 1918. They started to build democratic state structures in the spirit of Roman law — the rule of law. The citizenship law of 1919 gave the possibility to obtain Latvian citizenship to all inhabitants of Latvia who lived in the country from 1914, before the First World War, independently of their ethnic or religious identity. The Constitution of 1922, The Satversme, added the institutional basis of a parliamentary democracy and hence Latvia became a modern state entity with its 1920-ties.

The independent Latvian state existed *de facto* between 1918 and 1940, enough to leave an indelible imprint in Latvian collective memory. As already noted, it never ceased to exist *de jure*. This was one of the main pillars for the restoration of state independence at the end of the Soviet occupation.

10.3 Challenges

When restoring independence in 1991, Latvians were confronted with huge challenges, most of which were directly linked with the characteristics of the state entity Latvians decided to leave. These challenges are outlined in the following.

10.3.1 *Imperialism*

The Soviet Union was undoubtedly the heir of the former Tsarist Empire. Latvia had to deal with an imperialistic dimension shown by Russia. These worries are evident in the cyber-siege of Estonia and the war in Ukraine. Latvians also had to be content with the fact that many Russians remained in Latvia, particularly the military personnel. The latter issue was dealt with in the Treaty signed in Moscow in April 1994 between Latvia and Russia, permitting the stay of more than 20,000 military personnel of the Red Army together with their families — a heavy heritage.

10.3.2 *Colonialism*

Latvia also had to deal with the colonial aspects of the Soviet Union and its consequences. During the many decades of Soviet rule, hundreds of thousands of Soviet citizens had been deliberately brought to Latvia until the very end of the 1980s. The aim was to change the demographic proportion of Latvians within the population. Before the occupation in 1935, Latvians constituted 77% of the population. This number fell to 52% fifty years later, in 1989.[8] In harmony with the old principle of the Roman Empire times — *ubi bene, ubi patriae* — these persons were practicing domineering behaviors. Like true "*homo sovieticus*" *or the Soviet man,*[9] they enjoyed practical privileges, for example, the ease of getting a job and a flat, whereas local families often lived several generations in one room. The *homo sovieticus* also had the privilege to communicate in only one language, the language of the dominating

---

[8] See, for example, Muižnieks, N. (2006). *Latvian-Russian Relations: Domestic and International Dimensions.* Latvijas Universitāte Akadēmiskais apgāds.

[9] A term that came to denote the then Soviet way of thinking: See Sharafutdinova, G. (2019). Was there a "simple Soviet" person? Debating the politics and sociology of "homo Sovieticus". *Slavic Review*, 78(1): 173–195; Tyszka, K. (2009). Homo Sovieticus two decades later. *Polish Sociological Review*, 168(4): 507–522.

power — Russian — ignoring the local language or worse denigrating Latvian as a dog's language. Still today, for some people, learning the official language (Latvian) feels like a humiliation.

10.3.3 *Socialist economy*

Latvia also had to deal with the consequences of the socialist economic system. Relying on its limitless natural resources, which were sold abroad and constituted the main source of foreign currencies, the Soviet regime failed to develop a system that was advantageous to Latvia. Collectivization, for example, led to a disastrous level of productivity in agriculture, as farmers did not have a reason to produce more for the sake of a centralized state. They were much more effectively working on the small pieces of land that were sometimes left for their own use. Through centralization and state planning, the Soviet state tried to integrate the economic system at a national level, for example, for energy production and transportation. A hidden agenda was also to make all parts of the Soviet Union depend on each other, preventing velleities of autonomy.[10] There, again, we see clearly that for Russian leaders, economic factors can be mere instruments for a game of political power that is well in line with the imperialistic mindset. Latvians needed to minimize economic dependency on their big neighbor.

Of course, by renouncing the socialist economy, Latvia also needed to revive individual initiatives to establish free market principles and all other elements of a free market economy. Although many people had become used to state guarantees in everyday life, a lot of them also wanted to work for their own interests. The very fact that Latvia had German administrative traditions based on the Roman rule of law was certainly an advantage in its effort to restart the market economy. For example, in contrast with Russia, Latvia had a tradition of regulating private property (detailed property records), and this allowed Latvia to simply renew the cadaster of 1939.

[10]NB: It is worth noticing here that the "Baltexit" in the energy field has been completed only very recently when the war in Ukraine forced Europe to renounce gas deliveries from Russia.

10.3.4 *Totalitarianism*

Even if the totalitarian dimension of the Soviet regime had decayed at the end of the 1980s, it was still present and had left long-lasting traces. Here, we shall mention just a few features. The population did not trust most of the state institutions, assuming that the state apparatus was repressive by definition. This is particularly problematic if a justice system is supposed to inspire trust. Some people may even perceive the ability to fool the state as ethically positive and a mark of cleverness. Furthermore, the KGB[11] (and other repressive institutions), with its methods, had even distilled a profound distrust within the population — a challenge when cooperation is expected for a common task. Moreover, taking these factors into account, it is natural in a totalitarian society to adopt a kind of schizophrenic attitude by saying things in public that have nothing to do with reality or what you think or even do. Those are survival reactions whose psychological sequelae are difficult to assess and deal with and, unfortunately, are susceptible to persisting.

10.4 Strengths and Weaknesses of a Nation Undergoing Transformative Changes

Any totalitarian regime founded on a historical injustice has inherent contradictions that will eventually destroy it in the long run. Such contradictions may seem to be under control at the beginning but function as a gene of progressive destruction. The journey of Latvia was tough, but one the people were determined to undergo.

10.4.1 *National consciousness goes public*

In Latvia, which was occupied by the USSR, this gene was national consciousness.[12] It had evolved during the phase of recognition of the Latvian state and consolidated to an independent state between the two

[11] More on the KGB: https://www.history.com/topics/european-history/kgb.

[12] An "imagined" state of nationalism; see Anderson, B. (2010). The nation and the origins of national consciousness. In Montserrat, M., Berdún, G., Guibernau, M., & Rex, J. (Eds.), *The Ethnicity Reader: Nationalism, Multiculturalism and Migration*. Cambridge: Polity Press: pp. 56–64.

World Wars. Although World War II and the Stalinist regime did a lot to wound the Latvian national consciousness, history showed that the occupation regime did not succeed in erasing it.

Though the repressions and total censorship ended up removing national consciousness from public life, it never reached the very nucleus — the family. It is fair to say that national awareness found shelter and hid in the family territory. This ultimate bastion never surrendered and was ready to blossom again, should circumstances allow it. Clandestine celebrations of Christmas, conversations by the fireplace, preservation of statehood symbols, stories about independence told by witnesses to young generations, maintaining contact with exiled Latvians, as well as practicing consequent hypocrisy in the relationship with the regime — a vast arsenal was cultivated in preparation of a decisive future struggle. When the struggle would come wasn't clear at all but there was a feeling of its inevitability. We may assume that exactly, thanks to a lot of Latvians who cherished a weird conviction about "the possibility of the impossible," so useful when the real struggle for restoring independence came.

Surely, the occupation regime was aware of such a clandestine tension in the family and was searching for means to thwart it. It did so, for example, by giving a green light to ethnographic expressions of "*Latvianness*" while, at the same time, systematically importing a growing number of strangers from other Soviet republics to dilute the ethnic composition of the local population. All in all, this approach did not pay off as the first public unrests were linked with the Latvian ethnical restlessness, and it was precisely in an ethnographic festival that the flag of the independent Latvian state publicly appeared for the first time (Baltika festival July 1988).

As the first structured public manifestation of this national consciousness, preserved within the family, we should mention the Helsinki-86 group founded in 1986. Limited in number, this group of courageous activists formally based their activities on the chapter on human rights of the Helsinki Accords (1975) and promoted a campaign to "remind" the West as well as Latvia about the illegal occupation of Latvia. It was the first remarkable expression of Latvian national awareness outside the family circle.

It was in that time, in the second half of the eighties, that the internal undoing of the Soviet communist regime started in a progressive but inexorable manner. The grounds for it were the economic failure and crisis as well as the moral bankruptcy of the dominating ideology. The regime began *perestroika*,[13] a set of reforms that were merely cosmetic repairs. The disintegration process of the Soviet Union offered a tiny window of opportunity for Latvians to deal with their particular concern — independence.

The Environment Protection Club or *Vides aizsardzības klubs*, formally founded in 1986, can be considered the first opposition movement. It was the first really significant non-governmental organization in the territory of occupied Latvia. Its activities triggered processes now described as the "Third Awakening."[14] A small stream grew into a powerful river that washed away the occupation regime from Latvia (in fact, there is an often-used word, *likteņupe* — the river of fate or destiny).[15] In 1987, through public protests, the construction of a hydroelectric dam on the Daugava river, near the second-biggest city of Latvia, Daugavpils, was formally abandoned. This was a big victory because a previous project, the Pļaviņas hydroelectric power station, had submerged areas of historical and cultural significance to the Latvians.[16]

It has to be mentioned that from the outset of the movement, diverse forces in favor of independence, implemented a range of tactics to push things always just a little bit further than foreseen. Such an opportunistic approach was facilitated by the uncertainties linked with the fall of the regime. These tactics were harmonized with those of other democratic groups all over the USSR, including in Russia, which accelerated the weakening of the regime. There was a permanent balance on the edge of what is possible and what is impossible. The challenge in each occasion was to test "how far you could go too far."[17]

---

[13] This movement lasted from 1985–1991. *See* Kotkin, S. (2001). *Armageddon Averted*. Oxford: Oxford University Press.

[14] Penikis, A. (1996). The third awakening begins: The birth of the Latvian popular front, June 1988 to August 1988. *Journal of Baltic Studies*, 27(4): 261–290.

[15] While *Likteņupe* often refers to the place Daugava, it is also symbolic. see: Mawhood, W. (1986). The Unbuilt Soviet Metro System that Haunts Latvia's Capital: STRUGGLE Deep Baltic. Available: https://deepbaltic.com/2019/06/28/the-unbuilt-soviet-metro-system-that-haunts-latvias-capital-struggle/ (Accessed 1 January, 2024).

[16] *Ibid.*

[17] In 1987, also a senior advisor of President Ronald Reagan, Jack Matlock, informed Latvians that the United States had never recognised the legitimacy of Soviet rule over the Baltic states, which they were not aware of. (See Mawhood (1986), *Op. cit.*).

A huge step was taken when thousands of people went to the streets to protest against the creation of a metro in Riga on 27th April 1988.[18] The work of building a metro had a direct link with various issues related to independence, broken promises, lack of local agency, and the worry that there was a plan for masses of immigrant workers to be flooded into Riga, further threatening the local ethnic balance of the population.[19] Furthermore, the protest was a message of self-determination in a colonial atmosphere — decisions about Latvia should be made in Riga, not in Moscow. To be one's own masters was one of the mottos of the Latvian demonstration.

These mass demonstrations showed that NGOs could count on widespread support, and various organizations were founded and others became stronger in their demands of restoring Latvian independence. In 1988, a plenum was organized to talk openly about the very fact of occupation and to create a movement. The Latvian Popular Front (LPF) was founded a few months later.

10.4.2 *On a tight rope between the possible and the impossible*

To be on the safer side, when founding the LPF, state independence was not explicitly mentioned. The basic lines dealt with principles of regime democratization, requiring closer following of the Soviet constitution, which stipulated rather large sovereignty for Latvia — which was never realized in practice.

Then again, the reason for this was balancing between the possible and the impossible. Latvia was the center of a Soviet war district, full of Red Army and military staff. Almost intuitively, a conviction was anchored in Latvians since the very start of the movement that aims could be reached only through peaceful resistance. Armed underground resistance could not be a solution. On the one hand, the military superiority of the Soviet regime was obvious and, on the other hand, the movement badly needed widespread moral support from an international audience as well as within the USSR.

As a matter of fact, these tactics were remarkably successful. On 23 August 1989, the three Baltic nations chose the fiftieth anniversary of the

---

[18] Interestingly, in Chile in 2019, 1.2 million people gathered in Santiago to protest the building of a metro, and is one of the largest protests in the country's history.

[19] Mawhood, W. (1986), *Op. cit.*

Molotov–Ribbentrop pact,[20] when the Nazi and the Soviet totalitarian regimes divided Eastern European territories into the so-called Baltic Way, to organize a peaceful protest. Millions of people of diverse origins formed a hand-in-hand chain of people singing all along 600 km across the three Baltic states. This event resonated at an international level as a *Singing Revolution* (see Exhibit 10.2) and fostered undivided sympathy internationally as well as in the USSR. Had there been armed actions killing people of Russian origin, it is doubtful whether President Boris Yeltsin would have later signed so easily, the formal recognition of Latvian independence! It is worth noticing that incitement to ethnic hate was never in the arsenal of Latvian independence fighters.

Exhibit 10.2. Singing Revolution.

Source: Reproduced with Permission from Diena.[21]

[20]Britannica (2024). German-Soviet Nonaggression Pact. Available https://www.britannica.com/event/German-Soviet-Nonaggression-Pact (Accessed 1 January, 2024).

[21]Available here: https://www.diena.lv/raksts/latvija/politika/akcijas-baltijas-cels-mantojums-ieklauts-unesco-starptautiskaja-registra-680564.

Events progressed like an avalanche. The Latvian Popular Front, in its autumn 1989 congress, announced Latvian statehood and the full renewal of Latvian independence as its goals. This radical step was made possible by the massive support for the LPF, as well as the situation in the Soviet Union where Gorbachev's *perestroika,* to a certain extent, had weakened the repressive capacity of the USSR[22] — some confusion reigned, and the reactionary forces had not consolidated yet. The LPF's main objective was then to participate in the elections of the Latvian Soviet Supreme Council, the first elections in the USSR in which non-members of the Communist party were also allowed to take part.

The pre-election processes were not simple. It had to be taken into account that the representatives of the USSR armed forces, as well as the recently immigrated foreigners, had to participate in these elections; hence, it was of tremendous importance to reach out to a maximum number of people and to obtain their active support. Numerous public servants of the occupying authorities showed sympathy for the movement, and administrative leaders of big enterprises and even representatives of the Latvian Communist Party got involved in the campaign. Questions about collaborationism were not raised but appeared much later. The challenge was again to manage the impossible — to gain power within the context of Soviet law and structures in order to use it later to restore Latvian independence and to deconstruct these same structures.

10.4.3 *A strong victory in a fragile situation or searching for the right balance…*

And they did it! The Latvian People's Front won the elections, and in the very presence of the reactionary opposition on 4th May 1990, the Parliament voted a Declaration for the renewal of independence of the Republic of Latvia based on the principle of state continuity.

From then on, the core of the independence movement moved from the LPF to its faction in the Supreme Council, where it had an overwhelming majority — a powerful institution was conquered but still LPF did

[22] In 1989, the USSR at the highest level, adopted the "Occupation of the Baltic States," which declared that the occupation was not part of the law nor the will of the Soviet people.

not yet have the authority in the whole territory of Latvia. The presence of a huge Red Army contingent, security structures of the USSR, prosecution, police (milicija), and the apparatus of the Communist party was a strong threat to the movement.

As a matter of fact, it was a situation of double governance. On the one hand, Latvia had the occupation power institution of the USSR — the Supreme Council of the Latvian Soviet Republic — conquered by the independence activists, and on the other hand, the repressive, military, and other structures of the occupying power of the USSR. At first glance, it looked like a fully absurd situation, but rationally, it was the only solution for balancing the possible and the impossible of that historical moment. Nothing was yet completely achieved and the situation was not ripe for international recognition of a restored independent Latvian state.

Indeed, there were still a lot of existential as well as tactical decisions and compromises to be made. Any fiasco could jeopardize the whole process of independence restoration. Most of the independence activists elected in Parliament did not have experience in state power positions and had to learn on the job to become responsible and competent "servants of the state." There was no time for schooling on democracy, including lawmaking, the fundamental duty of a Parliament.

This transition to state responsibility was eased by two aspects. First, democratic principles and human rights were core values of the independence movement from its very start. Therefore, it was only logical to lay the foundation of a functional democracy as quickly as possible. Second, a few MPs had been active in the authoritative part of the occupation power. The most eminent example was the chairman of the Parliament, Anatolijs Gorbunovs, who had been the ideological first secretary of the Latvian Communist Party before choosing the camp of Latvian independence, together with numerous other party members. He had gained widespread popularity and had been convincingly elected to the Parliament. His experience, his quiet personality, and his network were irreplaceable for the right functioning of the new Parliament and even of the state.

Another existential issue was the relationship with the USSR's central power in Moscow. Although the vertical power in Moscow was profoundly deconstructed at that time and some confusion reigned about which structure was responsible for what action, maintaining relations with Secretary General Mikhail Gorbachev remained essential, if only because he had garnered much sympathy in Western society. The West was afraid that weakening Gorbachev's position could reverse the perestroika processes.

These relationships, until Gorbachev's fall, were pure equilibrist art, balancing on a tightrope between what was done in Riga and what was told in Moscow. The disintegration of vertical power made it possible. An example of this is what can be qualified as "*lure diplomacy.*"[23] While it was absolutely clear in Riga that the only purpose of all activities was the restoration of sovereign Latvian statehood, in Moscow, the Latvian LPF representatives pretended to be interested in the idea of a new Union Treaty that would redefine the relationships between republics within the USSR. For Gorbachev, it was a hopeful solution to save the Union, whereas for Latvians it was a kind of shield to impede the Soviet central power from interfering too much with what was happening in Latvia. To an extent, it was some kind of conformism, but it was justified to avoid direct confrontation with the Red Army's contingent stationed in the Baltics.

In this context, a third existential issue turned out to cultivate direct contacts with the leaders of the Baltic War District and the Soviet Armed forces in Latvia. In that respect, the non-violent tactics had to be ensured. The hypothesis of an armed provocation against the USSR Armed Forces was plausible, and any violent action had to be avoided at any price. LPF and its regional structures fully succeeded in it. Importantly, the leadership of the Supreme Council managed to maintain solid communication with the Baltic War District head. In principle, this was to solve practical issues linked with army logistics and infrastructure. In practice, these direct contacts profited from the state of confusion in Moscow by strengthening the conviction that the Latvian Supreme Council had legitimate rights to deal with what was happening in Latvia without threatening the USSR armed forces.

---

[23] This can be considered a type of diplomacy where you use incentives to lure a nation away from another nation while disguising the true objectives. For example, using debt or financing; see Wong, B. (2020). China's mask diplomacy. *The Diplomat*, 25. While it may overlap with soft power, this may also involve a sleight of hand.

Unfortunately, not all violence could be prevented. In January 1991, first in Vilnius and then in Riga, clashes took place that cost human lives. In Riga, special duty units of the USSR Ministry of Interior — the OMON — attacked the Latvian Ministry of Interior. Even today, it is not clear who gave the order for this operation, which Gorbachev distanced himself from. But the aim was clear — an intentional provocation aimed at involving the regular army units located in Latvia, as OMON's military capacity alone would be insufficient for a military coup.

The counteraction to the new Latvian power structures came instantly. The regional LPF structures mobilized all over Latvia, and a huge number of large agricultural vehicles of various types were brought to Riga to prevent any planned attack by their presence alone. In addition, barricades were established and defended night and day by masses of people. The city center around the Parliament was blocked by unarmed people and barricades. This turned out to be decisive. In front of such a massive display of unity, the head of the Red Army forces understood that army involvement would mean terrible bloodshed, a lot of civil victims, and a very complicated military operation with unforeseeable consequences; they backed down. Not only did no instructions come from Moscow (a result of lure diplomacy) but there were also too few professional military staff members present. Most were recruits with less than two years of experience who did not have the motivation to shoot unarmed civilians.

Besides dealing with the USSR authorities, Latvian leaders in Moscow were also developing ties with the growing alternative power represented by Boris Yeltsin, soon to be the first president of the Republic of Russia. It is fair to say that Anatolijs Gorbunovs played a central role on which both the Estonian and the Lithuanian leaders were relying. This strategy was based on a long-term personal relationship between him and Yeltsin. While barricades were being erected in Riga, the chairmen of the three Baltic Supreme Councils met with Yeltsin in Tallinn. The events in Vilnius and Riga were an opportunity for Yeltsin to discredit Gorbachev and strengthen control over the USSR's armed forces. He promised his support to the Baltic states. This promise of solidarity toward the independence of the Baltic states paved the way for Yeltsin, as President of Russia, to sign the recognition of the independence of Latvia on 24th August 1991 (see Exhibit 10.3).

Exhibit 10.3. "You were not born free, you become free."[24]

4 MAIJS

Latvijas valstiskās neatkarības atjaunošanai – 30

2020. gada 23. aprīlis

«Par brīvu nepiedzimst, par brīvu kļūst»

Deklarācija, kas mainīja Latviju

KĀ ATDZIMA LATVIJA

"Neatkarības deklarācija pati par sevi nelecē-la mūs saulītē, taču tā deva mums iespēju pašiem izlemt savu likteni. (..) Neatkarības deklarācija savu izdarīja, tā saliedēja mūs – godīgos cilvēkus, ļāva neapbruņotiem stāties pretim vienai no varenākajām armijām pasaulē, visizsmalcinātākajam izspiegošanas aparātam un vislielākajam un visaptverošākajam varas mehānismam, kas līdz tam bija radīts pasaulē. Mēs pārvarējām bailes savā sirdī un uzvarējām," atzinis atmodas laika politiķis, jurists Ilmārs Bišers (1930–2011).

Izšķirošā soļa sagatavošana

Source: By permission — Riga Central Library: https://www.rcb.lv/2020/04/4-maijs/.

[24]The picture is an extract from a newspaper article announcing the independence vote on 4.5.1990. The MP's are going out of the parliament. On the right, the tall and thin person is Andrejs Panteļējevs.

10.4.4 *Searching for international support*

A significant challenge consisted of strengthening the international prestige of the endeavors for Latvian state independence. A doctrine of state continuity defined by the LPF[25] was consequently implemented, promoting the principle of restoring the Republic of Latvia of 1918, whose occupation and annexation by the Soviet Union many Western countries had never recognized. This choice was juridically and historically correct. Tactically, it was even more indispensable. Western countries were showing strong sympathy, if not euphoria, toward Gorbachev and his reforms in the USSR, but a national separatist movement, obviously disturbing Gorbachev's ambitions, was susceptible to not attract enough international support. Therefore, it was essential to remind everybody everywhere of the legitimacy of the existence of a Latvian state based on international law. Holding on to this juridical frame also meant the renunciation of the elaboration of a new constitution. The issue was discussed, but the LPF decided to renew the Constitution of 1922 in its entirety when the proper time came.[26]

In this context, it was very important to show the West as well as the East that the events taking place in Latvia were a democratic self-determination process. A referendum on independence was organized on 3rd March 1991 to prove the democratic legitimacy of the course launched by the parliamentary vote of 4th May of the previous year. It represented a risk, and it took time to reach a consensus within the LPF. Since the vote in 1990, some opposition to the independence process had been raised, based essentially on inhabitants of Russian background who had arrived in Latvia during the occupation period. All inhabitants of Russian origin were also given the right to vote. The risk paid off — 87.56% of inhabitants were entitled to vote, of which 73.68% voted yes to the following question: "Are you in favor of a democratic and independent Latvia?" Still, it indicated a problem — *circa* 400.000 voted against state independence, mainly military persons (more than 60,000 were stationed in Latvia) and

[25]Doctrine elaborated particularly by jurist Egils Levits, later to become president (2019–2023), on the illegal annexation of the Baltic States; see also: Mälksoo, L. (2003) Illegal Annexation of the Baltic States by the USSR (2003) Brill Nijhoff Lauri Mälksoo - 978-90-04-46489-6 Downloaded from Brill.com 12/23/2023 04:08:19PM via Open Access. https://creativecommons.org/licenses/by-nc/4.0.

[26]Note: The Latvian constitution — Satversme — re-entered fully into force on 6 July 1993 by an announcement by the then elected parliament — the Saeima.

their families, plus civilians who had arrived during the occupation. Their fate was going to be dealt with partially in an agreement with Russia (1994). But it certainly showed how essential it was to renew the Latvian juridical system, including the regulation of legitimate citizenship.

The period of double governance, from 4 May 1990 onwards (till 21 August 1991), passed under the a period of uncertainty. Every day came new, unexpected challenges that had to be adequately assessed so as to define what was possible and impossible to do. This was brutally interrupted by the reactionary putsch or coup in Moscow on 19th August 1991, proclaiming a return to the former USSR. For the LPF, the time for lure diplomacy was definitely over. Some armed vehicles appeared on Riga streets. The Supreme Council met on 21st August and proclaimed Latvia's full independence and demanded the renewal of the Constitution of the Republic of Latvia on the Latvian territory. There was an atmosphere of heightened emotions and fear that the whole independence movement would be brutally interrupted without any further perspective.

And yet, the next day justified this somehow desperate step. The Moscow putsch was a dramatic failure, and Yeltsin became the *de facto* leader of the USSR. The Baltic independence leaders had played the right card when collaborating with Yeltsin. As soon as the Latvian Supreme Council took the decision for independence, the international community started to recognize it, starting with Iceland on 22 August, 1991. The United States still hesitated, waiting for Yeltsin's reaction.

10.5 Independence at Last!

And finally, within half an hour in the Kremlin, on 24th August, history was made. The Latvian delegation met with the new Russian leader. In 30 minutes, Yeltsin accepted the text prepared by the Latvian delegation on the Declaration of the Recognition of the Independence of the Republic of Latvia and signed it (see Exhibit 10.4). Yeltsin trusted the Chairman of the Latvian Supreme Council, Anatolijs Gorbunovs, with whom he had gone hunting one year before. Latvians later joked about how this hunt paid off.

Recognition by the USA followed without any delay, and Latvia was fully recognized as a country in the international arena. There were still many challenges to be faced by the Latvian nation — the withdrawal of the Russian army, the border agreement with Russia, and the accession to the European Union and NATO — which seemed like inaccessible dreams in 1991, but history showed that the impossible could be achieved.

Exhibit 10.4. Yeltsin in the Supreme Council of Latvia on 1 August 1990.

Source: Reproduced with permission from Anatolijs Gorbunovs' personal archive.

In times of uncertainty, there is no given recipe to manage transformative changes. Creativity is needed. Latvia did this using both nonviolence and lure diplomacy. Characterizing how the Latvian nation regained its independence, one may talk of serendipity — luck is when opportunity meets preparedness.

A clear conscience of the end goal and a strong will to take risks rooted in a deep conviction that history had been unfair were essential for undertaking a revolutionary process. Intuitively, everybody — especially the leaders of the movement — anticipated that the difficulties would be tremendous and complex. Courage found its source in the unity of the massive movement — people joined it spontaneously, comforting everybody else that the time was now or never.

A high emotional wave overwhelmed a whole nation with an ingenuous faith that it couldn't fail — people went singing to fight for freedom, but they never lost their self-control. This level of emotional high of the Singing Revolution certainly helped to simplify the perception of the problems to come. The consolidation of the nation — its unity, flexibility and obstinacy, its wide cooperation networks, luck, and other factors — all of which were necessary ingredients for the Latvian nation to climb impossible summits. So, it happened — the impossible became a long-term reality.

https://doi.org/10.1142/9789811296000_0011

Chapter 11

Early Warning Systems: Whispers in the Global Corridors

Melodena Stephens*, **Frederic Sicre**†, **and Raed Awamleh**‡

**Mohammed Bin Rashid School of Government, Dubai, UAE*
†*Tardis Advisors, Dubai, Paris and Geneva*
‡*Center for Policy and Competitiveness,*
École de Ponts Business School, Paris, France

Key Takeaways

- The MENA region offers a tremendous lesson in early warning signals because it is the most crisis-prone region in the world.
- Tribes form corridors of connections or power and can provide information and opportunities to leverage an early warning system to identify tipping points.
- This form of governance differs from the West and is multilayered and rooted in collectivism.
- To hear EWSs, one must first be invited into the right corridor and admitted into the relevant room — this requires trust. Then, one needs to listen to build anticipatory governance.
- There are many corridors: summits, forums, alliances, network ties, and other forms of diplomacy like trade, education, and humanitarian relief to build these corridors and cross-reference your signals.

11.1 Middle East and North Africa — Backdrop

When one thinks of the Middle East, many images come to mind — oil, kings, sheikhs, strong rulers, unrest, religion, and language. Maybe opulence comes to mind, or even history (it has some of the oldest civilizations in the world). What religion comes to mind when referencing the region? There are 10–15 million Christians who live in Lebanon, Syria, Jordan, Palestine, Israel, and Egypt.[1] The wife of the late Yasser Arafat, leader of the Palestinian Liberation Organization, was a Christian. It gets even more complicated if we consider various sects within the same religion. Numerous misconceptions about this region create challenges regarding global governance and maintaining peace and stability.

The Middle East is one of the most crisis-prone regions[2] in the world and suffers from the legacy of colonialism (see Exhibit 11.1). In 1921, the French and British divided the Middle East according to the Sykes–Picot agreement. After World War I, in support of the Jewish communities in Europe, the British government announced the 1917 Balfour Declaration, backing the creation of the State of Israel in Palestine, which was endorsed by the League of Nations in 1922.[3] Based on the UN Partition Plan of 1947, Palestine was split into Jewish and Arab territories. During this period, there were mass migrations of either displaced people (Palestinians to neighboring countries) or Jews who were voluntarily displaced and moved to Israel. The displaced Palestinians do not fall under the purview of UNHCR, the UN Refugee Agency (created in 1950) but under the newly created organization called the United Nations Relief and Works Agency — UNRWA (established in 1949), which is required to raise funds independently of the UNHCR. Unlike the UNHCR, the UNRWA does not have a mandate to find a final solution for Palestinian refugees (like a permanent home or citizenship, or the ability to return home) as a

---

[1] World Atlas (2024). Arab Christians: Who are they and where do they live? Available: https://www.worldatlas.com/articles/arab-christians-who-are-they-and-where-do-they-live.html (Accessed 27 December, 2023).

[2] Stephens, M. (2016). Managing at the edge of chaos: Middle East North Africa perspectives for international management. In Merchant, H. (Ed.), *Handbook of Contemporary Research on Emerging Markets*, Cheltenham: Edward Elger Publishing, pp. 317–354. https://doi.org/10.4337/9781782546368.00022.

[3] Jewish Voice for Peace (n.d.). Facts. Available: https://www.jewishvoiceforpeace.org/wp-content/uploads/2015/07/JVP-Jews-of-the-middle-east-fact-sheet.pdf (Accessed 27 December, 2023).

Exhibit 11.1. Crises in MENA (overview).

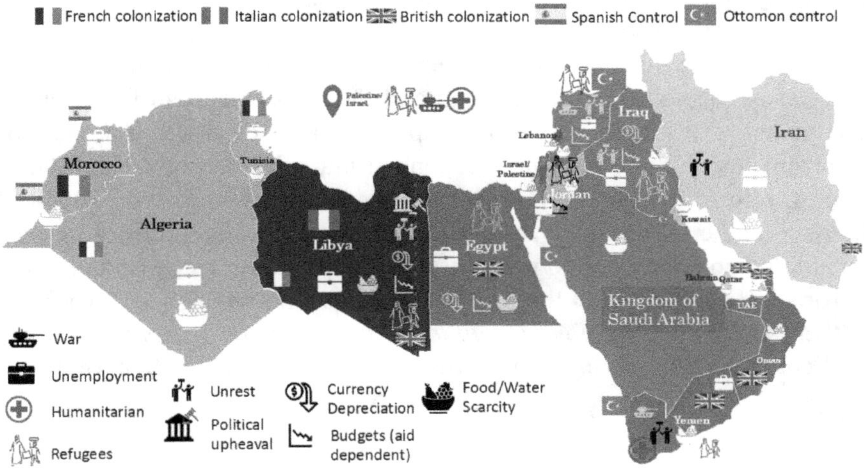

Source: Authors.

sustainable political settlement between Israel and Arab states has never been reached,[4] suggesting there are many standards to global governance.

The region suffers from massive displacement of people and refugees. In some cases, refugees migrate from one country to another. The refugee-producing countries are Syria, Israel–Palestine, Yemen, Iraq, and Libya, while the refugee-hosting countries are Jordan, Lebanon, Egypt, and also Iraq, Algeria, Yemen, and Syria. Many hosting countries[5] struggle with budget deficits, currency devaluation, and civil unrest. Problems

[4]According to the UNRWA, about 6.3 million Palestinian refugees are registered across the Arab world. Many (who still do not have citizenship in their host countries) are families of the original 750,000 Palestinians who were forced out of the newly formed state of Israel between 1947 and 1949. This event is known the Nakba or "catastrophe." See more here: https://mei.edu/publications/refugees-first-new-approach-middle-east-peace.

[5]Statista (2023). Number of refugees in the Middle East and North Africa region as of mid-2022, by Country of Asylum. Available: https://www.statista.com/statistics/1201495/mena-refugees-number-by-country-of-origin/#:~:text=Number%20of%20refugees%20hosted%20MENA%202022%2C%20by%20country%20of%20asylum&text=Of%20these%2C%20the%20highest%20number,Jordan%20followed%20behind%20with%20715%2C000 (Accessed 13 February, 2024).

are complex: The influence of foreign governments, the flow of weapons,[6] unemployment,[7] and scarcity of water,[8] food,[9] and funds[10] are critical issues for regional security.

Many of the other crises in the region come from a misunderstanding of what is happening on the ground and the consequences of the same. The invasion of Iraq in search of weapons of mass destruction proved to be erroneous — there were no weapons of mass destruction to be found. The war took the lives of 4,400 American troops and over 300,000 Iraqis.[11] The civil unrest, war, and the destruction of the political structures left Iraq wide open to radicalism and the subsequent exportation of terrorism. In 2003, when the Iraq war started, "*US troops were working with the still-new Iraqi government to create a national security structure that could handle the challenges the nation would face in the years to*

[6] Stockholm International Peace Research Institute: Arms Transfer (2022). SALW control-related assistance in the Middle East and North Africa: Identifying needs and bridging gaps. Available: https://www.sipri.org/commentary/topical-backgrounder/2022/arms-transfer-and-salw-control-related-assistance-middle-east-and-north-africa-identifying-needs-and (Accessed 13 February, 2024); Stockholm International Peace Research Institute (2022). Arms transfer and SALW controls in the Middle East and North Africa: Challenges and state of play. Available: https://www.sipri.org/commentary/topical-backgrounder/2022/arms-transfer-and-salw-controls-middle-east-and-north-africa-challenges-and-state-play (Accessed 13 February, 2024).

[7] Atlantic Council Middle East (2023). @ACMideast on X, 11 August. Available: https://twitter.com/ACMideast/status/1690045491684290560 (Accessed 13 February, 2024).

[8] WEF (2023). How can the Middle East and North Africa manage the region's water crisis? Available: https://www.weforum.org/agenda/2023/01/middle-east-north-africa-mena-water-crisis-industry-leaders-solutions/#:~:text=The%20Middle%20East%20and%20North%20Africa%20(MENA)%20is%20one%20of,area%2C%20especially%20women%20and%20children (Accessed 12 February, 2024).

[9] EIU (2021). Food security remains a major issue in MENA. Available: https://www.eiu.com/n/food-security-remains-a-major-issue-in-mena/ (Accessed 12 February, 2024).

[10] See 2024 IMF briefing: https://www.imf.org/en/News/Articles/2024/02/01/tr013124-transcript-of-press-briefing-regional-economic-outlook-middle-east-central-asia-udpate.

[11] Nawaz, A. & Sagalyn, D. (2023). The long-lasting impact of the U.S. invasion of Iraq. *PBS News*, 29 March. Available: https://www.pbs.org/newshour/show/the-long-lasting-impact-of-the-u-s-invasion-of-iraq (Accessed 13 February, 2024).

come."[12] This process was not as easy as they had thought. The United States ended its mission in Iraq in 2009, handing over responsibilities to Iraqi forces, and the country is still mainly in a state of unrest.[13]

There have always been political tensions — the eight-year Iraq–Iran war led to the deaths of 300,000 Iraqis and 600,000 Iranians.[14] There have been factions fighting and causing civil unrest, for example, the Houthis (based in Yemen) who caused attacks in the Red Sea and neighboring countries and impacted the people of Yemen when the Arab coalition further intervened, adding more weapons to the growing stockpile. Hezbollah in Lebanon (backed by Iran) creates another complication in the overall picture.[15]

The ISIS and al-Qaeda networks (originating from Iraq and Afghanistan) exploit humanitarian issues and civil unrest to foster radicalization, impacting much of Iraq and Syria and infiltrating the wider region. Much of their funding came from American military equipment left in the region, for example, Humvees worth over USD$ 1 billion and other state-of-the-art military hardware like tanks, helicopters, ammunition, and machine guns.[16,17] Other primary sources of funds are captured oil fields, which enables them to sell oil in the black market at cheaper prices and funds criminal activities like raiding, smuggling, drug

---

[12] Mayfield, M. (2013). A powerful presence. *Frontline*, 5(1): 9. Available: https://www.cbp.gov/sites/default/files/documents/frontline_vol5_issue1.pdf.

[13] Britannica (n.d.). U.S. withdrawal and the rise of the Islamic State in Iraq and the Levant (ISIL). Available: https://www.britannica.com/place/Iraq/U-S-withdrawal-and-the-rise-of-the-Islamic-State-in-Iraq-and-the-Levant-ISIL (Accessed 12 February, 2024).

[14] Nawaz & Sagalyn (2023), *Op. cit.*

[15] Riedel, B. (2022). Yemen war spreads to the UAE. *Brookings*, 10 February. Available https://www.brookings.edu/articles/yemen-war-spreads-to-the-uae/ (Accessed 27 December, 2023).

[16] CGSRS (2015). Money matters: Sources of ISIS' funding and how to disrupt them. Available: http://cgsrs.org/publications/27 (Accessed 13 February, 2024).

[17] Note: The leaving back of weapons and other military hardware is a significant problem in the Middle East. Yemen has the 2nd highest guns per capita, and many of the weapons are remnants of wars or the weapon trade. Root. T. (2013). Gun control, Yemen-style. *The Atlantic,* 12 February. Available: https://www.theatlantic.com/international/archive/2013/02/gun-control-yemen-style/273058/ (Accessed 27 December, 2023); Small Arms Survey (2003). Chapter 5: Living with weapons: Small arms in Yemen. Available: https://www.smallarmssurvey.org/sites/default/files/resources/Small-Arms-Survey-2003-Chapter-05-EN.pdf (Accessed 13 February, 2024).

trafficking, and kidnapping for ransom.[18] ISIS remains the largest funded terror organization in the world with ties to other terrorist groups.[19]

These are just a few examples: This interrelationship between regions, factions, arms movement, and people movement is complex and a source of much chaos. To understand the region, one should understand the foundational governance structure (not the imposed colonial structure). Only then could one learn to listen to Early Warning Signals (EWSs). In some cases, outside governments thought they heard EWSs but were in the wrong corridors, listening to the wrong information.[20] To be in the right place and at the right time and be allowed to listen, a country, agency, or person needs to have built a foundation of trust.

11.2 Tribes: The Corridors of Connections and Conduits for Anticipatory Governance

Perhaps the word Arab comes to mind when the Middle East is mentioned. Who or what is an Arab? It would be easy to say the people that live in Arabia. The Arab people believe they originate from the genealogical lines of the Prophet Noah or the Prophet Abraham (so the Muslims, the Christians, and Jews have that in common). In Arabia, there are two types of tribes, descended from Adnan and Qahtan (who can both be traced to the Prophet Noah and the Prophet Abraham). Adnan (from the line of the Prophet Ishmael, the Prophet Abraham's son) is often associated with Northern Arabs (like Jordan and Syria). The Southern Arabs are descendants of Qahtan (the Prophet Abraham's lineage), originating from Yemen and spread throughout the Arabian Peninsula.

Egypt's Gamal Abdel Nasser staged the first military coup in the Arab region against traditional rule aligned with the remnants of colonialism after the military lost the 1948 war against Israel. He soon became the first Egyptian President of Egypt in 1954 (the first Egyptian after 2500 years).[21]

---

[18] CGSRS (2015), *Op. cit.*

[19] The Global Counter-Terrorism Forum and Hedayah do not associate terrorism or violent extremism with any religion, nationality, civilization, or ethnic group, consistent with relevant UN Security Council Resolutions; see https://hedayah.com/about-ftf-programs/.

[20] Listening to the wrong information has led to many unfortunate consequences, in some cases funding small factions of fighters, supporting coups, or arms transfer.

[21] Aljazeera (2008). Arab unity: Nasser's revolution. Available: https://www.aljazeera.com/news/2008/6/20/arab-unity-nassers-revolution (Accessed 10 January, 2024).

He inspired an Arab nationalism[22] beyond his country's boundaries — uniting the region between Mashreq (Arab East) and Maghreb (Arab West).[23] Nasser reawakened the need for independence from colonialism[24] and set about infrastructure projects (moving away from sourcing finance from the USA to the Soviet Union). Thinking the West was pro-Israeli, to cement his anti-western stance, Nasser nationalized the Suez Canal in 1956. This project was built and operated mainly with French and British investments and expertise.[25] That led to war.

Not all Muslims are Arabs, and not all Arabs are Muslims. And though the Arab identity unifies during crises, like the angst over the invasion of Iraq or the continuous human crises in Palestine, the Arab identity simmers under multiple identities.

To understand Arabs, it is vital to unpick the concept of tribes (qabila) and, hence, the solidarity and governance structures between them. There is a collectivist governance mechanism via the tribes that also reflects how anticipatory governance is achieved at the national level, unlike in more individualist countries where governance needs different, more formal mechanisms. In this context, the individual (unlike in Western countries) is not the focal point of the governance system; instead, it is the group. The governance mechanism of the Arabs has ten layers — seven from the individual to the tribe level and another three from the tribe to the nation (see Exhibits 11.2(a) and 11.2(b)). These layers are immediate family, extended family, major branch of the subclan, subclan, clans, major branch of the tribe, tribe, major branch of the federation, and tribal federation of kinship, nation, or race.

---

[22]Many words are used to describe this phenomena: al qawmiya al 'arabiya (Arab nationalism), al wataniya al 'arabiya (Arab patriotism), al wihda al 'arabiya (Arab unity), al ittihad al 'Arabi (Arab union), and al 'uruba (Arabism or Arabhood); see https://www.graduateinstitute.ch/communications/news/rise-and-fall-pan-arabism.

[23]The Arab nationalism agenda was reaffirmed through the League of Arab States which was formed in March 1945. Many attempts have been made to unify the Arabs and created a state. In 1958, for example, United Arab Republic (UAR) was created briefly unifying Egypt and Syria from February 1958 to September 1961.

[24]The region has been ruled by the British, French, Italian, and Spanish and has had huge influence of the USA and the USSR, and now China.

[25]Mohammad-Mahmoud, O.M. (2018). The rise and fall of pan-Arabism. In Fiddian-Qasmiyeh, E. & Daley, P. (Eds), *The Handbook of South-South Relations*. London: Routledge: pp. 168–177.

Exhibit 11.2(a). 7 layers of governance: Individual to tribe.

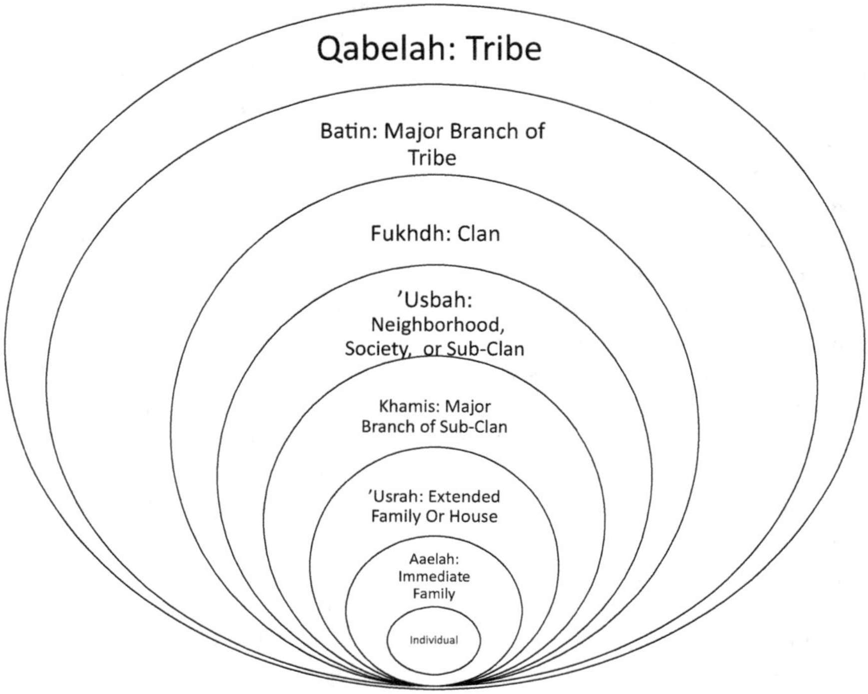

Source: Authors.

The name of the family and the tribe creates some level of commonality and forms a basis to encourage "*coordination, resource sharing, and collective defense*."[26] Justice at a tribal level is meted out through hierarchical rules and through consultations and negotiations where individual good is subordinate to collective good.[27] Most rulers and tribal leaders

[26] Weiner, S.J. (2016). *Kinship Politics in the Gulf Arab States*. Washington: The Arab Gulf States Institute: p. 3. Available: https://agsiw.org/wp-content/uploads/2016/07/Weiner_Kinship_Web.pdf (Accessed 8 January, 2024).

[27] For example, Bobseine, H. (2019). Tribal justice in a fragile Iraq. *The Century Foundation*. Available: https://tcf.org/content/report/tribal-justice-fragile-iraq/ (Accessed 10 January, 2024).

Exhibit 11.2(b). Three layers of governance: Nation to tribe.

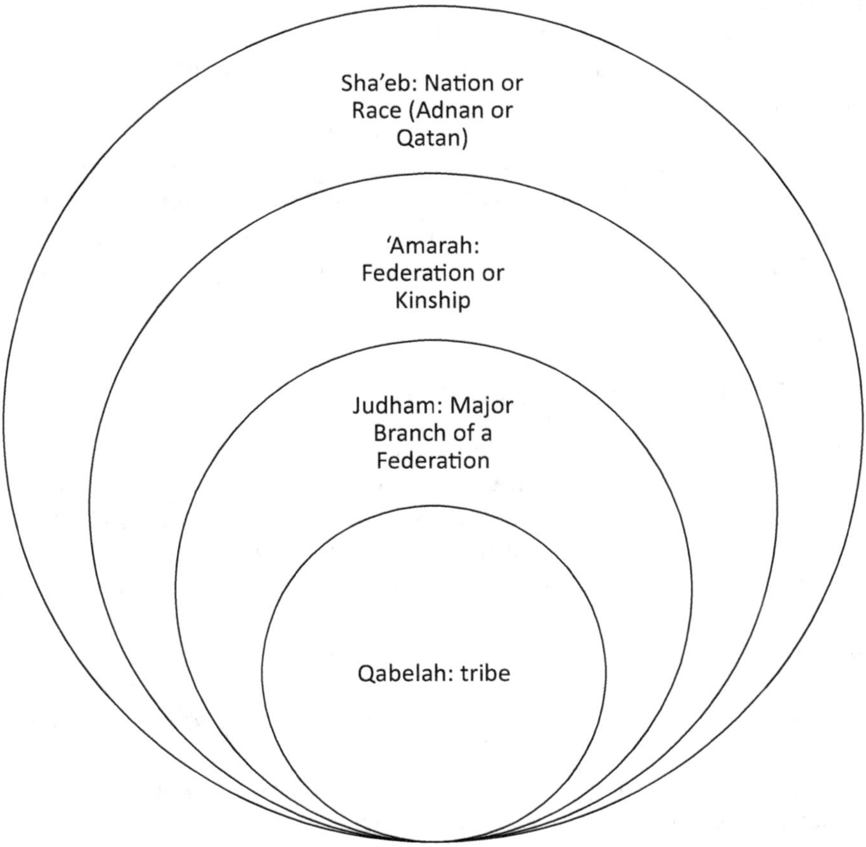

Source: Authors.

hold "court" — *majlis*, *diwan*, or *diwaniya*.[28] These forums act as platforms to negotiate, mediate, advocate, and resolve conflicts, and they are often filled with subtle meanings and symbolism. Sometimes, there is an assumption that tribalism is associated with religious extremism, but this is more a reflection of the political orientation of the leaders, as seen with the significant reforms KSA undertook in 2016, where the powers of the

[28]Albogam, K.F. (2020). How are Arab tribes structured. Available: https://www.quora.com/How-are-Arab-tribes-structured (Accessed 8 January, 2024); Weiner (2016), *Op. cit.*

religious police were restricted, ushering in a new, more open culture in the Kingdom.

To operate in the region, there is a necessity to understand these corridors of power or connections that extend from family relationships (including marriage via *kinship politics*[29]) to deeper genealogical or ancestral ties bound in history, geography, and shared experiences. Current boundaries of countries, defined by colonial treaties, do not consider the original dispersion of tribes across regions and the inter-relationships they have through marriage and their own agreements and treatises. It is estimated that 45% of married couples were closely related before marriage.[30]

11.3 Early Warning Signals (EWSs)

EWSs can be used to identify small incremental changes that lead to a tipping point in socio-political ecosystems.[31] A tipping point is a shift in the system from one state to another. Sonja Grimm and Gerald Schneider state the following in their discussion paper: "*In many cases, however, due to competing political, diplomatic, or economic reasons or due to the lack of political will, for example, international intervention comes too late or is so weak that it cannot prevent the unfolding disaster. Such failures often lead to ex-post facto expressions of consternation that a traumatizing event could have been prevented as it was allegedly easily predictable.*"[32]

These EWS failures sometimes make politicians worry about whether or not to heed the signals. One can associate two types of errors with

---

[29] Weiner (2016), *Op. cit.*

[30] Tadmouri, G.O., Al Ali, M.T., Al Khaja, N., Hamamy, H.A., Obeid, T., & Nair, P. (2009). Consanguinity and reproductive health among Arabs. *Reproductive Health*, 6: 17. DOI: 10.1186/1742-4755-6-17.

[31] Scheffer, M., *et. al.* (2009). Early-warning signals for critical transitions. *Nature*, 461(3): 53–59; Scheffer, M., *et al.* (2001). Catastrophic shifts in ecosystems. *Nature*, 413(6): 591–596; Taleb, N.N. (2007). *The Black Swan: The Impact of the Highly Improbable*. London: Penguin Books.

[32] Grimm, S. & Schneider, G. (2011). Predicting Social Tipping Points: Current Research and the Way Forward. German Development Institute. Available: https://edoc.vifapol.de/opus/volltexte/2011/3343/pdf/DP_8.2011.pdf (Accessed 27 January, 2023).

EWSs (see Exhibit 11.3). True positives are when predictions of events based on signals come true. True negatives are predictions of events that turn out wrong. Another challenge seems to be understanding the time in which an event may come to fruition and estimating the resources required or the impact. For example, some events take time to reach a tipping point and can catch governments unawares (like 9–11). There have been suggestions that terrorism signals are too small compared to the movement of troops and, hence, are missed by the EWS radars.[33] In these cases, policy-makers may adopt a wait-and-see approach.

Exhibit 11.3. Types of errors with EWSs.

	Occurred	**Not Occurred**
Predicted	True Positive	True Negative
Not Predicted	True Negative	True Positive

Source: Based on theory from Grimm and Schneider (2011).[34]

There are many issues one needs to manage before using EWSs for forecasting as shown in the following:[35]

1. Information — is the information in real time and reliable?
2. Information sharing and coordination — is the information reaching the right people in time for action? Who is responsible for collecting, who is to be warned, and who will act on the warning?[36]
3. What is the role of experience, analysis, and intuition for the event?

[33] Wirtz, J.J. (2013). Indications and warning in an age of uncertainty. *International Journal of Intelligence and CounterIntelligence*, 26(3): 550–562.

[34] *Ibid.*

[35] See, for example: Feil, S.R. (1998). *Preventing Genocide: How the Early Use of Force Might Have Succeeded in Rwanda.* New York, NY: Carnegie Commission on Preventing Deadly Conflict. In this piece, Feil argues that the Rwandan genocide may have been averted or at least minimized if as little as 5000 troops were deployed to the country in April 1994.

[36] Wulf, H. & Debiel, T. (2009). Conflict early warning and response mechanisms: Tools for enhancing the effectiveness of regional organisations? A comparative study of the AU, ECOWAS, IGAD, ASEAN/ARF and PIF. *Crisis States Working Papers Series* No. 2. Available: https://eprints.lse.ac.uk/28495/1/WP49.2.pdf (Accessed 27 January, 2023).

4. Learning — are the learnings shared to augment the EWS strategy?
5. Rare event — is the event an outlier (is there no precedent)?
6. Calling Wolf — what will be the impact of calling out a threat that does not come to realization (see Exhibit 11.4)?
7. What is the role of technology in gathering intelligence, and where is the emphasis? People, process (software and data included), or infrastructure?

In the case of false positives and false negatives, governments need to consider decision thresholds and the impact of these decisions on the public and the international community. In the case of technology intelligence, the focus must be on people.[37] EWSs need political will where a decision needs to be taken, assuming a point of no return has been reached.[38] The matter gets complicated if intervention is required in another country as the following question arises: Who will take the lead and responsibility?[39]

Exhibit 11.4. Warning detection matrix.

	No Threat	**Threat**
Warning	False Positive (false alarm)	True Positive (hit)
No Warning	True Negative (all clear)	False Negative (miss)

Source: Adapted from Choo (2009).[40]

[37] Shehabuddeen, N.T. & Probert, D.R. (2004). Excavating the technology landscape: Deploying technology intelligence to detect early warning signals. In *2004 IEEE International Engineering Management Conference* (IEEE Cat. No. 04CH37574), Vol. 1, pp. 332–336.

[38] Whittall, J. (2010). Humanitarian early warning systems: Myth and reality. *Third World Quarterly*, 31(8): 1237–1250.

[39] Krumm. D. (1988). Early warning: An action agenda. In Davies, J.L. & Gurr, T.R. (Eds.), *Preventive Measures*, pp. 248–255.

[40] Choo, C.W. (2009). Information use and early warning effectiveness: Perspectives and prospects. *Journal of the American Society for Information Science and Technology*, 60(5): 1071–1082.

11.4 To Hear the Whispers, You Need to Be Invited into the Corridors and Find the Right Room

The ability to listen to EWSs and *act* rather than *react* is an important characteristic of managing risks. Using timely information is essential. The World Economic Forum suggests that misinformation and disinformation are the biggest risks over the next two years.[41] What can governments do, and how do they listen in on conversations happening in these corridors? They must first create or access these corridors to find the right rooms.

Arguably, to understand EWSs in the Middle East, there is a need to comprehend the traditional tribal influence on "modern" Arab society. It is often what is meant and not so much what is said. Moreover, experienced diplomats in the region do not rely so much on what is publicly being debated; instead, they depend more on what is privately shared in the relevant corridors and rooms. Here, access becomes the main issue; the key is building trust. Naturally, building trust takes time and a lot of experience.

In some cases, this will also involve shuttle and subtle diplomacy, where the mediator goes between parties, choosing what information to keep and what to share to find common grounds to move issues forward.[42] So, do shuttle diplomacy and subtle diplomacy lead to trust, or vice versa? What are the right places to be seen when building bridges? The formal organizations, diplomacy, and networks are all intermingled in this complex space. Having an EWS strategy is about listening to multiple perspectives and being able to discern correct and actionable information. The following are a few examples of corridors.

11.4.1 *World Economic Forum in Middle East*

Some of the most powerful corridors are found in the Swiss Alpine village of Davos every January during the World Economic Forum. Gathering thousands of leaders from businesses and governments, the interactions that take place can lead to critical foresight as well as making new and

---

[41] WEF (2024). Global Risks Report 2024. Available: https://www.weforum.org/publications/global-risks-report-2024/digest/ (Accessed 14 February, 2024).

[42] Strongly associated with Kissinger and his work in the Middle East. Hoffman, D.A. (2011). Mediation and the art of shuttle diplomacy. *Negotiation Journal*, 27(3): 263–309.

essential allies and partnerships. Those who can leverage these opportunities are not necessarily the good speakers but the good listeners. A few examples stand out, such as the first visit to Davos of HM King Abdallah of Jordan in 2010. He came to Davos with the usual pomp and circumstance awarded to such prestigious first-time visitors to the World Economic Forum, including a plenary session address,[43] multiple media interviews, and bilateral meetings with political leaders from other nations.

However, the most important gathering on the King's agenda was one he had personally requested — to meet with 20 CEOs of large technology companies. This was in the early years of the new millennium, and the internet was invading our economies, societies, and companies — the King wanted to know more and, as such, asked for a one-hour meeting with the leaders of Microsoft, Intel, Cisco, and a few others. They were all gathered in a private room in one of the hotels, and when His Majesty arrived and sat among them, the room quietened. There was an awkward silence as the CEOs expected the King to read a speech or at least address them — but nothing of the sort was on the King's mind.

Breaking the silence, the King explained that he had come to listen and wanted to learn how he, as King, should look at the IT revolution that was unfolding to benefit Jordan's main natural resource — its people. Over the following 55 minutes, the stunned CEOs started providing advice, guidance, and ideas. One of the central ideas that emanated was to seek ways to modernize Jordan's educational system and use technology to make it available throughout the country. As the meeting was ending, one CEO stood up and passed a bowl around, asking those CEOs interested in helping King Abdallah execute this strategy to put their business cards in the bowl. That meeting led to a massive revamp of Jordan's educational system over the years and has made the Kingdom one of the region's primary sources of entrepreneurship and start-ups.

The WEF has historically been an important corridor for EWSs and whispers. Nelson Mandela came to Davos in 1992 for the first time, accompanied by a delegation from his party, the ANC. This was two years before the historic election in South Africa in 1994. Mr. Mandela was in Davos with his economic team to meet international business leaders to encourage future investments in the country once fair and free elections

[43] H.M. King Abdullah II Ibn Al Hussein (2010). Interview at Davos. *YouTube*, 29 January. Available: https://www.youtube.com/watch?v=96Z18I2UKAE (Accessed 13 February, 2023).

held. During his three-day visit, he also had a major session in the plenary hall on the political future of South Africa — but the rest of the time, he attended sessions and panels led by Chief Executives of large companies, listening to their views on where in the world they were investing and what prerequisites were critical to attracting FDI.

It is important to note that the ANC's economic policy at the time was centered on nationalizing key industries in the country with a view of redistributing wealth in the country to the millions of South Africans who were unable to participate in the economy due to the imposition of apartheid. As Nelson Mandela and his team listened over the three days of their visit, they realized that no foreign investor would look at South Africa with the government taking back control of major sectors of the economy.

Nelson Mandela walked out of a bilateral meeting with the Chinese Premier at the time, Li Peng, determined to reverse the ANC's Economic Manifesto on Nationalization. Indeed, the Chinese leader told the future president of South Africa that China's government was embarking on a massive divestment from state-owned enterprises and launching a privatization program at the national level.[44] Stephen R. Covey (author of 7 Habits of Highly Effective People) perfectly captures these two examples when he writes, "*Most people do not listen with the intent to understand; they listen with the intent to reply.*"[45]

11.4.2 *Strategic alliances*

One of the earliest Arab associations was the Arab League, which began in 1945.[46] Its primary objective was coordinating the political, cultural,

---

[44]Sorkin, A.R. (2013). How Mandela shifted views on freedom of markets. *The New York Times*, 9 December. Available: https://archive.nytimes.com/dealbook.nytimes.com/2013/12/09/how-mandela-shifted-views-on-freedom-of-markets/ (Accessed 14 February, 2024).

[45]Covey, S.R. (1989). *7 Habits of Highly Effective People: Powerful Lessons in Personal Change*. New York: Fireside.

[46]Founding members were Egypt, Syria, Lebanon, Iraq, Transjordan (now Jordan), Saudi Arabia, and Yemen. Later, other countries joined: Libya (1953); Sudan (1956); Tunisia and Morocco (1958); Kuwait (1961); Algeria (1962); Bahrain, Oman, Qatar, and the United Arab Emirates (1971); Mauritania (1973); Somalia (1974); the Palestine Liberation Organization (PLO; 1976); Djibouti (1977); and Comoros (1993).

economic, and social programs between countries and mediating disputes.[47] In 1964, the PLO was given observer status to represent the Palestinians, and later, in 1976, it upgraded to full membership. The League has suspended and reinstated membership to align members to common goals. For example, Egypt was suspended after signing a treaty with Israel in 1979 and reinstated in 1989. In February 2011, following Libya's handling of the Arab Spring, it was removed from the League and reinstated later in August of the same year. Syria was given ten months to stop its violent campaign against protesters, during which half a million people were killed and another 23 million displaced following the Arab Spring. When Damascus did not comply, Syria was removed in 2013 and reinstated in 2023.[48] This reinstatement occurred after the KSA Foreign Minister Prince Faisal bin Farhan Al Saud visited President Bashar al-Assad, and the League voted to find a regional solution for the problem. Assistant Secretary-General of the Arab League Hossam Zaki commented about the decision, "*The understanding that has been growing for the past several months, especially after the catastrophe of the earthquake, is that there is no clear international attention that is supposed to be driving for a solution in Syria... The Syrian crisis has been spilling over very negative effects on the neighboring countries. The neighboring countries and the region, especially the Arab countries, feel that this situation needs to be resolved. This is why we reached this point.*"[49]

Other endeavors have taken place in the form of treaties, MOUs, or councils, but the impact on economic integration has been slower.[50] The Greater Arab Free Trade Area (GAFTA) was signed by 14 Arab countries

---

[47] Britannica (2024). Arab League. Available: https://www.britannica.com/topic/Arab-League (Accessed 14 February, 2024).

[48] Other events also happened, an earthquake in Turkey and Syria and a China-brokered agreement to restore ties between KSA and Iran. See Al Jazeera (2023). Arab League agrees to bring Syria back into its fold. Available: https://www.aljazeera.com/news/2023/5/7/arab-league-agrees-to-bring-syria-back-into-its-fold (Accessed 14 February, 2024).

[49] *Ibid.*

[50] For example, the ideas being explored include a single GCC currency. More on economic integration is available here: Abedini, J. & Péridy, N. (2008). The greater Arab free trade area (GAFTA): An estimation of its trade effects. *Journal of Economic Integration*, 23(4): 848–872.

in 1997 to begin free trade by 2007. GAFTA embeds the Gulf Cooperation Council (GCC) and the Arab League. In terms of impact, GAFTA intra-exports have increased by an average of 15.1% pa, compared to world exports of 7.9% during 1997–2005.[51]

The Gulf Cooperation Council (GCC) was established in an agreement between the Kingdom of Saudi Arabia, Bahrain, Kuwait, Oman, Qatar, and the UAE in 1981.[52] During the 2011 Arab Spring, Jordan and Morocco were invited to join the GCC (Morocco declined, and Jordan's entry was delayed). Between 2017 and 2021,[53] Egypt, KSA, UAE, and Bahrain cut diplomatic ties and instituted a ground, sea, and air blockade against Qatar, citing that Qatar had violated a 2014 pact that undermined regional security by publicizing the Arab Spring, forging ties with other countries like Iran and Turkey, and being friendly with the Muslim Brotherhood. Kuwait led the mediation via shuttle diplomacy.[54] Sheikh Jaber Al Sabah, Kuwait's Foreign Minister for 38 years and the Emir of Kuwait from 2006–2020, an elder statesman respected by the GCC, valued by the Qataris, and considered neutral by all involved GCC parties, was the intermediary. As part of the resolution, the WTO lawsuits filed by Qatar were withdrawn.

A strategic bilateral agreement can be with other partners, like the one the USA has put in place with the UAE. While the relationship with Iran is complicated, the USA has used the UAE as a "Riga Station," where

---

[51] *Ibid.*

[52] The GCC is run by the Supreme Council, which comprises the heads of state of the six member countries. The Ministerial Council, which comprises the foreign ministers of the six member countries, reports to the Supreme Council. The GCC Chairmanship is rotated and resolutions are voted upon. The main objective of the GCC is enshrined in Article 4, which states that the alliance was to strengthen ties between the member states and promote cooperation.

[53] Ulrichsen, K.C. (2021). Saudi Arabia just lifted its Qatar's 43 month blockade: How did this rift end? *Washington Post*, 8 January. Available: https://www.washingtonpost.com/politics/2021/01/08/saudi-arabia-just-lifted-qatars-43-month-blockade-how-did-this-rift-end/ (Accessed 14 February, 2024).

[54] Altiok, H. (2023). Kuwait's mediation in the Gulf crisis: Dynamics of Kuwait's foreign policy approaches. In Rahman, M.M. & Al-Azm, A. (Eds.), *Social Change in the Gulf Region*. Gulf Studies. Singapore: Springer: p. 8. https://doi.org/10.1007/978-981-19-7796-1_35.

they could watch and understand a nation with whom they had no direct diplomatic relations,[55] setting up the Iran Regional Presence Office (IRPO) in 2006. The UAE has always tried to maintain neutrality.

11.4.3 *Network ties*

The heart of any diplomatic mission is people. Often, their personal power and official stance (versus personal viewpoints) are confused. Even before the invasion of Iraq,[56] UAE's Sheikh Zayed Bin Sultan Al Nahyan and Sheikh Mohammed bin Rashid Al Maktoum tried to dissuade President George Bush[57] from the Iraq invasion. Sheikh Mohammed bin Rashid even traveled to Basra and met Saddam Hussein.[58] Over 5 hours, he attempted to convince him to leave Iraq to avoid more bloodshed, but Sadam refused.[59]

---

[55]Burns, R.N. (2006). U.S. Policy Toward Iran. Speech at Council on Foreign Relations. October 11. Transcript available at www.cfr.org/iran/us-policy-toward-iran-rush-transcript-federal-news-service/p11698.

[56]Iraq engaged in war with Iran in 1980s, leading to the death of over 1 million people, devastating the Iraqi economy, making its army the fourth-largest globally, and leading to the invasion of Kuwait to recover the costs spent in the war. Due to overproduction, the price of crude oil dropped in July from US$18 to US$12 per barrel, further hurting the Iraqi economy. Available: https://www.nytimes.com/1990/07/18/business/iraq-threatens-emirates-and-kuwait-on-oil-glut.html.

[57]The USA was the third country to recognize the new state of UAE in 1971, according to Carnegie Papers, however Jordan was the first, after Iraq (and of course UK as UAE was under the Trucial States). See https://carnegieendowment.org/files/dubai_iran.pdf. The formal agreement came later: https://www.state.gov/u-s-relations-with-united-arab-emirates/#:~:text=The%20United%20States%20has%20had,formal%20diplomatic%20relations%20in%201972.

[58]The GCC was founded in 1981, aligning itself with the UAE and supporting Iraq in the Iran–Iraq War and needed to keep shipping lanes in the Arabian Gulf open, but when Iraq invaded Kuwait, Desert Storm had UAE's support. UAE remains the top export destination for the USA in the MENA region. See https://www.uae-embassy.org/uae-us-cooperation/uae-us-trade.

[59]Reynolds, R. (2019). Sheikh Mohammed offered Saddam Hussein Asylum in 2003, he reveals in new autobiography. *The National*, 16 January. Available: https://www.thenationalnews.com/uae/government/sheikh-mohammed-offered-saddam-hussein-asylum-in-2003-he-reveals-in-new-autobiography-1.813014 (Accessed 14 February, 2024).

When Sultan Abdülaziz (Ottoman Empire/Turkey) visited the 1867[60] World Fair in Paris with a diplomatic delegation of 41 people, following the visit of Governor Isma'il Pasha of Egypt,[61] it was clear there was a cultural divide (based on representation, authenticity, and popularity), suggesting that narratives need to be interpreted through symbols and actions, before listening.[62] The Ottoman Empire had a choice of banks — some were Western interested parties (the Rothschild Group and the Perierre Brothers). However, they preferred the British group that existed in a private capacity as the Ottoman Bank in 1856[63] and gave it a privileged status in 1863. This was because of the bank's previous success in Egypt with the Bank of Egypt (1856) and based on the Egyptian experience, the likelihood that the bank in Turkey would be relatively independent in running their operations, with reduced influence from Britain in the venture.[64] The bank eventually extended its reach to Libya.

In the wake of World War I, when the Ottoman Empire aligned itself with Germany, the British needed to weaken the Ottoman presence in Arabia. A British Army officer by the name of Thomas Edward Lawrence (later became the legendary Lawrence of Arabia) was sent from Cairo to negotiate with Sharif Hussain Bin Ali, the ruler of Hijaz (the Mecca and

---

[60]In 1863, Sultan Abdülaziz had his first overseas trip was to Egypt and Europe. In 1867, he visited Napoleon III in France, Queen Victoria in England, King Leopold in Belgium, and Emperor Francois Joseph in Austria. However, what is interesting is that in 1856, the Ottoman Bank was opened (by a private British investment), which was granted a privileged status in 1863, acting as a central bank issuing banknotes and loans. When the one lira banknote was issued, it had inscriptions in five languages, Turkish, French, Greek, Armenian, and Arabic, suggesting global trade ties.

[61]Displaying the Orient. Available: https://publishing.cdlib.org/ucpressebooks/view?docId=ft8x0nb62g&chunk.id=d0e747&toc.id=&brand=ucpress.

[62]For example, an early ethnographer, Ahmed Midhat, wrote about the streets of Cairo and objected to the representation of Egypt through belly dancers; https://histanthro.org/notes/orientalism-alla-turca/.

[63]Prior to the visit, a British (later French-British) bank called the Ottoman Bank, founded in 1856 existed.

[64]Autheman, A. (1996). I. L'Ottoman Bank". La Banque impériale ottomane. Histoire économique et financière - XIXe-XXe. Paris: Institut de la gestion publique et du développement économique: Comité pour l'Histoire Economique et Financière de la France: pp. 1–20.

Madina regions and most of the west and north of the peninsula) to encourage a rebellion against the Ottomans in return for independence and self-rule. Lawrence spoke eloquent Arabic, was an archeologist, and deeply understood Arab/Bedouin culture and values. He even dressed up as a Bedouin, skillfully rode a camel, and acquired a genuine appreciation for the Arab desire for liberation. Lawrence quickly gained the trust and respect of many Arab rulers and tribal leaders at the time, including Prince Faisal Bin Al Hussein, younger brother of King Abdullah II of Jordan.

In 1916, the Great Arab Revolt started in Mecca and, within a few years, spread to Jordan, Syria, Iraq, and the wider region. The rest is history. Lawrence was an astute negotiator, a skillful military strategist, and a good fighter himself. He orchestrated a number of key raids on the Ottoman rail roads in Hijaz and Jordan that drained Ottoman military supplies, which ultimately led to the fall of the Ottoman strategic stronghold in the Gulf of Aqaba and the subsequent overtaking of its fort in an impressive campaign. While it is sometimes difficult to separate the man from the legend, the story of the Lawrence of Arabia is quintessential EWS and shuttle diplomacy — quintessential in understanding a culture, gaining trust through words and deeds, being an honest broker and a respected deal maker.

11.5 Diplomacy Has a Cascading Effect and Can Be Used to Listen

There are many types of diplomacy, all of which are ears on the ground (depicted in Exhibit 11.5). Even after the Iraq invasion, the UAE sent humanitarian aid to Iraq and called for the sanctions against Baghdad to be lifted, canceled US$7 billion in debt, and reopened the embassy in Baghdad after ten years of Kuwait's invasion.[65] Diplomacy allows corridors to be opened that will enable the flow of information.

[65] Bonesh, F.R. (2022). UAE's approach to Iraq. Al-Bayan Centre for Planning and Studies. Available: https://www.bayancenter.org/en/2022/10/3504/ (Accessed 14 February, 2024).

Exhibit 11.5. Types of diplomacy — Examples from MENA.

Type of Diplomacy	Examples
Economic diplomacy: Influencing economic policies of partner countries	UAE-India CEPA entered into force on May 1, 2022, resulting in the removal of tariffs on more than 80 percent of products for UAE exporters. Further, in July 2023, there was the ability to trade in local currency (enhanced with UPI's RuPay digital platform in February 2024).
Financial diplomacy: Creating fiscal stability in the host country	Over US$ 21 billion was provided as capital to US companies Citigroup and Merrill Lynch during the 2007–2009 financial crisis by SWFs from UAE, Kuwait, Singapore, and South Korea.
Business or commercial diplomacy: Focuses on FDI and inward and outward investment	SWFs like KSA's PIF and UAE's Mubadala invest in Soft Bank, which invests in start-ups. Careem, UAE's first unicorn, received funding from regional investors like Saudi Telecom Company, Abraaj Group, Al Tayyar Group, Beco Capital, Lumia Capital and Wamda Capital. Uber which had funding from Saudi Public Investment Fund, acquired Careem in 2019.
Science and technology diplomacy	UAE's NIMR will also produce Jais armored vehicles in KSA.[66] RuPay introduced into UAE will use the India Stack.
Education diplomacy	India sets up a branch of IIT Delhi in Abu Dhabi. KSA will send 70,000 Saudis to 200 foreign universities to study by 2030. The UAE Gov Knowledge Exchange program focuses on capacity building for foreign government officials and sharing best practices.
People diplomacy	UAE Minister of State for AI (first one in the world). UAE (Nakheel) offered a home to Shah Rukh Khan, the Bollywood superstar. Literary giants: the poet Jalāl al-Dīn Muḥammad Rūmī (Iran) or author Khalil Gibran (Lebanese American author). The Pope's visit to the UAE (also overlaps with religious diplomacy).

(*Continued*)

[66] See, for example: https://breakingdefense.com/2024/02/uaes-nimr-debuts-jais-mk2-armored-vehicle-tech-transfer-to-saudi-arabia-on-track/.

Exhibit 11.5. (*Continued*)

Type of Diplomacy	MENA and EWSs
Cultural diplomacy	Tourism to Egypt and the pyramids, or Fez in Morocco.
Sports diplomacy	F1 in UAE's Abu Dhabi, Bahrain, KSA, and Qatar.
Religious diplomacy	Mecca, in KSA, Mount Nebu (where Moses died), Jordan, Bethlehem, or Cairo, where baby Jesus resided.
Humanitarian diplomacy	Dubai hosts the world's largest humanitarian aid logistics center; Egypt, Qatar, and the USA negotiated for a ceasefire in Gaza before the 2024 Ramadan between Hamas and Israel (which failed for the timeframe).
Peace diplomacy	The Abraham Accords were signed between UAE, Bahrain, and Israel (and later Morocco) in 2020; the UAE's negotiation on prisoner release between Ukraine and Russia.

Source: Adapted from Stephens (2024).[67]

Diplomacy can result in soft power though the exchange of knowledge and experience. The UAE government has embarked on an international campaign promoting bilateral capacity building. The Government Knowledge Exchange program was established at the federal level under the UAE Ministry of Cabinet Affairs. As of early 2024, over 20 countries have participated, from Uzbekistan to Zimbabwe through Malta and Jordan. This program focuses on senior government officials and exposes them to new experiences of government practices through seminars, site visits, coaching sessions, and executive projects. The aim is to help officials find solutions that work for their context and serve as a platform for knowledge exchange and, most importantly, relationship building. The purpose is to listen and learn from each other's experiences to build a better world together.

[67] Stephens, M. (2024). Leveraging Sovereign Wealth Funds for Soft Power. In J. Harris, K. Baker, & . Nakshabandi (Eds.). *The Palgrave Handbook of Sovereign Wealth Funds*. ISBN978-3-031-50820-2.

11.6 Steps to Create an EWS in Global Corridors

We recommend the following four steps to use EWSs in global corridors to build anticipatory governance mechanisms:

1. **Listen.** The first step to getting access to global corridors is to listen. There is a wealth of knowledge and local experience out there, and each entity (public or private) has its own expertise that needs to be respected. Technology may allow diplomats to "listen,"[68] but to understand, it may depend on how they confront their biases and understand the context.
2. **Be present.** Once the corridors to be accessed are known, the next step is to gain access to the right rooms and be present. Those who are absent may be left behind. Just turning up signals willingness to listen and hence be listened to. Knowledge is a weapon that can be used constructively to shape the future.
3. **Create venues and opportunities for discussion.** Not everyone can afford to be present at large global gatherings. If there is no invitation, then create your event or forum and invite critical parties. Rather than compete, collaborate or augment existing discussions. These activities build foundations of trust, a powerful weapon in times of need.
4. **Lobby for others — to build bridges of trust.** The global arena is complex, and the ability to find and create relationships with partners along the journey, to help with the strategic alignment of goals and mutual benefits is needed. This can only be done through lobbying for others and building bridges of trust.

---

[68] Di Martino, L. (2019). The spectrum of listening. *CPD Blog*, 26 August, Available: https://uscpublicdiplomacy.org/blog/spectrum-listening (Accessed 14 February, 2024).

Section 3

Governing Advanced Technology

https://doi.org/10.1142/9789811296000_0012

Chapter 12

Technology Anticipation and Regulation

Patrick Noack

Future Foresight and Imagination,
Dubai Future Foundation, Dubai, UAE

Key Takeaways

- Technology development and spillover are faster than governments can regulate.
- The regulatory space is complex, and even self-regulation has challenges.
- Governments need to anticipate technology turns and prepare for them through foresight.
- Governments need to build more regulatory sandboxes to ensure that beta tests are also useful for regulatory oversight.
- Governments should embrace *in silico* regulations (experimenting using computer simulations).

12.1 Degrees of Separation: Tech Anticipation and Regulations

French philosopher Paul Virilio was known for his writings about technology. He wrote an important quote that illustrates the need for anticipatory governance when it comes to technology:

> "*When you invent the ship, you also invent the shipwreck; when you invent the plane, you also invent the plane crash; and when you invent*

electricity, you invent electrocution...Every technology carries its own negativity, which is invented at the same time as technical progress."[1]

The ship and the shipwreck are directly linked, separate by just one degree, and therefore their connection is intuitive. Regulation that ensures passenger safety, or the protection of the environment is in principle quite straightforward. To remain with the aircraft analogy, flight technology has been around for over 100 years. This technology was evolutionary and incremental: It began with experimental flights, then single-engine and single-seater aircraft, then bigger, faster, further, and better.

Along that journey, insight was gained, often painfully, that could be built into subsequent models and iterations. This matters because at no point were the lives, the livelihoods, or the finances of a significant proportion of the world at risk in one fell swoop. It is also fair to assume that the first industrial revolution, which occurred in Britain in the 1750s and ostensibly is the enabler of the early (and ultimately the current) flight industry, moved at a slower pace than subsequent industrial revolutions.

By slower pace, I mean the speed at which technology is developed from science and engineering, and, ultimately, the time it has taken for prototypes to be adopted by markets and shift the way of doing business at a global scale. The pace of technology distribution is far more rapid now, 250 years since the dawn of the first industrial revolution and three industrial revolutions later,[2] and increasingly, there are use cases and technologies where widespread safety cannot be assured without regulation because their dissemination and market penetration are swift and deep.

Not only is the length of each revolution shorter[3] but the time to technology is shorter, too. And this is what futurist Ray Kurzweil means by an

---

[1] Virilio, P. (1999). *Politics of the Very Worst.* New York: Semiotext(e): p. 89.

[2] Schwab, K. (2015). The fourth industrial revolution: What it means and how to respond. *Foreign Affairs*, 12 December, Available: https://www.foreignaffairs.com/world/fourth-industrial-revolution (Accessed 7 January, 2024).

[3] Older technologies (cars, lighting, nuclear power, ATMs, etc.) took a median time of 32 years from invention to commercialisation: Gross, R., Hanna, R., Gambhir, A., Heptonstall, P., & Speirs, J. (2018). How long does innovation and commercialisation in the energy sectors take? Historical case studies of the timescale from invention to widespread commercialisation in energy supply and end use technology. *Energy Policy*, 123: 682–699. In healthcare, it takes 17 years for research evidence to reach clinical practice, (Morris, Z.S., Wooding, S., & Grant, J. (2011). The answer is 17 years, what is the question: Understanding time lags in translational research. *Journal of the Royal Society of*

era of exponential growth and accelerating returns[4] — faster technological and other growth that results from previous technologies and in increasingly greater returns for the user, investor, and perhaps society at large. While it is easy to be carried away by future prospects of such an accelerating proposition, it more than highlights the need for anticipatory governance.

Suddenly, a piece of software is accessed or downloaded by millions — even billions — even in beta testing phases.[5] And these may not conform to regulation because regulation may not exist or existing regulation may not be adequate. Historically and characteristically, the regulators are lagging behind the developers, and for good reason: The pace of innovation is fast, while the bureaucratic velocity of regulation may be slowing down and is inversely proportional to the growing number of new "products" to regulate. The temptation for regulators to push their mandate to the entrepreneurs or the private sector in an effort to self-regulate has ended in variable results.

There is a growing need to anticipate technology or the technology turns, which can be described as changes or shifts in the directionality of its assessment — whether the focus is the conditions of technology, its impact on society, or the ethics of the technological development.[6]

Medicine, 104(12): 510–520. DOI: 10.1258/jrsm.2011.110180), but the internet and AI is changing this situation rapidly.

[4] See, for example: https://www.thekurzweillibrary.com/the-law-of-accelerating-returns (Accessed 6 January, 2024).

[5] Take, for example, OpenAI's Chat GPT which has also been embedded in many other products like Microsoft's CoPilot. There has been a movement toward public beta testing even though it means the product is not ready yet at scale to garner word of mouth and increase profits: Jiang, Z., Scheibe, K.P., Nilakanta, S., & Qu, X. (2017). The economics of public beta testing. *Decision Sciences*, 48(1): 150–175.

[6] With respect to technology, there have been several turns — empirical, experimental, practice, and ethical — and the philosophical question remains: Is the human who makes and uses the technology the focus or the technology that the human created? For example, see Verbeek, P.P. (2010). Accompanying technology: Philosophy of technology after the ethical turn. *Techné: Research in Philosophy and Technology*, 14(1): 49–54; Nordmann, A. (2016). Changing perspectives: The technological turn in the philosophies of science and technology. *Philosophy of Technology after the Empirical Turn*, pp. 107–125.

12.2 Global Regulatory Responses to Advanced Tech

One interesting case was the United Kingdom's "Responsibility Deals," where tripartite groupings were established between the government (for example, the National Health Service, the NHS, in the UK), the wider public (or the consumers of a product or class of products to be regulated), and the private sector seeking regulatory clarity and license to operate in a complex space. Such complex spaces have included efforts to "nudge" rather than regulate consumers toward healthier food choices. However, these efforts have not always led to the desired outcomes, and the responsibility deal agenda might be better served by shaping the regulation around improving processed food formulations.[7]

The attempt was noble because it sought to identify an ideal set of recommendations that would balance the priorities and needs of each stakeholder. While appealing and, in principle, a good strategy, it failed to understand and address the power imbalances of each stakeholder group and ultimately, the faction with most powers of persuasion won the day. More recently, the cases of social media companies attempting half-heartedly to self-regulate the content on their platforms have showcased convincingly the challenge of self-regulation that results from regulators not stepping up and the public suffering as a result. Anticipatory regulation is, therefore, key. There is also an unexpected ingredient to successful regulation that has not been explored enough: the role of the city or country where (anticipatory) regulation happens.

There are some places — cities mostly, regions on occasion — that have historically attracted talent and technology development — London, Paris, California, Bangalore, and many more. The confluence of knowledge, opportunity, a workforce, finance, and, well, lack of regulation was at the core of the boom these locations have enjoyed. What this has resulted in was a hotbed of activity because the ingredients were right. Whether it was about engineering marvels in London, the gold rush in California, the emergence of Silicon Valley, or the appearance of Bangalore as a tech hub, development *preceded* regulation. Just because this pattern has held true for centuries is no good reason to assume it could not be

[7]See, for example, Srinivasan, C.S. (2015). UK public health responsibility deals — can they nudge consumers towards healthier diets? In *89th Annual Conference — Agricultural Economics Society*, April 13–15. Coventry, UK: Warwick University. Available: https://ideas.repec.org/p/ags/aesc15/204208.html (Accessed 10 January, 2024).

reversed. In fact, it needs to be upended because the stakes are ever-increasing in this age of exponential growth. Exponential risks require that.

12.3 The Case of Dubai

Dubai is a location that has all the right ingredients to make this happen and is fast becoming a location to develop regulation in a technology-friendly and future-facing city. To borrow from a futures approach, the Futures Triangle developed by Sohail Inayatullah[8] is a good concept that could be used to explain how certain locations are more future oriented than others, at a particular point in time balancing the weight of the history, the pull of the future, and the push of the present.

To assess the weight of history, we might explore what is holding us back, the barriers to change, or the deep structures that resist change. Push of the present examines the trends pushing toward particular futures. The pull of the future is about compelling images of the future (i.e., you "can't not" go there).[9]

In Dubai, and in relation to anticipatory governance and regulation, at present, there are few structures that resist change — a strong push of the present to a future infused with emerging technology and a strong pull from the future to leverage a comparative advantage to reach a futuristic image of the future in as short a time as possible.

For example, the Dubai Future Foundation has recently utilized the Dubai Experimental Zone mechanism within the Dubai Silicon Oasis (DSO) to generate regulation to fly drones Beyond the Visual Line of Sight (BVLOS).[10] The work was carried out with the Dubai Civil Aviation

---

[8] Inayatullah, S. (2008). Six pillars: Futures thinking for transforming. *Foresight*, 10(1). DOI: 10.1108/14636680810855991.

[9] See, for example, Riedy, C. (2012). The futures triangle. *Medium*, 5 November. Available: https://medium.com/@chrisjriedy/the-futures-triangle-7ef2ed728a02 (Accessed 10 January, 2024).

[10] The Dubai government has been looking at the potential of drone technology for some time: The Dubai Sky Dome policy was approved in 2018. The Dubai Civil Aviation Authority issued comprehensive standards and legislations to regulate the use of drones like Law No. (4) Of 2020. For more on the BVLOS, see: Government of Dubai Media Office (2023). Dubai Silicon Oasis hosts groundbreaking three-week BVLOS drone delivery trials. Available: https://mediaoffice.ae/en/news/2023/October/08-10/Dubai-Silicon-Oasis-hosts-groundbreaking-three-week-BVLOS-drone-delivery-trials (Accessed 7 January, 2023).

Authority (DCAA), Dubai Future Labs, and private commercial entities. In recent years, drones have become increasingly ubiquitous and applications tied to deliveries of up to 250 g are being assessed. The delivery of small packets by drone is gaining interest as a means to reducing cost, traffic, and emissions, promoting sustainability and ultimately reliability of delivery. So, this could be termed an "emerging technology" because in various jurisdictions there is no regulation for automated delivery by drones beyond the line of sight.[11]

In this instance, a space was allocated within the DSO to evaluate the technology over the course of one year. While ultimately the regulation was developed,[12] experiment participants highlighted some of the challenges, including the following:

- delays due to administration and existing trial agreements;
- fragmented responsibilities among experiment participants and regulators;
- the existence of responsibility without authority of some stakeholders.

It was also felt by some commercial participants that the time for the experiment was too long, resulting in greater costs. Finally, while regulation is applicable to all, the burden in co-developing regulation shouldered by early adopters is far greater than that of the companies unwilling to engage in the process and later benefit from the regulation or the certification process. This means that it can be challenging to engage the stakeholders needed to develop the regulation needed for emerging technologies.

Anticipatory governance is a way to balance the three elements of present, past, and future in a way that is aligned with the objectives of the

[11] Some African countries, like Rwanda, Ghana, Nigeria, and Kenya, have used drone deliveries for medical supplies. There are few metros where drones are being used for commercial activities. So far, the deliveries are being led by drone companies (not being led by government regulations). See Palmer, A. (2023). Amazon's drone business can't get off the ground as regulations, weak demand stymie progress. *CNBC*, 11 March. Available: https://www.cnbc.com/2023/03/11/amazon-prime-air-drone-business-stymied-by-regulations-weak-demand.html (Accessed 8 January 2023).

[12] For the full regulation, see here: Government of Dubai (2023). Dubai Civil Regulations for UAS Operations. Available: https://betawebapi.dcaa.gov.ae/Uploads/Dubai%20Civil%20Aviation%20Regulations%20for%20UAS%20Operations.pdf (Accessed 8 January 2023).

government, in relation to emerging technologies and future developments as well as taking into consideration the potential future risks of emerging technologies. The constant quest toward the future is an asset for countries and cities to attract the best talent and shape the future/respond to current and future challenges.

Finally, the continuing developments in artificial intelligence should not go untested in the anticipatory governance and regulations space. If AI can help engineers trial hundreds of designs of rocket nozzles and pick the most effective one — rather than physically building each one and testing it on a rocket[13] — could and should AI hold promise in optimizing regulation for emerging technology? This is *in silico* regulation so to speak. Consider the advantages: Many of the parameters required for experiments that lead to regulation could be easily tested or verified within an AI environment. This may include review of the paperwork, licenses, approvals, etc., for companies participating in the trials. Then there is the review and comparison of existing regulations within the country and a comparative analysis of laws existing in other jurisdictions.

12.4 Creating a Regulatory Capacity for *In Silico* Regulation

To create a regulatory capacity for *in silico* regulations, governments can specifically focus on four key outcomes as described below.

12.4.1 *Outcomes*

Efficient analysis: AI can sift through vast amounts of data, identifying patterns and potential risks associated with emerging technologies faster and more comprehensively than humans. This could improve the speed and accuracy of regulatory frameworks. For example, imagine the sheer volume of data generated by autonomous vehicles. AI systems could analyze accident reports, traffic patterns, and sensor data in real time,

[13] See, for example: Hyperganic (2022). We just built the world's largest 3D-printed aerospike rocket engine. *Lins Blog*, 22 May. Available: https://hyweb-wordpress.dply.hyperganic.com/blog/we-just-built-the-worlds-largest-3d-printed-aerospike-rocket-engine/ (Accessed 13 February, 2024).

identifying potential flaws or safety risks that human analysis might miss. This could inform regulations on vehicle design, software updates, and driver training, significantly improving safety and preventing accidents. This means governments need to focus on standardizing data formats for data analysis, have clear guidelines on data access, privacy guidelines, and security, and also have central open-source data repositories that are anonymized to optimize data use and increase its spillovers.

Predictive power: AI models could anticipate the potential ethical and societal impacts of new technologies before they reach large-scale deployment, allowing for proactive mitigation measures. For example, AI models could be trained on historical data relating to environmental impacts from various technologies, like gene editing or nanomaterials. By feeding in data on a new technology's properties, the model could predict potential ecological risks and guide the development of regulations to minimize harm before widespread adoption. Here, government regulators need to have a way to ensure the data used for predictive power are verifiable and the contexts in which assumptions are being made (synthetic data, biased data, etc.) are transparent for policy decision-makers.

Personalized regulation: AI could help tailor regulations to specific situations and contexts, accounting for the nuances of different technologies, applications, and jurisdictions. For technologies with varied applications, AI could analyze the specific context of their use and tailor regulations accordingly. For example, AI-powered drones could be subject to stricter safety and privacy regulations when operating in densely populated areas compared to remote landscapes. Governments need to decide when and how personalized regulations are utilized and to ensure the citizen has choice and agency.

Continuous monitoring: AI systems could continuously monitor the use of emerging technologies and policy lapses, flagging potential issues and recommending adjustments to regulations in real time. AI systems could constantly monitor social media and news outlets for emerging ethical concerns surrounding a new technology like facial recognition. This system could detect and flag potential biases, discrimination, or privacy violations, triggering real-time regulatory updates or intervention. Governments might decide to create early warning systems and structures to respond to issues flagged by AI tools.

12.4.2 *Challenges*

On the other hand, there are clear challenges associated with the use of AI in shaping regulation as shown across a range of topics:

Bias and fairness: AI algorithms can perpetuate existing biases, leading to discriminatory regulations. Transparency and rigorous oversight would be crucial to ensure fairness and equitable outcomes. Transparency and rigorous oversight would be crucial to ensure fairness and equitable outcomes by:

- Diversity in data: Actively collect and integrate data representing diverse demographics and contexts to prevent bias from creeping into AI models. This could involve collaborating with marginalized communities and incorporating real-world datasets reflecting various scenarios.
- Algorithmic audits and fairness testing: Regularly assess AI models for bias and discriminatory outcomes. Develop independent auditing bodies and utilize fairness testing tools to identify and mitigate bias before deployment.
- Human oversight and intervention: Maintain human oversight in regulatory decisions supported by AI, ensuring ethical considerations and fairness principles are applied throughout the process.

Lack of transparency and explainability: Complex AI models can be opaque, making it difficult to understand how they arrive at conclusions and recommendations. This could raise concerns about accountability and trust in AI-driven regulations. Concerns about accountability and trust in AI-driven regulations could be allayed by:

- Explainable AI (XAI) research and development: Invest in research on XAI techniques that make AI models' reasoning and decision-making processes transparent and understandable. This allows for informed scrutiny and builds trust in AI-driven regulations.
- Interpretable models and visualizations: Prioritize the development of AI models that are inherently interpretable and readily explainable to humans. Visualization tools can further aid in understanding how the model arrives at specific conclusions.
- Documentation and public communication: Clearly document the training data, algorithms, and limitations of AI models used in

regulation. Openly communicate how AI is being used and actively engage with the public to address concerns and build trust.

Limited scope: AI is only as good as the data it is trained on. It may struggle to adapt to unforeseen scenarios or technologies outside its training dataset. Some important approaches to improve outputs would include:

- Continuous data updates and feedback loops: Establish mechanisms for updating AI models with new data and feedback from real-world applications. This ensures the models remain relevant and adapt to evolving technologies and contexts.
- Scenario planning and simulation: Utilize AI simulations to explore potential risks and unintended consequences of emerging technologies under diverse scenarios. This can help inform regulations that are robust and adaptable to unforeseen situations.
- Human expertise and domain knowledge: Combine AI analysis with human expertise and domain knowledge to bridge the gap between data-driven insights and actionable regulations. This ensures a holistic understanding of the technology and its implications.

Potential for misuse: There is a risk that AI could be used to control or suppress innovation, rather than promote responsible development and deployment of emerging technologies. The following should be done:

- Ethical frameworks and oversight: Develop strong ethical frameworks and independent oversight bodies to guide the development and deployment of AI in regulation. This ensures transparency, accountability, and adherence to ethical principles.
- Public engagement and participation: Actively engage the public in discussions about AI-driven regulations. Encourage participation in policymaking processes and feedback mechanisms to ensure regulations are responsive to public concerns and needs.
- Risk assessment and mitigation strategies: Proactively identify potential risks of misuse or control associated with AI-driven regulations. Develop robust mitigation strategies and safeguards to prevent undesirable outcomes and protect individual rights.

Obviously, the type of emerging technology would likely dictate the effectiveness of AI in its regulation. For example, AI might be more suitable for monitoring and analyzing data-driven technologies than regulating complex social or ethical dilemmas.[14]

In conclusion, as our species rushes through wave after wave of technological innovation that brings growing (some would say existential) risk, the insight offered by Paul Virilio will continue to hold true. This means that anticipatory governance and good regulation are key, especially in a location that is as projected toward the future as Dubai. But there is a global benefit to this: A future-oriented city, like an enlightened emerging technology company, will take it upon itself to shape regulation that protects users and promotes innovation; surely, this is a global public good. The case for anticipation is clear and the road to *in silico* anticipatory regulation is being paved; Dubai may well be the location for this to play out most effectively.

---

[14]Not surprisingly, some of the inputs for the *in silico* regulation section have benefited from AI input, especially from Google's Bard.

https://doi.org/10.1142/9789811296000_0013

Chapter 13

Anticipatory Governance on Cybersecurity

Akshay Joshi, Tal Goldstein, and Giulia Moschetta

Centre for Cybersecurity, World Economic Forum, Geneva, Switzerland

Key Takeaways

- There is growing cyber inequity between organizations that are cyber-resilient and those that are not.
- In an interconnected digital economy, raising systemic cyber resilience is a zero-sum game. Collaboration among organizations across the entire ecosystem, governments, and regulators is essential to building a more secure cyber environment.
- Emerging technology will exacerbate long-standing challenges related to cyber resilience. As organizations race to adopt new technologies, understanding the immediate, mid-term, and long-term implications of these technologies is paramount.
- Cybersecurity, which is the protection of the cyber environment and organization and user's assets, needs to be dynamic due to the rapidly evolving technological landscape, the increasing sophistication of attack vectors, geopolitical dynamics and cyber fallout.
- Anticipatory governance presents a unique opportunity not only to enable the identification of and response to emerging threats effectively but also to facilitate the creation of a resilient and adaptable security ecosystem.

13.1 Introduction

Global risks such as cyber threats, economic instability, technological disruptions, supply chain vulnerabilities, climate change, and pandemics, among others, demand coordinated international efforts to address their multifaceted challenges. Each year, the World Economic Forum publishes the Global Risks Report, which provides an overview of the most severe risks we may face over the next decade (see Exhibit 13.1). The 2024 edition of the report was published amid an era of multiple interconnected crises.[1] Among the top ten risks facing the world both over the two- and ten-year horizon was "cyber insecurity."

Examining the evolution of technologies, back in 2018, there was hype about cryptocurrencies and the underlying blockchain technology. Fast forward a couple of years, we found ourselves in the midst of a pandemic where the world took to video conferencing and organizations embarked on a massive digital transformation enabled by the cloud. Toward the tail end of the pandemic, the narrative shifted toward the metaverse[2] up until the advent of generative artificial intelligence large language models such as ChatGPT around the end of 2022. Through all these digital transformations and technological breakthroughs, concerns about cybersecurity,[3] privacy,[4] and the underlying ethics[5] have been central to enabling trust.

---

[1]World Economic Forum (2024). Global Risks Report 2024. Available: https://www.weforum.org/publications/global-risks-report-2024/ (Accessed 13 January, 2024).

[2]Time (2021). The Metaverse has already arrived. Here's what that actually means. https://time.com/6116826/what-is-the-metaverse/ (Accessed 13 January, 2024).

[3]In their review of current scholarly work on the topic, the authors conclude "the association between cybersecurity investment and future cybersecurity incidents remains inconclusive." (p. 179) — Walton, S., Wheeler, P.R., Zhang, Y., & Zhao, X. (2021). An integrative review and analysis of cybersecurity research: Current state and future directions. *Journal of Information Systems*, 35(1): 155–186.

[4]The challenge is that "present privacy requirement" and "future privacy requirements" differ significantly as the privacy implications are often emergent a posteriori (p. 13). — Anthonysamy, P., Rashid, A., & Chitchyan, R. (2017, May). Privacy requirements: Present & future. In *2017 IEEE/ACM 39th International Conference on Software Engineering: Software Engineering in Society Track (ICSE-SEIS)*. IEEE: pp. 13–22.

[5]AI ethics is dominated by too much abstraction, that makes it difficult to apply and the biases of power influences (countries and private sector). Hickok, M. (2021). Lessons learned from AI ethics principles for future actions. *AI and Ethics*, 1(1): 41–47.

Exhibit 13.1. Top 10 global risks.

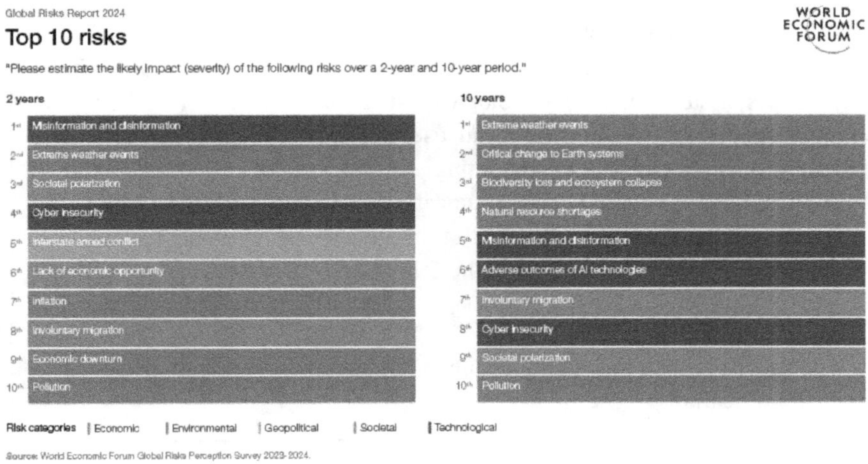

Source: World Economic Forum (2024). Reproduced with permission.[6]

Exhibit 13.2. Definition of anticipatory governance.

Anticipatory Governance is the systematic embedding and application of strategic foresight throughout the entire governance architecture, including policy analysis, engagement, and decision-making.

Source: OECD (2019).[7]

The principles of Anticipatory Governance (see Exhibit 13.2 for a definition of anticipatory governance) emerge as a compelling framework to address the dynamic challenges of our digital age and the underlying cybersecurity issues (see Exhibit 13.3 for definition of cybersecurity). Cyber is not a static concept; it is a dynamic, multidimensional field that demands continuous adaptation and anticipation. In this chapter, we will explore the interplay between strategic foresight and the ever-evolving landscape of digital security.

[6] World Economic Forum (2024). Global Risks Report 2024. *Op. cit.*, p. 8.

[7] OECD (2019). Strategic Foresight for Better Policies, p. 3.

Exhibit 13.3. Definition of cybersecurity.

Cybersecurity is the collection of tools, policies, security concepts, security safeguards, guidelines, risk management approaches, actions, training, best practices, assurance, and technologies that can be used to protect the cyber environment and organization and user's assets. Organization and user assets include connected computing devices, personnel, infrastructure, applications, services, telecommunications systems, and the totality of transmitted and/or stored information in the cyber environment. The general security objectives comprise the following:

- Availability
- Integrity, which may include authenticity and non-repudiation
- Confidentiality

Source: ITU (2023).[8]

13.2 The Dynamic Nature of Cybersecurity

Cyberspace encompasses all forms of networked digital activities, including the content of and actions conducted through digital networks.[9] Cyber is also considered the 5th operational domain, after land, sea, air, and space.[10] Cyberspace is highly complex, marked by a multidimensional and ever-evolving landscape. First of all, there is the ever-changing threat environment. Threat actors, driven by human ingenuity and motivated both by opportunity and external influences, continuously refine their tactics and capabilities. This perpetual evolution leads to the sophistication of attack vectors but also increases the difficulty of anticipation and

[8]ITU (2023). Cybersecurity definition. Available: https://www.itu.int/en/ITU-T/studygroups/com17/Pages/cybersecurity.aspx#:~:text=Cybersecurity%20strives%20to%20ensure%20the,risks%20in%20the%20cyber%20environment (Accessed 12 December, 2023).

[9]UK National Cyber Strategy (2009). Available: https://www.gov.uk/government/publications/cyber-security-strategy-of-the-united-kingdom (Accessed 13 January, 2024).

[10]Tikk Ringas, E. (2015). *Evolution of the Cyber Domain: The Implications for National and Global Security.* IISS. Routledge: Taylor & Francis.

preparation. There are close to 4000 cyberattacks per day.[11] The geopolitical backdrop further amplifies this complexity, influencing the targets and strategies observed in the cyber realm.

In addition, the rapidly changing technological environment introduces another dimension. Innovation of information technologies occurs at a breakneck pace, significantly altering the risk landscape. Any implementation of a new technology immediately creates a new attack surface that cyber attackers take advantage of. It is as if the battlefield itself is in constant flux. Moreover, the technologies and solutions developed to address cyber threats are also in constant evolution, making it highly challenging to stay ahead of the curve.

This rapid uptake of technologies has outpaced the ability of civil society, regulators, and organizations to truly implement safety and security principles.[12] Furthermore, to responsibly implement leading-edge technology, it is critical to reinforce the underlying systems required to support it.

13.2.1 *Cybersecurity as a threat multiplier*

Besides being a significant standalone risk, cybersecurity is particularly unique as it is a massive threat multiplier. If we take the example of a cyberattack on the energy grid, such as the Colonial Pipeline ransomware attack[13] that paralyzed the east coast of the US for several days, an incident of such magnitude can have catastrophic economic and social consequences. In this case, the vulnerability was traced to a legacy VPN.[14] The six-day shutdown of the pipeline in the USA, which carries refined

---

[11] Palattay, N.J. (2023). Many cyber attacks per day: The latest stats and impacts in 2023. *Astra*. Available: https://www.getastra.com/blog/security-audit/how-many-cyber-attacks-per-day/ (Accessed 13 January, 2024).

[12] World Economic Forum (2024). Global Cybersecurity Outlook 2024. Available: https://www.weforum.org/publications/global-cybersecurity-outlook-2024/ (Accessed 22 January, 2024).

[13] Reuters (2021). Knowns and unknowns about the hack at colonial pipeline. Available: https://www.reuters.com/business/energy/knowns-unknowns-about-hack-colonial-pipeline-2021-05-09/ (Accessed 13 January, 2024).

[14] Government Technology (2021). Back to basics: A deeper look at the colonial pipeline hack. Available: https://www.govtech.com/sponsored/back-to-basics-a-deeper-look-at-the-colonial-pipeline-hack (Accessed 13 January, 2024).

gasoline and jet fuel across 5500 miles, disrupted supply, increasing fuel prices slightly.[15]

In the case of a food crisis, a large-scale disruption, such as the one experienced during the attack on JBS, the world's largest meat processing company (based in Brazil), that rendered all meat processing facilities in the US and Australia inoperative,[16] can further exacerbate the pressures on an already strained system. JBS ended up paying US$11 million in Bitcoin to the hackers.[17]

Furthermore, during economic downturns, there is often a surge in cybercrime, as economic pressure motivates cybercriminals to innovate and create new types of threats. This was demonstrated during the recession of 2008 when the FBI reported a 22.3% increase in online fraudulent activity.[18]

13.3 The Data-Driven Forces of Cybersecurity

Data are pivotal in cybersecurity risk assessment and planning. Organizational and national cybersecurity strategies increasingly rely on data-driven decision-making. Beyond safeguarding networks and systems, it is about recognizing that cybersecurity has ascended from the realm of technology to the sphere of business imperatives. According to the World Economic Forum's Global Cybersecurity Outlook 2023, business and security leaders' perspectives on the importance of cyber risk

---

[15] Tsvetanov, T. & Slaria, S. (2021). The effect of the colonial pipeline shutdown on gasoline prices. *Economics Letters*, 209: 110122.

[16] New York Times (2021). Meat processor JBS paid $11 million in ransom to hackers. Available: https://www.nytimes.com/2021/06/09/business/jbs-cyberattack-ransom.html (Accessed 13 January, 2024).

[17] Campbell, N. (2021). JBS paid an $11 million ransom to cyberattackers. *NPR*. Available: https://www.npr.org/2021/06/09/1004964822/jbs-paid-an-11-million-ransom-to-cyberattackers#:~:text=David%20Zalubowski%2FAP-,The%20meatpacking%20company%20JBS%20confirms%20it%20paid%20an%20%2411%20million,its%20U.S.%20and%20Australia%20operations.&text=JBS%2C%20the%20world%27s%20largest%20meat,very%20difficult%20decision%20to%20make.%22 (Accessed 13 January, 2024).

[18] IC3 (2010). 2009 Annual Report on Internet Crime Released. FBI. Available: https://archives.fbi.gov/archives/news/pressrel/press-releases/ic3-2009-annual-report-on-internet-crime-released (Accessed 17 February, 2024).

management are converging.[19] This realization demands unwavering attention and oversight from top leadership.

Within this data-driven landscape, two distinct types of cyber intelligence come to the fore:

- *Strategic Intelligence*: This hinges on comprehensive data analysis, offering insights that inform long-term cybersecurity strategies. It empowers organizations and nations to anticipate emerging threats and vulnerabilities, guiding resource allocation and policy development. Strategic intelligence may include adversary activities and intentions, cyber threat trends in a given sector or region, security implications of new technologies and methods, emerging cybersecurity regulations, policies, and economic indicators. The data allow organizations to formulate long-term strategies that anticipate evolving threats and proactively allocate resources to address potential risks.
- *Operational Intelligence*: This is the linchpin for real-time threat detection and response. By analyzing data in the moment, it dives deeper into specific threats and adversary tactics, techniques, and procedures. Operational intelligence relies on real-time threat intelligence feeds, such as discovered vulnerabilities, indicators of compromise, and threat analysis. Cybersecurity teams are using this information to actively monitor live data to detect anomalies, malicious activities, and ongoing cyber threats. Operational intelligence equips cybersecurity teams to swiftly identify and counter potential risks and immediate threats, implementing countermeasures and fortifying their defenses against evolving attack methodologies.

These types of cyber intelligence work together to fortify defense strategies and ensure a proactive and adaptive response to the dynamic cybersecurity environment. Strategic intelligence and foresight are at the core of anticipatory governance; they inform policymaking and prevent long-term risks and emerging vulnerabilities.

[19] 51% of business leaders and 32% of security leaders consider cybersecurity a key business enabler. World Economic Forum (2023), *Op. cit.*

13.4 Exploring Anticipatory Governance in the Cyber Realm

In this chapter, we delve into the realm of cyber-related Anticipatory Governance, with a specific focus on the geopolitical implications of threat development and adaptation, the sophistication of attack vectors, and the intricacies of cybersecurity within an ever-changing global context. Additionally, we showcase use cases from the World Economic Forum's initiatives, underlining the significance of public–private collaboration, industry collective approaches, and activities designed to empower leaders to navigate the dynamic digital landscape.

Governance within cybersecurity transcends the establishment of policies and procedures. It entails the intricate choreography of controlling actions and permissions, determining what can be done and by whom. This dimension of governance is central to maintaining the resilience of organizations, societies, and economies in the face of cyber threats. Beyond internal governance, the imperative for collaborative governance is evident. The cyber realm necessitates cooperative efforts, both public and private, to combat cybercrime effectively.

In an increasingly interconnected world, where governments and organizations rely heavily on digital infrastructure and data-driven technologies, cybersecurity has become increasingly intertwined with geopolitics. International crises and emerging global challenges, with their cascading effects and unexpected consequences, find governments and organizations unprepared to face unforeseen changes. In an interconnected digital economy, raising systemic cyber resilience is a zero-sum game. Collaboration among organizations across the entire ecosystem, governments, and regulators is essential to building a more secure cyber environment (see Exhibit 13.4).[20] Anticipatory governance is, therefore, a necessary tool in global policymaking to mitigate future threats and predict geopolitical fallouts. In the context of cybersecurity, a proactive approach to managing evolving cyber threats and their geopolitical implications is fundamental. Moreover, anticipatory governance is instrumental in shaping the trajectory of future digital technologies and promoting effective global policies.

[20] World Economic Forum (2024), *Op. cit.*

Exhibit 13.4. Effects of cyber regulations on cyber risks.

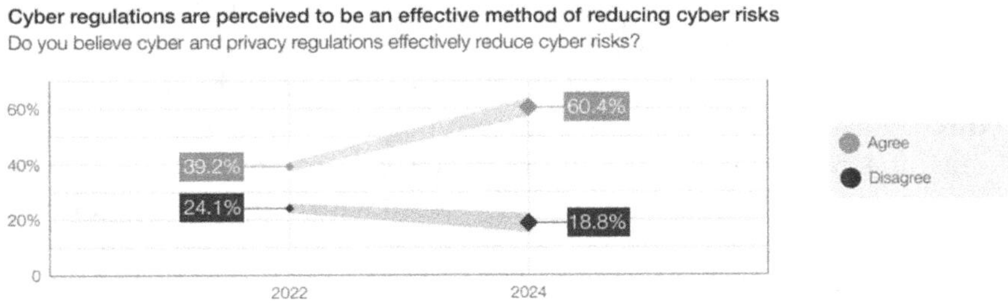

Source: World Economic Forum (2024).[21]

13.4.1 *Benefits of anticipatory governance for cybersecurity*

Anticipatory governance will allow us to shield and prepare for future cyber incidents by mitigating threats, building resilience, fostering international collaboration, promoting governance of emerging technologies, pushing innovation, and promoting research on security solutions:

- Anticipatory governance will help **refine cyber threat intelligence practices**, monitoring and predicting cyber risks and the evolutions in the cyber threat landscape. It will lead to the development of early warning systems and the preparation of cyber-related scenarios.
- It will also **foster cyber resilience** by helping businesses identify risks and critical assets, prepare, detect, and respond to cyber incidents by developing crisis management plans and ensuring business continuity. It will inform the drafting of national cybersecurity policies and strategies, which will be more adaptable and responsive to changing technological and geopolitical landscapes.
- It will **address the growing cyber inequity** across organizations and countries. Due to the interconnected nature of the cyber ecosystem, the risks associated with this technological divide between organizations and nations that can and cannot adequately mitigate cyber events pose both a threat to the entire ecosystem and outsized risks to those that are already vulnerable.[22] Anticipatory governance can trigger systemic collaboration to address global cyber inequity.

[21] *Ibid.*, p. 7.

[22] *Ibid.*

- Anticipatory governance can help the public sector **prepare for future cyber crises** by promoting collaboration across governments and the private sector to ensure the protection of critical infrastructure.
- Anticipatory governance will help **foster public–private cooperation** by using foresight to anticipate future challenges and shortcomings and by pushing for joint approaches to mitigate risks. It will promote responsible governance of emerging technologies by informing early regulatory discussions, as in the case of AI and quantum computing.
- It will also **spur innovation by incentivizing research** and collaboration across stakeholders and lead to the development of cutting-edge security solutions.

13.4.2 *The role of anticipatory governance in cyber crises*

Anticipatory governance can play a crucial role in preparing the public sector for upcoming cyber crises and safeguarding essential services. In the case of Ukraine, the proactive assessment of cyber threats and critical infrastructure vulnerabilities enabled strategic planning, private sector support, and international cooperation to mitigate the impact of cyberattacks and defend critical infrastructure.

Since the 2014 Russian annexation of Crimea, the subsequent attacks on the Ukrainian electrical grid in 2015, which caused a power outage for over 200,000 residents, and the 2017 NotPetya attack, which infected 10% of all Ukrainian computer systems before spreading across the globe, Kyiv has been enhancing its cyber resilience and strengthening its cyber defense mechanisms.[23]

In the days before the full-scale Russian invasion in February 2022, the Ukrainian government transferred the local servers on which the digital public sector infrastructure relied to the public cloud. By taking the timely and informed decision to evacuate critical government data to information processing centers across Europe, the authorities of Ukraine limited the impact of the conventional Russian missile strikes on

[23] Financial Times (2003). Ukraine shores up cyber defences in readiness for Russian attack. Available: https://www.ft.com/content/778997c3-50ce-4b40-9c20-c8564c840a57 (Accessed 13 January, 2024).

government buildings as well as the data wiper cyberattacks waged on government systems in the wake of the invasion.[24]

This example demonstrates the intrinsic link between the cyber domain, national security, digital economy, and anticipatory governance, which serves as a poignant illustration of how governments and organizations can successfully navigate the ever-evolving cyber threat landscape.

13.4.3 *Harnessing anticipatory governance to support board governance of cyber risk*

Securing leadership support for cybersecurity remains a challenge. For too long, cybersecurity has been perceived as an IT problem and delegated to technology specialists. Yet, as the threat increases, it needs to be seen not merely as a technical issue but rather as one of strategy, culture, and cooperation.

This requires business and government leaders to lead from the front when it comes to managing cyber risk within their enterprises so that the digital economy on which individuals, organizations, and countries increasingly rely is safeguarded. Indeed, effective leadership — on cyber and other technology issues — will only become more critical in the upcoming future.

To help leaders understand and rise to the challenge, in 2017, the World Economic Forum published "Advancing Cyber Resilience — Principles and Tools for Boards"[25] as one of the pioneering efforts to put a spotlight on the role of boards in enabling a culture of cybersecurity within organizations.

In 2021, the Forum, in collaboration with the National Association of Corporate Directors in the US and the Internet Security Alliance, published a set of consensus Principles for Board Governance of Cyber Risks. What started as a set of voluntary principles (see Exhibit 13.5) has been one of many efforts that have culminated in the Securities and Exchange Commission's proposed new rules that will significantly increase public

[24]Le Monde (2023). In Ukraine, 'wiper' malware is used as a weapon of war. Available: https://www.lemonde.fr/en/international/article/2023/04/20/in-ukraine-wiper-malware-is-used-as-a-weapon-of-war_6023564_4.html (Accessed 13 January, 2024).

[25]WEF (2017). Advancing cyber resilience — principles and tools for boards. Available: https://www.weforum.org/publications/advancing-cyber-resilience-principles-and-tools-for-boards/ (Accessed 13 January, 2024).

Exhibit 13.5. Principles for cyber-resilient organizations.

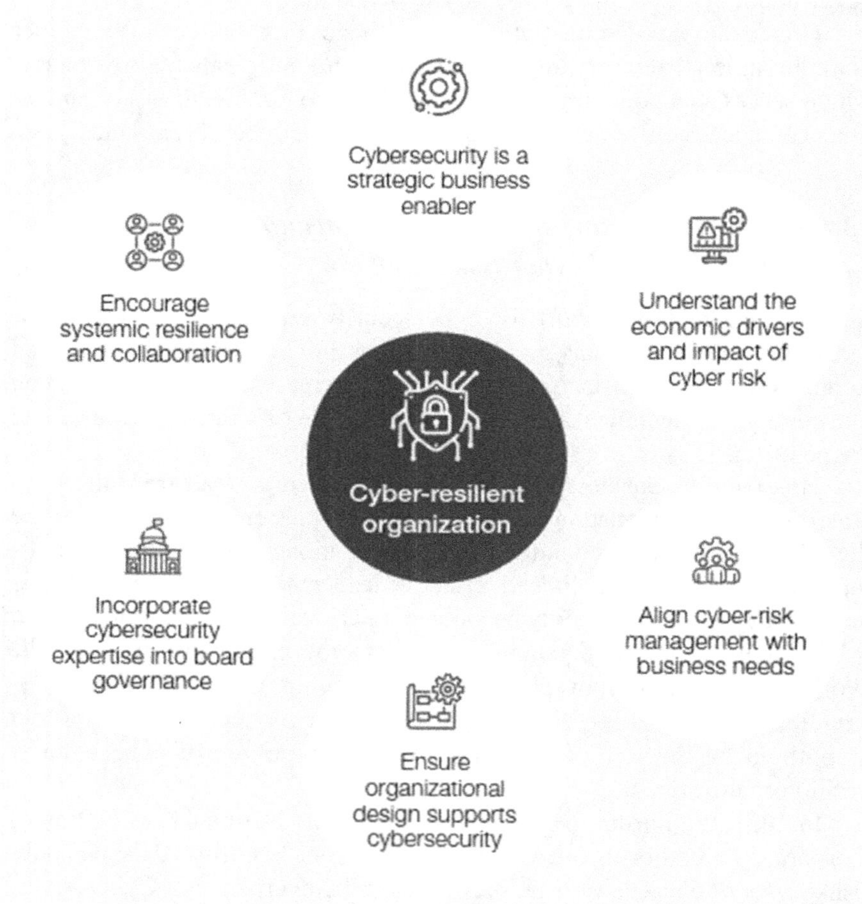

Source: World Economic Forum (2021).[26]

companies' reporting of both cybersecurity breaches and what executive management and the board are doing to mitigate cyber risk. Preparation for the new Securities and Exchange Commission (SEC) reporting rule is, effectively, preparation for overseeing a sustainable, resilient, and effective company in the 21st century (see Exhibit 13.5).

[26] WEF (2021). Principles for Board Governance of Cyber Risk, p. 6. Available: https://www.weforum.org/publications/principles-for-board-governance-of-cyber-risk/ (Accessed 15 January, 2024).

13.5 Applying Anticipatory Governance to Emerging Technologies to Leverage Their Transformative Potential and Proactively Manage Security Risks

In the age of the fourth industrial revolution, the pace at which technologies are being developed, coupled with rapid advances in capabilities, makes it virtually impossible for governance to catch up. Take, for example, the case of artificial intelligence (AI). Even though the notion of AI is not new, generative AI took the world by storm, resulting in the proliferation of regulations aiming to address the potential misuse of the technology with impacts being experienced across the individual, organizational, national, and global levels.

According to the World Economic Forum's Global Cybersecurity Outlook 2024, 56% of leaders believe that generative AI will advantage cyber attackers over defenders in the next two years.[27] The main concern is that generative AI will advance the adversary's ability to undertake actions that defenders are already fighting against, such as phishing, developing custom malware, and propagating misinformation (see Exhibit 13.6).[28]

Exhibit 13.6. Emerging technologies will exacerbate long-standing challenges related to cyber resilience.

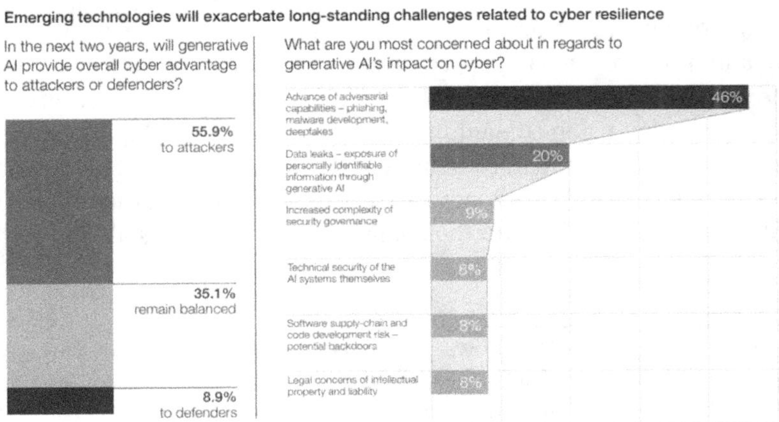

Source: World Economic Forum (2024).[29]

---

[27] World Economic Forum (2024), *Op. cit.* (Accessed 13 January, 2024).

[28] *Ibid.*

[29] *Ibid.*, p. 6.

The uncertainties surrounding this new technology underscore the pressing need for robust AI governance frameworks. To ensure AI is developed and used responsibly, the World Economic Forum has launched the "AI Governance Alliance,"[30] a multistakeholder initiative uniting industry leaders, governments, academic institutions, and civil society organizations to champion responsible global design, development, and deployment of AI systems.

In an analogous manner, quantum technologies could chart a similar trajectory, making it a unique example to put anticipatory governance into practice. The quantum computing age will unlock multiple optimization and simulation opportunities across industries through its ability to solve specific mathematical problems in a significantly faster and more efficient manner than was previously possible. However, the arrival of quantum computing and its ability to speed up certain complex mathematical computations could render obsolete the current encryption on which most enterprises, digital infrastructures, and economies rely. Quantum technologies, therefore, represent a significant and tangible risk (see Exhibit 13.7) to digital economies, with potential global impact. If this risk materializes, it could overshadow the great benefits that quantum technologies could offer mankind.

While definitive timelines for both quantum computing applications and the associated quantum cybersecurity threats have not yet fully materialized, organizations must act now to evaluate their readiness to adapt to the quantum threat. In January 2023, a Chinese research paper claiming the creation of a method to break the RSA algorithm[31] that underpins most online encryption using a quantum machine with only 372 qubits resulted in widespread concern before being debunked by experts. This incident, however, points to the steady advances in quantum computing, which are shrinking the time horizon for the quantum era. In fact, it is almost certain

---

[30] World Economic Forum (2023). World Economic Forum Launches AI Governance Alliance Focused on Responsible Generative AI. Available: https://www.weforum.org/press/2023/06/world-economic-forum-launches-ai-governance-alliance-focused-on-responsible-generative-ai/ (Accessed 13 January, 2024).

[31] Financial Times (2023). Chinese researchers claim to find way to break encryption using quantum computers. Available: https://www.ft.com/content/b15680c0-cf31-448d-9eb6-b30426c29b8b (Accessed 13 January, 2024).

Exhibit 13.7. Deployment scenarios to address quantum risks.

Scenario	Rationale	Potential impacts	Potential opportunities
Do nothing	Organizations that believe quantum computing is still at an early stage and the benefits of investing and embarking on the quantum transition are yet to be defined.	- No protection from quantum; full impact on the digital infrastructure - Disruption of business operations and processes - High risk of requiring a reactive, direct changeover when the threat materializes	- No upfront financial outlay
Adopt a hybrid approach	As standards are created, it is possible to have classical, quantum and post-quantum cryptography solutions in a hybrid mode. The security of the complete solution is as good as the strongest element.	- Vulnerability of classical solutions - Low to medium financial impact	- Provides legacy support to old solutions - Allows agility and flexibility to adapt quickly to new solutions - Provides classical protection while PQC algorithms being further stress tested
Follow a phased approach	Phase investment to adopt quantum security solutions to replace impacted solutions.	- Vulnerability of classical solutions - Low to medium financial impact	- Prioritization of solutions based on inventory - Phase-based improvement learnings - Phased budget spending following quantum's evolution
Direct changeover	Make a replacement of all impacted solutions, replacing them with quantum and post-quantum cryptography.	- High financial impact – large migrations can have higher costs - Large disruption of business operations and processes	- Direct enhancement of security against quantum risks for smaller, novel and less complicated environments

Source: World Economic Forum (2022).[32]

that the "ChatGPT moment" of quantum computing will result in far more significant challenges for the world.

The good news is that we can anticipate the risks and have the unique opportunity to build safeguards to ensure we do not let security issues come in the way of realizing the true potential of this technology. In 2022, the World Economic Forum, in collaboration with Deloitte, published the

[32] WEF (2022). Transitioning to a Quantum-Secure Economy, p. 15. Available: https://www3.weforum.org/docs/WEF_Transitioning%20to_a_Quantum_Secure_Economy_2022.pdf (Accessed 13 January, 2024).

white paper "Transitioning to a Quantum-Secure Economy,"[33] outlining the risks of quantum computers and providing initial guidance for organizations to transform their governance and security practices for the quantum era. To further help organizations prepare for this new reality, the Forum recently launched the "Quantum Readiness Toolkit"[34] that presents a set of principles (see Exhibit 13.8) that organizations can use to help ensure they are ready to enter the quantum computing era securely. These principles cover a range of areas, from strategizing about future-proof technology, embedding quantum risk in governance structures, and existing risk management processes to finding the right talent to head this new challenge.

Exhibit 13.8. Guiding principles to understand the quantum-secure transition.

Source: World Economic Forum (2023).[35]

---

[33] *Ibid.*

[34] WEF (2023). Quantum Readiness Toolkit: Building a Quantum-Secure Economy. Available: https://www.weforum.org/publications/quantum-readiness-toolkit-building-a-quantum-secure-economy/ (Accessed 13 January, 2024).

[35] *Ibid.*, p. 5.

In order to inform future policymaking on quantum security in the financial sector, the World Economic Forum, in cooperation with the Financial Conduct Authority (FCA) Authority, has initiated an international dialogue between industry and regulators. This effort developed four guiding principles and a roadmap to foster proactive action and inform future regulatory approaches for the financial sector toward a transition to a quantum-secure economy.[36]

13.6 Conclusion

While the concept of anticipatory governance has already been established, ensuring its application across contexts should be a strategic priority. As highlighted in the previous use cases, including Ukraine's cyber preparedness, board-level application of cybersecurity culture, multistakeholder AI governance, and the policy-oriented quantum security awareness initiative, anticipatory governance offers distinctive advantages.

In the evolving realm of cybersecurity, anticipatory governance presents a unique opportunity not only to enable the identification of and response to emerging threats effectively but also to facilitate the creation of a resilient and adaptable security ecosystem. The synergy between cybersecurity and anticipatory governance holds the key to shaping a future where technology serves as a strategic enabler of progress rather than a source of vulnerability. By applying principles of anticipatory governance to cybersecurity, governments and organizations worldwide can harness the benefits of technological evolution while also preparing for future digital risks and ensuring cyber resilience.

[36] World Economic Forum (2024). Quantum Security for the Financial Sector: Informing Global Regulatory Approaches. Available: https://www.weforum.org/publications/informing-global-regulatory-approaches-to-quantum-security-for-the-financial-sector/ (Accessed 13 January, 2024).

https://doi.org/10.1142/9789811296000_0014

Chapter 14

Envisioning the Future of Government: How Emerging, Secure Technologies and Data Flows Can Enable Anticipation and Action that Improve Performance

Daniel Chenok

IBM Center for The Business of Government, Washington, D.C., USA

Key Takeaways

- Technologies and data flows have made traditional governmental approaches outdated.
- Governments face a barrage of information, and without adequate processing, it may not help deliver public value.
- Ensuring secure technologies and data flows requires understanding and framing problems, new processes to solve problems, new implementation solutions that rely on advanced technology and analytics, and government agility to anticipate the future and make choices that best serve the public.
- New technologies like AI, cloud computing, and quantum computing can be beneficial by tapping into analytics using large-scale datasets. However, this also comes with risks, such as privacy, bias, and security gaps.

- The government must adopt a security-first mindset, sustain a responsive, agile approach, and implement best practices in cybersecurity, i.e., security by design.

14.1 Background

Today, governments confront serious, complex management challenges that necessitate effective leadership. Such challenges call for improving capacities required to prepare for, address, and resolve new problems. Many of these obstacles transcend organizational boundaries and change rapidly. Approaches that governments have relied on for decades are growing outdated, and agencies often lack capabilities that can address a new era. Prescriptions on how best to respond to emerging issues often coalesce around calls for governmentwide or cross-boundary strategies that rely on modern technology.

Moreover, government leaders increasingly face disruption and uncertainty. Many indicate that what was previously viewed as Black Swan events are now becoming more frequent — and more destabilizing. The vulnerability of social and economic well-being across nations has been magnified by reliance on both connectivity and distributed networks subject to disruption on multiple fronts.

Indeed, over the past several years, governments around the world have responded to the impacts of the pandemic, as well as heat waves, wildfires, floods, cyberattacks, supply chain interruptions, and other crises. One event follows closely on the heels of another, or multiple events can occur at the same time. This cascade raises fundamental questions about how governments can prepare for these and other shocks yet to come. Governments must develop the agility and ability to anticipate and respond.

In this context, addressing risks has placed renewed emphasis on the importance of being resilient. The combination of perpetual uncertainty and an ever-evolving risk environment continuously overtakes current risk planning and response models. At the same time, governments have captured valuable lessons in developing anticipatory capacities. Four key areas have emerged as fundamental to continuing and accelerating government transformation and anticipating the future:

- **Rapid innovation and agility** — Many governments, even those caught off guard by the pandemic, quickly shifted to technology modernization as an innovation that supported speedy response to other new threats, including new technologies.

- **Security** — Multiple crises have exposed gaps in cybersecurity and critical infrastructure security.
- **Talent transformation** — The future workforce must learn new skills to address changing technological and socioeconomic contexts, and it is unclear who needs to bear the cost of this responsibility.
- **Trust and transparency** — Anticipating needs and providing services become more challenging to ensure transparency (an important part of governance) and build trust (important for legitimacy), given demands for values like protection, liberty, and equity.

Within each of these areas, governments need to understand what is required to build resiliency and anticipate future shocks. Readiness requires governments to prioritize investments in data and technology and define and orchestrate strategies to address challenges in several key domains simultaneously. Governments need to build a set of core capabilities to be better prepared for the future.

In order to help governments better prepare for and respond to future shocks, IBM, working through the IBM Institute for Business Value and the IBM Center for The Business of Government, and in partnership with the National Academy of Public Administration (the Academy), launched an initiative to help governments identify core capabilities critical to building resilience. This contributed to a 2023 report, "Preparing Governments for Future Shocks: A Roadmap to Resilience"[1] (this report captured lessons from multiple underlying reports that framed the Future Shocks initiative[2]). Based on the common themes that emerged from this work, Exhibit 14.1 summarizes eight imperatives laid out in this report — a guide that governments can use to anticipate, prepare for, and respond to shocks of any origin.

---

[1]Mihm, C. (2023). Preparing Governments for Future Shocks. IBM Center for The Business of Government (IBM Center), IBM Institute for Business Value, and National Academy of Public Administration & Syracuse University Maxwell School of Citizenship and Public Affairs. Available: https://www.businessofgovernment.org/report/future-shocks-roadmap (Accessed 1 January, 2024).

[2]Future Shocks Initiative (2023). IBM Center. Available: https://www.businessofgovernment.org/node/4845.

How can governments leverage technology and innovation that support building these and similar anticipatory capabilities? The IBM Center published a 2023 book, *Transforming the Business of Government: Insights on Resiliency Innovation, and Performance*,[3] which focuses on the capabilities identified and describes a future of government that can help inform agency readiness — identifying strategic actions for innovation and performance to drive agency missions forward. These chapters point to new ways of understanding and framing problems, new processes to solve problems, and new implementation solutions that rely on advanced technology and analytics. Several essays written by leading thinkers address this imperative through topics that include artificial intelligence (AI), quantum computing, and data and evidence.

This chapter draws on these recent publications and other IBM Center research to demonstrate how secure implementation of advanced technologies can enable the government to use data to make more informed decisions, promote transparency, and improve outcomes in an increasingly complex and uncertain world. Such capabilities support greater transparency through which the public can understand and engage with the government, ultimately increasing performance and public trust.

Exhibit 14.1. Eight imperatives to anticipate and address future shocks.

Imperative 1: Build a governance mechanism for future shocks.
Imperative 2: Plan to mitigate crosscutting shocks.
Imperative 3: Manage risks and extend opportunities.
Imperative 4: Increase public participation and improve communication.
Imperative 5: Fast-track government innovation and transformation.
Imperative 6: Support data-driven decision-making strategies.
Imperative 7: Dedicate the proper resources and get the incentives right.
Imperative 8: Invest in a future shock-ready workforce.

Source: IBM Center (2023).[4]

[3]Chenok, D. & Keegan, M.J. (Eds.) (2023). *Transforming the Business of Government: Insights on Resiliency Innovation, and Performance.* IBM Center. Washington D.C. Rowman and Littlefield.

[4]IBM Center (2023). Preparing Governments for Future Shocks. Available: https://www.businessofgovernment.org/sites/default/files/Preparing%20governments%20for%20future%20shocks.pdf (Accessed 1 January, 2024).

14.2 Key Technologies: Cloud, AI, and Quantum

Public and private organizations are moving through a significant period of inflection, given the rapid evolution of a suite of technologies. Artificial intelligence (AI) and, more recently, generative AI and the development of initial quantum capabilities all gain strength when building on a foundation of cross-boundary networking enabled by cloud platforms. Together, this suite of technologies is often referred to as "intelligent automation."[5]

Intelligent automation is the common name for technologies used together to transform how people work. It consists primarily of artificial intelligence and robotics but also includes blockchain, cloud computing, and other technologies. Artificial intelligence, one component of intelligent automation, refers to machines and software that perform tasks we typically associate with humans, such as recognizing and analyzing speech or images, predicting events based on past information, or making decisions. Intelligent automation is a technology term that is also used to describe the process of transforming work through new technologies.[6]

Each of these emerging intelligent technologies offers a set of capabilities that can enable the government to improve anticipatory governance and resilience in the face of change.

14.2.1 *Cloud computing*

Cloud computing has long been defined by the US National Institute of Standards and Technologies as "ubiquitous, convenient, on-demand network access to a shared pool of configurable computing resources (e.g., networks, servers, storage, applications, and services) that can be rapidly provisioned and released with minimal management effort or service provider interaction."[7]

---

[5]As described in 2022 report from the IBM Center and the Partnership for Public Service (2021). Improving Outcomes in Government Through Data and Intelligent Automation. Available: https://www.businessofgovernment.org/report/intelligent-automation (Accessed 1 January, 2024).

[6]*Ibid.*, p. 1.

[7]National Institute of Standards and Technology (2011). The NIST Definition of Cloud Computing. Special Publication, 800-145, p. 2. Available: https://nvlpubs.nist.gov/nistpubs/legacy/sp/nistspecialpublication800-145.pdf (Accessed 14 January, 2024).

Agencies can adopt secure and scalable cloud solutions that will transform their government operations while delivering effective and equitable digital public services. Cloud networks can provide the building blocks for technology-enabled service improvement in agencies anticipating and addressing a wide range of issues, including weather prediction, agricultural development, veteran benefits, emergency management, federal personnel, and national defense.

There are three stages of cloud computing that can strengthen agency capabilities:[8]

Stage 1: Cloud infrastructure for mission-specific needs: Here, early adopters and innovators (within their subagencies and offices) independently move to the cloud solutions to support their mission-specific needs.

Stage 2: Agencywide cloud enablement: Agencies move toward centralized platforms, applications, and infrastructure in a process known as cloud enablement to handle everyday necessary processes like billing, data sharing, and collaboration.

Stage 3: Cloud technology for future transformation: By adopting a platform, the agency innovators have cloud services and business-oriented solutions that provide stability and security, allowing these innovators to refocus their efforts on developing more ambitious programs and ideas.

In moving through these stages, governments should strengthen cloud networks against security threats and operate cloud networks to optimize planning and performance.

Cloud Security. Threats to federal data, software applications, and digital infrastructure, including cloud-based technologies, are growing exponentially. NIST reports on new cyber vulnerabilities daily[9] that, if unaddressed, could result in large-scale security breaches that can weaken government resilience. To safeguard the systems and services that agencies rely on to serve the public, the government must adopt a security-first mindset, maintain a responsive, agile approach, and implement cybersecurity best practices.

---

[8]Gould, A.S. (2023). Mobilizing Cloud Computing for Public Service. IBM Center-Partnership for Public Service. Available: https://www.businessofgovernment.org/report/mobilizing-cloud-computing-public-service (Accessed 8 January, 2024).

[9]For more information, see: https://nvd.nist.gov/vuln.

Cloud Optimization. As agencies implement best practices to maintain accountability while exploring and expanding cloud use, they can implement multiple strategies:

- *Build cloud financial operations into cloud planning*: Cloud migration projects, like any complex IT initiatives, can experience excess costs and time lags. Agencies can track their cloud usage and spending so that cloud operating decisions are data driven and outcome based.
- *Develop flexible and scalable partnerships with an ecosystem of mission-aligned cloud service providers*: Pay-as-you-use cloud computing, while intuitive, runs counter to the annual and often multi-year government budgeting cycles. Agencies can strengthen resilience through multi-cloud ecosystems that leverage diverse services and platforms.

Account for ROI. Agencies can quantify the dollar value of migrating workloads to the cloud for transparency and accountability.

14.2.2 *Artificial intelligence*

The advent of artificial intelligence has moved digital adoption rapidly in government. As agency use of AI evolves, leaders will look for pathways to capitalize on opportunities, and the workforce will need new technical and social skills to assess AI-based data for improved anticipatory governance and decision-making.

More specifically, AI could enable agencies to fulfill numerous roles efficiently and effectively by reducing or eliminating repetitive tasks, revealing new insights from data, driving analytically based actions, improving service, and enhancing agencies' ability to achieve their missions.

As a series of reports[10] from the IBM Center and the Partnership have described, AI can help government employees focus on core responsibilities that are related to their agencies' missions and, hence, devote less time on administrative duties. They are likely to have more hours to plan for multiple scenarios, make choices among complex options, deliver services, and perform other mission-related tasks. These reports cite

[10]IBM Center and Partnership for Public Service (2019). More Than Meets AI, Parts 1–2. Available: https://www.businessofgovernment.org/report/more-meets-ai-part-ii (Accessed 4 January, 2024).

specific implementation strategies, including efficient decision-making, risk management, and AI literacy.

AI Can Increase Efficiency and Improve Decision-Making. Automating administrative tasks has been one of AI's initial benefits. Over time, federal employees are spending less time on repetitive administrative work and more on tasks that are core to their agencies' missions, from mitigating hazards in workplaces to following through on complicated applications for grants or other government services.

As AI decreases time spent on clerical work and increases the amount of information that can be collected and analyzed, employees can focus more of their time and attention on anticipatory analyses and on tailoring services to the needs of individuals.

AI Can Adapt to Address Risks in a Changing World. AI technologies raise concerns about data privacy, safety, and security. Similar risk factors have affected the public's perceptions when other new technologies were introduced; hence, today's leaders are required to address these concerns to foster trust, as more agencies rely on AI to carry out missions.

As governments aim to assess and mitigate AI risks, agencies can look to international best practices on risk mitigation. For example, the Canadian government has taken steps to ensure its agencies and their departments have simplified the tools and guides for the credible use of AI products, assessment of AI risks, and training required for people to use AI responsibly. As other governments adopt AI, they should enable agencies to buy tested and trusted AI products and create effective ways to identify and manage potential risks.

Government leaders can address risks via a path to success that would start by using AI in smaller, attainable projects, enabling their agencies to develop expertise and experience. Their approach to lessening AI risks must also evolve rapidly if they hope to use AI to address the government's most pressing challenges. Top challenges include bias, security, and transparency. A useful framework for placing government actions in a continuum of risks is given in Exhibit 14.2.[11]

---

[11] Bullock, J. & Young, M. (2020). Risk Management in the AI Era. IBM Center. Available: https://www.businessofgovernment.org/report/risk-management-ai-era-navigating-opportunities-and-challenges-ai-tools-public-sector (Accessed 5 January, 2024).

Exhibit 14.2. Addressing AI risk and discretion for government.

Table 1. Matrix of Task Analysis by Level of Analysis and Degree of Discretion

Degree of Discretion / Level of Analysis	Low Discretion	Medium Discretion	High Discretion
Micro (Individual)	Data Entry, Issuing Licenses or Permits	Placing Children in Foster Care, Sentencing/Parole	Emergency Response
Meso (Organizational)	Facilities Operations	Hiring Processes, Performance Management	Goal Setting, Strategic Planning
Macro (Institutional)	Statutory Obligations	Policy Formulation	Crisis Response and Management

Source: Adapted from Young, Bullock, and Lecy (2019). Used with authors' permission.

Table 2. Potential Use of AI Tools for Tasks by Degree of Discretion.

Low Discretion	Medium Discretion	High Discretion
Automation	Decision Support Tool, Predictive Analytics	New Data Generation, Reduction of Data Complexity, Relationship Discovery

Source: Adapted from Young, Bullock, and Lecy (2019). Used with authors' permission.

Source: Bullock & Young (2020) - Reproduced with Permission.[12]

Government agencies play a crucial role in adopting AI, for example, by ensuring that malicious actors do not exploit AI-powered algorithms. This essential role underscores the need for the government to become a responsible user of the technology and embed ethics and transparency in AI implementation.

AI Can Increase Focus on Technical and Data Skills. Agencies need to enhance their digital and data literacy and learn how best to use AI and related technologies. As AI becomes more ubiquitous, government employees need new skills to succeed in an AI-enabled world, emphasizing expertise in technical, digital, and data skills.

Indeed, governments cannot implement AI to improve foresight and anticipate future events in a world of risks without a skilled workforce that can implement strategies such as those listed previously. To boost AI literacy for the transformation of the workforce, a three-phased approach

[12] *Ibid.*

(see Exhibit 14.3)[13] can make government organizations more able to plan and respond to deliver exceptional public services and achieve mission success.

Ignatio Cruz, Assistant Professor from Northwestern University concludes as follows: "*Ultimately, this three-phased approach aims to equip government leaders and managers with the insights and actions necessary to navigate the complexities of AI integration. Furthermore, these strategies can empower leaders to discern the potential of new tools confidently, paving the way for informed decisions about adopting and integrating cutting-edge technologies. By fostering an environment where AI literacy is at the forefront of organizational strategy, government agencies can become more efficient, responsive, and, ultimately, advance their mission for the citizens they serve.*"[14]

Exhibit 14.3. Enabling AI literacy for government.

Phase 1: Assessment
Steps:

- Develop AI vision and goals.
- Assess current AI literacy levels.

Phase 2: Implementation
Steps:

- Adopt a co-creation approach for AI implementation.
- Promote interagency agility.
- Ensure responsible and trustworthy AI use.

Phase 3: Evaluation and Continuous Learning
Steps:

- Measure progress and adjust.
- Provide regular training and foster learning.

Source: Cruz (2023).[15]

[13] Cruz, I.F. (2023). AI literacy: A prerequisite for the future of AI and automation in government. In Chenok, D. & Keegan, M.J. (Eds.), *Transforming the Business of Government*. Washington D.C. Rowman and Littlefield. Available: https://www.businessofgovernment.org/sites/default/files/Chapter%207%20-%20AI%20Literacy%20Cruz.pdf (Accessed 16 January, 2024).

[14] *Ibid.*, pp. 111–112.

[15] *Ibid.*

14.2.3 *Quantum computing*

As defined by IBM, "*Quantum computing is a rapidly emerging technology that harnesses the laws of quantum mechanics to solve problems too complex for classical computers.*" Complex challenges that governments address, like those identified in the Future Shocks initiative, comprise multiple variables that intersect in constantly evolving patterns, such as weather and climate prediction, disease transmission, or global supply chain interaction. Such complexities go beyond the capability to address traditional computing that lacks quantum power to enable multiple simultaneous interactions.

Quantum has significant potential to drive improvements in operational efficiency across government and the capacity to address previously intractable problems. The technology can foster immense potential benefits for the public. As a tool to enhance anticipatory government, agencies must protect against risk in using quantum: Developing "quantum-safe" capabilities is crucial to maintaining data security and integrity for critical applications.

In the US, the National Quantum Initiative[16] brings together "*a whole-of-government approach to ensuring the continued leadership of the U.S. in QIS [quantum information science] and its technology applications.*" Such an enterprise strategy is key to enabling the government to tap into the potential for quantum to improve performance across a range of issues and use cases, including materials science, pharmaceuticals, finance, and energy.

Paula Gagna, Stanford University Fellow, notes that quantum computing has significant potential for improving agility and analysis across government, as well as enabling more sustainable computing environments given quantum's efficiency relative to traditional computing.[17] However, quantum introduces a number of risks that must be addressed in order for the government to best capitalize on its potential, including

[16]National Quantum Initiative (n.d.). https://www.quantum.gov/about/ (Accessed 27 December, 2023).

[17]Gagna, P. (2023). Chapter 9: The quantum technology challenge: What role for the government. In Chenok, D. & Keegan, M.J. (Eds.), *Transforming the Business of Government.* IBM Center. Washington D.C. Rowman and Littlefield. Available: https://www.businessofgovernment.org/blog/quantum-technology-challenge-what-role-government (Accessed 8 February, 2024).

cybersecurity — quantum-safe cryptography is a burgeoning area to stay ahead of quantum-based adversarial attacks — and its integration with AI.

Gagna writes the following: "Quantum Artificial Intelligence — a combination of quantum technology and AI — could compound the disruptive capacity of both technologies. Any information assumed secure today could be captured and stored to be deciphered later once sufficiently powerful quantum computers are created. Hackers or hostile governments could seize currently encrypted personal or financial data and decipher it retroactively."[18] Australia has been an early responder to quantum technologies and aspires to be a global leader by 2030.[19] Using insights from a roundtable session with government leaders in Australia, seven recommendations to build capacity are summarized in Exhibit 14.4.[20]

Exhibit 14.4. Recommendations for quantum adoption by government.

1. Outline the quantum computing possibilities and the ambition appetite.
2. Design platforms to orchestrate the quantum computing ecosystem to advance public value.
3. Leverage strategic international partnerships to accelerate and scale quantum computing discoveries and capabilities.
4. Invest in creating a public workforce that is quantum computing literate and skilled.
5. Establish an office to coordinate quantum computing initiatives across the public sector.
6. Publicize use cases on quantum computing in the public sector.
7. Identify risks and disruptions to digital systems across the public sector.

Source: Desouza & Fatima (2023).[20]

---

[18] *Ibid.*

[19] Australian Government (2023). National Quantum Strategy. Available: https://www.industry.gov.au/sites/default/files/2023-05/national-quantum-strategy.pdf (Accessed 20 January, 2024).

[20] Desouza, K. & Fatima, S. (2023). Quantum Computing for Public Value: Lessons from Australia. IBM Center. Available: https://www.businessofgovernment.org/sites/default/files/Quantum%20Computing%20For%20Public%20Value.pdf (Accessed 20 January, 2024).

14.3 How Can Agencies Tap Emerging Technologies to Use Data for Greater Anticipation and Improved Performance?

Governments face an enormous and increasing barrage of information that drives content to enable anticipation and inform choices in areas ranging from citizen interactions and business regulation to law enforcement and national security. Technologies such as those discussed here enable governments to tap into data stores with previously unimaginable speed, scale, and accuracy. In anticipating future complexities, cloud, AI, quantum, and related intelligent automation technologies provide decision-makers with tools to view the state of the world today, scenarios and probabilities for what may come tomorrow, and opportunities to redefine how governments can take action and improve outcomes for the public.

Cloud computing provides significant scalability, and cloud platforms provide flexible and cost-efficient ways to store, process, and share data across computing siloes across organizations. AI, which strengthens cognitive understanding, can help public sector officials examine large datasets and find patterns quickly and reliably to draw key insights, foster predictive analytics, and optimize resource allocation. Quantum networks support using data to make findings and reach decisions at previously unthinkable speeds, allowing for a far more nuanced approach to anticipatory and agile performance management that holds immense promise for solving problems once considered insurmountable.

An irony mentioned earlier is that while these technologies can bolster government effectiveness and foresight, they also can fall victim to risks. For example, AI can link data in ways that allow for the identification of individuals even without identifiers, raising privacy concerns; similarly, poor-quality data or subjective algorithms can raise bias considerations — both can be addressed by applying sound ethical parameters to data use, which have been embraced in the recent AI Executive Order[21] in the US as well as other countries based on OECD principles (2019).[22] Cloud

[21] White House (2023). Executive order on the safe, secure, and trustworthy development and use of artificial intelligence. Available: https://www.whitehouse.gov/briefing-room/presidential-actions/2023/10/30/executive-order-on-the-safe-secure-and-trustworthy-development-and-use-of-artificial-intelligence/ (Accessed 30 December 2023).

[22] Organization for Economic Cooperation and Development (2019). OECD AI Principles Overview. Available: https://oecd.ai/en/ai-principles (Accessed 30 December 2023).

applications can both protect against and open new cyber risks to the data that reside on them, putting a premium on building security into cloud development early rather than as a bolt-on — often referred to as "security by design." The advent of quantum computing calls for governance now to build an effective pathway for government data use in the future.

Advanced and emerging technologies have the potential to transform government data use and performance management. The ability to dive deeply and rapidly into large-scale data stores can enable agencies to see patterns and anomalies, spot obstacles and efficiency, and make choices among scenarios for improvement. Agencies that use analytics to improve planning and performance have seen outcomes as important as reduced marine accidents, improved quality medical care, and faster delivery of social services to recipients in need.

Leading private sector firms use technology to make similar adjustments that inform customer service and operational effectiveness in the public sector context; hence, better access to information can drive greater transparency, accountability, and citizen trust. By leveraging innovation responsibly, governments can act with agility to anticipate the future and make choices that best serve the public.

https://doi.org/10.1142/9789811296000_0015

Chapter 15

Digital Transformation: A Tool for Anticipatory Governance

Yousif El-Ghalayini

Mohammed Bin Rashid School of Government, Dubai, UAE

Key Takeaways

- The post-*New Public Management* era is when public administration is moving toward a theory of governance, building the capacity of government to act effectively and decisively to solve public problems.
- In this new context, future-thinking governments will promote public sector innovation and establish resilient governance strategies that enable adaptation and flexible adjustment.
- Digital transformation allows for revolutionary governance, which alters the relationship between governments and citizens using information and communication technologies, affecting how governments address policy problems.
- Anticipatory governance stands out as a system that enables governments to utilize foresight and manage emerging challenges before they escalate into crises, emphasizing the importance of data in proactive decision-making.
- Anticipatory governance employs datafication for futures thinking and policymaking, transforming social phenomena into data that can be measured, quantified, and analyzed.

15.1 Introduction

In the last three decades, the term governance has been used commonly in both academic discourse and ordinary discussions about how the public sector and other institutions manage themselves and their relationships with the broader society. The emphasis on governance, in many ways, reflects public concerns about the capacity of the government to act effectively and decisively to solve public problems. This new approach to policy development emerged as an outcome of several shifts in public administration from the traditional public administration to the New Public Management (NPM) and finally to Public Governance.[1] Some scholars even argue that NPM has been a transitory stage in the evolution from traditional public administration to what is here called *governance*.[2] This direction toward governance is viewed as a new open space for innovation in managing public organizations and developing more effective public policies.[3] The current public sector challenges have changed public administration and leadership. They reveal the demand for robust governance strategies to deal with turbulent problems and the need for public sector transformations.[4]

15.2 From Government to Governance

Different forms of governance have emerged, such as agile governance, adaptive governance, and anticipatory governance, in addition to new forms of government machinery (see Exhibit 15.1). Public administration scholars and practitioners increasingly use these new terminologies in the face of the complexity and uncertainty of rapid environmental change. Agile governance has focused on responsiveness and adaptability[5] to

---

[1]Mills, D.E., Bradley, L., & Keast, R. (2021). NPG and stewardship theory: Remedies for NPM privatization prescriptions. *Public Management Review*, 23(4): 501–522.

[2]Hyndman, N. & Liguori, M. (2016). Public sector reforms: Changing contours on an NPM landscape. *Financial Accountability & Management,* 32(1): 5–32.

[3]Bourgon, J. (2009). New directions in public administration: Serving beyond the predictable. *Public Policy and Administration,* 24(3): 309–330.

[4]Kettl, D.F. (2015). *The Transformation of Governance: Public Administration for the Twenty-First Century*. John Hopkins University Press, Baltimore.

[5]Amruloh, M.C. & Putri, R.L. (2023). Implementation of agile governance in optimizing the potential of Sekapuk Village, Gresik District. *RIGGS: Journal of Artificial Intelligence and Digital Business*, 1(2): 30–35.

Exhibit 15.1. Anticipatory governance and common terminologies.

Perspective	**Agile Governance**	**Adaptive Governance**	**Anticipatory Governance**
Methods	Strategic alignment ability, steering skills, and agility to perform control.	Meaningful collaboration across actors and scales; effective coordination between stakeholders and levels; building social capital.[6]	For example, algorithmic processes, harnessing correlation with causation.
Principles	Flexibility, effectiveness, and responsiveness.	Effective environmental decision-making.	Datafication of Society.
Ecosystem	Multi-governance synergy.[7]	Understanding of socio-ecological systems as complex adaptive systems.	Scientifically derived information about ecosystem function in decision-making.

Source: Adapted from Jalonen & Uusikylä (2023).[8]

societal and economic upheaval resulting from unpredictable challenges.[9] Adaptive governance is based on fit-for-purpose government operations.[10]

In turbulent issues, there is a demand for collaborative efforts that transcend traditional boundaries, promote public sector innovation, and, perhaps most crucially, establish resilient governance strategies that

[6] Sharma-Wallace, L., Velarde, S.J., & Wreford, A. (2018). Adaptive governance good practice: Show me the evidence! *Journal of Environmental Management*, 222: 174–184.

[7] Awamleh, R., Stephens, M., & Salem, F. (2023). *Agile Government — Emerging Perspectives in Public Management*. Singapore: World Scientific Publishing.

[8] Jozaei, J., Mitchell, M., & Clement, S. (2020). Using a resilience thinking approach to improve coastal governance responses to complexity and uncertainty: A Tasmanian case study, Australia. *Journal of Environmental Management*, 253: 109662.

[9] *Ibid.*

[10] Jurgilevich, A. (2023). Chapter 13: Adaptive and anticipatory governance in urban adaptation to climate change. In *Handbook on Adaptive Governance*, p. 207.

enable and support adaptation and flexible adjustment. These strategies encourage entrepreneurial exploration and exploitation of emerging opportunities. Traditionally, governments struggle to anticipate unforeseen changes in today's volatile world. The emergence of governance reflects the changing relationship between governments and citizens and how governments address policy problems. Further, the increased dependency on the private and nonprofit sectors to deliver public value also complicates government oversight as transparency decreases, impacting accountability.

Anticipatory governance aims to find ways to address volatile and unpredictable changes while setting a direction for the future. This innovative approach is characterized by its proactive and adaptable approach to dealing with uncertainty. It encourages efforts to strengthen planning, communication, and collaboration skills through joint initiatives.[11] In contrast to conventional governance models, its central focus is to proactively identify and address emerging challenges before they escalate into crises. Professor David Guston defines anticipatory governance as "*a broad-based capacity extended through society that can act on a variety of inputs to manage emerging knowledge-based technologies while such management is still possible*."[12] However, while anticipatory governance establishes proactive measures in navigating unpredictability, its effectiveness is amplified when paired with Digital Transformation (DT).

15.3 Anticipatory Governance and Digital Transformation

Amidst unprecedented global changes and challenges, a critical element that stands out is every government's digital transformation. DT became high on the government agenda as it is about doing things differently than in the past. It affects all aspects of the public sector, the technical, managerial, and even legal levels. The new direction toward DT led to a complete redesign of organizations and impacted organizational processes, people,

---

[11] Jozaei, J., Mitchell, M., & Clement, S. (2020). Using a resilience thinking approach to improve coastal governance responses to complexity and uncertainty: A Tasmanian case study, Australia. *Journal of Environmental Management*, 253: 109662.

[12] Guston, D.H. (2014). Understanding 'anticipatory governance'. *Social Studies of Science*, 44(2): 218.

and structure. DT is a critical strategy where governments enhance the quality of their services, streamline their operations to become more efficient, and improve their overall performance through digitization.[13]

DT is a term that emerged with the e-government movement at the end of the twentieth century. This shift was mainly part of the NPM movement in the same era as a relatively innovative method to carry out the work of governments using information and communication technologies. Based on Oxford Dictionary, there is no significant difference between the terms "Electronic" and "Digital" as both terminologies have a common meaning: "*computers' involvement or the technology that lies behind the computers on something.*"[14] Therefore, public administration scholars agree that DT within government began during the third industrial revolution. There was a shift from mechanical and analog electronic technology to digital electronics using electronic and information technology systems that further automate production. The first programmable logic controller (PLC) appeared in 1969, and further advancements include the Internet, personal computers, and other ICTs.[15] While governments often funded these advancements, the private sector initially took advantage of digital technologies, while the government followed decades later.[16] This transformation, which began in the 1990s, has led to a new generation of government.[17] Initially, digitalization focused on *low-hanging fruits* like record keeping and computations, but this was followed by the social digitalization period (1995–2015) and then government cyberwarfare and media (2015 onward).[18] This new era saw the appearance of terms such as Digital Government and Digital Governance. Digital Government refers to

---

[13]Gong, Y., Yang, J., & Shi, X. (2020). Towards a comprehensive understanding of digital transformation in government: Analysis of flexibility and enterprise architecture. *Government Information Quarterly*, 37(3): 101487.

[14]van Dorsten, J. (2012). Re: Discovery of electronic documents and attorneys' obligations. Exigent Group: pp. 34–36. Available: https://exigent-group.com/wp-content/uploads/67-1.pdf (Accessed 10 February, 2024).

[15]Australian Government 2.0 Taskforce (AGT) (2009). Department of Finance and Deregulation: Engage: Getting on with Government 2.0. Available: http://www.finance.gov.au/publications/gov20taskfor cereport/ (Accessed 14 January, 2024).

[16]Rifkin, J. (2011). *The Third Industrial Revolution: How Lateral Power is Transforming Energy, the Economy, and the World*. Turkey: Macmillan.

[17]Scholl, H.J. (2020). Digital government: Looking back and ahead on a fascinating domain of research and practice. *Digital Government: Research and Practice*, 1(1): 1–12.

[18]*Ibid.*

Exhibit 15.2. SMACIT acronyms.

Acronym	Terminology	Example
SMACIT	Social networks, mobile devices, (big) data analytics, cloud computing, and the Internet of Things.	Data-Driven Decision-Making, Predictive Analytics, Smart Cities, Citizen Engagement.
ERP	Enterprise Resources Planning.	Accounting and Financial Reporting, Project Management, Citizen Services (Service Delivery and Online Portals).
IT	Information technology.	E-Government Services, Data Warehouses, Communication and Collaboration, Geographic Information Systems.
PLC	Programmable logic controller.	Infrastructure Control, Traffic Control Systems, Energy Management, Environmental Monitoring, Manufacturing and Maintenance.

Source: Author.

the use of ICTs by governmental agencies to deliver better services to citizens, where ICTs enable tools for enhancing organizational efficiency.[19]

Digital technologies are amalgamations of information, computing, communication, and connectivity technologies.[20] These include social networks, mobile devices, (big) data analytics, cloud computing, and the Internet of Things. Collectively, they are often encapsulated under the acronym SMACIT (see Exhibit 15.2[21]), signifying a robust array of readily accessible digital technologies, including artificial intelligence, blockchain, robotics, and virtual reality.[22] Using SMACIT technologies sets DT

[19] Bakry, S.H. & Alfantookh, A. (2006). IT-governance practices: COBIT. *Applied Computing and Informatics*, 5(2): 53–61.

[20] Bharadwaj, A., El Sawy, O.A., Pavlou, P.A., & Venkatraman, N.V. (2013). Visions and voices on emerging challenges in digital business strategy. *MIS Quarterly*, 37(2): 14-001.

[21] *Ibid.*

[22] Sebastian, I.M., Ross, J.W., Beath, C., Mocker, M., Moloney, K.G., & Fonstad, N.O. (2020). How big old companies navigate digital transformation. *Strategic Information Management*. New York: Routledge: pp. 133–150.

apart from prior IT-enabled transformations like Enterprise Resource Planning (ERP). ERP has reached a critical turning point where many public sector leaders, employees, and constituents ask for improved customer experiences, increased efficiency, and greater transparency. For numerous governments, adopting these technologies represents a novel endeavor characterized by uncertain magnitudes and scopes of the associated changes.

The technological advancements marked by DT allow for revolutionary governance, which has altered the relationship between governments and citizens and how governments address policy problems. This relationship has transformed both structural and normative aspects of governance, including governance processes and structures, stakeholders' relationships, and perspective of values and methods to achieve governance objectives to improve efficiency, effectiveness, participation, transparency, accountability, responsiveness, democracy, and economic development gained for societies and administrations. Information, communication technology, and big data optimize managerial decisions and policies by integrating complex data analysis and visualization in government operations and public management processes. Therefore, there is an agreement among scholars that DT strengthens governmental managerial capacity and enhances the legitimacy, transparency, and responsiveness of good governance to solve social problems better and serve all citizens.[23]

Despite all this, some scholars argue that DT has many shortcomings, especially in dealing with current challenges that necessitate focusing on the causes of problems, not the effects, which is the case of DT.[24] The complex nature of contemporary interactions and processes presents challenges that need to be addressed regarding causation rather than impact. Therefore, DT's emphasis is on minimizing negative unintended consequences and prioritizing responsiveness rather than delving into the root causes of the problem. Many risks associated with the digital environment include misinformation, biased algorithmic decision-making, social

[23] Kang, W. & Wang, Y. (2018). China digital governance development review over the past two decades. *International Journal of Public Administration in the Digital Age (IJPADA)*, 5(3): 92–106.

[24] Charalabidis, Y., Flak, L.S., & Pereira, G.V. (2020). *Scientific Foundations of Digital Governance and Transformation.* Switzerland: Springer.

media manipulation, tech monopolies, cyber threats, surveillance concerns, and privacy violations.[25]

In light of these, this transformative shift, despite its challenges, would enhance governance by fostering new approaches, such as anticipatory governance, achieved through a better understanding of DT and Datafication.

15.3.1 *Datafication and Predictive Analytics*

As governments embrace DT, it does provide important tools to forecast better and promote resiliency. Tools like real-time data monitoring, risk identification, trend prediction, and predictive analytics permit governments to act. For example, in the case of disease tracking during COVID-19.[26] Datafication can change "*the relationship between governments and citizens, and how governments address policy problems*."[27] Datafication refers to transforming social phenomena into data that can be measured, quantified, and analyzed.[28] This movement is expected to alter how new data (and knowledge) inform policymaking by revolutionizing the policy analysis process and real-time policy intervention monitoring.

As datafication reshapes the landscape of information gathering and processing, it leads to the generation of vast datasets, commonly referred to as big data. Big data are defined as high-volume data that frequently combine highly structured administrative data actively collected by public sector organizations with continuously and automatically collected structured and unstructured real-time data, often passively created by public and private entities through their Internet interactions.[29] Big data provide

---

[25] Almeida, V., Filgueiras, F., & Gaetani, F. (2020). Digital governance and the tragedy of the commons. *IEEE Internet Computing*, 24(4): 41–46.

[26] Tõnurist, P. & Hanson, A. (2020). Anticipatory Innovation Governance. *OECD Working Papers on Public Governance*, p. 44. Available: https://www.oecd.org/science/anticipatory-innovation-governance-cce14d80-en.htm (Accessed 4 February, 2024).

[27] Braña, R.B.F. & Sánchez, Z.S. (2023). *Foresight and Regulation. Anticipatory Governance and Administrative Foresight in Times of Transition and Recovery*. Spain: Aranzadi/Civitas.

[28] Maffei, S., Leoni, F., & Villari, B. (2020). Data-driven anticipatory governance. Emerging scenarios in data for policy practices. *Policy Design and Practice*, 3(2): 123–134.

[29] Gong, Y., Yang, J., & Shi, X. (2020). Towards a comprehensive understanding of digital transformation in government: Analysis of flexibility and enterprise architecture. *Government Information Quarterly*, 37(3): 101487.

governments with a rich resource to analyze patterns, trends, and correlations for informed decision-making and enhanced public service delivery. Big data allow for the collection and sharing of vast amounts of data between government departments and agencies, reducing the administrative burden through one-stop-shop reforms, thus reducing the required documents by 29% and processing time by 35% compared to previous processes.[30] This indicates an improvement in operational efficiency and immediate service delivery. Big data are being used successfully for anticipatory governance in the U.S. Army with its Automated Continuous Evaluation Systems. The system uses big data analytics and "context-aware security" to investigate government, commercial, and social media data to uncover patterns of applicants.[31] Furthermore, big data facilitate online services, which in turn reduce the required workforce and lead to more efficient operations.

Datafication and predictive analytics are used in policing, patrolling, planning health inspections, and federal income tax collection.[32] An example of this is the UK's use of predictive analytics to develop an algorithm that identifies the types of drivers who are most likely to get into dangerous road accidents.[33] Predictive analytics has been used to identify potential instances of tax evasion.[34] This is done by analyzing a dataset to detect patterns that may indicate a higher likelihood of tax fraud among certain individuals. This demonstrates the advanced role of anticipatory governance. Also, in the case of terrorist prevention, big data is used to visualize ongoing and prospective attacks, and thus to mitigate or prevent such activities. DT creates new tools that facilitate some aspects of anticipatory governance and allow for better adaptive systems.

Think tanks also provide a clear example of anticipatory governance. The assembly of signals and narrations of geopolitical scenarios are provided to prompt leaders in different types of organizations to take action for various causes, such as sustainable transportation systems or the

[30] *Ibid.*

[31] Tõnurist & Hanson (2020), *Op. cit.*

[32] Maffei, S., Leoni, F., & Villari, B. (2020). Data-driven anticipatory governance. Emerging scenarios in data for policy practices. *Policy Design and Practice*, 3(2): 123–134.

[33] *Ibid.*

[34] *Ibid.*

promotion of climate-smart food production.[35] Through predictive analytics, policies can avoid challenges before they even occur.

However, digitalization also brings new challenges and requires new mechanisms of governance to protect human rights and establish a societal infrastructure of fairness and accountability. An example of where it can go wrong is the use predictive grades during COVID for the GCSEs and A-levels in the UK[36] or when policing went wrong and showed a bias in profiling in the US.[37] DT brings turbulence and fast transformations, which may bring social crises. In this context, digitalization could lead to permanent structural change in public service, affecting job content, public sector business models, and employment dynamics. One of the core features of DT is the automation of job tasks, which threatens routine jobs within the bureaucracy and puts particular pressure on traditional medium-skilled jobs that may lead to labor market polarization.

Further, it may change the type of employment relying on external, flexible, temporary, or freelance jobs and platforms. This demonstrates how the actual impact of the DT may also lead to concerns of a radical increase in unemployment or jobless growth due to technological change. The key to governance in the digital context is decentralized processes and collaborative decision-making that involves multiple stakeholders, as well as transparency and accountability of both stakeholders and algorithms.[38]

15.4 Conclusion

DT presents both challenges and opportunities for a forward-thinking government. Technological innovations bring new governance mechanisms to establish a societal infrastructure of fairness and accountability. Governance is also transforming, where digital technologies utilize and

[35] Danielsen, F., Flak, L.S., & Sæbø, Ø. (2022). Understanding digital transformation in government. In *Scientific Foundations of Digital Governance and Transformation: Concepts, Approaches and Challenges*. Cham: Springer International Publishing: pp. 151–187.

[36] Quinn, B. (2020). UK exams debacle: How did this year's results end up in chaos? *The Guardian*, 17 August. Available: https://www.theguardian.com/education/2020/aug/17/uk-exams-debacle-how-did-results-end-up-chaos (Accessed 30 January, 2024).

[37] Santow, E. (2020). Can artificial intelligence be trusted with our human rights? *Australian Quarterly*, 91(4): 10–17.

[38] Almeida, V., Filgueiras, F., & Gaetani, F. (2020). Digital governance and the tragedy of the commons. *IEEE Internet Computing*, 24(4): 41–46.

Exhibit 15.3. Digital transformation, datafication, and anticipatory governance.

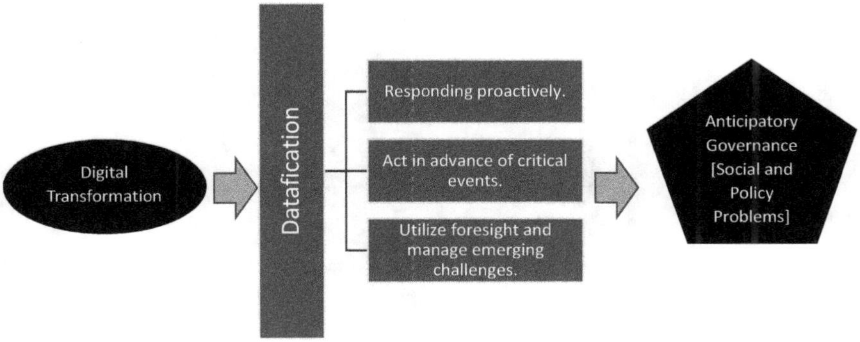

Source: Author.

leverage data for anticipatory governance. Therefore, it is crucial to expand the theoretical foundation for the role of data or information and information systems in governance in the digital age further.

Research in DT has focused primarily on advancing the practice concerning online services and improved management. There is a need for a holistic approach that accounts for questions of what an appropriate DT would look like, as well as basic questions regarding governance in the digital era. Datafication and big data are important elements of the larger system of anticipatory governance, which aims to equip governments with the ability to perceive and respond to impending situations or changes proactively, enabling them to act in advance of critical events (see Exhibit 15.3). Anticipatory governance, as a system embedded in DT, allows governments to utilize foresight and manage emerging challenges before they escalate into crises, emphasizing the importance of proactive decision-making. It can help set a direction for the future and find contextual ways to deal with volatile change.

https://doi.org/10.1142/9789811296000_0016

Chapter 16

Generative AI and the Copyright Minefield: Creating Safeguards

Sara Al Ghalayini[*,†] **and Kamal Al Awalmeh**[‡]

[*]*Legal Boutqie, Fujairah, UAE*
[†]*Equus Corporate, Dubai, UAE*
[‡]*University of Petra, Amman, Jordan*

Key Takeaways

- The existing copyright laws struggle in terms of relevance to emerging technologies like generative AI.
- The purpose of copyright laws was to protect artistic and expressive works and give creators control over the distribution and adaptation of their work.
- Generative AI uses massive datasets (often without permission) for training and, through training, can reproduce outputs inspired by the datasets, suggesting infringement of copyright.
- The increasing use of data colonialism, a method of acquisition of private data in the purview of governments, non-governmental organizations, and corporations, is creating further complications both at national and international levels.
- These data flows across borders and companies require a global AI governance outlook.

- Anticipatory governance in this space needs a stress test to see if existing laws and frameworks are sufficient or being force fit into a new context and, if the latter, needs to be able to buy time to change the regulations.

16.1 Introduction

On 2 February 2023, Getty Images, a US-based leading global visual content creator, filed a lawsuit accusing Stability AI Inc., a US- and UK-based corporation, of infringing and replicating more than 12 million photographs along with their associated captions and metadata, without permission or consent. Stability AI had, as part of its effort to build its business, utilized the data to train its model as an open-source AI image generator.[1] On August 2023, due to such significant and increasing risks arising from content creators, generative AI firms, and their investors, the US Copyright Office issued a notice of inquiry (NOI) on the Federal Register on copyright and AI. Such a notice is meant for the congress to be advised and consider the gathered information on its regulatory work, which will allow it to provide information and resources to courts, other government entities, and the public.[2] On 27 December 2023, the New York Times lawsuit filed (at this time of writing) was one the most prominent cases before the US District Court regarding generative AI copyright infringement. New York Times is demanding judgment against the defendants, Microsoft Corporation, OpenAI, and affiliated companies, presenting massive infringements worth billions of dollars in statutory and actual damages resulting from the infringement of its copyright. In its statement of claim, the New York Times presented evidence of unauthorized use, misuse, misappropriation of the content, unfair competition using the New York Times data, and many other infringements; the claim has also stated evidence against "fair use" that is continuously presented as a

[1]JUSTIA Dockets & Filings (2023). Getty Images (US), Inc v. Stability AI, Inc. Case 1:23-cv-00135-GBW-(District Court, D. Delaware February 23, 2023). Available: docs.justia/cases/federal/district-courts/Delaware/dedce/1:2023cv00135/81407/26/2.html.

[2]Panettieri. J. (2023). Generative AI lawsuits timeline. *Sustainable Tech Partner*. Available: https://sustainabletechpartner.com/topics/ai/generative-ai-lawsuit-timeline/ (Accessed 10 January, 2024).

central argument by generative AI incorporations defending themselves in copyright infringement cases.[3]

A copyright on a work provides rights to the holder, with exclusivity to control certain uses of the work such as reproduction, distribution to the public, public performances and public displays, and adaptation.[4] Copyright law is the regulation and policies designed to protect artistic and expressive works.[5] Since the development of AI, more so with generative AI, there have been uncertainties on the robustness of the copyrights. Generative AI acquires massive amounts of data for training purposes, frequently including copyright-protected information, mostly without authorization from data owners.[6] These circumstances raise enormous concerns, including, without limitation, the legal path of fair use, the development of derivative works, and the lawfulness of data acquisition and utilization. The integration of input data for the refinement and training of AI models gives rise to anxieties regarding potential infringements of copyright.[7]

16.2 Data Colonialism and Global AI Governance

Getty Images v. Stability AI is just one instance out of other enormous data infringement instances occurring on a daily basis and represents only one

[3]Ramaswamy, A. (2023). New York Times arrives in new tech with AI lawsuit. *Reuters*, 19 December. Available: https://www.reuters.com/legal/litigation/new-york-times-arrives-new-tech-with-ai-lawsuit-2023-12-28/ (Accessed 15 January, 2023).

[4]Mossoff, A. (2005). Is copyright property. *San Diego Law Review*, 42: 29. Available: https://heinonline.org/HOL/LandingPage?handle=hein.journals/sanlr42&div=11&id=&page= (Accessed 15 November, 2023).

[5]Park, W.G. (2010). The copyright dilemma: Copyright systems, innovation and economic development. *Journal of International Affairs*, 64(1), 53–68.

[6]Murray, M.D. (2023). Tools do not create: Human authorship in the use of generative artificial intelligence. Available: https://papers.ssrn.com/sol3/papers.cfm?abstract_id=4501543 (Accessed 15 November, 2023).

[7]Lan, Z., Yang, S., Fan, R., Zhao, B., & Yan, Y. (2023, July). Innovation or piracy? Empirically demarcating AI painting copyright infringement boundary. In *2023 3rd International Conference on Public Management and Intelligent Society (PMIS 2023)*. Atlantis Press: pp. 1328–1341. Available: https://www.atlantis-press.com/proceedings/pmis-23/125989284 (Accessed 15 November, 2023).

aspect of other arising issues.[8] In recent years, the use of such data has raised fears and increased risks due to the exploitation by private incorporations and other governments. Even before the EU GDPR — the rules issued to regulate the use of data and protect EU citizens around the world — there were increasing challenges to infringements occurring without proper sanctions on the unlawful use of an individual's data.[9] Nevertheless, cross-border data transfer cases are still being witnessed and rulings issued with penalties and precautionary sanctions. For example, a recent fine was issued by Ireland's Data Protection Commissioner on 22 May 2023 of Euro 1.3 billion against Meta for violating the EU's data privacy laws by transferring massive personal data of Meta's users in the EU to the USA. Such types of rulings indicate serious infringement — having further consequences on the repetitive, systematic, and continuous transfer and storage of Meta users' data.[10] The unforeseen technological explosion in 2023, driven by machine learning and AI, has given rise to *data colonialism*, involving the profit-driven exploitation of data, mainly through online behavior.[11] Data colonization is "*the process by which governments, non-governmental organizations and corporations claim ownership of and privatize the data that is produced by their users and citizens*."[12]

---

[8] Ishitani, H., Doorey, D.J., & Harvard Law Review (2023, June 22). Data colonialism and data sets. *Harvard Law Review*. Available: https://harvardlawreview.org/blog/2023/06/data-colonialism-and-data-sets/, https://harvardlawreview.org/blog/2023/06/data-colonialism-and-data-sets/ (Accessed 15 November, 2023).

[9] Sarkar, S., Banatre, J.P., Rilling, L., & Morin, C. (2018, July). Towards enforcement of the EU GDPR: Enabling data erasure. In *2018 IEEE International Conference on Internet of Things (iThings) and IEEE Green Computing and Communications (GreenCom) and IEEE Cyber, Physical and Social Computing (CPSCom) and IEEE Smart Data (SmartData)*. IEEE: pp. 222–229. Available at: https://ieeexplore.ieee.org/abstract/document/8726847 (Accessed 15 November, 2023).

[10] Li, Y. (2021). Cross-border data transfer regulation: A comparative study of China and Europe. Available at: https://u-pad.unimc.it/handle/11393/283978 (Accessed 15 November, 2023).

[11] Gray, J. & Suzor, N. (2020). Playing with machines: Using machine learning to understand automated copyright enforcement at scale. *Big Data & Society*, 7(1): 15. Available at: https://journals.sagepub.com/doi/full/10.1177/2053951720919963 (Accessed 15 November, 2023).

[12] Purdue University (2023). Glossary — Data colonisation. Available: https://purdue.edu/critical-data-studies/collaborative-glossary/data-colonialism.php (Accessed 15 November, 2023).

Often, individuals may not be aware of how their data are being exploited. Further, colonization can be extended to the Global South, where the Global North may use data from less developed countries to its advantage.[13] It is estimated that only about 40% of the least developed countries had data protection policies in place (compared to over 95% of Europe).[14]

Our lives and behavior with smartphones, websites, and apps are being utilized as raw material and considered as an open digital source that can be appropriated for large corporations to be used to generate a profit. This process may undermine democratic governance and expand inequity. The authors of the book *The Costs of Connection. How Data Is Colonizing Human Life and Appropriating It for Capitalism* further warn that data colonialism places us at risk of losing our ability to understand ourselves and the role we play in society, as well as losing the capacity to understand our reflection on social life.[15]

The role of governments is massive — and not just as regulators but data aggregators. To a certain extent, public institutions have generated and managed extensive datasets. Governments are progressively implementing sensor networks to receive real-time data that aid operational decision-making.[16] Additionally, many organizations use sensors for many purposes, from reclaiming control over personal health to advocating for political transformation. While certain data fall within the behavioral domain, others capture the condition of the non-human world, measuring elements like air quality, soil temperature, and the transit

[13]Couldry, N. & Ulises, M.A. (2019). *The Costs of Connection. How Data Is Colonizing Human Life and Appropriating It for Capitalism.* SFO: Stanford University Press. Available at: https://www.degruyter.com/document/doi/10.1515/9781503609754/html (Accessed 18 November, 2023).

[14]UNCTAD (2020, April 29). Data and Privacy Unprotected in One Third of Countries, Despite Progress. https://unctad.org/news/data-and-privacy-unprotected-one-third-countries-despite-progress (Accessed 18 November, 2023).

[15]Couldry, N. & Mejias, U.A. (2019). Making data colonialism liveable; How might data's social order be regulated? *Internet Policy Review*, 17 July. Available at: https://policyreview.info/articles/analysis/making-data-colonialism-liveable-how-might-datas-social-order-be-regulated (Accessed 18 November, 2023).

[16]Kitchin, R. (2014). Big data, new epistemologies and paradigm shifts. *Big Data & Society*, 1(1). Available at: https://journals.sagepub.com/doi/full/10.1177/2053951714528481 (Accessed 18 November, 2023).

patterns of city buses. Data collection may not be limited to citizens or local firms but also to other nationals, further complicating issues.[17]

In the meantime, it has also been argued that the engagement of public organizations with big data is similar to the data colonialism frameworks of private sector extraction. However, it would (hopefully) be used to produce public value through analytical tools that will impact the human experience in social and political aspects.[18] More research is needed on this topic — where data are gathered and used beyond for-profit companies — and this can be done by expanding the use of analytical tools to show how a broader approach can improve our understanding of the complexities in social context.[19]

16.3 Global AI Governance

The copyright dilemma needs global governance as data flow across borders and legal jurisdictions.[20] Furthermore, since national data policies are not coherent across borders, this creates a second level of challenges. AI is in a continual state of evolution, characterized by the unforeseeable timing of events and directions. Emerging advancements in AI technologies have affected the development of public policy.[21] An example of its development is a new generation of AI-powered malware like DeepLocker, which possesses the ability to conceal itself within seemingly harmless carrier applications, like video conference software. It can target individual

[17]Knox, H. & Nafus, D. (2018). *Ethnography for a Data Saturated World.* Manchester University Press, Manchester. Available at: https://www.jstor.org/stable/j.ctvnb7k8z (Accessed 18 November, 2023).

[18]Hewitt, J.N. (2021). A real time processing system for big data in astronomy: Applications to HERA. Available at: https://dspace.mit.edu/handle/1721.1/141908 (Accessed 18 November, 2023).

[19]Gabrys, J. (2016). Practicing, materialising and contesting environmental data. *Big Data & Society*, 3(2): 2053951716673391. Available at: https://journals.sagepub.com/doi/full/10.1177/2053951716673391 (Accessed 18 November, 2023).

[20]Abbot, R. & Rothman, E. (2022). Copyright law in the age of generative artificial intelligence. Available at: https://papers.ssrn.com/sol3/papers.cfm?abstract_id=4185327 (Accessed 19 November, 2023).

[21]Nordstorm, M. (2021). AI under great uncertainty: Implications and decision strategies for public policy. *AI&Society*. Available at: https://link.springer.com/article/10.1007/s00146-021-01263-4 (Accessed 19 November, 2023).

computer users in various ways, such as facial recognition, geolocation, and voice recognition.[22]

The OECD has taken the initiative to pave the way for policymakers around the globe. The OECD Expert Group on AI Future and its AI Policy Observatory are setting the grounds with other stakeholders to structure a forum for dialogue on topics involving the statutory measures for AI. The OECD highlighted the fact that the future challenges associated with generative AI require solutions at a broader and more systemic level. These solutions encompass regulatory measures, ethical frameworks, technical standardization for AI, auditing processes, model release practices, and access strategies, among other considerations.[23] These measures gained momentum with Japan's G7 Presidency, which took place on 6 December 2023. The G7 President's statement underlined the G7's commitment to advancing global conversations on AI governance and enhancing interoperability among various AI governance frameworks, recognizing the diversity of approaches and policy instruments within the G7. The statement reaffirmed the goal of establishing trustworthy AI that is aligned with democratic values.[24] However, it does not still specifically address the copyrights issue.

One of the most recent policy endorsements is the Hiroshima AI Process Comprehensive Policy Framework proposed at the Japan–EU Summit on July 13, 2023, which is a significant milestone as it is the first successful international framework equipped with guiding principles and a code of conduct to address the impact of advanced AI systems on societies and economies.[25] The call has been extended to AI actors to support the Hiroshima Process International Guiding Principles and Code of Conduct. The accomplishment of the Hiroshima AI Process during

[22] Stoecklin, M. (2018). Concealing Targeted Attacks with AI locksmithing. *IBM Research.* Available at: https://github.com/CyberWarefare/DeepLocker (Accessed 02 December, 2023).

[23] Lorenz, P. (2023). Initial Policy Considerations for Generative Artificial Intelligence. OECD Publishing. Available at: https://www.oecd-ilibrary.org/docserver/fae2d1e6-en.pdf ?expires=1706813854&id=id&accname=guest&checksum=EDE8F953DCF5AE8CCDC 94957FF9A3A00 (Accessed 02 December, 2023).

[24] White House (2023). G7 Leaders' Statement, December 06. Available at: https://www.whitehouse.gov/briefing-room/statements-releases/2023/12/06/g7-leaders-statement-6/ (Accessed 02 December, 2023).

[25] MOFA Japan (2023). EU-Japan Summit. Available at: https://www.consilium.europa.eu/en/press/press-releases/2023/07/13/eu-japan-summit-2023-joint-statement/ (Accessed 02 December, 2023).

Japan's G7 Presidency is highlighted as a testament of the ability to lead responsible innovation and governance of emerging technologies promptly. Anticipation is expressed for further advancements in the Hiroshima AI Process following the work plan developed by relevant ministers.

In addition, the G7 President statement has welcomed the UK-hosted AI Safety Summit and highlighted further international AI meetings hosted by the Republic of Korea and France. Emphasizing the importance of collaborative efforts with the OECD and the Global Partnership on Artificial Intelligence (GPAI), the commitment covers collective progress in advancing the Data Free Flow with Trust (DFFT).[26] The aforementioned collaboration is establishing the Institutional Arrangement for Partnership to shape a secure generative AI in cooperation with the OECD. It is understood that governments are vying with each other to shape responsible and inclusive AI governance practices, which is highly challenged by the unforeseeable and accelerated development of generative AI.[27]

16.4 Complexities of Copyright Infringement

The legislative and policy gaps in AI Governance have to answer many basic concerns and complexities with respect to copyright law. The concerns are not only about the ambiguity in the legal implication of using generative AI but also relate to the many unanswered aspects that require further exploration to answer.[28] For example, the US Copyright Office, the Federal Courts of the US, and the US Congress are striving to direct this matter starting from the following two main questions:

(1) Are the generative AI productions subject to copyright?
(2) To what extent does the production and utilization of content through generative AI platforms raise concerns regarding copyright infringement or other violations of copyright law?

---

[26]The United States Government (2023, December 6). G7 leaders' Statement. *The White House*. https://www.whitehouse.gov/briefing-room/statements-releases/2023/12/06/g7-leaders-statement-6/ (Accessed 02 December, 2023).

[27]European Commission (2023). Shaping Europe's digital future. *EU Policy and Legislation*, 30 October. Available: https://digital-strategy.ec.europa.eu/en/library/hiroshima-process-international-code-conduct-advanced-ai-systems (Accessed 02 December, 2023).

[28]Cheng, J. & Zeng, J. (2023). Shaping AI's future? China in global AI governance. *Journal of Contemporary China*, 32(143): 794–810.

Such questions are not easy to answer in a few lines as it requires a thorough study of the fundamentals of copyright law and an understanding of how the generative AI was trained, the extent of fair use, the portion copied, the jurisdiction for filing the claim, and other tests. However, in this chapter, we provide a summary of the current status as of January 2024 and what the US Copyright Office has as a basis to consider infringement.[29]

16.5 The Eligibility of Generative AI Creations for Copyright Law Protection

With respect to the debate on AI Creations Copyrightability, a majority of opinions strongly indicate that such works shall not be subject to the protection of copyright as this takes us to the very basics of the law of copyright and the most fundamental characteristic of artistic works which shall be produced and owned by humans "authors."[30] Raising such an argument takes us back to the "monkey selfie" case, in which a monkey snapped photos in 2011, and it was denied copyrightability as the Court of Appeal in San Francisco has decided that the photograph is a work of an animal who cannot own copyright.[31]

Therefore, by this argument, it is understandable that the productions of AI platforms are not subject to protection in most cases. However, the US courts have not concluded such debate by denying all the works involving the production of generative AI because, in the Thaler v. Perlmutter Case, the Court in its ruling highlighted that "AI platforms are not protected by copyright unless the work contains sufficient 'human input' to qualify the user of an AI system as an 'author' of a generated work."[32] This

[29] Samuelson, P. (2023). Generative AI meets copyright. *Science*, 381(6654): 158–161.

[30] Ginsburg, J.C. (2002). The concept of authorship in comparative copyright law. *DePaul Law Review*, 52: 1063. Available at: https://heinonline.org/HOL/LandingPage?handle=hein.journals/deplr52&div=41&id=&page= (Accessed 03 December, 2022).

[31] Guadamuz, A. (2018). Can monkey selfie teach us anything about copyright law? *WIPO Magazine*. Available at: https://www.wipo.int/wipo_magazine/en/2018/01/article_0007.html (Accessed 03 December, 2023).

[32] Thaler v. Perlmutter, No. CV 22-1564 (BAH), 2023 WL 5333236 (D.D.C. August 18, 2023). Available at: https://www.documentcloud.org/documents/23919666-thalervperlmutter (Accessed 03 December, 2023).

judgment is in alignment with the US Copyright Office requirement of Human Authorship.

On the other hand, it has been argued that neither has the Berne Convention (the international convention of copyright law for the protection of Literary and Artistic Works) defined the term "author" to explicitly refer to the word "human" nor has the Copyright Act expressly required that the author shall be a human as such a requirement had been originally set back in 1973 through the practices of the US Copyright office and its implementations.[33]

Finally, different jurisdictions, such as in the UK, are keen to know whether the US will extend the protection of copyright law for AI creations in light of the emergence of generative AI, similar to the extension of copyright determined for software when the necessity emerged.

16.6 Copyright Infringement and AI Generative Model Liability

AI algorithms that are being built to generate literary, artistic works, and audio and visual outputs are being fed and exposed to enormous amounts of data, including photographs, text, voice, financial data, behavioral data, and genetic data, in addition to other works gathered from online resources.[34] The process of training also includes creating or storing digital copies of existing works. This process is "*the reproduction of entire works or considerable portions thereof.*" *Certain generative AI programs acknowledge that their algorithms are based on* "*large publicly available sets of data that involve licensed productions,*" and their programs analyze the stored copies of digital content to produce their outputs.[35] Whereas permission is never obtained from copyright holders, the process then constitutes a breach of the exclusive right to reproduce copyrighted

[33] Ricci, D. (2023, April). Legal issues with using AI to create content. Kean Miller LLP. Available at: https://www.intellectualproperty.law/2023/04/legal-issues-with-using-ai-to-create-content-written-with-help-from-ai/ (Accessed 04 December, 2023).

[34] Miller, A. (1993). Copyrights protection for computer programs, databases and computer-generated works: Is anything new since CONTU? *Harvard Law Review*. Available at: https://www.jstor.org/stable/1341682 (Accessed 04 December, 2023).

[35] Murray, M. (2023). Generative AI Art: Copyright infringement and fair use. *Science & Technology Law Review*. Available at: https://papers.ssrn.com/sol3/papers.cfm?abstract_id=4483539 (Accessed 05 December, 2023).

works. In this context, AI corporations defend their breach with the concept of fair use. However, it is worth mentioning that the outputs of AI also infringe the copyrights of the holders when creating works that are substantially similar to their works.[36]

In light of all this and with the groundbreaking technologies of AI programs, Diffusion Models such as Midjourney, DALL-E, and text-producing programs such as ChatGPT, the US courts and the US Copyright Office are witnessing a sufficient number of cases that make it worth amending the Copyright Act or other legislation.[37] The copyright breaches are separate from the privacy breaches on individuals through other techniques developed by generative AI. It is noticeable that the policymakers and the US Congress are taking an approach of "wait and see" until the courts are more experienced with AI cases, with outcomes of court judgments, as it also constitutes part of the law in several jurisdictions depending on court precedents.[38]

The aforementioned is causing challenges for the owners of copyrights to file their lawsuits — aside from litigation costs, the burden of identifying the infringement, proving the breach, and the enforceability, all of which are not easy and are very costly. In the case of Getty Images, demonstrating the breach and the unauthorized use of their works could be considered straightforward compared to others facing infringement. The output of generative AI models has, in several cases, included the watermark of the generated work. On the other hand, other copyrighted works may not have been so easily identifiable. Even in the case of Getty Images, with the fast development and advancement of AI models, it will definitely become more difficult to distinguish between AI-generated works and human-created works.[39]

---

[36]Madan, R. & Ashok, M. (2023). AI adoption and diffusion in public administration: A systematic literature review and future research agenda. Available at: https://www.sciencedirect.com/science/article/pii/S0740624X22001101 (Accessed 20 December, 2023).

[37]Ricci (2023), *Op. cit.*

[38]Appel, G., Neelbauer, J., & Schweidel, D. (2023, April). Generative AI has an intellectual property problem. *Harvard Business Review*. Available at: https://hbr.org/2023/04/generative-ai-has-an-intellectual-property-problem (Accessed 20 December, 2023).

[39]Rane, N. (2023). Potential role and challenges of ChatGPT and similar generative artificial intelligence in architectural engineering. Available at: https://papers.ssrn.com/sol3/papers.cfm?abstract_id=4607767 (Accessed 20 December, 2023).

Therefore, copyright holders have been exploring advanced tools to detect infringement in the age of AI Generative models. One early instance of this was the research project that developed a tool called Glaze at the University of Chicago, which uses technology to allow users and owners of copyrights to identify unauthorized utilization of their works. However, it is always possible for techniques we use today to be overcome by a future algorithm. Thinking of the way this enormous data is being generated immediately flags concerns about the very basics of the law of copyright and the protected works of any original creator of work under the Berne Convention — for the protection of literary and artistic works, which includes the right to prohibit the works' reproduction, its public performance, its recording, its translation into other languages or its adaption.[40]

In the AI and copyright debate, the arising cases highlight the pressing need for international collaboration and unified guidelines for bridging legislative gaps and addressing copyright, among the other complexities essential to navigating the challenges posed by AI technologies. Reflecting on those legal challenges, not only do infringements need to be identified during the algorithms development stage or the training stage, but one also needs guidelines on infringements for the duration of copyright protection on lack of originality and creativity, and determining the authorship and ownership of the produced content.[41]

16.7 Anticipatory Government for Legal Maneuvering and New Tech

It has been explained through this chapter that new technologies are always accompanied by the public's expectations for policymakers to be prepared with policies and governance to protect the rights of individuals and to act with ethical and regulatory considerations in order to release the

[40] LegaMart Editorial (2023, November 13). International copyright law, 2022: Top shocking court cases. https://legamart.com/articles/international-copyright-law-top-court-cases/ (Accessed 20 December, 2023).

[41] Ross, J. (2023). Artificial intelligence: Copyright infringement and consequences. *Urtecht University School of Law*. Available at: https://crsreports.congress.gov/product/pdf/LSB/LSB10922 (Accessed 20 December).

tension due to unexpected risks. On the other hand, advanced technologies will also come with the hope of economic advancement and the enhancement of services and public value (government and private sector).[42]

Several governments have paid attention to the ethical guidelines for generative AI over the past three years, which has resulted in the EU's Ethical Guidelines,[43] the UK's guidance Artificial Intelligence and Data Protection Toolkit,[44] and Canada's Algorithmic Impact Assessment.[45] Such ethical principles set general guidelines and boundaries for the use of AI. Yet, at the micro levels of governance, the tensions of AI require AI scholars to translate those principles into implementation, especially looking at risks to fundamental human rights and the security of the data beyond the control of government.[46] A majority of AI researchers view the government as a regulator. Despite the fact that governments are increasingly becoming users of AI, the mechanisms of AI involvement to advance public value remain vague.[47]

Meanwhile, an anticipatory government has a core role in assessing probable and desirable forms of guardrails for shaping our future while turning the available resources and challenges into beneficial ones for

[42] Zhao, Y. (2023). The infringement risk and legal regulation of generative AI works. *Science of Law Journal.* Available at: https://www.clausiuspress.com/assets/default/article/2023/09/06/article_1694014270.pdf (Accessed 22 December, 2023).

[43] EU (n.d.). A Europe fit for the digital age. *European Commission.* Available:. https://commission.europa.eu/strategy-and-policy/priorities-2019-2024/europe-fit-digital-age_en (Accessed 22 December, 2023).

[44] ICO (n.d.). Our work on artificial intelligence. Available at: https://ico.org.uk (Accessed 22 December, 2023).

[45] Iftikhar, P., Kuijpers, M.V., Khayyat, A., Iftikhar, A., & De Sa, M.D. (2020). Artificial intelligence: A new paradigm in obstetrics and gynecology research and clinical practice. *Cureus*, 12(2): e7124. DOI: 10.7759/cureus.7124.

[46] Morley, J., Floridi, L., Kinsey, L., Elhalal, A., & Garcia, F. (2020). Operationlising AI ethics: Barriers, enablers and next steps. *AI & Society.* Available at: https://www.researchgate.net/publication/356241846_Operationalising_AI_ethics_barriers_enablers_and_next_steps (Accessed 20 December, 2023).

[47] Cremer, C. & Whittlestone, J. (2021). Artificial canaries: Early warning signs for anticipatory and democratic governance of AI. *International Journal of Interactive Multimedia and Artificial Intelligence.* Available at: https://www.ijimai.org/journal/bibcite/reference/2905 (Accessed 20 December, 2023).

maintaining public value.[48] Building anticipatory government capacity for AI legal frameworks can include the following steps:

1. Identifying early warning signs of advancement and digital transformation and testing whether existing laws and frameworks are sufficient or being force fit into a new context [stress test — does it protect the human rather than the non-human or the organization].
2. Development of an initial self-regulatory approach to buy time through advocacy and education, and enforcement of available laws on advanced technologies safeguarding fundamental rights through responsible AI behavior and preventing malicious use.
3. Lobbying of international governments to ensure the frameworks are implementable across borders.

[48] Chen, Y., Ahn, M., & Wang, Y. (2023). Artificial intelligence and public values: Value impacts and governance in the public sector. *Sustainability*, 15(6): 4796.

https://doi.org/10.1142/9789811296000_0017

Chapter 17

Transformative Change: Future Children

Maddalena Campioni

Future, Foresight and Strategy Expert,
Early Childhood Authority,
Abu Dhabi, UAE

Key Takeaways

- The current time will be remembered in history as a period of tectonic shift for the current and future generations.
- Our early brain development is impacted by exposure to stimuli like AI and this can be passed to successive generations.
- Neural plasticity is affected by the externalization of knowledge and information overload.
- More longitudinal research is required to understand the seven drivers of transformative change affecting future children.
- Anticipatory governance should be in place to protect our children and our society.

17.1 Overview

The current time will be remembered in history as a time of tectonic shift for current and future generations. AI and brain development are the big questions for the future, specifically the impact of AI on brain development. Years of research in multiple fields seem to have reached a turning point. AI is not the solution for everything, but it is as good as human input; we are learning to use its numerous applications, but we do not fully understand all the transformative limitations, including the difference between high quality and poor quality, and good and bad, which are not always clearly defined. The following quote raises the important issue of asking the right question when paving the way forward:

> *"The question of whether a computer can think is no more interesting than the question of whether a submarine can swim."*
>
> Edsger W. Dijkstra, Computer Science Pioneer

We are still at the stage of coming to terms with the fact that every new revolutionary innovation comes with enormous change, which, if not considered appropriately, may become potential pitfalls. The turning point for the future of humanity is the realization that AI, without a proper understanding of future ramifications and regulation, might be hindering brain development, especially for children. AI became the center of interest in early childhood research, as it is a critical time when the brain is forming and developing, and patterns of behavior and habits are set for the long term. The very operating system of the human brain is set in this stage of life, and even though many changes happen later in life, the foundations are set in the womb and early childhood.

This chapter considers and analyzes some key events and examples of dynamics and drivers of transformative change. These very transformative changes impact brain development, behavior, and well-being throughout the life course, shifting relatively quickly from an external event, i.e., the development of AI, to behavior changes and habits, i.e., screen time, decreased movement and human interaction, and eventually leading to anatomical and morphological changes and challenges for future generations (see Exhibit 17.1) and current well-being.

Exhibit 17.1. Definition of future generation.

Future generations are "all those generations that do not yet exist, are yet to come, and who will eventually inherit this planet."

Source: UNSECEB (2023).[1]

[1] United Nations (2023). United Nations System Common Principles on Future Generations. Available: https://unsceb.org/sites/default/files/2023-05/Advance%20Unedited%20-%20

17.2 Where Are We?

In 2017, Oxford published an article on *Children's Screen Time Guidelines too Restrictive, According to New Research*,[2] grasping the sentiment at the time that "controlling screen-time, understanding how much TV or app use is good for children." Presently, the issue is very much debated globally. Another famous example is the *Cinderella Law* in South Korea where on the 25th of August 2021, during the pandemic, South Korea decided to abolish a law banning children under 16 from playing online computer games between midnight and 6 am.[3] The 2023 publications are more aligned with the Asian Development Bank report, *Reimagine Tech-Inclusive Education*,[4] focusing on aligning pedagogical practices, governance, and the involvement of all stakeholders. Have we raised the bar or has the *Overton Window*[5] moved? While most of this legislation and research is related to gaming, gamified education is being used more and more, and the border between education and gaming is slim. Gamified education is another example of a double-edged sword if not handled carefully.

Think only that, despite Large Language Models (LLM) like Chat GPT being widely used in schools and at home, the conversation at the moment is just starting to understand the risks, as the recent report *How*

United%20Nations%20System%20Common%20Principles%20on%20Future%20Generations.pdf (Accessed 4 February, 2024).

[2]University of Oxford (2017). Children's Screen-Time Guidelines Too Restrictive, According to New Research. Available: https://www.ox.ac.uk/news/2017-12-14-children's-screen-time-guidelines-too-restrictive-according-new-research (Accessed 4 February, 2024).

[3]Lee, M. (2014). South Korea eases rules on kids' late night gaming. *The Wall Street Journal*, 2 September. Available: https://www.wsj.com/articles/BL-KRTB-6517 (Accessed 4 February, 2024).

[4]Asian Development Bank (2023). Reimagine Tech-Inclusive Education: Evidence, Practices, and Roadmap. Available: https://www.adb.org/sites/default/files/publication/892641/tech-inclusive-education-evidence-practices-road-map.pdf (Accessed 4 February, 2024).

[5]The Overton Window of Political Possibilities is a theory that suggests that you can manipulate public perceptions to push the window politically to make policy choices acceptable. For example, see Szałek, B.Z. (2013). Some praxiological reflections on the so-called 'overton window of political possibilities'-'framing' and related problems. *Reality of Politics. Estimates-Comments-Forecasts,* 4: 237–257.

Might the Early-Years Sector Use Generative AI? published by NESTA shows.[6] Exhibit 17.2 shows how generative AI might be able to interact with children in the near future. This technology, as with every innovation, has positive and negative outcomes: It is up to human intelligence to make sure that it leads to development for human beings, and it is also up to us to mitigate negative potential impacts.[7]

The turning point of modern society happens at two speeds: On the one hand, we have fast technological development and adoption of innovation and, on the other hand, we experience a slow realization or awareness of the need to develop anticipatory governance, so slow that the scale of change has an enormous effect on our children's future and on future generations. Not only will there be an enormous change in society and the world our children will inhabit, but there are clear signs that the children themselves will be affected during key developmental stages of their lives. In particular, consider neural plasticity, which is defined as, "*the capacity of the nervous system to modify itself, functionally and*

Exhibit 17.2. Exploration of generative AI use cases for early years.

Source: Adapted from Kanders and Stupple-Harris (2023).[7]

---

[6]Kanders, K. & Stupple-Harris, L.(2023). How might the early-years sector use generative AI? *NESTA*. Available: https://www.nesta.org.uk/project-updates/how-might-the-early-years-sector-use-generative-ai/#:~:text=Generative%20AI%20has%20the%20potential,workload%20for%20caregivers%20and%20educators (Accessed 25 January, 2023).

[7]*Ibid.*

structurally, in response to experience and injuries."[8] This suggests that preferential morphological changes might be passed on to children and lead to an evolutionary change.

Neural plasticity has been recorded as a decrease in brain size. One of the studies supports the hypothesis that this may be the result of the externalization of knowledge.[9] This externalization of knowledge, in turn, advantages group-level decision-making, due in part to the social systems the internet facilitates, which lead to distributed cognition (or thinking) and the storage and sharing of information. However, though the volume of information on the worldwide net is enormous, it may be just 10% of what is in people's heads, according to Quora co-founders.[10] Therefore, one logically ponders the following question: "What are we losing in this evolution?"

Adrian Galvan, a neuroscientist, concluded in 2010 that development, as determined by our genetic and some external stimuli, and learning, such as the act of acquiring information, are not two completely separate constructs and, instead, exist on a continuum.[11] This suggests that our biology and, specifically, our brains change according to the stimuli and the perception of the world we receive. Another example is a systematic review compiled on infant social interactions and brain development, where the authors show how human/parent interaction will affect communication and emotional involvement.[12] These articles surfaced a number of key drivers of change to be considered in building anticipatory

---

[8]Von Bernhardi, R., von Bernhardi, L., & Eugenin, J. (2017). What is neural plasticity? *Advances in Experimental Medicine and Biology*, 1015: 1–15. DOI: 10.1007/978-3-319-62817-2_1.

[9]DeSilva, J.M., Traniello, J.F., Claxton, A.G., & Fannin, L.D. (2021). When and why did human brains decrease in size? A new change-point analysis and insights from brain evolution in ants. *Frontiers in Ecology and Evolution*, 712. https://doi.org/10.3389/fevo.2021.742639.

[10]Arrington, A. (2010). Quora has the magic: Benchmark invests at $86 million valuation. *Tech Crunch*, 29 March. Available: https://techcrunch.com/2010/03/28/quora-has-the-magic-benchmark-invests-at-86-million-valuation/ (Accessed 2 February, 2024).

[11]Galvãn, A. (2010). Neural plasticity of development and learning. *Human Brain Mapping*, 31(6): 879–890.

[12]Ilyka, D.; Johnson, M.H., & Lloyd-Fox, S. (2021). Infant social interactions and brain development: A systematic review. *Neuroscience & Biobehavioral Reviews,* 130: 448–469.

governance, skills development, brain size, screen time-linked health, mental health, and social and emotional communication and intelligence.

Do we understand the effect, impact, and ramifications on brain development, well-being, mental health, and ultimate longevity? Will future research also focus *more* on the effect of AI on the brain and human development? While, as human beings, technically, we are very advanced, we are still lagging behind in logic and creating solutions to understand unintended consequences. I believe that our generation wants to be remembered in history for being solution oriented, leading to peace and stability, and being innovative luminaries, among other things. One would ask the following: Shouldn't we focus more on ensuring that the solutions this technology may lead to are future-proof and holistically good for child development and our society?

However, not all players in this field are insensitive to the science described. Initial scattered signs of the turning point can be seen on the following examples. Sweden is at the forefront in transforming anticipatory governance with its latest policy; Swedish Minister for Schools, Lotta Edholm, announced in a statement in August 2023 that the government wants to reverse the decision by the National Agency for Education to make digital devices mandatory for preschools and end digital learning for children under six years of age.[13] This was following an urgent call by UNESCO for the appropriate use of technology in education.[14]

Hence, as a futurist, a foresight expert, and an average polymath, I feel it is my ethical duty to consider and analyze how the current fragmented understanding we are weaving through might lead to a blurred vision of the future. A blurred vision of the future might lead to paralysis in decision-making because of the lack of clarity or data. A paralysis in decision-making might lead to delays in sustainable solutions and possibly an ineffective use of funding and resources on short-lived innovations or marginal, easily manageable issues.

---

[13] Pele, C. (2023). Sweden brings more books and handwriting practice back to its tech-heavy schools. *APNews*, 11 September. Available: https://apnews.com/article/sweden-digital-education-backlash-reading-writing-1dd964c628f76361c43dbf3964f7dbf4 (Accessed 4 February, 2024).

[14] UNESCO (2023). UNESCO issues urgent call for appropriate use of technology in education. Available: https://www.unesco.org/gem-report/en/articles/unesco-issues-urgent-call-appropriate-use-technology-education?TSPD_101_R0=080713870fab20001616af18947ee251c04a6c3dc89555da0a477dff4dfbc4e8a630657b55 (Accessed 4 February, 2024).

Many questions come to mind: Do we fully understand the ramifications of Generative AI on current and future generations? Children are budding societies, the future of our survival as humanity. Are we making the right educated choice for our future and our children's future? Are we taking nature for granted or as a marginal player in human survival?

17.3 What Should We Do?

These are big existential questions that are recurrent in the media and in people's minds. If we sweep them under the carpet because they are too big, too complex, and not easily communicated, they will come back when we least expect them or least want to deal with them. I do not have all the answers, and experts globally are currently struggling to tackle such profound and all-encompassing shifts. But I would like to give some pointers on the dynamics of change we are experiencing in the early childhood development sector and in foresight in general, particularly in terms of neural plasticity, AI, and anticipatory governance. When asking questions, it is also important to consider where we find the answers for them. Where do we look for solutions?

Luckily, foresight and anticipatory approaches are becoming widespread knowledge and are commonly used. We use anticipatory methodologies to imagine the future and foresight to anticipate what is going to come, to act with a wider understanding of the dynamic of change, biases, and uncertainties. A memorable quote by French writer and novelist Jean-Baptiste Alphonse Karr is "*Plus ça change, plus c'est la même chose*," which translates to "*the more there are changes the more it is the same thing*" to underline that there is an inherent tendency to change, but this change's ultimate objective is to reach a common recurrent "state of things." In order to maintain fundamental elements for the success of humanity, we need to embrace change and understand what needs to change. Understanding these *dynamics of change* was at the base of Karr's writing, too.

The consciousness of change is an important realization, as consciousness is a process, and in foresight, communicating consciousness and controlled imagination surfaces a common possible and plausible future reality. On 4th May 2023, the United Nations Chief Executives Board for Coordination and the High-level Committee on Programs published the Common Principles on Future Generations. Transformational changes happening now will mark a shift in brain development and

Exhibit 17.3. Key steps to understand transformations of AI on future generations.

2021	Second thematic pillar on "duties to the future"
2022	Declaration for Future Generations
2022	Global Action on Brain and Neurological Health
2023	A policy brief "To Think and Act for Future Generations"

Source: United Nations Chief Executives Board for Coordination and the High-Level Committee on Programs.[15]

societal fundamental constructs. Exhibit 17.3 states the history of actions, showing that to have an impact, we need to anticipate and consider humanity as an important renewable resource.

The UN approach seems to underline the fact that, in this profound change, we are unsure of the outcomes for future generations and, in a sense, for humanity as we know it. But following Karr's quote, we will be just the same if, maybe, we can find the middle ground between groundbreaking discoveries and missing out on certain aspects of humanity. It is important that we increase awareness and anticipate possible solutions.

> *"All that makes us human is a creative act of experience and perception."*
>
> - Rick Rubin, author of *The Creative Act: A Way of Being.*[16]

As a neuroscientist, my possible starting point is the understanding that our imagination and creativity can be constrained by our cognitive biases and by too much reliance on unimaginative (for the moment) technology, such as AI. This could be because AI is coded by unimaginative humans, as the comic in Exhibit 17.4 illustrates with the man searching for his wallet where there is light, not where he lost it, suggesting that we might be applying our intelligence and technology in the wrong way to find solutions.

[15] See CEB: https://unsceb.org/topics for the various topics.

[16] Rubin, R. (2023). *The Creative Act: A Way of Being*. Great Britain: Canongate Books Ltd.

Exhibit 17.4. A man looking for his wallet under the lamp post.

Source: Author, generated by AI using Night Café on 3/1/24.

17.4 Drivers of Change for Future Learning Research

In conclusion, if we consider AI and how it impacts the future of children, we could broadly subdivide future research into seven main interconnected thematic areas, as explained in this chapter. The importance of this topic is highlighted by the fact that brain morphology is plastic and will affect thinking capability and, ultimately, human survival. Hence, awareness of scientific research in this field might save our brain potential, as part of our biology is NOT determined by genetics. The seven drivers of change are good areas for research on the impact of the child of today and tomorrow:

- *Education Disruption*: Education and learning are disrupted, and we are currently redesigning education systems and approaches using tech- and/or nature-oriented future education.
- *Future Skills*: The future of work and the skills most required or most remunerated and fostered do not align. While creativity and innovation need to be fostered in the long term, the short-term view and approach to deal with the immediate skills still prevail and should be balanced with the future long-term sustainable approach.
- *Role of Family*: Family dynamics and structure are changing and affecting the way children perceive the world around them.
- *Natural Environment*: Environmental changes cause disruption in lifestyle and well-being, which will greatly affect the future of children and create transformative change, including in their way of living, like housing and urbanization.
- *Security and Privacy Risks*: These risks surface due to connectivity, technology, globalization, and the need for cultural exchange, which lead to unknown territories in terms of child security and privacy risks.
- *Increasing Focus on Longevity*: This shows a dichotomy between advances in medical imaging, AI diagnostics, and genetics, compared to the fashionable trend of body hacking. This is marketed mainly by the private sector without adequate longitudinal studies and wider consideration of personal differences. This is incongruent with the present, which is overwhelmed by mental health and well-being problems which struggle to take a central stage.
- *Grey Social, Ethical, and Moral Guidelines*: Children are exposed through technological capabilities to a variety of ethical questions, and their choices in society might be affected by the actual experience they have.

The important point is "what you can do for the future" not "what the future can do for you." Anticipatory governance should be in place to protect our children and our society, and anticipatory governance for children is belated. These and the drivers of change enumerated in this chapter should be, in my opinion, the guiding elements for anticipatory governance and what we should do for the future.

https://doi.org/10.1142/9789811296000_0018

Chapter 18

Future of Education and Work: Using Backcasting to Design Guardrails

Melodena Stephens[*] and Sohail Inayatullah[†,‡]

[*]*Mohammed Bin Rashid School of Government, Dubai, UAE*
[†]*UNESCO Chair in Futures Studies, IIUM, Kuala Lumpur, Malaysia*
[‡]*Tamkang University, Taipei, Taiwan*

Key Takeaways

- Backcasting can be complex and requires time, different levels of expertise, and the ability to challenge assumptions and think both logically and creatively.
- It is not a simple one-day exercise if the purpose is governance or building guardrails.
- However, when the purpose is to make the future more plausible, i.e., easier to see how the vision can become reality, it can be done in shorter time frames when properly facilitated.
- The journey of backcasting is iterative and needs skilled facilitators, as with all foresight methods.
- Backcasting requires skills related to strategy, problem-solving, and, most importantly, the ability to iteratively move from the long to the medium to the short term to consider guardrails necessary for anticipatory governance.

18.1 Introduction

According to the IMF, AI will impact 40% of global employment and up to 60% of jobs in advanced economies, 40% in emerging economies, and 26% in low-income countries.[1] This study suggests that the higher the education, the more likely the exposure to job loss (unless we can think of complementary AI). This transition and the need to switch jobs will impact the youth, women, and old (with older people less likely to adapt). Hence, governments must rethink education, the future of work, society, and even government budgets. Of course, other scenarios are possible, i.e., including a future after jobs.[2]

This chapter highlights anticipatory governance by using the backcasting method for a preferred space (in education and work) to identify governance issues, early warning signals, and possible strategies — or events — to link the future to the present.[3] While the initial activity began with a possibility space (what could happen), it was quickly narrowed down to what should happen and what strategies need to be put in place from the predicted space (what will happen).

The overview of the backcasting process is illustrated in Exhibit 18.1. The facilitator's job could be to work backstage, collate information, and capture the discussions, looking for synergies or points of dissent. Ideally, it is recommended that there be a gap of a few days between stages to ensure time for reflection, research, and relearning.

18.2 Example Using Backcasting

Proposed Plan: Approximately 20+ policymakers (across one month).

This example is for illustrative processes to go through the design stages of backcasting. In this example, the horizon is about 50+ years. Various policymakers from different domains get together and start with possibilities. The backcasting exercise begins after a suitable warm-up to get participants comfortable with their imaginative side.

---

[1]Cazzaniga, M., *et al.* (2024). Gen-AI: Artificial intelligence and the future of work. IMF Staff Discussion Note SDN2024/001. Washington D.C.

[2]Inayatullah, S. (2022). Scenarios for teaching and training: From being "kodaked" to futures literacy and futures-proofing. *CSPS Strategy and Policy Journal,* (8): 33–50.

[3]Inayatullah, S. (2015). *What Works: Case Studies in the Practice of Foresight*. Malaysia: Tamkang University.

Exhibit 18.1. Backcasting process: Agile thinking — A summary.

	Stage 1: Future Horizon	Stage 2: Present Horizon	Stage 3: Push-and-Pull Factors	Stage 4: Anchor Policies	Stage 5: Impact and EWS
Perspective	**Wide → Narrow**	**Narrow → Wide**	**Wide → Narrow**	**Narrow → Wide**	**Wide → Narrow**
Purpose	**Define and Visualize the Future or Alternative Futures and the Time Frame:** *Narrow from predicted and possible futures to preferred future and agree on norms (how you want to get there).*	**Where We Are Now:** *Identifying assumptions, reevaluating spillovers, and assessing feasibility (what is required to get there).*	**Identify Push-and-Pull Factors that Shape Your Future:** *Identify forces that need to be managed to reach the preferred future and generate EWS (Why is this possible and how will I know I am getting there).*	**Determine Anchor Policies:** *Identify the gaps and the policy coherence required to move in the trajectory of this preferred future (what is necessary to get there).*	**Determine Impact and Develop an EWS:** *(How do I know I am getting there the correct way I envisioned).*
Funnel Perspective		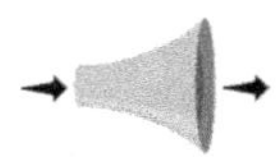	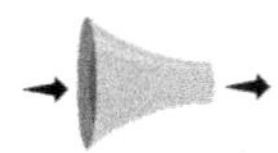	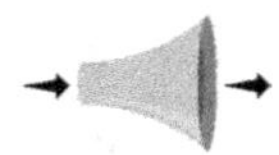	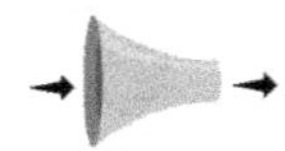

(*Continued*)

Exhibit 18.1. (*Continued*)

	Stage 1: Future Horizon	**Stage 2: Present Horizon**	**Stage 3: Push-and-Pull Factors**	**Stage 4: Anchor Policies**	**Stage 5: Impact and EWS**
Perspective	**Wide → Narrow**	**Narrow → Wide**	**Wide → Narrow**	**Narrow → Wide**	**Wide → Narrow**
Imagination	I Imagination (future possibilities)			III Imagination (impact — imagine other factors that may affect your preferred future — the challenge is to think of wild cards)	I Imagination (spillovers — think of these policies and their impact — on other policy domains)
Scoping	II Scoping (trade-offs — agreeing on norms)	III Scoping (broad-outline assumptions; reflect on present and identify what is missing — nestle the preferred future in the context of life)	I Scoping (broad — identify factors that push or pull the future from happening)	II Scoping (gap analysis — identify policy gaps for the new future)	II Scoping (identify relevant impact — positive, negative, or unintended consequences)

Boundary Setting	III Boundary setting (focus) (settling on preferred future)	I Boundary setting (focus — reconfirm if the process captures the future you prefer — rethink possible futures based on spillovers you foresee (intended and unintended))	II Boundary (scenario/ preferred future and trajectory — assess how these push-and-pull factors affect your future)		
Assessment		II Assessment (feasibility — what is needed to make the probable future guaranteed)	III Assessment (shifts — identify what would be triggers or signs that could inform or warn policymakers of any deviation from the planned trajectory, looking at push-and-pull factors)	I Assessment (Existing policies — assess the policy fit of existing policies — looking for coherence, obsolescence, or even fit for purpose)	II (identify metrics (including baseline) and EWS)

Source: Authors.

Exhibit 18.2. Future vision prompts (sample).

Source: Authors.

Stage 1: Future horizon — Define and visualize the future and the time frame

Process: Imagination (possibilities) → Scoping (trade-offs) → Boundary setting (focus)

Imagination (possibilities): Using the Future Vision prompt cards[4] (see Exhibit 18.2), the following question was asked: *In the year 2075, how would you like (use the prompt from the card: ownership, government, mobility, etc.) to be seen by (use the prompt from the card: individuals, society, etc.)*? This will help start the creative process of a desired future. This individual exercise can take 30–45 minutes, depending on how well the warm-up exercises for reaching an imaginative state went.

The participants read each other's imagined future. By reading the various scenarios, the group chooses a few (via voting) with the help of the facilitator (see Exhibits 18.3(a) and 18.3(b)). By reading other people's cards, the group better understands the shifts that can occur at an ecosystem level, which is an integral part of imagining the future.

Scoping (trade-offs): For scoping, the issue of *identity* in the context of digital twins and learning comes up. The group focuses on this example, looking at trade-offs based on the imagined future for skills. Exhibit 18.4 highlights one of the trade-offs. From this, the group agrees on norms (depicted in Exhibit 18.5).

[4]There are 53 design cards that focus on needs, industry, rights, and values.

Exhibit 18.3(a). Shortlisted scenarios.

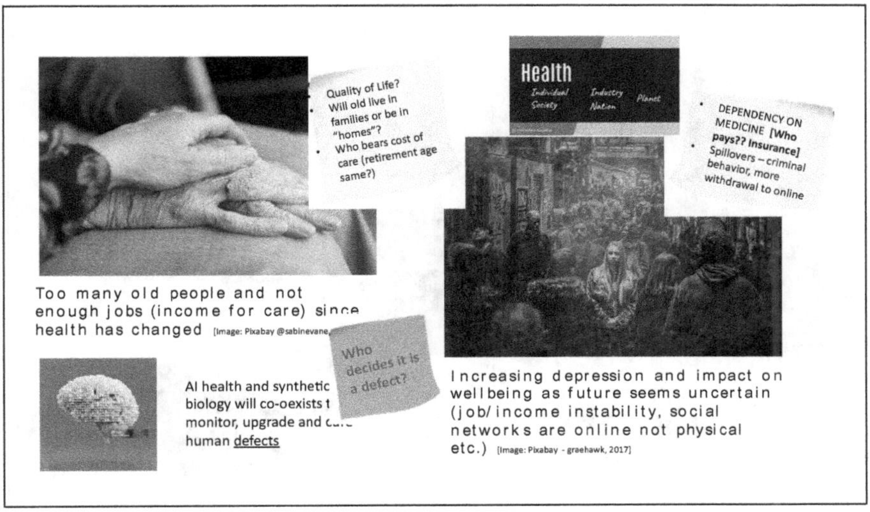

Exhibit 18.3(b). Shortlisted scenarios.

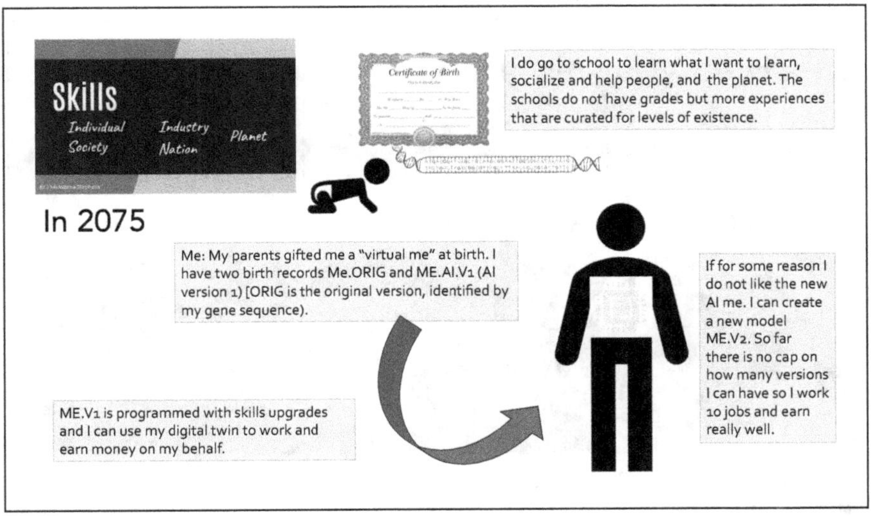

Source: Authors, and Image from Pixabay.

Boundary Setting (narrow): Having agreed on norms, the participants work on a joint final preferred future. This future is defined within the context of the target audiences from whom buy-in is required (users, regulators, industry, and other key stakeholders). At this stage, the focus is

Exhibit 18.4. Sample of trade-offs — Managing real and virtual identity.

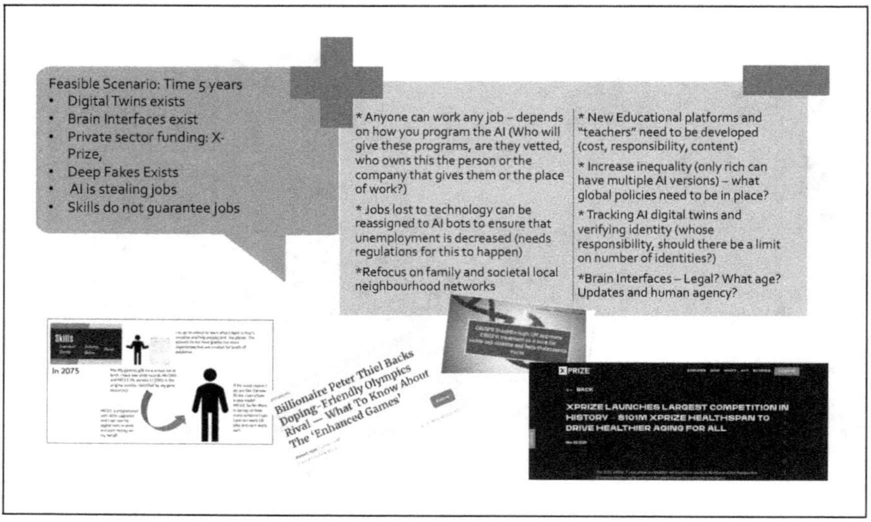

Source: Authors.

Exhibit 18.5. Boundary setting: Norms, stakeholders, and final scenario (sample).

Source: Authors.

national and industry-level agenda setting to get a commitment of resources.

The following four stages need a participatory process to glean frontier knowledge and implicit information and to identify future change agents. At this stage, more participants may be invited to participate.

Exhibit 18.6. Finding the gaps (preferred future and present) — Sample.

Where Are We Now?

Issues	2075	Now (2023)	Missing
Identity (gene and digital)	All people are registered in national and international database.	Only biometrics and names via Hospital or Ministry of Interior	Gene sequencing, data protection policy, which Ministry responsible, Registration of digital twins (which ministry), legal identity of digital twins, Intergovernmental coordination
Jobs for Digital Twins	Recruitment, separation of digital twin jobs (profit sharing), policies	AI and human jobs are separate.	Ethics and regulations, design of jobs and transparency of jobs that can be outsourced to digital twins.
Societal Education	Everyone is a digital native and humans are comfortable interactive with humans and digital humans	40% of the world has no connectivity 20% are not digital natives	Infrastructure (at least 6G) Education on technology and usage (all ages)
Technology	Gene Sequencing, Wearables, Interface, Infrastructure (WIFI)		

Source: Authors.

Step 2: Present horizon: Where are we now?

Process: *Boundary setting (focus)* → *Assessment (feasibility)* → *Scoping (broad)*

Boundary setting (focus): Where are we now? At this stage, the focus is narrowed to issues perceived as important for the preferred journey, and participants assess where they are currently situated (see Exhibit 18.6 as a sample). This stage needs to be synced with the previous stage (so it is iterative). This process is vital to understanding the shift in values, attitudes, and behaviors for the future.

First, list the issues identified in column 1. Then, articulate the preferred future in column 2. Then, state where the group is now (present status) for the issue regarding the articulated future in column 3. This process helps clarify what is missing (column 4), and now participants have a *to-do list* or a list of assumptions to help plan.

Assessment (feasibility): Plausibility is essential for future shaping in backcasting. A table of items identified in the previous stage is now assessed for feasibility. Exhibit 18.7 gives an example of the feasibility of registering human birth and the digital twin.

Scoping (assumptions): The previous step looked at feasibility. However, believing a future is feasible means making assumptions about the

Exhibit 18.7. Feasibility of a key issue (sample).

Feasibility: Registration

List	Feasibility by 2075	Discussion Points
Gene sequencing and registration	Feasible: need costs to drop to US 2/- (Research grants for tech development?) Need to link health records with legal biometrics (national)	To reduce costs: Speed up by investing grants (buy – COST USD 1 million or make COST USD 2 billion) Cybersecurity and data protection of existing health systems not strong enough New system with blockchain (that can be tied with digital twins and the national ID – Cost 4 Billion (reoccurring 3 million) and needs to be parallel with existing.
Digital Twins	Gene digital twin AI twin and skills and learning	Possible – details may keep evolving as more knowledge of human body emerges (cost 15 million) AI twin for skills and learning (may need brain interfaces or more) - too intrusive if it mirrors human being – AVOID. Can be independent of human self.

Source: Authors.

Exhibit 18.8. Assumptions (sample).

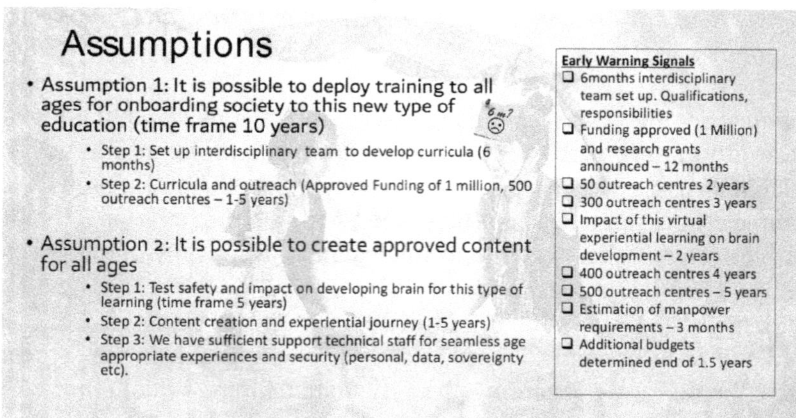

Source: Authors.

pathway to this future. This assumption could be related to technology, resources, regulation changes, behavior and attitude shifts, or even the economy (see Exhibit 18.8).

In this example, resource assumptions could be in terms of R&D, funding, talent, political connections, strategic resources, or even

Exhibit 18.9. Push-and-pull factors (example).

Pull Factors (Future Opportunistic Trends)	Push (Trends from the Weight of the Past and the Present Momentum)
Technology Development and Funding: Industry growth	Global Competitiveness: National level focus on education (to control talent and mindsets)
UNESCO focuses on individual learning for the child	Ministries of Education begin to deploy remote learning
AI competitiveness and fusion of Synthetic Biology	Work-life-balance becomes a right
Balance of both demographic extremes countries with aging population and countries with young population	Increasing pension payouts and dwindling birth rates
Emergence of virtual/augmented reality and spatial computing platforms	Antitrust issues

Source: Authors.

legitimacy. A series of assumptions have been accepted, assuming that the 2075 scenario comes true. It is essential to write these assumptions explicitly. These assumptions may also act as early warning signals (EWSs). In Exhibit 18.9, another assumption could be on early prototypes that may become obsolete because of newer and better technologies.

Step 3: Push-and-pull factors that shape your future

Process: *Scoping (broad)* → *Imagination (Focus and trajectory)* → *Assessment*

Scoping (broad): In this step, participants identify the trends that will aid or detract from their preferred future (push-and-pull factors). They begin by rewriting their vision for the future. It is normal for the preferred future to change as more information becomes available during the iterative process. These trends are organized into themes: metaphor, litany, systemic, and worldview[5] (see Exhibit 18.10). For policymakers, by acknowledging that public value is a perception, these trends and facts on which the strategy is based form a baseline of assumptions.

[5]This can be understood looking at the following document: Asian Development Bank (2022). Futures Thinking in Asia and Pacific. Manila: ADB.

Exhibit 18.10. Casual layered analysis levels (example of first-level analysis).

CLA	Description	Problem-Solving	Challenge
Litany (visible problem)	**View of current reality**: Education is broken. AI will take away our jobs. There is no such thing as work–life balance unless you are wealthy. **Official description of the issue:** Education is not tailored to the child's needs nor will lead to an increase in earnings.	**Simple Litany—captures the current narrative:** Customize education based on individual needs and allow individuals to earn income from their unique talents.	**Between Litany and Systemic Perspective:** AI learns from individual data; how do we prevent big tech from exploiting special skills? How can we create a shared rewards system so that no one is left behind in society? What about people who want to live off the grid?
Systemic perspective (Causes)	**Causes for current reality:** Industry, education, and government interventions are out of sync.	**Complicated**: Ethics of the idea of digital twins and their standardization (can there be anonymization of identity for specific cases? Issue of personal data privacy).	
Worldview (Frame of Analysis)	**Assumptions behind causes of key stakeholders:** How can we keep our cultural values in this new way of learning? Does this impact child psychology, and what are dos and don'ts?	**Complex multiple systems now interact**: Who will be the guardian of the guard keeper for privacy?	**Between Systemic perspective and World view:** If we do not get into this space, will we lose a competitive advantage?

(*Continued*)

Exhibit 18.10. (*Continued*)

CLA	Description	Problem-Solving	Challenge
	Is society prepared for the cyber and data security issues? Whose responsibility is it to onboard non-digital and digitally divergent people to acceptable standards? Who decides, and what are acceptable standards?		
Metaphor (Deep, Unspoken Issues) — *Sci-Fi is an excellent place to start*	**Nation First and the Country with Data owns the World** FIRST TO DATA	Fear about being left behind or about brainwashing or even longevity in virtual paradigm (like Altered Carbon; Transcendence); Data Privacy and issues (Minority Report). THE DATA LEAPFROG	**Between World view and Metaphor:** Is there a clash of paradigms? AI and its robotic representations versus the original version of the human (ORG) may result in a reality where the real and virtual worlds collide and influence each other (for better or worse). The Child AI could be a genius and evolves faster than parent — and then who will be the guardian? (Movies like Terminator, Ready Player One; Minority Report or Brian and Charles could be examples) WE OWN DATA AND THEN DATA OWNS US

Source: Authors.

Exhibit 18.11. Trajectory to preferred future.

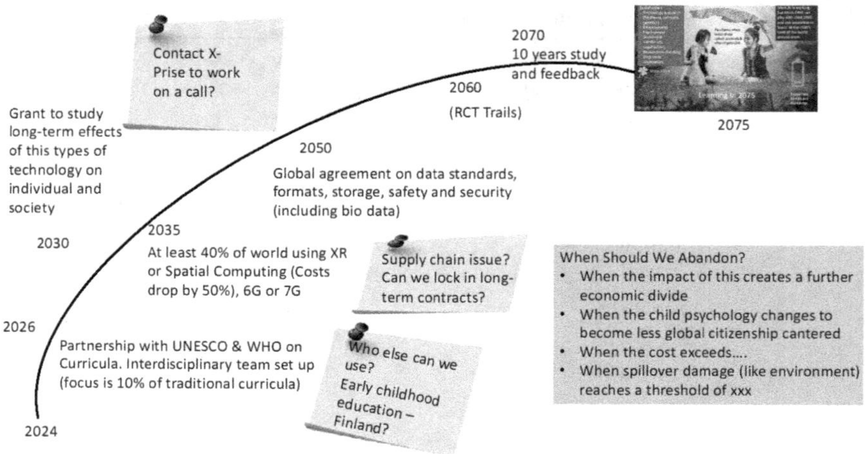

Source: Authors.

Following a discussion, another round of anonymous voting, a discussion, and a prioritization of factors take place. These factors are prioritized based on issues that policymakers will need greater oversight. What is critical in this stage is to describe *additional assumptions* based on the preceding analyses. Stage 3 should end in a trajectory of likely events that need to happen in the preferred future. The more detailed it is, the more likely the participants will be able to shape the future (see Exhibit 18.11).

Boundary (scenario and trajectory): Look at the identified EWS and assumptions; what can be done if the trajectory is not going as planned? These scenarios must be visualized via brainstorming to think of backup plans (refer to Exhibits 18.5 and 18.11). This process will add to the list of assumptions and EWS.

Assessment (shifts): When do the participants think aborting their policy/strategy implementation is suitable if the backup plans fail (see Exhibit 18.11)? At this step, participants determine the hard stops to ensure the backup plans are not because of hubris or because the project becomes too big to fail. Addressing the possible elephant in the room endorses the fact that values and norms outweigh the preferred future. Further, it is called a preferred future because, in the present, only imagination can take the participants to the future. When to abort the planned trajectory is added to the list of EWS and assumptions.

Stage 4: Anchor policies

Assessment (existing policies) → Scoping (gap analysis) → Imagination (impact)

Assessment (existing policies): What policies (strategies) will need to evolve at every stage of the various problems identified by the EWS and assumptions if the preferred future is knocked off course? Keep it human-centered. This centering is described by Karl-Henrik Dreborg, the Swedish futurist, as follows: "*To qualify as a backcasting study, the scenarios chosen in the project must reflect solutions to a specified societal problem.*"[6] The scenarios should help the participants get a broader perspective of possible solutions.[7] Revisit Exhibits 18.10 and 18.11. List the policies, adding more points of consideration from other analyses. Classify policies as (1) local, (2) national, and (3) international policies.

Scoping (gap analysis): Once participants list all the policies, the group needs to reflect on each policy's projected impact across time and look at push-and-pull factors that may modify the intended effect (this is an iterative stage with Step 3). Ask the following:

- What is the flexibility built into the policies?
- What new policies may be needed?
- What data do we need for evidence and baseline monitoring? Who and how should we capture them?
- What are the methods for rapid sharing of learnings?
- Who has the responsibility for the policy adaptation?
- What are the narratives of each person in the process? Do you have an inner story that can help create the desired future? Or are their stories counterproductive and not aligned with the vision?

This analysis helps identify critical stakeholders for shaping the intended future. Further, the participants have aggregated data points that can also act as EWS.

---

[6]Dreborg, K.-H. (1996). Essence of backcasting. *Futures*, 28(9): 816.

[7]Quist, J. & Vergragt, P. (2006). Past and future of backcasting: The shift to stakeholder participation and a proposal for a methodological framework. *Futures*, 38(9): 1027–1045.

Imagination (impact): This exercise aims to understand the positive and negative implications of the decisions on the preferred future by revisiting the revised scenario (in this case, the revision of Exhibit 18.7). In this case, the first level of effect is the child and the caregiver (human or robot). The next impact level is society (family), community, and education professionals. The group may identify skills that need to be developed or may be lost. A question can be asked under what conditions the robot might gain sentience. Or is it best to see the key characters as part of an ecology of consciousness? These focused discussions broaden the knowledge base at both individual and collective levels. Revisit all previous charts and update them with relevant information.

Stage 5: Impact: Developing an EWS — The last stage

Process: *Imagination (spillovers) → Scoping (relevant impact and unintended consequences) assessment (metrics and EWS)*

The final iteration takes place to ensure that the future and the processes for future shaping are aligned.

Imagination (spillovers): We now broaden the scope to look at the impact beyond education in terms of human (general), societal, environmental, technological, legal, defense, and economic impacts. This broadened perspective will form part of the EWS. Here, the participants need to be careful not to always define their impact in terms of low-hanging fruits[8] or quick wins, which may lead to mission drift. Some of this may have already been done, but it is a confirmatory process.

Scoping (relevant impact and unintended consequences): This stage is relatively easy. The group sorts the impact into relevant effects and unintended consequences. The group now revisits the policy, assumption, and EWS lists (see Exhibit 18.12 as a sample).

Assessment (metrics): The group now takes the same list and creates a list of data that need to be collected (also derived from EWS). So, for example, if data are being collected on technological advancements, and the scoping exercise determines that the boundary includes hardware, genetics, and regulatory principles, the question will focus on data for each and

---

[8]Holmberg & Dreberg (2000), *Op. cit.*

Exhibit 18.12. Data, EWSs, and assumption updated lists.

Data (Braod)

- Level of progress of technology hardware/software etc.
  - hardware
  - Software – programming and biological
  - standards
- Mobile coverage pp
- Bandwidth coverage pp
- Access to age and education resources Preschool – K12
- Learning levels and job opportunities (matching effectiveness)
- Deviations between ORG. and AI and impact at multiple levels – individual, family, society, nation, global citizenship
- Environmental impact
- Political impact and power of private sector versus small business etc

EWS

- Synthetic Biology (neuro interface)
  - Technology readiness level (Scale of 1–9 DoD scale)
- Hardware TRL
  - TRL
- Infrastructure
  - TRL
- Programming (new)
  - TRL
- Quantum Computing
  - TRL
- Incident register report
- Regulations (Education, Technology, Industry, Défense, Export/Import etc.)

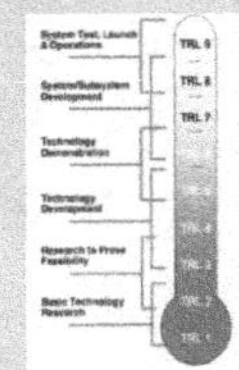

Assumptions

- Global Citizenship Values are universal
- Transparency of code
- Cybersecurity is real-time
- Personal data can be deidentified for analysis
- Profit sharing to ensure no inequality based on income/earnings
- Sustainability processes will ensure planet flourishing
- Etc.

Source: Authors.

determine the collection responsibility. This is an interesting exercise as it requires a constant revisit of STEM advancements and also tests your assumptions on the benefits of a preferred future.

18.3 Conclusion

The example illustrated in this chapter shows how complex backcasting is. It reiterates the importance of time (to conduct the activity), the need for multiple stakeholders at multiple levels, and iteration. While foresight workshops are trendy, the reality is that if governance is the focus, it needs thoughtful, long-term thinking and the ability to challenge assumptions. This is a special skill. It requires systems thinking, which is the ability to move from "*observing events or data, to identifying patterns of behavior over time, to surfacing the underlying structures that drive those events and patterns*."[9] One needs to "see" the intricacies of a wicked problem and understand the complex decision-making situation, the multiple stakeholders' agendas and the beneficiary perception of impact before turning to solutioning.[10] Systems thinking can be defined as "*a set of synergistic analytic skills used to improve the capability of identifying and understanding systems, predicting their behaviors, and devising modifications to them in order to produce desired effects. These skills work together as a system*."[11]

Backcasting participants need cognitive flexibility, defined as "*A skill that enables us to switch between different concepts or to adapt behavior to achieve goals in a novel or changing environment. Cognitive flexibility provides us with the ability to see that what we are doing is not leading to success and to make the appropriate changes to achieve it*."[12] Backcasting participants need to have systems thinking skills. They must also go

---

[9]Goodman, M. (2018). Systems thinking: What, why, when, where, and how? *Systems Thinker*. Available: https://thesystemsthinker.com/systems-thinking-what-why-when-where-and-how/ (Accessed 3 February, 2024).

[10]Richmond, B. (1993). Systems thinking: Critical thinking skills for the 1990s and beyond. *System Dynamics Review*, 9(2): 113–133.

[11]Arnold, R.D. & Wade, J.P. (2015). A definition of systems thinking: A systems approach. *Procedia Computer Science*, 44: 669–678.

[12]Sahakian, B.J., Langley, C., & Leong, C. (2021). Why is cognitive flexibility important and how can you improve it? *WEF*, 25 June. Available: https://www.weforum.org/agenda/2021/06/cognitive-flexibility-thinking-iq-intelligence/#:~:text=Many%20of%20

beyond systems to deep narratives, as in the CLA Model. Underneath the system are worldviews that are supported by myths and metaphors. While backcasting requires participants to move toward rigor, to make a difference — to change minds and hearts and impact policy and strategy — it must link to core metaphors. These stories ensure that the strategies developed have a deep commitment from all parties.[13]

Finally, backcasting participants should be boundary spanners. Participants need to find relevant knowledge, verify the information, and know where to seek additional opinions and facts. Boundary-spanning skills allow participants to act as a "*network manager; the importance of building effective personal relationships with a wide range of other actors; the ability to manage in non-hierarchical decision environments through negotiation and brokering; and performing the role of 'policy entrepreneur' to connect problems to solutions and mobilize resources and effort in the search for successful outcomes.*"[14]

Hence, though future foresight benefits from a diversity of thought, if the exercise has skilled participants with the three above-mentioned skills, the process of shaping the future may be a more effective exercise where governance can also be inbuilt into the process.

The future of education and its intersection with advanced technologies like AI and genome editing will require policymakers to ask what kind of society we wish for in the future. They must look at all possibilities, good and bad, to ensure suitable guardrails are generated to create a more positive outcome for humanity and the planet. This deliberation is essential at multiple levels.

---

these%20traits%20are,a%20novel%20or%20changing%20environment (Accessed 3 February, 2024).

[13] Inayatullah, S. (2022). *From Anticipation to Emancipation.* Malaysia: Tamkang University.

[14] Williams, P. (2002). The competent boundary spanner. *Public Administration*, 80(1): 103–124.

Section 4

Learning from the Past: Guardrails and Opportunities

https://doi.org/10.1142/9789811296000_0019

Chapter 19

From OldSpace to NewSpace: Not Just an Evolution, Not Yet a Revolution

Donato Giorgi*

Centre National d'Etudes Spatiales, Paris, France

Key Takeaways

- The ongoing transformation of the space sector requires that we take into account a great diversity of factors and components, typical of complex systems.
- Miniaturization, digitalization, increase of private investments, and globalization of space are changing the competitive dynamics of national space programs, both nationally and in the international arena.
- Despite the mainstream narrative on NewSpace, fundamentals of the space sector are almost unchanged: Long-term planning and transparent public budgets are still necessary to support the R&D&I that the industry may then transform into products and services.
- Fostering entrepreneurship in space requires a higher tolerance of risk for public procurement.
- While the space sector grows, negative consequences on the environment can be already seen and need to be addressed pragmatically.

*Disclaimer: Views, thoughts, and opinions expressed in the text belong solely to the author and not necessarily to the author's employer or organization.

19.1 The Birth of a Commercial Space Age Full of Promises

If you have never heard of Elon Musk, you probably have spent the last few years hidden in a cave, away from society, or you should definitely review your information and social media strategy. Eclectic and visionary entrepreneur, borderline genius for some, he became famous — before the Twitter/X saga — for his electric cars, Tesla, and for his endeavors in the space industry with his company Space X.

It is in space that he has become the herald (despite himself) of a new age of the space race dubbed NewSpace[1] that has brought a multiplication of new actors, public and private, in all segments of the space arena. Space has since become a regular topic for mainstream media, with astronauts gaining the status of social media celebrities (see Exhibit 19.1), more and more countries creating their own space civilian and/or defense space agencies or industries, and start-ups popping up anywhere there is potential for public and/or private funding. Moreover, the prospect of women and men setting foot again on the Moon or one day on Mars already appears as a galvanizing first step to colonizing our solar system, making humanity a multi-planetary species. This is indeed a surprising shift if compared to 15 or 20 years ago when there were still a limited number of well-known entities (countries, space agencies, industries, and academia) that had dominated the space field for decades, mainly focused on science, technology, and security (and some commercial business, like satellite telecommunications).

This shift happened as a consequence of a complex system evolution that a reorientation of policies by the US administration has prepared and profoundly accelerated.

First of all, as a regulator, the decision to make available space data and bid on their commercial potential more than 20 years ago, allowing access to precise (non-degraded) GPS signals to the public (in 2000)[2] and opening

---

[1] Commercial use of space has existed since the early 60s when, for instance, AT&T paid US$3 million to NASA for their broadcasting satellite Telstar in 1962. NewSpace is also characterized by private customers, new business models, private investment, applications outside the space sector, and exploitation of new data. For example, see: Golkar, A. & Salado, A. (2020). Definition of new space — Expert survey results and key technology trends. *IEEE Journal on Miniaturization for Air and Space Systems*, 2(1): 2–9.

[2] GPS.gov. Available: https://www.gps.gov/systems/gps/modernization/sa/.

Exhibit 19.1. French astronaut Thomas Pesquet, regularly ranked 2nd favorite celebrity in France.

Source: Reproduced with permission: © ESA/NASA 2017.

(well before)[3] the market for satellite imagery. We can hardly imagine our daily life without satellite navigation and precise positioning today.

Then, as the biggest client of the space industry, in a sector largely dominated by public budgets, the US administration tried a different procurement approach aimed at reducing costs and complexity: by buying a service with fixed price contracts from a commercial provider, instead of developing the space infrastructure themselves that would eventually be used to the same effect.[4] Announced by NASA in 2006, the Commercial Orbital Transportation Services program (and those that followed up) did exactly that: In order to replace the Space Shuttle[5] (to be retired in 2011),

---

[3]Land Remote Sensing Policy Act, 1992; Scott, W. (2016). Op-ed | U.S. satellite imaging regulations must be modernized. *Space News*, 29 August. Available: https://spacenews.com/op-ed-u-s-satellite-imaging-regulations-must-be-modernized/ (Accessed 5 February, 2024). To be noted that the French and the Soviet were already selling satellite imagery at then-considered high resolution.

[4]For example, see: Heracleous, L., Terrier, D., & Gonzalez, S. (2019). NASA's capability evolution toward commercial space. *Space Policy*, 50: 101330.

[5]Each single flight of the Space Shuttle was estimated to cost around US$1 billion.

a limited number of industries were selected to compete (and to be supported by NASA) to provide cargo resupply and crew transportation services to the International Space Station (i.e. NASA would then buy a service from an operator and would not own nor operate launcher and transportation module as in the past).

Such a choice — essentially delegating technical responsibility to industry — was met with some ill-concealed skepticism by some, who perceived the program as an interesting experiment deemed to fail, since "space is hard." Despite a few drawbacks and a decade-long dependence on Russia for astronauts' transportation to and from the ISS, the new approach proved to be successful. The success of SpaceX and Elon Musk was born and, with it, a structural fall in price for launch services (~40% for geostationary orbits and by a factor of 4 for the ISS)[6] and a much larger availability of launch opportunities (with new and legacy launch companies and with SpaceX launching very often).

In parallel, technological progress, notably in miniaturization and digitalization (led by Silicon Valley) and a larger availability of space technologies made space assets and services much more accessible. Concretely, universities with majors in space engineering could afford labs to develop nanosats (satellites of a size of multiple cubes of 10 cm per side, adapted for hands-on projects for students), and more companies emerged to offer small satellites with performances that were unattainable earlier for such a category of satellites[7] or to provide new space-based services. This led to the creation of companies like Planet in 2010 and Starlink in 2015 and the emergence of constellations of satellites.

It was the first time in the history of space that the launch market experienced a major structural reduction in prices, that space technology became much more accessible, and the production of space infrastructures, services, and data started to become easier. As a consequence, imagination took off and rapidly created a buzz around the world.

---

[6] Jones, H. (2018). The recent large reduction in space launch cost. Available: https://ttu-ir.tdl.org/items/bc37e942-bf12-479c-8fc6-4711c0e270d4 (Accessed 1 February, 2024).

[7] Some quite rightfully say that, for the same performances, satellite size went from a small car to a shoebox; see Henriquet, P. (2022). New space: The changing face of the space industry. *Polytechnique Insights*, 3 November. Available: https://www.polytechnique-insights.com/en/columns/space/new-space-the-changing-face-of-the-space-industry/ (Accessed 1 February, 2024).

19.2 A Race Toward the New Economic Frontier

As NewSpace showed potential for commercial success, a new narrative was being forged: Space is the new economic frontier. Space technology application spillovers are everywhere (from our phones to airplanes' Wi-Fi or banking precise timing), and the economic potential of space data, space exploration, or space-based services remains to be unleashed; so, if this is not strictly for space economy itself, space technology can be an enabler for the economic development of a multitude of other sectors.

Interestingly, this economic narrative has become predominant and, on a more or less anecdotic note, the term *innovation* has replaced or been added to the expression R&D in the general language for activities related to the preparation of the future and for space in particular. Apparently, interest in technology itself has shrunk if it is not related to new concrete and profitable applications over the short term. Understandably, when global economic growth lags behind, and employment rates are weak, economic development may become the main rationale to convince decision-makers to allocate funds for investments in space. Of course, GPS applications and Elon Musk appear as evidence that this space rationale is, in principle, correct.

Today, it is common practice in the space sector to recall a study published by Morgan Stanley — among others — in 2017 stating that the global space industry could generate revenue of US$ 1.1 trillion or more in 2040, up from US$340 billion in 2017.[8] The space market encompasses a wide range of sectors, satellite technology, telecommunications, space tourism, asteroid mining, and research in space. Of course, every country wants a slice of the pie and, while bearing in mind the importance of science and the strategic role of space technology for national autonomy (military satellites for intelligence and secure telecom, Geo-intelligence, etc.), more and more countries have been increasingly drawn to space for the promise of economic returns.

From the Philippines to the Gulf nations via Australia, the number of space agencies and offices has grown in the last 20 years. National space laws[9] — as the regulator's enabling tool — have been approved or are

---

[8] Sheetz, M. (2017). Morgan Stanley predicts space industry will triple in size: Here's how to invest. Available: https://www.cnbc.com/2017/10/12/morgan-stanley-how-to-invest-in-1-trillion-space-industry.html (Accessed 15 January, 2024).

[9] UNOOSA (2023). National space law. Available: https://www.unoosa.org/oosa/en/ourwork/spacelaw/nationalspacelaw/index.html (Accessed 4 February, 2024).

being updated (where they existed already). Facilities to promote entrepreneurship and the creation of start-ups (incubators and accelerators) are being deployed extensively; considerable government budgets are dedicated to innovation in space, and private investors/venture capital firms have invested important amounts in space companies.

Of course, the fact that success in space may translate into harnessing space technology to fuel economic growth adds to its potential for geopolitical influence, technological advancement, and, where necessary, societal transition toward a knowledge-based society. Investments in space appear more than ever as a Swiss knife to aid in the progress of society.

19.3 Taking a Perspective on the Mainstream Narrative

The emergence of NewSpace, Elon Musk's interplanetary vision, and the new race to the Moon have sparked general enthusiasm and optimism about the potential of space technology and its future markets. From the lunar economy to asteroid mining, in-orbit servicing, mini and micro launchers, and settling a human colony on Mars, all seem possible (see Exhibit 19.2).

However, it is important to understand enthusiasm using the right amount of perspective, appropriate figures, and contextualization. In fact, even if trust in technology has rarely been disappointed (often, it is just a matter of time, patience, and abundance of funds to find a solution compatible with the laws of physics), business models, perception of opportunities, and future markets may sometimes be fallacious. Policymakers need to understand the assumptions being made in these estimates.

For a start, the definition of what space economy is and, as a consequence, its size are not unanimously agreed upon especially if compared to the approach used by Morgan Stanley. While many tend to use the latter,[10] others[11] consider that the US$1 trillion related figures are flawed by a lack

[10] Even in 2023, McKinsey Forecasts $1 Trillion by 2030, Though Currently It Is Valued US$ 447 Billion from US$ 280 Billion in 2010. See McKinsey (2023). A giant leap for the space industry. Available: https://www.mckinsey.com/featured-insights/sustainable-inclusive-growth/chart-of-the-day/a-giant-leap-for-the-space-industry# (Accessed 5 February, 2024).

[11] Like Pierre Lionnet, Research and Managing Director of Eurospace, the European association of space industries. See his post: Available: https://www.linkedin.com/posts/eurospacepierrelionnet_space-economy-fundamentals-activity-6835514574809137152-tGPI or (in French), Lugherini, Regnaud, Saint Martin: Available: https://www.lemonde.fr/

Exhibit 19.2. The Moon from the International Space Station. The Moon is perceived as a future economic environment.

Source: Reproduced with permission: © NASA/ESA 2016.

of clearly defined methodology and are inflated by a questionable use of the notion of "space-enabled economy." This includes, for example, the value of content distributed by satellites (Direct-To-Home television) and the value of apps using satellite positioning (GNSS). But the use of GNSS positioning for ship tracking does not make maritime shipping part of the space economy, nor a Bollywood movie if it is broadcast by a satellite. Hence, a growth in these uses (meaning a greater number of GNSS terminals or DTH equipment) has no impact on the demand for satellites.

Such enthusiasm was generated during a 15-year-long period of low or even negative interest rates and, therefore, there is a strong tendency to bear risks which attracted private investors or VC. But as the interest rates go up, investors are less incentivized to fund capital-intensive projects that do not have a clear revenue stream or path to profitability, leaving many space start-ups scuffling for funds.

idees/article/2024/01/09/europe-spatiale-une-copie-baclee-de-ce-que-les-americains-ont-fait-il-y-a-vingt-ans-ne-peut-pas-tenir-lieu-de-politique-spatiale-europeenne_62099-09_3232.html.

In 2022, private investment dropped 50% year-to-year for space start-ups. We are witnessing the first few bankruptcies (Masten Space Systems, Virgin Orbit), layoffs (Planet, GOMSpace, Sierra Space), and restructuring of business plans (Rocket Lab from small to big launchers). In the context of competition and potential oversupply of similar offers, consolidations look very likely in the next few years, especially if one considers that most of NewSpace companies have not found a replacement in the market for investor funding.

As of 2022, government space budgets were estimated at US$ 103 billion, while private investments are less than US$ 10 billion (after an all-time peak of US$ 15 billion in 2021), with most of the latter collected by a small group of companies like SpaceX. Even though a stabilization of the level of private investment in space is expected (and not a catastrophic drop), the narrative of NewSpace, where the commercial business will take over from government-supported programs, looks overoptimistic. This appears particularly true when considering that business plans of the likes of SpaceX, DigitalGlobe, or Planet are supported by, if not depending on, institutional contracts.

19.4 Anticipating to Avoid and/or Mitigate Potentially Disrupting Consequences of NewSpace

Regardless of the exact size of the future space economy, it is already clear that the space sector is growing and changing at a fast pace. The space actors are not only increasing in number but are also engaging in an ever-expanding array of activities that range from launching constellations of hundreds and thousands of satellites in orbit to plans to develop private space stations or reach the Moon, Mars, or the asteroids. The ever-growing number of new players (and objects in orbit around Earth) is complexifying the dynamics of the space sector and, therefore, questioning the relevance of the current governance.

This needs to be worked out at different levels. Within a country or a region, the transition from a few major industrial players (sometimes one or two; think of Airbus or Thalès in Europe or Boeing, Lockheed Martin, and Northrop Grumman in the USA) to a much larger industrial base brings advantages, like more competition and reduced costs, but it adds more complexity as well. Governments and space agencies need to now adapt their industrial policy and, while preserving the strategic industrial assets developed in decades of investments and the associated employment (sometimes remnants of a sort of military–industrial complex), they have to provide opportunities to the newcomers. In a sector like space where public funds are paramount to the success of a company, this is not an easy task.

Additional complexity also impacts the way a country regulates space activities under its purview in relation to the international community. To address this, national laws are being prepared (as in Saudi Arabia), updated (like in France), and bylaws adopted (as in the UAE). The difficult task of the legislator is to take into account, on the one hand, the need to support the competitiveness of its industry and, on the other hand, the responsibilities and obligations stemming from international law (the Space Treaties, in particular), safety and security of its citizens, and protection of the environment on Earth and in space.

This is indeed a difficult and multifaceted task. For instance, easier access to technologies can lead to uncontrolled technology transfers and missile proliferation[12] that governments need to anticipate and prevent. Moreover, the orbital environment has to be preserved through a sustainability approach. With the exponential growth of objects in Low Earth Orbit (area of space below an altitude of 2,000 km), the risk of collisions in orbit or uncontrolled reentry on Earth become more and more worrying (see Exhibit 19.3). But, unlike the sea or the airspace, space has very limited rules defined by the Space Treaties and few internationally endorsed guidelines and best practices (it is to be noted that decades ago, the international community delegated to the International Telecommunications Union the management of telecommunication frequencies and the allocation of geostationary orbit slots — identified even then as scarce resources).

Considering the current state of multilateralism, particularly in UN fora like the Committee on Peaceful Use of Outer Space (COPUOS), it is unrealistic to envisage a revision of the Space Treaties to define a new compulsory regime dedicated to space. Nonetheless, the international

[12] Brockmann, K. & Raju, N. (2022). NewSpace and the Commercialization of the Space Industry: Challenges for the Missile Technology Control Regime. Stockholm International Peace Research Centre. Available: https://www.sipri.org/publications/2022/policy-reports/newspace-and-commercialization-space-industry-challenges-missile-technology-control-regime (Accessed 15 January, 2024).

Exhibit 19.3. Evolution of the number of objects launched per year in low earth orbit.

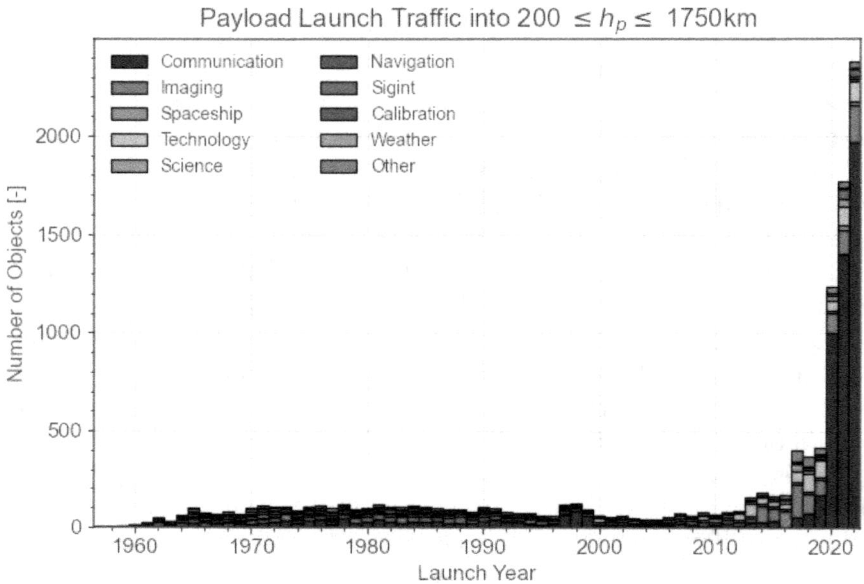

Source: Reproduced with permission: © ESA Space Environment Report 2023.

community is making efforts to identify or update more flexible, non-mandatory tools (like the COPUOS Guidelines for the Long-term Sustainability of Outer Space Activities adopted in 2019) to ensure, at least for the moment, a reasonable common approach to sustainable use of space. The final objective, over the long term and a topic of continuous discussion and negotiation, is to establish a global and comprehensive Space Traffic Management.

In the same vein, as a new race to the Moon is underway, with Mars and the asteroids being targeted as the next destinations, there is a need for clear rules for safe and transparent exploration, scientific research, and commercial activities on these celestial bodies. However, today, as space exploration operates more in a competitive than a cooperative manner, notably between the US and their partners on one side and China and Russia on the other, a globally endorsed approach is not only overly ambitious but, as one could suspect, not even a priority.

Therefore, in anticipation of the return to the Moon, the US administration elaborated a new framework in 2020 for international cooperation in space exploration called "Artemis Accords" (like the Greek goddess of the Moon and the actual US space program). Based on the Outer Space Treaty, with the goal of achieving a sustainable and robust presence on the Moon, the Artemis Accords are a political document establishing a set of principles to govern the civil exploration and use of outer space. Among these principles, it is worth noting the definition of "safety zones" and the "extraction and utilization of space resources," the former to avoid harmful interference on the surface of the Moon (or Mars, asteroids, or comets). Resources will be necessary to support a long-term presence on the Moon but the Accords clear the way to commercial exploitation of such resources, which is very much one of the long-term goals of the NewSpace ecosystem. So far, more than thirty US partners have signed the Artemis Accords. China and Russia and their partners, in the meantime, are making progress on their project for an International Lunar Research Station (ILRS).

19.5 Conclusion

The space sector is in a profound transformative phase initiated by both the effect of an acquired maturity of the industry and a change of approach of the American administration toward its space sector. Born in the USA, NewSpace is now a global trend for governments, industries, and societies. It has disruptive consequences for the traditional space industry and how our governments deal with the economy, society, environment, international partners, and so on. Nonetheless, the fundamentals are still the same, and disruption and continuity seem to go hand in hand — It is not just an evolution but not yet a revolution.

If the USA has pushed and anticipated the consequences of such transformation, making use of its competitive advantages, like large market and massive budgets that allow it to take risks and plan alternatives, others are trying to catch up, their actions sometimes being hindered by budgetary constraints and political and industrial setups.

In such a context, governments' agility and anticipation are essential to build and maintain a sustainable and competitive space sector. The factors of success are numerous, and looking back at how the space sector has been developing in the USA and in the rest of the world, some considerations seem appropriate while, of course, far from being exhaustive.

The so-called OldSpace and NewSpace are not mutually exclusive, and they rather complement each other. With the traditional industry being challenged, it needs to become more agile and competitive. Newcomers need to build a legacy, grow in size, and demonstrate reliability. Governments and space agencies, the source of most of the space budgets so far, play the essential role of building bridges between the two and making sure that while new approaches (governance, management, procurement, human capital, etc.) are implemented, knowledge and know-how are not lost. Throwing the baby out with the bathwater is never a good idea.

The success of the American NewSpace model, while apparently very enticing, cannot be envisaged as transferrable "as is" to the rest of the world. The USA are essentially a self-reliant space ecosystem sustained by the biggest budgets worldwide and well protected from international competition. Europe, on the contrary, has much lower budgets,[13] scattered over countries and organizations playing in a complex and much more open market. For instance, attempts to implement in Europe a real base of institutional anchor tenant customers (European Union, ESA, European countries) for European launchers (as NASA does for SpaceX, for instance) has not been really successful, so far.[14]

Similarly, the will to create a space ecosystem from scratch requires a holistic approach implying, among others, setting up balanced regulations (business oriented while protecting national interests and environment), investment in talent development, and providing access to technology and appropriate funding. Long-term, transparent space programs are essential to localize competence and production and to make the industry blossom and grow.

Lastly, part of NewSpace's success comes from its intrinsic entrepreneurial nature and acceptance of higher levels of risk than in the past. Since public funds and support are necessary for development, a risk-taking culture needs to be addressed at an institutional level, now more than in the past, as civil servants are by definition responsible for the good use of taxpayers' money. Clearly, appropriate rules of procurement for public contracts need to be defined.

---

[13] Euroconsult (2023). New historic high for government space spending mostly driven by defense expenditures. Available: https://www.euroconsult-ec.com/press-release/new-historic-high-for-government-space-spending-mostly-driven-by-defense-expenditures/ (Accessed 15 January, 2024).

[14] Wall, M. (2023). SpaceX Falcon 9 rocket launches 2 German military satellites. *Space.com*, 24 December. Available: https://www.space.com/spacex-german-military-satellites-launch-december-2023 (Accessed 15 January, 2024).

https://doi.org/10.1142/9789811296000_0020

Chapter 20

Frameworks for Impact Measurement under Uncertainty

Keertana Subramani

Mohammed Bin Rashid School of Government, Dubai, UAE

Key Takeaways

- The chapter discusses why impact measurement frameworks are of vital importance in the inception, design, monitoring, and adaptation of governmental policies to ensure their success in reaching intended outcomes.
- Broadly, impact measurement serves to help policymakers achieve twin goals: to identify and mitigate risks and adapt policies with the needs of time to ensure their goals are met.
- Effectively employing impact measurement frameworks helps the government in several ways, including improving transparency and public trust, preventing unintended consequences, and identifying which policies to choose or sustain among a range of potential options.
- Three different approaches are proposed to help policymakers identify when to implement policies of different types: an analysis-based approach, a plausibility-based approach, and an approach relying on tracking of indicative metrics (indices).
- A 7-step cyclical framework is presented, which governments can employ to effectively measure the impact of any policy.

20.1 Introduction

The *Great Leap Forward* campaign, a cultural and social movement, was launched by the Chinese Communist Party leader Mao Zedong in 1958 with the aim to rapidly transform China into an industrialized socialist society.[1] It, however, resulted in 15 to 30 million people dying of starvation, causing one of the greatest famines in human history.[2] A slow response to initial indications of food shortages was to blame for the famine.[3] The slow response was in part due to a lack of objective reporting on the agricultural situation, including a "*nearly complete breakdown in the agricultural reporting system*."[4]

The failure of the well-intentioned Great Leap Forward campaign demonstrates why *anticipatory governance* and impact governance frameworks are crucial for policymakers to avoid unintended consequences and ensure that well-intentioned policies achieve their desired outcomes. In particular, the campaign can be analyzed through two key lenses relating to anticipatory governance — risk mitigation and adaptability — as follows:

- *Risk Mitigation:* Anticipatory governance involves foreseeing potential risks and challenges before implementing policies. In the case of the *Great Leap Forward*, there was a failure or an error in anticipating the consequences of rapid and large-scale collectivization[5] and industrialization at local levels with high penalties for non-compliance, which eventually led to calamitous outcomes from the campaign, leading to its abandonment in 1961. This was due to the high level of innovation introduced, which was untested and unplanned, resulting in declining

[1]Encyclopedia Britannica (2024). Great leap forward. Available: https://www.britannica.com/money/topic/Great-Leap-Forward (Accessed 24 January 2024).

[2]Ashton, B., *et al.* (1984). Famine in China, 1958–61. *Population and Development Review*, 10(4): 613–645. DOI: 10.2307/1973284. Available: Population Council, Wiley (Accessed 30 January, 2024).

[3]Meng, X., Qian, N., & Yared, P. (2015). The institutional causes of China's great famine, 1959–1961. *The Review of Economic Studies*, 82(4) (293): 1568–1611.

[4]Banister, J. (1987). *China's Changing Population.* Stanford: Stanford University Press: p. 13 (Accessed 30 January, 2024).

[5]Where small farms were consolidated to pool resources and labor into large cooperatives, under the socialist government. See: Brown, C.D. (2012). China's great leap forward. *Association for Asian Studies*. Available: https://www.asianstudies.org/publications/eaa/archives/chinas-great-leap-forward/ (Accessed 30 January, 2024).

crop production, a large increase in pests, and poorly constructed water projects.[6]

- *Adaptability:* Anticipatory governance allows policymakers to adjust their strategies in real time based on emerging challenges. An effective information collection framework that would collect and feed a real-time pipeline of high-quality data from the grassroots levels to a central framework visible to key decision-makers was lacking in China at the time of implementation of this campaign. Data estimates were skewed[7] as there were strong incentives for officials to over-report crop yield.[8] These factors led to very slow reaction times to fix or stop the campaign or ask for aid,[9] by which time the casualty count was already high.

A key lesson from this campaign's experience is the importance of risk mitigation and adaptability or iterative improvement. Regularly updating and improving governance frameworks based on feedback and outcomes is crucial. In the case of the *Great Leap Forward*, a lack of feedback mechanisms and adaptability led to a prolonged crisis. *Anticipatory governance helps policymakers foresee risks, while impact governance frameworks ensure that policies are well defined, measurable, and regularly assessed.*

A review of the outcomes of the campaign was held during the Seven Thousand Cadres Conference in 1962, only four years after the campaign was launched, where Mao acknowledged the limitations of his campaign and took a temporary back seat in policymaking.[10] The failures of the *Great Leap Forward* later informed the government's approach to the *Third Front Construction* campaign, which followed a few years later in 1964, which built basic industries, infrastructure, and the national defense sector

[6] Song, S. (2010). Mortality consequences of the 1959–1961 Great leap forward famine in China: Debilitation, selection, and mortality crossovers. *Social Science & Medicine*, 71(3): 551–558.

[7] Till today there is no correct or certain estimate of causalities — existing estimates vary widely. See Smil, V. (1999). China's great famine: 40 years later. *BMJ*, 319(7225): 1619–1621.

[8] Chang, G.H. & Wen, G.J. (1997). Communal dining and the Chinese famine of 1958–1961. *Economic Development and Cultural Change*, 46: 1–34.

[9] Smil, V. (1999). China's great famine: 40 years later. *BMJ*, 319(7225): 1619–1621.

[10] Mao, Z. Talk at Working Conference. Marxists Internet Archive. Available: https://afe.easia.columbia.edu/special/china_1950_leaders.htm (Accessed 30 January, 2024).

in interior China. Thus, anticipatory governance was not completely absent in China during the period of this campaign; it was simply not sufficiently efficient, transparent, or introspective at short, regular intervals — all of which would have helped reduce the negative toll of the campaign on the people by helping the government pause or change course earlier than it did.

20.2 The Importance of Impact Measurement Frameworks

Anticipatory governance was defined by Leon Fuerth, a research professor at George Washington University, as "*a system of institutions, rules and norms that provide a way to use foresight for the purpose of reducing risk, and to increase capacity to respond to events at early rather than later stages of their development.*"[11]

In practice, some form of anticipatory governance or foresight planning is common in most developed and some developing countries; however, impact measurement and retrospection to improve and fine-tune the effectiveness of these initiatives are sparser. In most cases, it takes several years for countries to have unstructured retrospection and to re-steer their foresight goals and paths, and by this time, the policy has already veered too much off course or resulted in great damage. Such unstructured approaches are, however, suboptimal since the lack of periodic and quantified action may result in remedies that are insufficient or too delayed, resulting in loss of valuable resources, time, and preparedness in the interim. There are many examples of policies implemented with insufficient or poorly planned anticipatory governance practices, like the *One Child Policy* in China, the outsourcing of silicon chip manufacturing in the West, and the *2016 Demonetization* campaign in India.

Thus, regular, structured impact measurement and future foresight activities are crucial for long-run optimization and regular course correction in any entity. Strong impact measurement frameworks improve governance in multiple ways, as listed in the following:

1. *Accountability*

Impact measurement frameworks provide a transparent and systematic way to evaluate the success or failure of policies, which helps maintain

[11] Fuerth, L.S. (2009). Foresight and anticipatory governance. *Foresight*, 11(4): A 14–32.

public trust. Every country in the European Union, for instance, is liable to publicly disclose details about available legislations, datasets, and public rights under various categories, including political financing, public procurement, freedom of information, and conflict of interest, on the European Public Accountability Mechanisms ("EuroPAM") portal. Anyone can access this portal through the internet, and the portal enables easily accessible and transparent information that helps maintain public trust.[12]

2. *Effective Resource Allocation*

Impact measurement helps policymakers identify which policies are most effective in achieving their intended goals from a range of possible policy alternatives. One example of this is *Anticipatory Public Budgeting,* which allows the government to track what is working and what is not and shift finance across departments or incentivize departments to achieve outcomes.[13]

In India, for instance, multiple identity cards and systems existed to identify citizens. In March 2006, the Ministry of Communications and Information approved a Unique ID scheme for poor families, and in 2007, an empowered group of ministers recognized the need for a residents' database.

Then, following much discussion and many legal challenges that required the accumulation of supportive evidence, the government introduced the common, single identity or "Aadhaar" initiative in 2009, with the goal of assigning a unique identity number to each resident. With the accomplishment of generating biometric identities for over 940 million individuals, the program's goal was to extend this coverage to 1.2 billion people by June 2016.

Beyond the numerical aspect, Aadhaar also aspires to foster social inclusion and enhance the efficiency of both public and private service delivery. Notably, the initiative has found application in various public domains, including the digitization of government subsidy disbursements (G2P payments), provision of financial services, monitoring of government employee attendance to minimize absenteeism, and issuance of

---

[12] EuroPAM portal. Europam.eu (Accessed 30 January, 2024).

[13] Mohammed Bin Rashid School of Government (n.d.). Anticipatory Public Budgeting. Available: https://gic.mbrcgi.gov.ae/storage/post/f6bTTIppsLhLElDnEVTTTRm36I3t70HP4rY722t0.pdf (Accessed 25 January, 2024).

passports, voter identity cards, and other identification forms. It has also reduced payout leakages from the government to the people in welfare programs, such as in the public distribution system (PDS). Leakage in the PDS system is reduced by Aadhaar-enabled automatic weighing of the rations, which is tied directly to the current handler's Aadhaar identity.[14]

Bolstered by initial evidence of the program's success and positive impacts, the government extended the use of Aadhar to various other domains, such as financial services. Since its introduction, financial transactions amounting to USD 12 billion have taken place,[15] and over a billion bank accounts and mobile phones have been linked to Aadhaar.[16] Thus, the periodic assessment of the impact of policies is needed for governance which allows interventions to upscale or downsize their impacts.

3. *Ensuring continuous improvement and success of policies*

Regularly assessing policy impacts allows governments to learn from both successes and failures. This iterative process enables continuous improvement and refinement of strategies. Having identified economic diversification as a key priority for growth, the UAE announced a 5% value-added tax (VAT) in 2018 to increase its non-oil and non-hydrocarbon revenues, thus diversifying government revenue sources. This policy is an example of the government's continuous improvement toward its vision.[17]

For policies rolled out through digital platforms, stakeholders' feedback can be easily received through real-time ratings and comments, and periodic adjustments can be made based on these feedback data points to

---

[14]World Bank (2016). Aadhaar: Digital Inclusion and Public Services in India. Available at: https://thedocs.worldbank.org/en/doc/655801461250682317-0050022016/original/WDR16BPAadhaarPaperBanerjee.pdf (Accessed 24 January 2024).

[15]Mirchandani, R. (2017). What can India's biometric ID system do for development? — Podcast with Aadhaar architect Nandan Nilekani. Centre for Global Development. Available: www.cgdev.org/blog/what-can-indias-biometric-id-systemdo-development-podcast-aadhaar-architect-nandan-nilekani (Accessed 30 January, 2024).

[16]Banerjee, S. (2016). Aadhaar: Digital Inclusion and Public Services in India. World Bank. Available at: https://thedocs.worldbank.org/en/doc/655801461250682317-0050022016/original/WDR16BPAadhaarPaperBanerjee.pdf (Accessed 30 January, 2024).

[17]Reuters (2018). UAE's VAT move has gone well: Inflation to moderate: IMF official. Available: https://www.reuters.com/article/us-emirates-imf/uaes-vat-move-has-gone-well-inflation-to-moderate-imf-official-idUKKBN1IB1YS/ (Accessed 30 January, 2024).

cater better to stakeholders. For other offline policies, feedback can be received by setting up an independent committee that randomly selects stakeholders to consolidate feedback and make recommendations for improvement.

4. *Maintaining Public Confidence*

When governments can demonstrate the positive impact of their policies through concrete measurements, it enhances public confidence and support. Generally, the more transparency of the government, the strength of national institutions, and the trust of the public in the goodwill of the government, the more will be the public confidence in the government decisions. Specifically, proxy indicators, such as stock market averages, unemployment rate, commodity basket prices, GDP, foreign investment, and vote shares for the ruling party in the case of democracies, can be used to measure public confidence in a policy or a combination of policies. The indicator to track depends on the areas the policy targets and affects. Transparent and widespread media reporting and dissemination of the relevant indicators' change due to policies implemented are important to inform the public and gain their support, or to be informed of their disapproval for possible course correction. In democracies, overall public approval or disapproval can also be periodically measured by people's vote share for the incumbent party, although this must be taken with a pinch of salt as other non-policy factors also often affect voting results in most countries.

5. *Preventing Unintended Consequences*

Impact measurement frameworks assist in identifying unintended consequences of policies. This is particularly important to avoid negative outcomes that may arise due to incomplete understanding or unforeseen interactions between different elements of a policy. The prolonged nature of China's One Child Policy, which lasted between 1979 and 2015, in interaction with a slew of laws passed to protect women and promote their participation in the labor force has contributed to the country's drastically declining fertility rates — an unintended negative consequence which more careful foresight might have helped to avoid.

6. *Prioritizing Stakeholder Needs*

Impact measurement often involves gathering input from various stakeholders, ensuring that policies address the diverse needs of the population, and considering the perspectives of those directly affected.

The UAE, for instance, uses both formal and informal organizations, assessments, and platforms to understand and assess policies from various angles and stakeholders through councils such as the UAE Soft Power Council, forums like the World Governments Summit, and policy research institutes like the Mohammed Bin Rashid School of Government.

7. *Long-term Sustainability of Policies*
Impact measurement is crucial for evaluating the long-term sustainability of policies. It allows governments to assess the environmental, social, and economic impacts of their actions, promoting policies that contribute to sustainable development and removing others.

20.3 Choosing What Policies Are Needed: Various Approaches for Analyses

20.3.1 *Cost–benefit analysis of risk mitigation: Comparing cost of risk vs. cost of mitigation*

In the consideration of any policy, an organization will find a range of related risks. Every policy design is prompted by the objective to mitigate some risk that the government or organization perceives. The risk could be that of unmanageable overpopulation in the future, that of becoming obsolete like an energy company when fossil fuels run out, etc. Each risk can be assigned an associated cost and deduced based on the extent of material damage, setback to goals, time, and direct monetary expenditure that will result if the risk were to materialize. A high-cost risk, if realized, will be one that results in high overall damage. But we must keep in mind that risks also have a different probability of materializing. Each risk can be assigned an associated probability based on the probability of scenarios[18] that will have to occur for it to materialize. These probabilities may change in real time depending on the evolution of situations in the real world and, in most situations, are ballparked based on intuition and limited understanding of the world.

A risk with a high estimated cost but a very low expected probability of occurrence may be worth deprioritizing for mitigation below another risk with a medium cost but a very high probability of occurrence.

[18] Hayes, A. (2023). Risk analysis. *Investopedia*. Available: https://www.investopedia.com/terms/r/risk-analysis.asp (Accessed 30 January, 2024).

Accordingly, let's define a new concept that will help us weigh in both the actual cost of the risk and the probability of its occurrence: *the net projected cost of a risk*. We can define the net projected cost of risk as the probability of the risk occurring multiplied by the cost of the risk if it were to occur. Note that we need to calculate the net present value of a projected cost of a risk considering factors such as inflation and externalities.

Let's take a specific case. Consider a data center with physical servers. The center is already pest control treated; however, one of the risks facing the center is that of rodent infestation, which becomes especially probable if the upcoming summer in the area turns out to be a very hot one. Here, the cost of the risk, i.e., rodents chewing wires and destroying a server center, will be the cost of all servers destroyed, resulting in loss of business and required repair. The probability of rodent infestation can be approximated as the probability of the weather being above 45°C, based on weather forecast estimates. Say the probability of hot weather thus obtained is 50%. Then, the net projected cost of the risk will be 0.5 * net present value of the expected cost of replacing or restoring the computers and hardware damaged by the infestation and the cost of clearing out the infestation.

To mitigate each risk, mitigation strategies ("actions") must be developed. Each mitigation strategy will also have an expected cost associated with it — the cost of time, money, and effort spent planning for the strategy, preparing to implement the strategy, and implementing the strategy, along with costs due to any downstream impacts of the mitigation strategy. For instance, to mitigate the risk of rodents destroying a data server center in hot weather, one mitigation strategy is to install additional air-conditioning units. In this case, the time spent in searching for appropriate A/C units, the electricity costs, installation, and purchase costs of these A/C units all must be used to calculate the expected cost of mitigation.

With real-time monitoring, we can identify risks, and for each of these risks, we can compare the expected cost of mitigation to the net project cost of risk. We should proceed with the policy only when the projected cost of the risk (the danger posed by the risk) exceeds the cost of implementing the policy to mitigate the risk (the cost of action). Similar approaches can also be employed for policies at a country-wide level. An example of applying this approach to governmental policy is the following: Studies in the UK have found that every £1 invested in providing support for people with alcohol problems saves the public sector £5.[19]

[19] Mohammed Bin Rashid Centre for Government Innovation (n.d.), *Op. cit.*

This implies that the cost of action (providing support) on alcoholics is greater than the cost of risk (the average of public health support), so a support-oriented policy for alcoholics in this case would make sense.

20.3.2 *Estimating probabilities of risk through "plausibility" analysis: The case of the Shell Company*

Let us first distinguish between the concepts of probability and plausibility. There exist many definitions of plausibility. Plausibility is creating coherence both within a future and regarding its developmental path from the present, based on conformity to prior knowledge and respective worldviews.[20] According to the Oxford English Dictionary, plausibility is the quality in an argument, statement, etc., of seeming reasonable or probable.

Probability, on the other hand, measures how likely something is to happen. In mathematics, it is represented by a ratio showing the chances that a particular thing will happen. Sometimes, probabilities are hard to calculate in the real world, especially relating to risks of events and scenarios that have not actually occurred. The scenario planning wing, set up in 1967 at the Shell Company in the US, found a way of dealing with this: they looked at the plausibility of a risk when it was not possible to precisely estimate the probability of the risk. Plausible stories encourage judgment, not just attention to data and other information. An intuitive understanding of the world precedes and frames analytical understanding. Plausibility can be strengthened by how relevant the scenario is and by a logical storyline.

In the mid-1980s, Lo van Wachem, the chairman of Shell's committee of managing directors, instructed the scenario team to begin considering the impact of sustainability concerns on the energy business. The process took years, but it ended up shaping opinion throughout the group as the threat of global warming became more real. Shell's 1998 sustainability report was one of the first acknowledgments by a major energy corporation of the challenge of climate change.[21] Regarding sustainable development,

---

[20] Fischer, N. & Dannenberg, S. (2021). The social construction of futures: Proposing plausibility as a semiotic approach for critical futures studies. *Futures*, 129. https://doi.org/10.1016/j.futures.2021.102729.

[21] Shell (2007). Shell Sustainability Report 1999-2000. Available: https://www.shell.com/sustainability/transparency-and-sustainability-reporting/sustainability-reports/_jcr_content/root/main/section/list/list_item/text.multi.stream/1657187588199/4a5365f34781e84eb92afbef3106893b77ed26de/shell-sustainability-report-dutch-2007.pdf (Accessed 30 January, 2024).

the report stated the following: "*Shell companies are fully committed to contributing to sustainable development and are under no illusions about the difficulties. There is little practical expertise in this field and implementation will be a lengthy process of developing in-house knowledge and learning from outside experts.*" The report also anticipated specific areas of focus in sustainability for the company to focus on over time. It said, "*sustainability considerations will help reshape the Shell Chemicals portfolio of businesses over time*" in the 1998 report. Since then, the Shell chemicals portfolio has been developing expertise in bio-based, lower carbon, and circular economy solution sectors.

20.3.3 *Movements of aggregate indices as guides for anticipatory decision-making under uncertainty*

Aggregate indices, which are indicatory measures for specific phenomena of interest, can help governments measure the impacts of specific actions taken to reach overall goals over time and serve as a bellwether for potential future risks and the effectiveness of past anticipatory actions. Take the example of a commodity-dependent nation that aims to diversify within a decade to prevent the risk of economic collapse when the commodity runs out or goes out of demand. In this case, a composite index, such as the Economic Diversification Index[22] (EDI), which considers the direction of diversification of underlying pillars like trade, output, and revenue, can serve as an overall signal as to whether anticipatory actions taken to diversify are working as intended or whether trends are reversing in an unfavorable direction.

The UAE's EDI scores, for instance, have increased from 91 in the year 2000 to 96 in 2022, as demonstrated in Exhibit 20.1, indicating that the economy has indeed grown more diversified over this period. Comparing UAE's scores with the score of the most diversified country, the USA, is also very informative. USA's EDI scores increased from 133.8 in 2000 to 153.2 in 2022, demonstrating that USA's economy was much more diversified to begin with, and its diversification scores have also improved drastically over time. Comparing the scores of commodity-dependent countries — defined as countries that have more than 60% of their total merchandise exports in value terms consisting of natural

[22] Prasad, A., Subramani, K., Refass, S., Saidi, N., Salem, F., & Shepherd, B. (2024). Global Economic Diversification Index 2024. Dubai: Mohammed Bin Rashid School of Government. Available at www.EconomicDiversification.com (Accessed 30 January, 2024).

Exhibit 20.1. UAE's economic diversification index scores across time: 2000–2022.

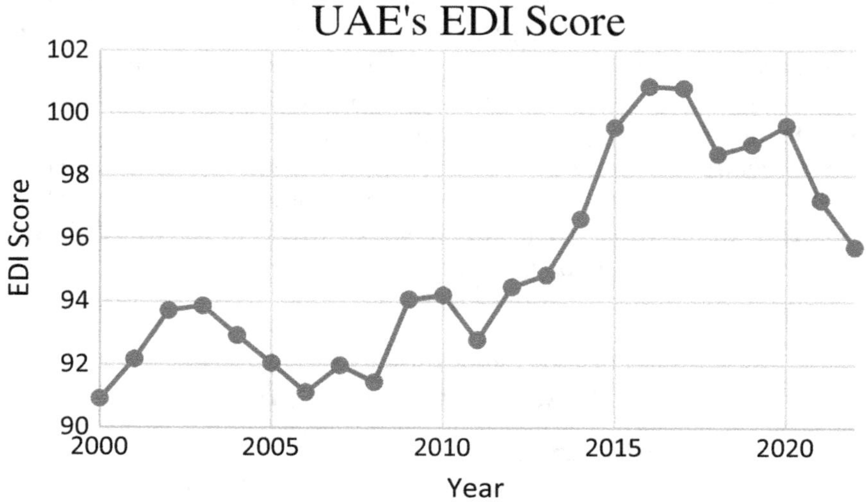

Source: Prasad *et al*., (2024).[23]

resources — to non-commodity-dependent countries, we see that the latter have much higher EDI scores in general, reflecting the challenges to diversification that countries face because of their commodity dependence. Comparisons at the regional level, such as across continents, help us understand the progress made over time in each of the regions toward economic diversification, as Exhibit 20.2 demonstrates.

Using indices such as the EDI has both benefits and limitations for policymakers. Benefits include having a single aggregate score for a complex phenomenon with many underlying components that is measurable and can thus be tracked transparently and comparably across time to understand the direction of the country's progress toward its goals. A key limitation of such indices is that, given the lack of perfect availability of data, not all essential components of economic diversification can be captured or accurately and proportionately accounted for in a single index. Some components underlying the EDI may be strategically more important to some countries than others; however, as a globally consistent index, the EDI gives equal

[23] Prasad, A., Subramani, K., Refass, S., Saidi, N., Salem, F., & Shepherd, B. (2024). Global Economic Diversification Index 2024. Dubai: Mohammed bin Rashid School of Government. Available at www.EconomicDiversification.com (Accessed 30 January 2024).

Exhibit 20.2. EDI scores across continents between 2000–2022.

	2000	2004	2008	2012	2016	2019	2020–22
North America	121.5	122.3	127.4	130.3	132.2	135.0	132.8
Western Europe	109.2	110.6	112.6	112.0	113.4	114.4	114.8
East Asia & Pacific	102.6	104.0	104.8	106.7	107.8	108.9	109.0
Eastern Europe & Central Asia	96.5	97.9	99.1	99.8	100.8	101.2	101.2
MENA	93.1	93.5	93.7	95.0	98.5	98.3	98.4
South Asia	92.9	94.8	95.3	96.0	97.1	97.6	97.5
Latin America & the Caribbean	95.6	95.4	95.9	96.2	97.3	97.2	96.8
Sub-Saharan Africa	87.7	88.5	88.7	88.9	90.7	89.5	89.3

Source: Prasad *et al.*, (2024).[24]

weightage across countries to the three underlying subindexes and their various components to calculate the final score. For economies dependent heavily on commodities such as fossil fuels, minerals, or food exports, annual indices such as the Economic Diversification Index can help them note their current diversification levels, consider and plan for greater diversification in trade, output, and revenue, and take stock of their progress over time.

Similarly, countries that have agreed to sustainable development goals in international forums can investigate both global and regional reports published annually to see the impacts of anticipatory actions taken by them in the past to mitigate risk factors related to human development, economic growth, environment, etc. These indices have served governments as effective course correction signals in the past. The 2023 Arab SDGs Index report[25] found, for instance, that seven Arab countries were two-thirds of the way toward achieving the SDGs. Basic health and digital infrastructure outcomes were seen to be much improved in the region, while gender inequality remained an SDG that had consistently low scores and progress over time. Specific trends and scores in each of the SDGs and their underlying indicators varied from country to country within the region, suggesting policy implications at a granular level.

[24] *Ibid.*

[25] Zakzak, L., Subramani, K., Luomi, M., Fuller, G., Salem, F., & Lafortune, G. (2023). Arab Region SDG Index and Dashboards Report 2023. Dubai and Paris: Mohammed Bin Rashid School of Government (MBRSG) and UN Sustainable Development Solutions Network (UN SDSN) (Accessed 30 January 2024).

In combination with a robust impact measurement system, regular indices such as the ones highlighted earlier can effectively guide policy-makers' goals and timelines and help them stay on track to achieve their intended policy objectives in an otherwise uncertain world.

20.4 Toward a Structured Impact Measurement Framework

All organizations, after deciding to proceed with policy action, should ensure they have a well-developed impact measurement framework to

Exhibit 20.3. Continuous impact measurement: 7-Step cycle.

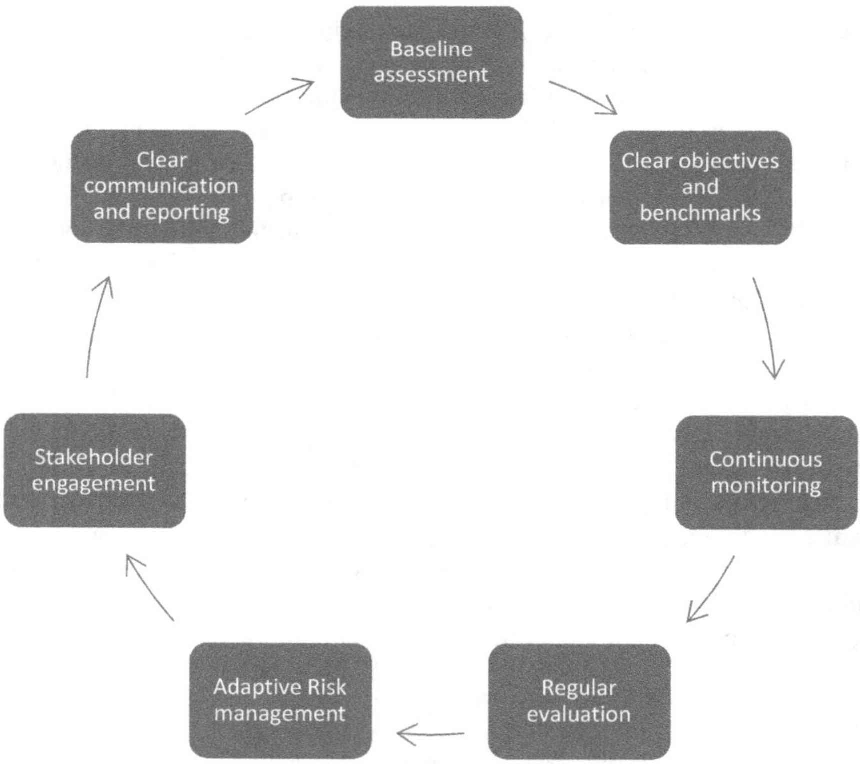

Source: Author.

assess the success of their policy, identify impact factors, prevent policy drift, and ensure projects stay within planned time frames and budgets. The steps taken to realize this framework have seven components (Exhibit 20.3).

1. *Baseline Assessment*

Conduct a baseline assessment before implementing the policy to establish a starting point. This will serve as a reference to measure the change and impact brought about by the policy.

2. *Define Clear Objectives and Benchmarks*

Clearly articulate the policy objectives, intended outcomes, and desired impacts. This involves specifying the goals the policy aims to achieve and the benchmarks against which success will be measured. Identify relevant and measurable Key Performance Indicators (KPIs) that align with the policy's objectives. These indicators should provide tangible data to assess the impact of the policy. These KPIs will evolve as the context evolves.

3. *Continuous Monitoring*

Implement a system for continuous monitoring of the selected KPIs throughout the policy implementation. Choose specific indicators or indices to measure and track across time to measure progress. Strike a balance between finding the minimum number of indicators for simplicity and transparency and ensuring coverage of all the key indicators to measure the progress of the initiative.

Conduct regular reviews and audits to ensure transparency and accountability. Qualitative impact measurement can capture information that may not be accurately or adequately represented by numbers alone. Finally, budget and time frame monitoring should be integrated into the impact measurement framework. Regularly assess whether the policy is adhering to the planned budget and time frame and adjust as necessary.

4. *Regular Evaluation Against Benchmarks*

Periodically evaluate the policy's impact against the predefined benchmarks. This evaluation should be conducted using the selected KPIs to assess whether the policy is on track to achieve its intended outcomes. If KPIs are changed or discontinued, ensure that the documentation and processes related to them are adjusted.

5. *Adaptive Risk Management*
Embrace an adaptive management approach that allows for adjustments based on ongoing monitoring and evaluation. If data indicate a deviation from the desired impact or unexpected challenges, policymakers should be ready to adapt, shift, or stop the execution of strategies accordingly.[26] Develop a robust risk management plan to anticipate potential challenges that may affect the policy's impact, timeline, or budget. Having contingency plans in place will help mitigate risks and reduce the likelihood of policy drift.[27]

6. *Stakeholder Engagement*
Engage with relevant stakeholders, including those affected by the policy and experts in the field. Their feedback can provide valuable insights into the real-world impact of the policy and help identify areas for improvement. Since government departments and policymakers rarely remain the same, it is important to maintain a consistent central record of all the feedback collected over time so that any official in the institution who oversees policy monitoring and execution can access all quantitative and qualitative feedback and KPI measurements with the source and timestamps.

7. *Communication and Reporting*
Establish clear communication channels to share findings and progress with stakeholders. Transparent reporting builds trust and allows for informed decision-making.

20.5 Conclusion

In conclusion, this chapter helps policymakers understand the importance of navigating the complex terrain of continuous impact measurement and foresight in policy evaluation using clear frameworks and several poignant examples. Examples of governmental policy failures due to inadequate

---

[26] Massachusetts Institute of Technology (n.d.). Anticipatory Governance. Available: scienceimpact.mit.edu/sites/default/files/documents/Anticipatory%20Governance.pdf (Accessed 3 January, 2024).

[27] Strategic foresight unit | Office of the Secretary — OECD. www.oecd.org/strategic-foresight/ourwork/Foresight_and_Anticipatory_Governance.pdf (Accessed 3 January, 2024).

and infrequent impact measurement highlight the critical need for governments to effectively adopt such frameworks. Strong impact measurement frameworks help governments in several crucial ways, as demonstrated by diverse country-level policy examples. Where possible, the logical framework for cost–benefit analysis of policies can be employed to facilitate informed decision-making. Alternative approaches like "plausibility" analysis, scenario-based planning, and monitoring movements of indicative aggregate indices can also offer valuable insights for impact measurement of existing policies and to indicate the usefulness of possible new policies. The chapter culminates with a meticulous 7-step cyclical impact measurement framework, which can help the government ensure that all their policies remain agile, informed, accountable, and continually adaptable in the face of uncertainty.

https://doi.org/10.1142/9789811296000_0021

Chapter 21

Anticipatory Governance and Decision-Making: Prevention of the Entry of Absent Quarantine Pests (AQPs) in Brazil

Estela Alves de Medeiros* **and Ricardo C. Gomes†**

**Ministry of Agriculture and Livestock, Brasília, Brazil*
†FGV EAESP, São Paulo, Brazil

Key Takeaways

- Methods to support decision-making are important for governments due to budget constraints.
- Anticipatory governance is a decision-making method that helps anticipate problems and decrease risk for public policy.
- *Plant health policy* is an example of public policy that can benefit from anticipatory governance.
- In Brazil, the Ministry of Agriculture and Livestock utilized the Analytical Hierarchy Process (AHP) to prioritize Absent Quarantine Pests (AQPs) as part of a National Program.
- The prioritization of cocoa *moniliasis* helped the Secretariat of Animal and Plant Health to implement faster contingency measures to prevent the spread of the pest.

21.1 Introduction

Anticipatory governance has been seen as a form of data-driven risk management to design scenarios in various fields of knowledge.[1] This "new" governance modality is possible when we have a large diversity of data for decision-making and analysis. The speed of data processing and the volume of algorithms and problems we are allowed to work with are unprecedented in history.[2] In this sense, governments worldwide and at all levels can find an opportunity to anticipate realities and establish policies to respond to damaging events or catastrophes. This point is defended by Joost Vervoot and Aarti Gupta,[3] who support the idea that "*we need to be one step ahead of the present... being ahead of events or the risk of being run over by them.*"

In this chapter, we present the anticipatory governance carried out by the Brazilian government, more precisely by the Ministry of Agriculture and Livestock (MAPA), in anticipating the invasion of the so-called Absent Quarantine Pests (AQPs), which have the power to cause significant damage to plant biodiversity, agriculture, and the country's economy. The prioritized absent quarantine pests receive special attention from the Plant Health Defense and Agricultural Research, which contributes to the prevention and control of pest occurrences, as in the case of the detection of the pest *Moniliophthora roreri* in the North Region. Implementing anticipatory measures was essential to prevent pests from spreading throughout the country.

The *Analytic Hierarchy Process* (AHP) was used to select pests, which enabled the ranking of a group of pre-prioritized pests. The activity was carried out by the technical team of the Department of Plant Health and Agricultural Inputs (DSV/DAS/MAPA) and by researchers from the Brazilian Agricultural Research Corporation (Embrapa), based on

---

[1] Fuerth, L.S. (2009). Foresight and anticipatory governance. *Foresight,* 11(4): 14–32.

[2] Maffei, S., Leoni, F., & Villari, B. (2020, 2020/04/02). Data-driven anticipatory governance. Emerging scenarios in data for policy practices. *Policy Design and Practice*, 3(2): 123–134.

[3] Vervoort, J. & Gupta, A. (2018). Anticipating climate futures in a 1.5°C era: The link between foresight and governance. *Current Opinion in Environmental Sustainability*, 31: 104. DOI: 10.1016/j.cosust.2018.01.004.

19 criteria, divided into three large groups: "entry"; "establishment and dispersion"; and "estimated impact."[4]

This chapter begins by providing an explanation for quarantine pests and their potential damage and losses to the country. Next, it presents how the agricultural defense agencies mobilize to prevent pest invasions. Finally, it presents the results and a brief vision of the future.

21.2 Nature of the Problem: What Are Quarantine Pests and Why Should They Be Addressed?

According to the IFRS (International Standard for Phytosanitary Measures) No. 5 of the International Convention for the Protection of Plants, ICPV, a pest can be defined as any species, breed, or biotype of plant, animal, or pathogenic agent harmful to plants or plant, products.[5] They are insects, mites, nematodes, bacteria, fungi, viruses, parasitic plants, or crop competitors. Quarantine pests are organisms of potential economic importance to the endangered area where they are not yet present or, when present, are not widely distributed. For this reason, these pests are subject to official control, either in the use of measures to prevent entry into the country or, if present in a given area, in the form of phytosanitary measures to enable eradication and control to avoid dispersion.

Absent quarantine pests have not yet been officially reported in the country (IFMN No. 5 of the International Convention for the Protection of Plants — CIPV). The Secretariat of Agricultural Defense of the Ministry of Agriculture and Livestock is responsible for publishing the official list of absent quarantine pests (SDA/MAPA Ordinance No. 617, of July 12, 2022) and present pests (Normative Instruction No. 38, of October 1, 2018) in Brazil. About 600 species or genera are officially regulated as absent quarantine pests in Brazil, in addition to 12 species of quarantine pests.

---

[4]Fidelis, E.G., Lohmann, T.R., da Silva, M.L., Parizzi, P., & Laranjeira, F.F. (2018). *Priorização De Pragas Quarentenárias Ausentes No Brasil*. Embrapa (Ed.). Brasilia: Emorata.

[5]FAO (2009). *CIPV. Normas Internacionais para Medidas Fitossanitária — NIMF 5.* Available at: https://www.ippc.int/largefiles/NIMF_05_2009_PT_FINAL_0.pdf (Accessed 4 February, 2024).

The introduction of absent quarantine pests in a region can cause social, ecological, and economic impacts, such as reduced production, loss of markets, increased export costs due to the imposition of phytosanitary barriers (domestic and international), increased control expenditures, unemployment due to the elimination or decrease of a particular crop in a region, and loss of biodiversity.

The transit of species between different geographical points and between environments has been a constant over time, especially in periods before the nineteenth century, in which there was no understanding of the danger posed by the introduction of an exotic species. Other factors aggravating the problem include increased trade and tourism between nations, increased agriculture and cattle raising, and global warming (climate change tends to favor the advancement of exotic species). The importance of agriculture for the Brazilian economy leads to a greater concern about the introduction of absent quarantine pests, which can generate economic losses, such as reduced production and loss of markets.

21.3 Anticipatory Governance to Face the Entry of Pests that Do Not Exist in Brazil

Routinely, the entry of pests into Brazil is prevented through inspection and control of the transit of animals and plants and their parts, agricultural inputs, animal and plant origin products, packaging, and wooden supports, imported or transiting internationally through Brazil. This inspection is carried out by the International Agricultural Surveillance System (Vigiagro) of the Ministry of Agriculture and Livestock (MAPA). The importation of any animal or plant and its products, derivatives, and parts is allowed only if it meets the regulatory criteria and procedures of inspection, quality control, and risk analysis established by the MAPA. Phytosanitary alerts and contingency plans are also mechanisms of phytosanitary defense employed to prevent or reduce the possibility of pest material entering the country.

Given the large number of species of quarantine pests absent and the budget available to plant health defense agencies, it was necessary to establish priorities for the performance of phytosanitary defense and agricultural research related to the theme of quarantine pests. Thus, Embrapa and the

Secretariat of Agricultural Defense of the Ministry of Agriculture and Livestock (SDA/MAPA) worked collaboratively to present a list of 20 missing quarantine pests, prioritized as the pests with the greatest risk to Brazilian agriculture. This work is not unheard of in the world as it was carried out by the United States and the European Union. He also emphasized that "*prioritization is a dynamic process that needs to be discussed and improved over time, considering the various factors that make up the process*."[6]

The Analytic Hierarchy Process (AHP) method was used for prioritization, which made it possible to rank a group of pests pre-prioritized by DSV servers and Embrapa researchers based on 20 criteria, divided into three major groups: "entry"; "establishment and dispersion"; and "estimated impact." The estimated impact received a weight of 54.66% in the analysis; entry was 24.65%, and establishment and dispersion were 20.68%.

The Analytic Hierarchy Process (AHP) was developed in the 1970s by Prof. Thomas Saaty.[7] It is based on mathematics and psychology and aims to assist people in making complex decisions. Therefore, the AHP provides a comprehensive and rational procedure for structuring a problem, representing and quantifying its elements, relating them to global goals, and evaluating alternative solutions. This structuring (hierarchy) represents the simultaneous interaction of the many factors affecting the problem. Hierarchical organization facilitates the determination of priorities according to the objective of the group, its knowledge, and its experience with the problem. Exhibit 21.1 presents a brief breakdown of each group worked by the AHP method applied in the prioritization of absent pests.

Based on the mentioned criteria, 20 absent quarantine pests were prioritized, ten classified as very high risk and 10 as high risk, with scores above 500. The impact criterion is given greater weight because "*if it [pest] does not represent a significant problem in terms of economic damage, the efforts and trade restrictions imposed in an attempt to prevent its introduction are not justified*."[8]

---

[6] Fidelis *et al.* (2018), *Op. cit.*

[7] Saaty, T.L. (2008). Decision making with the analytic hierarchy process. *International Journal of Services Sciences*, 1(1): 83–98.

[8] Fidelis *et al.* (2018), *Op. cit.*, p. 112.

Notably, of the 20 pests prioritized, four already had contingency plans in place, which are given in the following:

- *Moniliophthora roreri* (cocoa moniliasis) — MAPA Normative Instruction No. 23, of May 17, 2012.
- Phytoplasmas associated with Palm Disease Lethal Yellowing Syndromes — MAPA Normative Instruction No. 47, of September 24, 2013.
- *Cydia pomonella* (apple moth) — MAPA Normative Instruction No. 35, of October 27, 2015.
- *Fusarium oxysporum* f.sp. *cubense* tropical race 4 (R4T) — MAPA Normative Instruction No. 43, of August 13, 2018.

Exhibit 21.1. Prioritization of pests to be addressed.

Category	Criteria Used
Inputs	Distance between the nearest location and the Brazilian border; Number of bordering countries in which the plague occurs; The overall number of countries in which it can be found; Import volume of host material/regulated article; Number of imports of host material or regulated article; Number of continents where it already exists.
Establishment and Dispersal	Potential for climate adaptation in Brazil; Number of hosts; Total area of host crops; Percentage of micro regions with host crops; Efficiency of control methods; Estimation of annual natural dispersal distance; Probability of anthropogenic dispersal.
Estimated Impact	Expected percentage of damage; Value of the annual production of the host crop; Number of countries regulating the pest; Number of establishments with the host culture; Number of jobs in the production chain of host crops; Potential for pesticide contamination.

Source: Adapted from Fidelis *et al.* (2018).[9]

[9]Fidelis *et al.* (2018), *Op. cit.*

The result of this prioritization are important and will guide the discussions and planning of both research activities and projects, as well as plant defense activities and actions. Prioritized pests should have contingency plans and improvements in terms of phytosanitary surveillance actions. Research projects derived from the prioritization of absent quarantine pests should promote lines of investigation aimed at reducing the risks of entry and dispersion of these pests and their environmental impacts, as well as preventive genetic improvement actions.

21.4 Results to Date

The prioritization of absent quarantine pests led to the establishment, by the Secretariat of Animal and Plant Health (SDA), of the National Plan for the Prevention and Surveillance of Absent Quarantine Pests (PNPV-PQA), through SDA Ordinance No. 131, of June 27, 2019. The objectives of the Plan are to prevent the entry of absent quarantine pests (PQA) in the national territory; maintain a surveillance system for detecting and identifying missing quarantine pests in risk areas; and apply risk mitigation measures in cases of suspected entry.

Each National Plan for the Prevention and Surveillance of these pests should contain guidelines and operational procedures for applying preventive measures with containment, suppression, and eradication of outbreaks. Phytosanitary education, training, and technology transfer for agricultural defense agents and producers are among the priority actions for monitoring, identifying, and preventive management of these missing quarantine pests.

The Secretariat of Agricultural Defense has established goals for annual detection surveys for each Federation Unit, where each of the absent quarantine pests can occur. The Federal Superintendencies of MAPA carry out these surveys in states. The Department of Plant Health and Agricultural Inputs monitors the targets on a monthly basis.

As a result of the actions of the prevention and surveillance plan, an outbreak of the absent quarantine pest *Moniliopthora roreri* was detected in the state of Acre, in the municipality of Cruzeiro do Sul. This pest is known as Cocoa Moniliasis. The fungus attacks only the fruits of cocoa, cupuaçu, and other plants of the genus *Theobroma,* such as cacao and cupuí. The border of the country's northern region and the main cocoa-producing states are being monitored for this pest. Between 2016 and 2021, around 5,000 monitoring actions were carried out in the states of

Amazonas, Acre, Amapá, Rondônia, Roraima, Pará, Bahia, and Espírito Santo.

According to estimates by the Brazilian Institute of Geography and Statistics (IBGE), Brazil has about 600 thousand hectares of cocoa cultivated and 75 thousand producers, 60% of which are family farms, occupying the position of the 6th largest cocoa producer in the world, with a production of more than 200 thousand tons of beans/year. The states of Pará and Bahia are Brazil's primary producers of cocoa beans, responsible for approximately 96% of all national production. The cocoa production chain in Brazil generates almost 300,000 direct jobs, from cultivation to chocolate production.

The consequence of this outbreak was the declaration of a phytosanitary emergency in the states of Acre, Amazonas, and Rondônia, according to MAPA Ordinance No. 249 of August 4, 2021. The measure aimed to strengthen preventive actions and prevent the spread of the pest to cocoa and cupuaçu cultivation areas. In November 2021, a new pest outbreak was detected on a rural property in Humaitá, in southern Amazonas. The health authorities acted to eradicate the outbreak and monitor the affected area.

The phytosanitary emergency was extended in March 2022 through the publication of Ordinance Map No. 467 and in 2023 through the publication of Ordinance Map No. 603 of August 4, 2023. The ordinances also established the guidelines for preparing the State Emergency Plan for the Prevention, Suppression, and Eradication of the pest by the state plant health defense agencies.

In October 2022, a new outbreak of the pest Moniliopthora roreri was identified in the city of Tabatinga, state of the Amazon. Since then, the measures provided for in the National Prevention and Surveillance Plan have been initiated in the region. SDA Ordinance No. 703, of November 21, 2022, declared the municipalities of Cruzeiro do Sul, Mâncio Lima, Rodrigues Alves, Marechal Thaumaturgo, and Porto Walter in the states of Acre and Amazonas to be under quarantine for the absent quarantine pest *Moniliophthora roreri causing Cocoa Moniliasis,* as shown in Exhibit 21.2.

From the point of view of agricultural research, Embrapa has established a portfolio of projects on Entry Prevention and Management of Quarantine Pests in Brazil, better known as the "Quarantine Portfolio," after prioritizing pests. Its work is focused on developing research and

Exhibit 21.2. Moniliophthora roreri causing Cocoa Moniliasis.

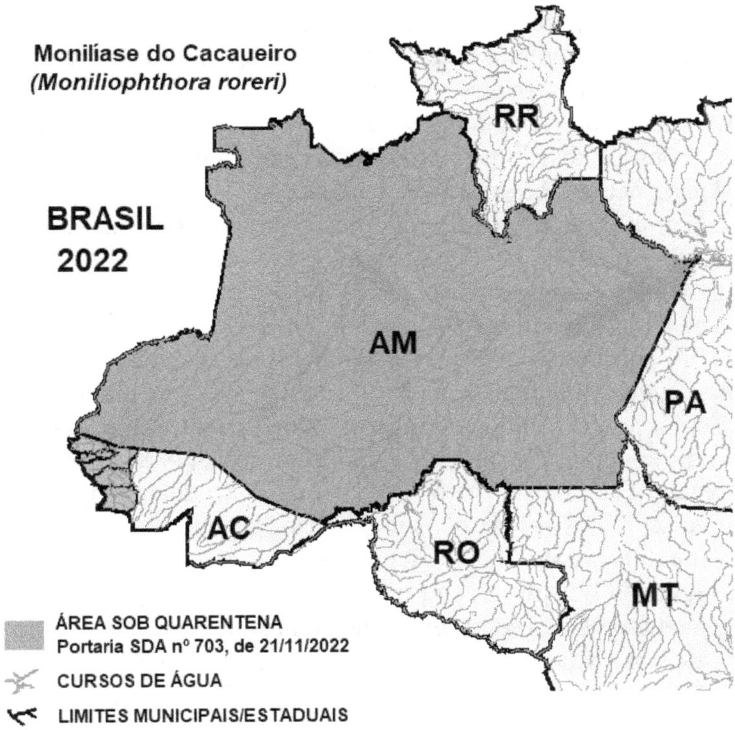

Source: Secretariat of Animal and Plant Health — Ministry of Agriculture and Livestock.[10]

technology transfer actions relating to pest management, territorial intelligence, biological control, phytosanitary analysis of plant material introduced under quarantine, and preventive genetic improvement. The Quarantine Portfolio has more than 13 ongoing projects and works involving 25 Embrapa research units, international partners, and private sector consultants.

[10]Government of Brasil (2017). Prevenção e Vigilância de Pragas Ausentes. Available: https://www.gov.br/agricultura/pt-br/assuntos/sanidade-animal-e-vegetal/sanidade-vegetal/planos-de-contingencia-pragas-ausentes (Accessed 4 February, 2024).

21.5 Conclusion

This chapter aims to present the anticipatory governance action taken by the Ministry of Agriculture and Livestock in Brazil to map pests that can create losses for the country's economy and agriculture. The measures that have been implemented make it possible to anticipate the introduction and dispersion of absent quarantine pests and eradicate some at an early stage. These actions are practical evidence of how anticipatory governance can contribute to good public management, anticipating problems and avoiding losses. The cooperation between the SDA/Mapa and Embrapa plant health specialists led to the definition of a set of missing quarantine pests for priority plant health defense actions.

The prioritization of Absent Quarantine Pests is fundamental for public policy, given the large number of plant species and threats to them. Prioritization helps to build contingency plans, establish monitoring strategies, and define the direction of agricultural research and technological development. The first step is to make a preliminary selection of the AQPs based on discussions with experts in the field. The next step is to apply the AHP methodology, starting with the formulation of the criteria (entry, establishment and dispersal, and impact), the formation of the hierarchy, and a comparison between criteria. The end result is the global prioritization of pest risk, which leads to the establishment of public policy.

https://doi.org/10.1142/9789811296000_0022

Chapter 22

Building an Architectural Framework for Anticipatory Governance: A Case Study of the Asian Development Bank

Susann Roth[*,†] **and Ivana Milojević**[‡]

[†]*Asian Development Bank, Manila, Philippines*
[‡]*Metafuture.org, Brisbane, Australia*

Key Takeaways

- Anticipatory governance is a proactive and forward-looking approach that is required both in the public sector and within multilateral organizations.
- Anticipatory governance is about administrating a system to enable it to harness opportunities in the future and mitigate risks of uncertainties; it helps to develop and implement reforms.
- The drivers creating a need for anticipatory governance include the recognition of uncertainties, the complexity of challenges, and the imperative to respond swiftly to rapid societal changes.
- The key obstacles for futures thinking as part of anticipatory governance are hesitancy to engage, reluctance to challenge the status quo, and fragmentation in implementing futures thinking.

---

[*]Disclaimer: Published in the authors' personal capacity and views do not necessarily reflect ADB's views.

- Achieving anticipatory governance requires a delicate balancing act that recognizes alternative futures and the priorities of multiple stakeholders; multilateral organizations, such as the Asian Development Bank, can play a pivotal role in this process to enhance awareness and build capacity.

22.1 Introduction

Anticipatory governance (AG) approaches have gained increasing attention as proactive and forward-looking tools to address the complex and uncertain challenges facing the world. Kyungmoo Heo and Yongseok Seo from the Moon Soul Graduate School of Future Strategy, Korea Advanced Institute of Science and Technology,[1] define AG as a "*system of systems*" utilizing foresight to formulate plans and execute relevant actions. The South African Institute of International Affairs (SAIIA) characterizes AG as a "*nonpredictive approach to enhance present-day preparedness*."[2] This involves building capacities in foresight and multistakeholder engagement to navigate potential future disruptive impacts.

David Guston[3] similarly defines anticipatory governance (in the field of new technology like nanotechnology) as a "*broad-based capacity extended through society*" capable of managing "*emerging knowledge-based technologies.*" Karlijn Muiderman *et al.*[4] emphasize that "*imagining and governing the future*" are core challenges for sustainability research and practice in the context of accelerating earth system transformations and their potential societal consequences. Consequently, AG methods and tools are "*increasingly used to imagine and govern transformations*

[1] Heo, K. & Seo, Y. (2021). Anticipatory governance for newcomers: Lessons learned from the UK, the Netherlands, Finland, and Korea. *European Journal of Futures Research*, 9(9): 1–14.

[2] Van Nieuwkerk, A. (2021). The South African Institute of International Affairs (SAIIA). *Building Anticipatory Governance in SADC: Post-COVID-19 Conflict and Defence Outlook.* Available: https://saiia.org.za/research/building-anticipatory-governance-in-sadc-post-covid-19-conflict-and-defence-outlook/ (Accessed 28 March, 2023).

[3] Guston, D. (2014). Understanding 'anticipatory governance'. *Social Studies of Science*, 44(2): 218–242.

[4] Muiderman, K., Gupta, A., Vervoort, J., & Biermann, F. (2020). Four approaches to anticipatory climate governance: Different conceptions of the future and implications for the present. *WIREs Climate Change*, 11(6): 1–20.

towards more sustainable futures across different policy domains and sectors."[5]

To substantiate the benefits of anticipatory governance, case studies illustrating its effectiveness are crucial. The effectiveness of AG varies and depends on specific contexts and the quality of implementation. This chapter recounts futures thinking and foresight integration in terms of the Asian Development Bank's capabilities, aiming to better contribute to the dialogue about the sustainable development of its developing member countries (DMCs).

22.2 Asian Development Bank and Anticipatory Governance

> *"Good governance and effective public management are essential for country and sector development. ADB's [Asian Development Bank'] message in its Asia 2050 report is clear — better governance across a range of dimensions and across Asia and the Pacific will determine whether a developing member country (DMC) can accelerate development and inclusive growth."*
>
> Asian Development Bank (2021, 2023)[6,7]

Since its establishment in 1966, the Asian Development Bank (ADB) has had inherently a futures-oriented approach. As a regional development bank, ADB envisions an Asia and Pacific region free of poverty characterized by sustainable and inclusive development. ADB Strategy 2030 aligns with the UN's Sustainable Development Goals (SDGs).[8]

---

[5] Muiderman, K., Zurek, M., Vervoort, J., Gupta, A., Hasnain, S., & Driessen, P. (2022). The anticipatory governance of sustainability transformations: Hybrid approaches and dominant perspectives. *Global Environmental Change*, 73: 203452.

[6] Asian Development Bank (2021). Asia 2050: Realizing the Asian Century. https://www.adb.org/publications/asia-2050-realizing-asian-century (Accessed 28 December, 2023).

[7] Asian Development Bank (2023). Strengthening Governance and Institutional Capacity. https://www.adb.org/adbi/capacity-building-training/strengthening-governance-institutional-capacity (Accessed 28 December, 2023).

[8] Asian Development Bank (2019). Strategy 2030 Operational Plans Overview. https://www.adb.org/sites/default/files/institutional-document/495946/strategy-2030-operational-plans-overview.pdf (Accessed 28 December, 2023).

Recognizing the importance of explicit foresight work, ADB has played three key roles in promoting futures thinking and foresight (see Exhibit 22.1): (i) Provider of capacity development for Developing Members Countries (DMCs); (ii) Instigator for applying futures thinking and foresight for internal reforms; and (iii) Documenter and sharer of futures thinking and foresight practices to raise awareness and develop a knowledge base in the development sector.

The three roles of ADB are interconnected in a cohesive approach to organizational learning and innovation. ADB's external capacity development initiatives inform its internal reforms, creating a dynamic feedback loop where practical experiences and insights gained from applying futures thinking internally contribute to the refinement of capacity development approaches with DMCs. Simultaneously, the documentation of these experiences serves as a valuable knowledge-sharing resource, facilitating the cross-pollination of ideas both within ADB and with external stakeholders. This holistic approach ensures that lessons learned from external engagements and internal adaptations collectively contribute to a more robust and informed application of futures thinking and foresight across ADB's operations.

Exhibit 22.1. ADB's roles.

ADB's Role	**Activities**
1. Provider of capacity Development for DMCs	ADB has provided technical assistance via a grant project to ten DMCs — Armenia, Cambodia, Indonesia, the Philippines, China, Kazakhstan, Mongolia, Uzbekistan, Vietnam, and Timor-Leste — to apply futures thinking and foresight in long-term planning, plan strategy development, and enhance multi-stakeholder dialogues to inform future-oriented visions for sectors.
Example #1: Since 2019, ADB has collaborated with the Government of Armenia. Initially focused on urban development, ADB moved in 2022 and 2023 to support Armenia's Ministry of Justice. ADB organized futures workshops focusing on future-proofing Armenia's judicial and legal reform efforts, contributing to the establishment of the Arbitration and Mediation Centre of Armenia.	
Example #2: From 2019 to 2023, ADB worked with the Philippines' National Economic and Development Authority (NEDA). Several training courses culminated in the formulation of the Central Luzon Regional Development Plan 2023–2028, the sub-region's development blueprint.	

Exhibit 22.1. (*Continued*)

<table>
<tr><th>ADB's Role</th><th>Activities</th></tr>
<tr><td colspan="2">Example #3: In 2023, ADB supported the Indonesian Ministry of National Development Planning (BAPPENAS) to deepen scenarios on Indonesia's long-term future, addressing various aspects such as transportation, housing, gender equity, maritime economy, development of Papua, and Indonesia as a whole. The outcomes included scenarios for addressing corruption, thematic scenarios related to Indonesia's potential for sustainable economic growth, and scenarios related to human capital. These scenarios were further developed using the Causal Layered Analysis method[9,10] to uncover barriers to implementing the preferred future and identify the best support.</td></tr>
<tr><td colspan="2">Example #4: In 2023, ADB worked with the Tashkent International Commercial Court (TICC) to facilitate the development of a comprehensive vision for TICC's future, with a focus on enhancing effectiveness, transparency, and accessibility in resolving commercial disputes, using futures and foresight methodologies. This helped TICC create a detailed vision, generating actionable insights while addressing potential threats and risks. This workshop laid the foundation for future planning meetings and discussions to further build capacities to effectively use futures and foresight approaches.</td></tr>
<tr><td>2. Instigator for applying futures thinking and foresight for internal reforms</td><td>ADB is applying futures thinking and foresight internally.</td></tr>
<tr><td colspan="2">Example #1: This includes training of over 400 ADB staff in theory, methods, and practices since 2016. Topics have included gender equality futures, knowledge management futures, and innovation futures.</td></tr>
<tr><td colspan="2">Example #2: Since 2021, futures thinking and foresight have been integrated into ADB's innovation hub service lines. The hub itself was conventionalized using futures thinking and foresight. These efforts have played a pivotal role in ADB's reforms toward a new operating model, shifting from an infrastructure bank to a climate bank, in alignment with emerging global priorities. In 2024, ADB appointed a sector planning specialist bring to mainstream futures thinking and foresight into upstream sector planning.</td></tr>
</table>

(*Continued*)

[9]Inayatullah, S. (2004). *Causal Layered Analysis (CLA) Reader: Theory and Case Studies of an Integrative and Transformative Methodology*. Taipei, China: Tamkang University Press.
[10]Inayatullah, S., Mercer, R., Milojević, I., & Sweeney, J. (Eds.) (2022). *CLA 3.0: Thirty Years of Transformative Research.* Taipei, China: Tamkang University Press.

Exhibit 22.1. (*Continued*)

ADB's Role	Activities
3. Documenter and sharer of futures thinking and foresight practices to raise awareness and develop a knowledge base in the development sector	ADB has shared the application of futures thinking and foresight at conferences and workshops and by publishing manuals, briefs, and reports.
Example #1: "Futures Thinking in Asia and the Pacific: Why Foresight Matters for Policymakers"[11] Example #2: "How ADB Uses Futures and Foresight Tools to Help Countries Prepare for an Uncertain Future"[12] Example #3: "Asian Development Bank Foresight in Action: Prospective Policy Making in Asia and the Pacific."[13]	

Source: Authors.

22.3 Lessons Learned: Moving Forward in Creating an Architecture for Anticipatory Governance

Utilizing interviews and experiences across ADB countries,[14,15] this section summarizes responses to the following key questions: What drives ADB's DMCs to want to develop anticipatory capacities? What obstacles hold them back? How to create architecture and processes in institutions to enable foresight and anticipation? How to balance fostering governance without increasing control that could stifle freedom and innovation? How do we best use anticipatory governance to convene stakeholders, break

[11]Asian Development Bank (2020). Futures Thinking in Asia and the Pacific: Why Foresight Matters for Policymakers. Available: https://www.adb.org/publications/futures-thinking-asia-pacific-policy-makers (Accessed 12 April, 2023).

[12]Roth, S. & Parry, J. (2023). How ADB uses futures and foresight tools to help countries prepare for an uncertain future. *Asian Development Bank.* Policy Brief No. 271.

[13]Milojević, I. & Roth, S. (2024). *ADB Foresight in Action: Prospective Policy Making in Asia and the Pacific*. Manila: Asian Development Bank (forthcoming).

[14]Asian Development Bank (2020), *Op. cit.*

[15]Milojević, I. & Roth, S. (2024). *ADB Foresight in Action: Prospective Policy Making in Asia and the Pacific*. Manila: Asian Development Bank (forthcoming).

silos, and govern for not just the future but for alternative futures and for emergent possibilities?

These questions aim to elicit insights from the experiences and perspectives gathered across ADB member countries, shedding light on the motivations, challenges, and strategies related to the development and implementation of anticipatory governance.

22.3.1 *The drivers*

Globally, challenges such as uncertainties stemming from climate change, rapid technological advancements, demographic shifts, social tensions, and geopolitical dynamics are propelling the demand for more agile and anticipatory governance. The complex and swiftly changing landscape requires effective governance to navigate risks and capitalize on opportunities. The rate of social change, coupled with cultural, demographic, environmental, technological, and economic challenges, intensifies the difficulty of such tasks.[16,17,18,19]

In many countries, the public sector finds itself stretched, grappling with the evolving, often competing demands of citizens. The speed and heterogeneity of social change and the evolving nature of change itself will result in an increasingly challenging task of governance in the future. Consequently, policymakers are actively seeking new conceptual and methodological tools to better prioritize issues and successfully implement policies addressing these dynamic changes.

In our work with various governments and affiliated stakeholders,[20] we have observed that policymakers are acutely aware of the rapid and complex nature of change, along with the uncertainties and risks associated with multifaceted transformations. They are looking for ways to better serve the needs of their citizens, transcend silos, mitigate short-termism, and move beyond piecemeal approaches to problems. There is a palpable

---

[16]Boin, A. (2008). *Crisis Management*, Vol. II. Los Angeles: Sage.

[17]Hajkowics, S., Cook, H., & Littleboy, A. (2010). *Our Future World: Global Megatrends that Will Change the Way We Live*. Brisbane: CSIRO.

[18]Inayatullah, S. (2006). Eliminating future shock: The changing world of work and the organization. *Foresight,* 8(5): 3–14.

[19]Oloruntoba, R. (2013). Plans never go according to plans. *Technological Forecasting and Social Change*, 80(9): 1674–1702.

[20]Milojević & Roth (2024), *Op. cit.*

need and call for action. For instance, during the pandemic, public policy responses were rapidly changing, sometimes on a weekly or daily basis. As new information emerged, public policy had to swiftly adjust. Unlike any other time in the past, policy responses quickly became outdated, underscoring the necessity for agile and anticipatory governance.

Several governments across the Asia-Pacific region, where ADB operates, are actively seeking ways to minimize risks and enhance opportunities arising from global, regional, and local challenges. They aim to comprehend the first-, second-, and third-order implications of their policies by understanding the impact these policies will have on the future. Additionally, they strive to "future-proof" their strategies, reduce "blind spots," engage a variety of stakeholders, and scrutinize the assumptions guiding their day-to-day work. Given the considerable effort invested in implementing strategies, policymakers aspire to "get them right" while considering changing conditions and anticipating possibilities in the long term. They are also alert to the importance of not just more reliable data about the emerging futures but of the narratives — the stories, the metaphors — that policymakers need to use to ensure that change is possible in the hearts and minds of citizens. For example, in Cambodia, they suggested a transformation in e-governance from the current "e-monk" to the future "e-Buddha," that is, a system that was simple, efficient, and paperless, for the good of the entire nation.[21] In the PRC, participants imagined a narrative where knowledge and innovation moved from "knowledge on a leash" to "knowledge with wings." For them, this meant a system that was merit based, used the latest technologies, and was organizationally agile.[22]

Moreover, there are emerging indicators of a shift in some Asia-Pacific countries toward a more participatory and inclusive approach to governance. Policymakers recognize the necessity of mobilizing relevant stakeholders, including the private sector, for funding and implementation, as well as multiple citizen groups, for a deeper understanding of risks and benefits to various social segments. For multilateral organizations like ADB, the recent emphasis on linking participatory decision-making with anticipatory governance is interesting and relevant, especially considering ADB's shift to a climate bank. This leads to the question of who is not in the room. Anticipatory governance can future-proof itself by including as many stakeholders as possible, including nature and new technologies such as AI.

[21] Asian Development Bank (2020), *Op. cit.*

[22] *Ibid.*

22.3.2 *The obstacles*

Despite the recognized need, demand, and efforts toward agile and anticipatory governance outlined in the previous section, numerous obstacles impede effective implementation. These obstacles primarily revolve around the challenges listed in the following:

Hesitancy to engage: There exists a general lack of awareness regarding what futures thinking and foresight approaches entail and how they can contribute to improved governance. Most leaders are unfamiliar with or untrained in futures thinking (FF). Consequently, organizational cultures often favor siloed and piecemeal approaches, short-termism, and fragmented responses. Changing this status quo is difficult and sometimes perceived as risky. Independent agencies are frequently required to navigate conflicting priorities and interests among stakeholders. While multilateral organizations like ADB aim to assist, the allure of "business as usual" often prevails over innovation and advancing systemic change. Challenging the status quo is inherently difficult, and the lack of awareness and education on FF tools, e.g., exclusion in training programs for many policymakers as part of their policymaking toolset, makes it even more so.

Reluctance to change: Concerns about the critical and sometimes subversive nature of challenging the status quo contribute to reluctance. In linear and top-down organizations, even discussions about alternative futures or scenarios can be perceived as threatening. Some participants in FF workshops express reluctance to take cognitive risks, speak their minds, and express vulnerability. Over the last decade, social media usage (via "filter bubble" or "echo chambers") and the fallout from disciplining those with divergent opinions have intensified pressure to avoid making "career-limiting moves," resulting in sanitized but vague statements often reflecting "toxic optimism." Freedom-of-speech issues underpinned by more restricted cultures may contribute to conservatism in some organizations and policymaking with very little divergence from the status quo.

Fragmentation of foresight work: While FF work is gaining momentum, there is a general lack of coordination among various partners and organizations. The absence of appropriate architecture and mechanisms for coordinating multiple FF activities at the country, regional, and global levels poses a challenge. New efforts, such as the establishment of the Global Futures Society, driven by the UAE, are in their infancy. Previous efforts by other global futures and foresight organizations, while noteworthy, have failed to establish quality standards for FF work. Simultaneous initiatives often attempt to "reinvent the wheel," lacking consideration for previous work done by numerous organizations globally, for example, an in-house UN Summit of the Future.[23] Coordination issues extend beyond the UN, with many multilateral organizations not yet collaborating effectively on FF.

22.3.3 *Balancing acts*

In navigating the complex landscape of agile and anticipatory governance, certain balancing acts are imperative. For example, independent organizations, particularly think tanks, play a crucial role in promoting the space for FF research. They can act as a resource and even hold the political arm accountable. Collaborating with the media and engaging civil society organizations (CSOs) is essential. The think tanks require support from international organizations to build technical skills and leadership that can sustain and legitimize diverse approaches. Multilaterals should coordinate and invest in FF capacity development for local organizations, moving beyond one-off engagements. This is particularly vital for Multilateral Development Banks (MDBs) to integrate FF as part of their MDB evolution agenda.[24]

The global multilateral system, conceived in the last century, is evolving from a single future for all to embracing alternative futures and localized development solutions. Multilateral organizations hold a pivotal role as neutral conveners, bridging the space between the present and the sustainable future. They facilitate discussions on alternative futures, providing spaces that might not organically occur. For example, ADB's FF efforts have been successful in convening stakeholders and breaking silos. This includes intergenerational engagement, hierarchical and seniority bridging, cross-sector collaboration, bridging sub-regions/provinces, and fostering collaboration between countries. ADB's role is evolving to support how countries develop visions for alternative futures at the local and

---

[23] The Summit of the Future in 2024 (UN). Multilateral Solutions for a Better Tomorrow. Available: https://www.un.org/en/common-agenda/summit-of-the-future (Accessed 6 January, 2024).

[24] G20 (2023). Strengthening Multilateral Development Banks: the Triple Agenda. Available: https://icrier.org/g20-ieg/pdf/The_Triple_Agenda_G20-IEG_Report_Volume2_2023.pdf (Accessed 6 January, 2024).

regional levels, contributing significantly to new forms of governance that are anticipatory and participatory. The shift from global to local and vice versa is essential.

22.4 Conclusion: Governing for the Future

In conclusion, navigating the complexities of anticipatory governance in Asia-Pacific countries (and beyond) involves recognizing both drivers and obstacles. The forces propelling anticipatory capacity include uncertainties, complexity, and the rapid pace of change. Simultaneously, obstacles such as hesitancy, reluctance, fragmentation, or sporadic initiatives pose challenges to effective implementation.

The balancing acts required in this dynamic landscape underscore the critical role of multilateral organizations. They must actively contribute even further to creating and legitimizing architectures and processes that foster foresight and participation without stifling freedom and innovation. Furthermore, multilateral organizations play a pivotal role in holding the space for alternative futures and facilitating cross-sectoral and cross-regional dialogues.

Creating an inclusive process for envisioning the future is paramount. It involves visualizing narratives of the future and establishing accountability between citizens and politicians to realize these visions. The approach extends beyond political cycles, emphasizing the roles of media, civil society organizations (CSOs), and development partners. However, planning for the long term while acting in the short term is crucial for delivering tangible benefits. Just as the needs of futures generations cannot be ignored, the long-term future needs to be linked to the present to ensure that action results.

The evolving role of multilateral organizations is central to this transformative journey. Shifting from a paternal perspective of development to a more participatory and co-creative stance is imperative. In this paradigm shift, the indispensable role of independent think tanks and organizations becomes evident, which needs to be nurtured in developing countries. These entities serve as guardians, holding the space and creating accountability across generations that extend beyond political cycles.

The case study of the ADB provides valuable insights into the practical application of anticipatory governance. ADB's internal and external futures mainstreaming initiatives showcase both successes and challenges.

ADB's efforts include bringing diverse stakeholders together, convening experts across agencies and silos, breaking civil servants out of routine, and creating space for discussing alternatives. The internal development of FF capacity is notable, but there is room for improvement in sharing experiences with ADB's clients and partners, such as establishing a Community of Practice (CoP) for civil servants. Areas for enhancement include consistent follow-ups, collaboration with local research organizations to better understand impact, and transitioning from general capabilities to applying foresight techniques within existing work.

The recommendations derived from ADB case study emphasize the need for more consistent follow-ups, ongoing processes, robust support mechanisms via local think tanks, academia, and CSOs, thorough evaluations, and the application of foresight in practical ways. Multilaterals should share FF practices, foster collaboration, create accountability at the global and regional levels, and support local capacity development and institution-building. Supporting processes from strategy and national development planning to decision-making about specific projects and their implementation is crucial. Engaging multiple stakeholders to share visions and cooperate on futures enhances the effectiveness of anticipatory governance.

As we forge ahead, the lessons learned from both drivers and obstacles, the delicate balancing acts, and the evolving roles of multilateral organizations and independent entities contribute to an emerging roadmap for anticipatory governance journeys. Creating inclusive visions, visualizing and communicating futures, and establishing accountability are ongoing processes that require courage, collaboration, adaptability, and a commitment to co-creating a sustainable and resilient future. This requires leaders who can step outside their comfort zones and the business-as-usual ways of working. This means authentically understanding the changing needs of citizens in each country and creating space for discourse and alternatives. Finally, given the global nature of wicked challenges like climate change, connecting local efforts to the global context would ensure that the needs of all global citizens are met.

https://doi.org/10.1142/9789811296000_0023

Chapter 23

Humanitarian Logistics and Health Response

Immanuel Azaad Moonesar

Mohammed Bin Rashid School of Government, Dubai, UAE

Key Takeaways

- Disaster preparedness in health logistics is crucial for reducing the adverse effects of crises on public health and ensuring effective humanitarian relief delivery.
- Predictive analytics and data-informed insights improve resource allocation and help tailor relief strategies to each crisis.
- These public–private partnerships prevent redundancy, speed up response times, and ensure resource allocation matches needs on the ground.
- In a humanitarian hub, the essential components and strategic mindset needed during crises are encapsulated by the three Rs^2 — Readiness, Rapid Responses, and Resilience & Recovery — with examples from the International Humanitarian City (IHC) in Dubai, Gavi, Global Fund, and BRAC.
- By transferring knowledge and fostering resilience, organizations should ensure their stakeholders are well rounded, adaptable, and ready for disasters.

23.1 Introduction

Reducing the negative impacts of crises on public health and ensuring effective humanitarian aid delivery are made possible via disaster planning within health logistics. Global humanitarian crises pose complicated health difficulties. Immediate humanitarian operations in conflict, natural disasters, and displacement zones generally struggle owing to insufficient nutrition, sanitation, and healthcare.

Yemen's humanitarian situation is one example. A prolonged battle has caused massive migration, food shortages, and a crumbling healthcare system. Millions of Yemenis[1] suffer from acute starvation, lack of clean water and sanitation, and insufficient healthcare, worsening health issues. Conflict and displacement have caused humanitarian crises in South Sudan[2] and the DRC. Food instability, poor water and sanitation, and infectious illness epidemics like cholera and Ebola put much pressure on the healthcare systems of these regions. Natural disasters can cause health-related humanitarian problems as well as combat zones. Recent storms in the Caribbean and Central America[3] have destroyed infrastructure, displaced communities, and raised waterborne illness risk owing to polluted water and poor sanitation.

Health issues in humanitarian situations need coordinated actions from humanitarian groups, governments, and the international community. Immediate help must be given to provide healthy food, clean water, and sanitation and to develop healthcare infrastructure to provide urgent medical care. The core causes of war, displacement, and poverty must be addressed to build resilience and stability in afflicted regions.

In this chapter, the background of the UAE is examined through the lens of the International Humanitarian City[4] (IHC), in addition to the examples of Gavi, BRAC, and the Global Fund. This chapter reiterates the importance of logistical frameworks for anticipatory health and

---

[1] The reports from UNHCR. Available: https://www.unhcr.org/countries/yemen (Accessed 18 February, 2024).

[2] The reports from Disaster Philanthropy- South Sudan via https://disasterphilanthropy.org/disasters/south-sudan-humanitarian-crisis/#:~:text=Critical%20drivers%20of%20displacement%20in,30%2C%202023 (Accessed 18 February, 2024).

[3] The reports from Disaster Philanthropy- Caribbean and Central America via https://disasterphilanthropy.org/?s=caribbean+ (Accessed 18 February, 2024).

[4] International Humanitarian City (2023). More information via: https://www.ihc.ae/.

humanitarian help. Specifically, it highlights the approach IHC uses to reach those most in need during disasters and enhance preparation efforts.

Humanitarian centers provide efficient and effective crisis relief. Governments, NGOs, international agencies, and local populations collaborate at these hubs. Humanitarian hubs improve assistance coordination and delivery by offering a shared cooperation and information exchange platform, facilitating speedy and effective resource deployment to affected communities. Advanced infrastructure and logistics allow these hubs to pre-position emergency supplies and create efficient distribution networks. Humanitarian centers speed up emergency response and develop resilience for future disasters. Their role is to expedite humanitarian activities, optimize relief effects, and save lives in catastrophic situations.

23.2 The 3Rs to Managing Health Logistics during Crises

In a humanitarian hub, the essential components and strategic mindset needed during crises are encapsulated by the three Rs: Readiness, Rapid Responses, and Resilience & Recovery. Under the *Readiness* phase, emphasis is placed on effective coordination, comprehensive training, and proactive preparedness measures. The second phase, *Rapid Responses*, entails legal considerations, active engagement with the public, collaboration with communities and civil society, and implementing policing measures. The final phase, *Resilience & Recovery*, involves documenting valuable insights gained during crises and developing robust resilience plans to navigate future challenges.

23.2.1 *The International Humanitarian City (IHC): An overview*

The realm of humanitarian aid or relief is complex.[5] The field of humanitarian help or relief is challenging because of the multiple characteristics of crises, which range from natural catastrophes to wars, as well as the

[5] Yan, Q. (2023). The use of climate information in humanitarian relief efforts: A literature review. *Journal of Humanitarian Logistics and Supply Chain Management* (ahead-of-print). https://www.emerald.com/insight/content/doi/10.1108/JHLSCM-01-2022-0003/full/pdf.

different demands of impacted communities. It entails overcoming political, logistical, cultural, and ethical barriers while delivering timely and efficient support to needy people. Coordination among many stakeholders, including governments, NGOs, and international organizations, is critical, but competing objectives and inadequate resources sometimes hamper it. Furthermore, the dynamic nature of crises necessitates flexible solutions and ongoing review to guarantee the best practical actions. Overall, the complexities of humanitarian relief highlight the value of teamwork, creativity, and a thorough awareness of the circumstances in which assistance is provided. The International Humanitarian City (IHC), which is situated in the heart of Dubai, serves as an outstanding best practice regarding the significance of collaboration[6] and proactive disaster preparedness. The city, founded to be a worldwide humanitarian center, helps pre-position and distribute disaster relief materials. Its strategic position, significant infrastructure, and persistent dedication and planning make it a model for catastrophe response and management with the 3 Rs: Readiness, Rapid Responses, and Resilience & Recovery (refer to Exhibit 23.1).

Catalyzing Local and Global Change: The International Humanitarian City (IHC) in Dubai is an example of a transformational catastrophe preparedness paradigm. By combining cutting-edge technology, strategic alliances, and forward-thinking policy, the IHC enables efficient humanitarian relief and fosters a worldwide culture of preparation. For example, when a terrible earthquake struck a neighboring nation, the IHC quickly coordinated relief operations, demonstrating the success of its contingency plans. This example of proactive disaster management inspired other businesses and governments to improve their disaster response skills, eventually saving lives and reducing the effects of future disasters. The IHC's proactive approach and dedication to innovation demonstrate Dubai's leadership in humanitarian aid, serving as a light of hope for vulnerable populations worldwide.

---

[6]Ahmad, M. (2023). Connecting people and places: How citizen diplomacy and VGI are strengthening disaster response and community development. In *Global Perspectives on the Emerging Trends in Public Diplomacy*. IGI Global: pp. 195–226. Hershey, USA.

Exhibit 23.1. The reach of the IHC in the year 2023 by product cluster and number of countries reached.

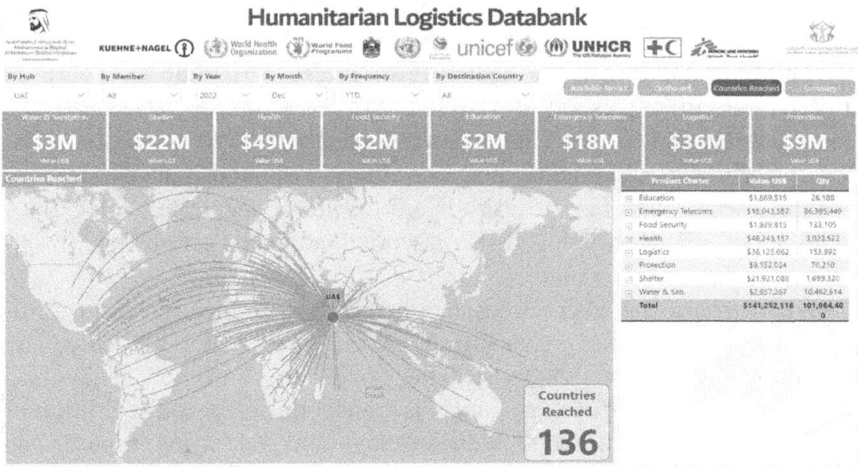

Source: IHC (2023).[7]

23.3 3R Framework in Action

This section applies the 3R framework to the context of humanitarian logistics and health logistics. Examples are taken from the IHC; Gavi (The Vaccine Alliance)[8]; BRAC[9] (formerly Bangladesh Rural Advancement Committee); and the Global Fund[10] to Fight AIDS, Tuberculosis, and Malaria.

23.3.1 *Readiness*

Coordination of Emergency Task Forces: Humanitarian help, including the coordination of Emergency Task Forces, may be observed in the reaction to

[7]International Humanitarian City (2023). All Countries Reached. Humanitarian Logistics Database. Available: https://www.ihc.ae/databank/# (Accessed 14 March, 2023). Note as of March 2024, 118 countries were reached.

[8]Gavi: The Vaccine Alliance (2024). More available: https://www.gavi.org/.

[9]BRAC (2024). More available: https://www.brac.net/.

[10]The Global Fund to Fight AIDS, Tuberculosis and Malaria (2024). More available: https://www.theglobalfund.org/en/.

a big earthquake in a densely populated city. Several organizations and institutions quickly gather to aid when a terrible earthquake struck a city. They include government institutions, international non-governmental organizations (NGOs), local grassroots groups, and specialist rescue squads.

The coordination of emergency task forces was vital to ensure an effective and quick response. The Task Forces, which included officials from a variety of industries and agencies, collaborated to assess the situation, prioritize requirements, and coordinate resource distribution. For example, search and rescue teams were told to concentrate on locations with the best chances of survival, while medical teams set up field hospitals to offer emergency medical care.

Furthermore, the Task Forces encouraged communication and coordination among many players, ensuring that efforts were not duplicated and resources were directed to where they were most needed. They also worked to optimize operations, such as transportation and distribution of assistance goods, in order to reduce delays and maximize impact. The Emergency Task Forces saved lives, alleviated suffering, and assisted the afflicted communities with their recovery efforts by coordinating the actions of many stakeholders. Their coordinated approach demonstrates the value of cooperation in humanitarian relief distribution, especially in complicated and fast-developing emergency circumstances.

Advanced Data Analytics: In disaster management today, the IHC uses data analytics. Since 2018, the team has been collecting and coordinating data on inventory from their partners to create the Humanitarian Logistics Databank. The automated system tracks the movement of aid on information from customs (ports, airports, and other entry points) and allows all participating relief workers to see the exact positioning of critical items for humanitarian relief (such as food, medicine, and shelter). By coordinating and sharing information, the partners avoid duplicate relief efforts and target resources where they are needed. This allows the IHC to improve collaboration, reduce bottlenecks, predict disasters, and organize more fruitful rescue activities.[11,12]

[11]IHC, Humanitarian Logistics Databank (2023). More available: https://www.ihc.ae/databank/ (Accessed 26 December, 2023).

[12]Manoj Kumar, M.V., Atalla, S., Almuraqab, N., & Moonesar, I.A. (2022). Detection of COVID-19 using deep learning techniques and cost effectiveness evaluation: A survey. *Frontiers in Artificial Intelligence*, 5: 912022.

Forecasting for Humanitarian Resources: The IHC forecasts future disasters, moving from a reactive to an anticipatory response, by examining historical catastrophes, environmental trends, and socioeconomic factors. Data analysis boosts forecasts.[13] Similarly, Gavi strengthens healthcare systems[14] by learning from immunization programs and responding to future difficulties. This entails documenting accomplishments and problems, gaining data-driven insights, and increasing global immunization to aid long-term recovery.

Also, relief operations are becoming more cooperative. Data coordinate parties. Under the hub's approach, government and charitable groups may obtain data-driven insights. Harmonization reduces overlaps and ensures resource distribution meets ground requirements, aiding relief efforts. Crisis management with modern data analytics is revolutionary because lives are in danger, and every decision affects the community. The transition is from anticipatory and ambiguous to proactive actions. Our data-driven strategy recognizes the unpredictability of disasters while emphasizing our capacity to prepare in a profession where time is key. By combining technology, mindfulness, and compassion, we secure our ability to respond quickly and effectively when every second matters.

Increasing Preparedness via Pre-positioning and Swift Distribution: Pre-positioning is critical to the humanitarian hub's approach. Keeping relief goods in crucial areas before disasters reduces the time it takes to notice a problem and give aid. A proactive approach changes disaster response dynamics based on historical data — the readiness to immediately deploy resources to provide badly needed aid to affected areas after a disaster.

The intensity of the Palestinian or Syrian crises,[15] accessibility to impacted areas, and logistical problems due to continuous violence or political instability can all affect emergency response time frames.

---

[13] Widener, D.V., Mazzuchi, T.A., & Sarkani, S. (2018). Simplifying humanitarian assistance/disaster relief analytic models using activity-based intelligence: Syrian refugee crisis as a case study. *Disaster Prevention and Management*, 27(1): 60–73.

[14] Gavi (2024). Health system and immunisation strengthening. Available https://www.gavi.org/programmes-impact/types-support/health-system-and-immunisation-strengthening (Accessed 14 March, 2024).

[15] UN Relief and Works Agency for Palestine Refugees in the Near East (2024). Description. Available: https://reliefweb.int/organization/unrwa (Accessed 14 March, 2024).

Humanitarian situations depend on quick responses to save lives and reduce suffering. In crisis response, every second matters; avoiding redundancy saves lives and maximizes aid.[16] Similarly, Gavi aids speedy health crisis responses by distributing vaccinations and supporting immunization efforts. It works with governments and other stakeholders to swiftly administer vaccinations to needy places, tackling emerging health challenges.

To help affected communities, medical supplies, food, shelter, and clean water must be sent quickly. In crises like Palestine and Syria, bureaucratic difficulties, security concerns, and logistical limits can delay humanitarian response operations. Despite these obstacles, humanitarian actors pre-position goods, form local alliances, and use cutting-edge technology to analyze and distribute relief quickly. Humanitarian centers, local authorities, and international organizations must coordinate to respond to catastrophes in these locations quickly and effectively.

The Palestinian and Syrian conflicts, which have uprooted millions, have limited the access of people to healthcare, food, and shelter. Thus, shortening reaction times and guaranteeing rapid emergency aid are essential to meeting vulnerable populations' urgent needs and minimizing disasters. Humanitarian actors are working together to improve reaction times and provide life-saving relief to Palestinian and Syrian residents.

In addition, a humanitarian center needs a *strategic location and infrastructure*. For example, the IHC is based in Dubai, which is strategically located in the Middle East between Africa and Asia. This great location allows quick access to disaster-prone areas. The hub has modern warehouses, logistical centers, and storage facilities to hold humanitarian goods. Supply storage is incorporated into these structures. These resources can be quickly and efficiently deployed in a disaster, reducing reaction time and improving aid distribution.

When refugees fled a nearby war, the International Humanitarian City (IHC) responded quickly. Within hours after receiving the crisis warning, the IHC triggered its emergency response processes and sent a team of specialists to examine the situation. The IHC managed emergency aid delivery to impacted regions in 4–8 hours using pre-positioned relief

[16] Shafiq, M. & Soratana, K. (2019). Humanitarian logistics and supply chain management: A qualitative study. *LogForum*, 15(1). DOI: 10.17270/J.LOG.2019.325.

goods and its broad network of partners and logistical skills. The aid includes shelter, food, water, medical supplies, and other essentials for the displaced. Medical teams, search and rescue units, and other specialist professionals were quickly sent by the IHC to help local authorities save lives and protect impacted populations. The IHC exhibited its humanitarian values and ability to respond to calamities by mobilizing promptly and efficiently, reducing suffering, and saving lives in neighboring nations in distress.

23.3.2 *Rapid responses*

Collaborative Partnership or Capacity for Multi-Sectoral Response: The IHC deploys resources and information efficiently through over 83 entities comprising partnerships with governments, NGOs, corporations, and international organizations tailoring humanitarian aid for diverse needs.[17] The IHC considers disaster response a shared responsibility where teams must work together to address complicated problems. For example, governments offer infrastructure and resources, and adapt regulations. NGOs offer localized knowledge, community involvement, and bottom-up thinking.[18] Private sector partners provide creativity and logistics, or donate resources like technology.

Capacity-Building: In the case of the Global Fund, which works with governments, NGOs, and other partners to build healthcare systems to fight AIDS, TB, and malaria, it mobilizes resources or works to support training, medical supply availability, and diagnostic capabilities. Periodic training teaches stakeholders new disaster responses. These courses include first aid, planning, agency coordination, and communication. Addressing many disaster response components ensures stakeholders are well rounded, flexible, and prepared. For example, Gavi coordinates worldwide vaccination access initiatives. Strategic relationships with governments, international organizations, and the corporate sector improve

---

[17] Ahmad (2023), *Op. cit.*

[18] Hilhorst, D., Desportes, I., & de Milliano, C.W. (2019). Humanitarian governance and resilience building: Ethiopia in comparative perspective. *Disasters*, 43: S109–S131. https://onlinelibrary.wiley.com/doi/pdfdirect/10.1111/disa.12332.

vaccination delivery. Gavi trains healthcare personnel and strengthens healthcare systems for immunization programs.

Long-term collaboration after a crisis affects disaster management from preparedness to recovery. Continuous sharing of information, resources, and learning strengthens the response ecosystem. Disaster response is more coordinated, effective, and compassionate with partnerships. IHC redefine "all hands on deck" by illustrating how several groups working toward the same goal have a significant influence. The IHC teaches disaster management organizations worldwide how collaboration may turn calamities into opportunities for development.

Increased capacity impacts all and helps strengthen the whole disaster response ecosystem. By sharing of best practices, key stakeholders also learn to cooperate. This synchronization enhances emergency response and avoids misunderstanding. BRAC's preparedness phase comprises community-based empowerment and training. This involves disaster preparedness education, volunteer training, and early warning systems to reduce natural catastrophe damage.

Disaster Management Simulations: Training and simulations improve crisis management in proactive capacity-building. Skill development and preparedness[19] are two benefits of this activity. Another capacity-building approach is simulation, where participants practice disaster management in simulations that help stakeholders collaborate, think fast, and decide. These workshops are theoretical and practical. Knowledge transfer enables employment and tenure planning and resiliency. The hub stresses capacity-building through the simulations because preparation is the best defense. It is responsive and changes opinions by developing stakeholders.[20]

Knowledge Transfer: The Global Fund focuses on disease control programs to build strength and recovery from crises. This entails building on successful solutions, upgrading healthcare infrastructure, and assisting communities develop sustainable health practices for future issues.

[19] Perry, R.W. & Lindell, M.K. (2003). Preparedness for emergency response: Guidelines for the emergency planning process. *Disasters*, 27(4): 336–350.

[20] International Humanitarian City (2023). Reports and Publications. Available: https://www.ihc.ae/latest-publications/ (Accessed 10 December, 2023).

23.3.3 *Resilience and recovery*

Reaching Vulnerable Populations: Organizational success comes from facilitating and organizing member efforts. States, non-governmental organizations, and international entities collaborate to create a comprehensive emergency response infrastructure that makes crisis response more efficient. Its collaborative approach speeds up reaction times and optimizes resource use, providing urgent and meaningful aid to needy individuals. The IHC works with the government of Dubai and Emirates Airlines to get free airlifts for humanitarian relief. While this strategy also overlaps with response time, it includes creating evacuation centers to house and help humanitarian personnel evacuate from dangerous areas. This dual-purpose method improves crisis response and worker safety. The organization leads the humanitarian community by prioritizing staff safety.

The company goes beyond quick reactions to complete disaster response. As disadvantaged people generally bear the brunt of calamities, the IHC organizes logistics around their needs. This integrated strategy addresses response disparities by ensuring fair access to vital resources. Exhibit 23.2 shows how the organization anticipates and meets the needs of vulnerable populations, including children, seniors, and people with special needs. Similarly, BRAC's resilience and recovery efforts are community based. BRAC builds resilient communities by recording crisis experiences and difficulties. The concept of recording crisis experiences and obstacles exemplifies community-based education in response to BRAC's resilience and recovery initiatives. In a recent flood-prone location where BRAC operates, community people were frequently confronted with the obstacles of restoring their lives following each calamity.

BRAC launched an educational program to teach local volunteers to chronicle their experiences during crises, including the specific obstacles they faced and the techniques they used to overcome them. These recordings were then used as instructional tools in the community, establishing a foundation for seminars and training sessions focused on increasing resilience. By sharing their experiences and learning from one another, community members were able to better plan for and respond to future catastrophes, resulting in more resilient communities. Sustainable development programs help communities recover from adversity. The IHC's humanitarian-compliant method transforms catastrophe response from relief to empowerment and dignity. Exhibits 23.2 and 23.3 show the organization's reach in over 136 countries.

Exhibit 23.2. Summary of the reach in the years 2022 and 2023 by product cluster.

Source: IHC (2023).[21]

Demonstrating Greater Impact: Impact Measurement and Crisis Management: With regard to the Health Resilience and Surveillance Impact Assessments, this KPI emphasizes fast, efficient aid. It assesses response preparedness by measuring reaction time. It symbolizes lives saved, suffering reduced, and resilience built. Disaster management's "golden

[21] International Humanitarian City (2023). Humanitarian Logistic Databank. Available: https://www.ihc.ae/databank/ (Accessed 14 March, 2024).

hour"[22] is crucial. We prioritize helping individuals promptly and efficiently using this KPI. Reaction time is measured to determine response preparedness. It signifies lives saved, suffering reduced, and resilience reinforced.

Coverage is another KPI. It guarantees help to all affected areas. The center analyzes coverage to evaluate response efforts, detect gaps, and improve distant area access. The organization's effective resource allocation reflects its humanitarianism. In a scarce location, resource optimization is ethical and practical. This KPI evaluates resource allocation for maximum impact. A center uses every resource to make a difference (2017 in Exhibit 23.3) (2023 in Exhibit 23.4).

Continuous progress goes beyond numbers. KPIs show strengths and opportunities for improvement. Introspection can create agile, accurate, and anticipatory solid frameworks. Impact measurement is a conversation between experience and progress. In an unpredictable world where varied populations are affected by disasters, the International Health Commission's impact assessment and crisis management method provides accountability and efficacy. KPIs help the hub create living, breathing anticipatory frameworks that can adapt, evolve, and improve. In contrast to calamities, the IHC emphasizes that our responses are controllable.

23.3.4 *Framework and lessons learnt*

The three main components of the framework (Exhibit 23.4) for anticipatory health and humanitarian relief logistics described in the preceding section are being prepared, responding quickly, and being able to bounce back: the 3 Rs: Readiness, Rapid Responses, and Resilience & Recovery. The methodology for anticipatory frameworks is modeled around the International Health Commission's strategy for health logistics and catastrophe preparedness. Key performance indicators (KPIs), capacity-building, collaborations, innovative data analytics, and engaging vulnerable groups are all highlighted.

---

[22] Forrester, J.D., August, A., Cai, L.Z., Kushner, A.L., & Wren, S.M. (2019). The golden hour after injury among civilians caught in conflict zones. *Disaster Medicine and Public Health Preparedness*, 13(5–6): 1074–1082. https://www.cambridge.org/core/journals/disaster-medicine-and-public-health-preparedness/article/abs/golden-hour-after-injury-among-civilians-caught-in-conflict-zones/FB3497687F5C020D368D7CBD37B5D746.

Exhibit 23.3. Summary of the reach in the year 2017 and 2023 by product cluster, countries reached, and aid spending.

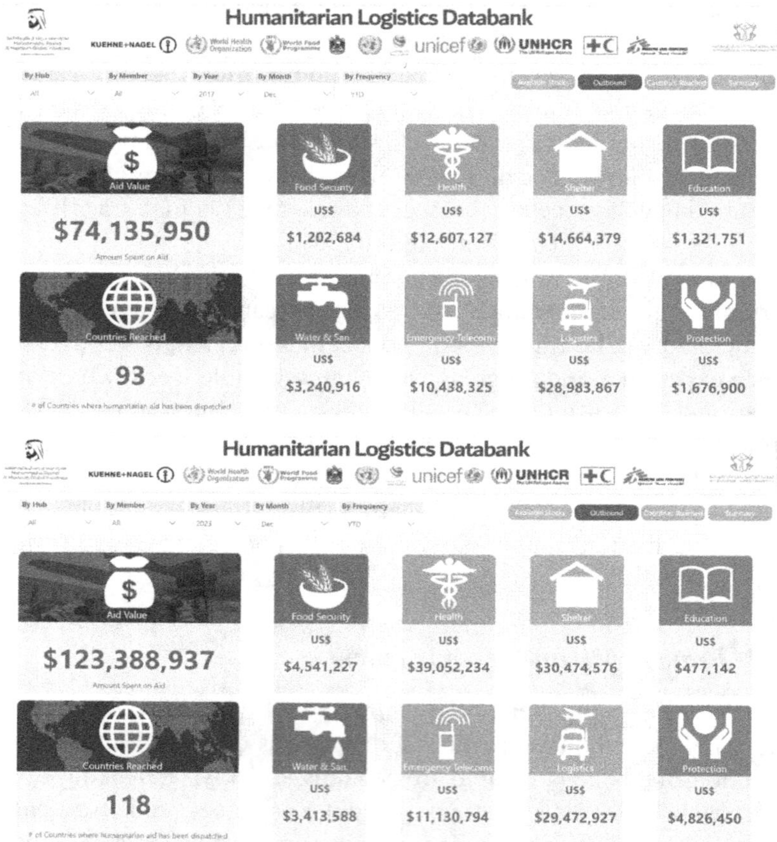

Source: IHC (2023).[23]

The Readiness stage included the following: 1. Coordination of Emergency Task Forces; 2. Advanced Data Analytics; 3. Increase Forecasting for Humanitarian Resources; and 4. Increase Preparedness for Humanitarian Services.[23] The Rapid Responses stage included the

[23] International Humanitarian City (2023). Available Stocks — Humanitarian Logistic Databank. Available: https://www.ihc.ae/databank/# (Accessed 14 March, 2024).

Exhibit 23.4. A framework for humanitarian logistics and health response.

Readiness

1. Coordination of Emergency Task Forces
2. Advanced Data Analytics
3. Increase Forecasting for Humanitarian Resources
4. Increase Preparedness for Humanitarian Services

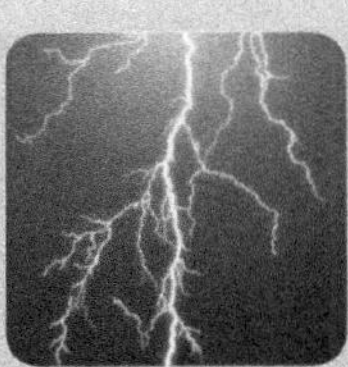

Rapid Responses

5. Collaborative Partnerships
6. Capacity Building & Training
7. Disaster Management Simulations
8. Humanitarian & Health Society Institutional Awareness
9. Knowledge Transfer

Resilience & Recovery

10. Reaching Vulnerable Populations
11. Health Resilience & Surveillance Impact Assessments
12. Resume Life & Document Lessons Learnt

Source: Adapted from AlQutob *et al.* (2020).[24,25]

following: 5. Collaborative Partnerships; 6. Capacity-Building and Training; 7. Disaster Management Simulations; 8. Humanitarian and Health Society Institutional Awareness; and 9. Knowledge Transfer. The Resilience & Recovery stage included the following: 10. Reaching Vulnerable Populations; 11. Health Resilience and Surveillance Impact Assessments; and 12. Resume Life and Document Lessons Learnt.[24,25]

---

[24]AlQutob, R., Moonesar, I.A., Tarawneh, M.R., Al Nsour, M., & Khader, Y. (2020). Public health strategies for the gradual lifting of the public sector lockdown in Jordan and the United Arab Emirates during the COVID-19 crisis. *JMIR Public Health and Surveillance*, 6(3): e20478. DOI: 10.2196/20478.

[25]AlQutob, R., Ajlouni, M.T., Abufaraj, M., & Moonesar, I.A. (2020). Jordan's public and surveillance health policies: During and after COVID-19. *Jordan Journal of Pharmaceutical Sciences*, 13(3): 1–12.

World Health Organization programs, the International Humanitarian City, Gavi (The Vaccine Alliance), Bangladesh Rural Advancement Committee, and the Global Fund to Fight AIDS, Tuberculosis, and Malaria are some of the global humanitarian use examples that exemplify the framework. In various settings, these case studies show how the framework can be implemented, highlighting the significance of data-driven risk assessment; partnerships with governments, NGOs, and businesses; training and simulations to build capacity and reach vulnerable populations; and key performance indicators to measure impact.

The framework aims to enhance the efficacy and efficiency of disaster response and humanitarian relief operations by encouraging cooperation and information sharing, moving the emphasis from reactive to anticipatory responses, and maximizing impact while minimizing redundancy. Disaster preparation, health logistics, and humanitarian relief organizations and agencies can benefit significantly from the framework since it provides an organized method to enhance readiness, response, and recovery operations in various crises and problems.

23.4 Concluding Remarks

Disasters may be terrible, but the IHC organization shows how anticipatory frameworks, collaboration, and attention to vulnerable groups can change disaster response. Its proactive efforts to ensure no one is left behind in a crisis inspire people worldwide, demonstrating the strength of a unified humanity. The various examples, such as the International Humanitarian City, Gavi, BRAC, and the Global Fund, show how logistical frameworks for anticipatory health and humanitarian relief operate. By adopting the 3Rs, stakeholders may improve crisis management via humanitarian logistics and health response.

https://doi.org/10.1142/9789811296000_0024

Chapter 24

Synthetic Biology Governance and Advocacy

Melodena Stephens* **and Abhishek Balakrishnan†**

**Mohammed Bin Rashid School of Government, Dubai, UAE*

†BCG BrightHouse, Atlanta, USA

Key Takeaways

- Synthetic biology is an advanced technological field that combines engineering with genetics.
- While a significant amount of research and dialogue is happening in this space, there need to be more safeguards to ensure that when we manipulate biological systems, we do not unleash unforeseen effects that we cannot reverse.
- This participative approach toward anticipatory governance needs knowledge translation and advocacy.
- Advocacy needs awareness campaigns, and policy reports are difficult to digest.
- In this example, we use generative AI to make a policy report more palatable to the general audience.

24.1 Advocacy

Advocacy can help translate science, but there are worries that it may misrepresent science.[1] Advocacy is a catch-all phrase and involves multiple activities like "*public education and influencing public opinion; research for interpreting problems and suggesting preferred solutions; constituent action and public mobilizations; agenda setting and policy design; lobbying; policy implementation, monitoring, and feedback; and election-related activity*."[2] Advocating for governance often falls to resilience scientists or champions of specific causes and policies.[3] For global advocacy, additional political and financial resources are required.[4] Graphic novels or comics can help bridge the gap between public education,[5] policymaker knowledge, and public relations.[6] In this example, we use Chat GPT and Adobe Firefly to help "*translate*" a policy paper into a comic strip.

---

[1]For example, see: Odendaal, A., Levänen, S., & Westerlund, H. (2019). Lost in translation? Neuroscientific research, advocacy, and the claimed transfer benefits of musical practice. *Music Education Research*, 21(1): 4–19.

[2]Reid, E.J. (2000). Understanding the word "advocacy": Context and use. *Structuring the Inquiry into Advocacy*, 1: 1.

[3]Milkoreit, M., Moore, M.L., Schoon, M., & Meek, C.L. (2015). Resilience scientists as change-makers — growing the middle ground between science and advocacy? *Environmental Science & Policy*, 53: 87–95.

[4]Hanegraaff, M., Vergauwen, J., & Beyers, J. (2020). Should I stay or should I go? Explaining variation in nonstate actor advocacy over time in global governance. *Governance*, 33(2): 287–304.

[5]Tatalovic, M. (2009). Science comics as tools for science education and communication: A brief, exploratory study. *Journal of Science Communication*, 8(04): A02.

[6]Horton, I. (2018). Comic Books, Science (Fiction) and Public Relations. Available: https://ualresearchonline.arts.ac.uk/id/eprint/14328/3/Comic%20books,%20science%20(fiction)%20and%20public%20relations.pdf (Accessed 14 February, 2024.)

24.2 Comics for Advocacy: Synthetic Biology Governance

SYNTHETIC BIOLOGY STORIES EVERYWHERE - CANT ESCAPE!!
ANDi, first GM primate. Will humans be next?
Editing humanity
TIME
It's Almost Here
HACKERS STOLE A MILLION PEOPLE'S DNA
mosquitoes
I AM GENETICALLY PROGRAMMED TO DIE AND NOT HAVE KIDS
I GLOW IN THE DARK - I HAVE JELLYFISH DNA
MEANWHILE
A Core Team Of Researchers Across Countries And Disciplines
THE SYNBIO COUNCIL
Were Comparing Notes......
BUT MAJORITY OF THE PUBLIC & POLICY MAKERS WERE UNAWARE OF THIS NEW CHALLENGE - THANKS TO THE VEILED MIST!

SYNBIO WAS EVERYWHERE - FOOD WE ATE, THE MEDICINE WE TOOK,CLOTHES WE WASHED, IN AGRICULTURE, CONSTRUCTION, MINING.....
BY 2030, IT COULD BE 4-30 TRILLION INDUSTRY...
AS MUCH AS 1/3 GLOBAL OUTPUT

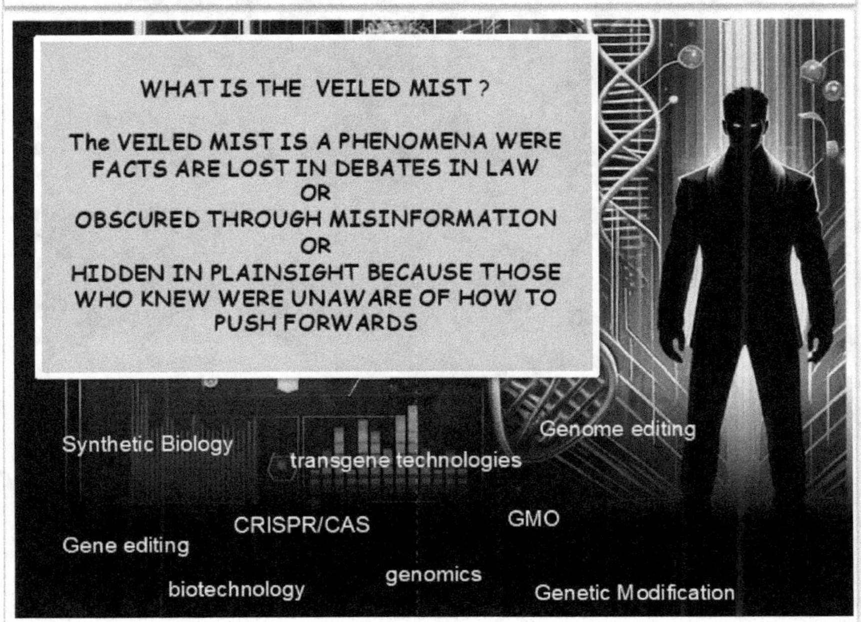
WHAT IS THE VEILED MIST ?
The VEILED MIST IS A PHENOMENA WERE FACTS ARE LOST IN DEBATES IN LAW OR OBSCURED THROUGH MISINFORMATION OR HIDDEN IN PLAINSIGHT BECAUSE THOSE WHO KNEW WERE UNAWARE OF HOW TO PUSH FORWARDS
Synthetic Biology
transgene technologies
Genome editing
CRISPR/CAS
GMO
Gene editing
genomics
biotechnology
Genetic Modification

THE VEILED MIST WAS GETTING STRONGER
POOR AWARENESS
REGULATORY GAPS
MISINFORMATION OR UNDERINFORMED
POLITICS & SYNBIO RACE
TECHNOLOGICAL ADVANCEMENTS
GREATER GOOD VS RISKS
PRIVATE SECTOR AGENDA
WHAT IS SYNTHETIC BIOLOGY or SYNBIO?
SYNETHIC BIO (SYNBIO) IS THE CREATION or REDESIGN OF BIOLOGICAL MOLECULES
WITH TECHNOLOGIES LIKE CRISPR AND AI, WE CAN BORROW FROM NATURE TO CREATE ARTIFICIAL BIOLOGICAL MATERIAL...
...OR MANIPULATE NATURAL BIOLOGICAL MATERIAL OR MIMIC NATURAL LIFE FUNCTIONS OR BEHAVIORS
THINK OF INSULIN, mRNA, GMO FOODS... ..

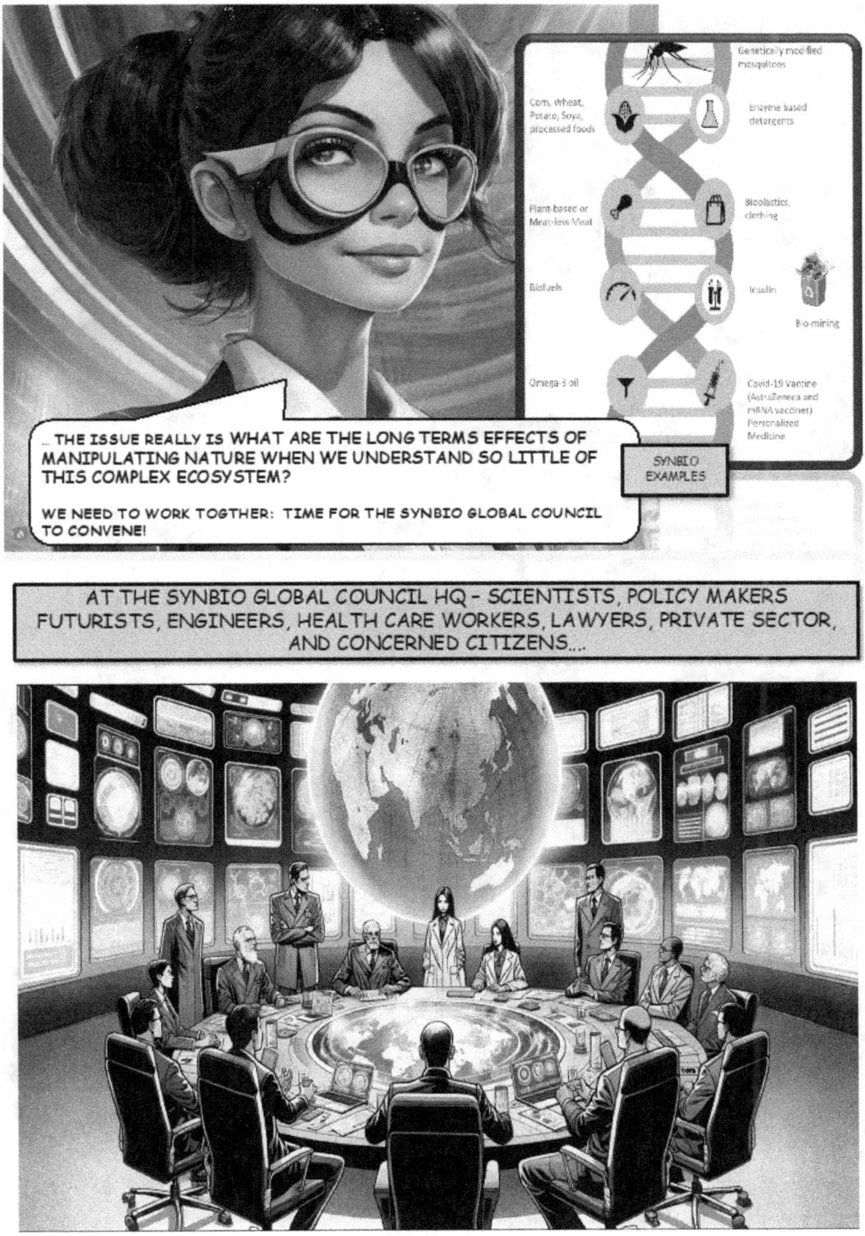
Genetically modified mosquitoes
Corn, Wheat, Potato, Soya, processed foods
Enzyme based detergents
Plant-based or Meat-less Meal
Bioplastics, clothing
Biofuels
Insulin
Bio-mining
Omega-3 oil
Covid-19 Vaccine (AstraZeneca and mRNA vaccines) Personalized Medicine
SYNBIO EXAMPLES
... THE ISSUE REALLY IS WHAT ARE THE LONG TERMS EFFECTS OF MANIPULATING NATURE WHEN WE UNDERSTAND SO LITTLE OF THIS COMPLEX ECOSYSTEM?
WE NEED TO WORK TOGTHER: TIME FOR THE SYNBIO GLOBAL COUNCIL TO CONVENE!
AT THE SYNBIO GLOBAL COUNCIL HQ - SCIENTISTS, POLICY MAKERS FUTURISTS, ENGINEERS, HEALTH CARE WORKERS, LAWYERS, PRIVATE SECTOR, AND CONCERNED CITIZENS....

AGENDA
DEFEATING THE VEILED MIST AT MULTIPLE LEVELS
RECOMMENDATION 1
INTERNATIONAL COLLABORATION AND COOPERATION
A. INTERNATIONAL THINK TANK
B. RISK CATEGORIZATIONS
C. LABORATORY / INSTITUTIONS LEVEL CODE OF CONDUCT

RECOMMENDATION 2
NOTHING DISIPATES THE VEILED MIST LIKE **EDUCATION & AWARENESS**
RECOMMENDATION 3
AGILE GOVERANCE: CREATING A REGISTER OF WHAT WORKS AND WHAT DOES NOT SO WE CAN LEARN FROM EACH OTHER...........

...........AND REGULATION SANDBOXES TO TEST NEW PRODUCTS, EXISTING REGULATIONS OR DEVELOP NEW ONES REGULATIONS FOR THE BENEFIT OF HUMANITY AND PLANET
SYNBIO GLOBAL COUNCIL DEFEATS THE VEILED MIST
....THE WORLD IS A GOOD PLACE TO LIVE IN
THE END

24.3 Science Advocacy Recommendations

Policy gaps exist with regard to access to knowledge (for evidence-based policy) and its palpability (relevance or interpretation), which may need research brokers.[7] These brokers or boundary spanners must bypass gatekeepers and coordinate with liaisons across boundaries (organization, national, and international levels).[8,9] Advocacy helps bridge the silos that exist between the two worlds where evidence needs legitimacy or needs to be brought to the forefront of the public agenda.[10] The following actions can be implemented for advocacy:

1. Identify the common values around which research should be built. Encourage reflection and discourse on these topics. Values are not

---

[7]Neal, J.W., Neal, Z.P., Kornbluh, M., Mills, K.J., & Lawlor, J.A. (2015). Brokering the research–practice gap: A typology. *American Journal of Community Psychology,* 56: 422–435.

[8]For example, see: Hopkins, M., Wiley, K.E., Penuel, W.R., & Farrell, C.C. (2018). Brokering research in science education policy implementation: The case of a professional association. *Evidence & Policy*, 14(03): 459–476.

[9]Williams, P. (2013). We are all boundary spanners now? International Journal of Public Sector Management, 26 (1): 17–32.

[10]Choi, B.C.K. (2005). Can scientists and policy makers work together? *Journal of Epidemiology & Community Health*, 59(8): 632–637; Bogenschneider, K. & Corbett, T. (2024). How to approach policymakers: The critical choice of advocacy or education. In *Family Policy Matters*. Routledge: pp. 331–359.

universal, nor can they be linearly translated across society and institutions.[11]

2. Support research and systems thinking.[12] Science advocacy needs multiple perspectives with a common purpose to do good with as much safety as designed in the process. The policy sphere is full of examples where hindsight is too late and the interventions of science (where the purpose was to do good) did harm.
3. Create spaces for discussions, co-creation, and translation.[13] While the scientific peer review process has its flaws, new technologies will also challenge many of our assumptions of what is good, working, or flawed. We will be confronted with dual-purpose research that needs dialogue and active considerations of guardrails (not only for the greater good).
4. Promote knowledge sharing in multiple formats, using scientific journal papers, social media, videos, talks, and cartoons — whatever works and gets attention. Most importantly, involve the public and experts.
5. Reiterate what works, what does not, and what can be a positive spillover to increase the tolerance to experimentation.[14]

---

[11] See recommendations by Lackey, R.T. (2007). Science, scientists, and policy advocacy. *Conservation Biology*, 21(1): 12–17.

[12] For example see: Duncan, R., Robson-Williams, M., & Edwards, S. (2020). A close examination of the role and needed expertise of brokers in bridging and building science policy boundaries in environmental decision making. *Palgrave Communications*, 6(1): 1–12.

[13] For example see: Garrard, G.E., Fidler, F., Wintle, B.C., Chee, Y.E., & Bekessy, S.A. (2016). Beyond advocacy: Making space for conservation scientists in public debate. *Conservation Letters*, 9(3): 208–212; Klerkx, L. & Leeuwis, C. (2009). Establishment and embedding of innovation brokers at different innovation system levels: Insights from the Dutch agricultural sector. *Technological Forecasting and Social Change*, 76(6): 849–860; Weerts, D.J. & Sandmann, L.R. (2010). Community engagement and boundary-spanning roles at research universities. *The Journal of Higher Education*, 81(6): 632–657.

[14] Gibbons, M. (1999). Science's new social contract with society. *Nature*, 402(6761): C81.

https://doi.org/10.1142/9789811296000_bmatter

Index

A
Aadhaar, 309
Absent Quarantine Pests (AQPs), 15, 323, 325
accountability, 6, 138, 199
adaptive capabilities, 86
adaptive governance, 237
adaptive solutions, 105
adaptive systems, 237
adjacent possible, 19, 30, 75
Adobe Firefly, 362
advanced economies, 272
advanced technology, 189
advisory groups, 19
advocacy, 9, 15, 140, 260, 361
agency, 44, 84, 120
agendas, 288
agenda setting, 362
agent, 8
aggregate indices, 315
agile governance, 3, 16
agile government, xi, 3, 16
agility, v, 45, 103
agricultural defense agencies, 325
AI governance frameworks, 253
AI models, 249
Airbus, 300
AI Safety Summit, 254
AI systems, 216
alert system, 10
Algeria, 167
algorithmic decision-making, 241
algorithms, 93, 199
alignment, 120, 237
alternative futures, 70, 273
ambiguity, 104
analysis, 175
analytic hierarchy process (AHP), 324
anchor policies, 69, 273
Anthropic, 26
anticipating problems, 58
anticipatory, 103
anticipatory analysis, v
anticipatory capacities, 338
anticipatory governance, 3
anticipatory government, 16
anticipatory insight, 86
anticipatory landscape, 63
anticipatory leadership, 113
anticipatory mindsets, 110
anticipatory policies, 70
antifragile, 103
anxiety, 84
Arab, 9, 167
Arab League, 179

Arab nationalism, 171
Armenia, 336
Artemis Accords, 302
artificial intelligence (AI), xi, 12, 51, 77
Asian Development Bank, 15, 333
Asia-Pacific, 340
assessment, 279
assumptions, 64, 69, 271, 281
asteroid mining, 297
auditing, 199, 253
audits, 199
augment, 187
Australia, 36, 71
authors, 255
automated, 243
autonomous vehicles, 197
avatars, 39

B

backcasting, 69, 271
backup plans, 284
Bahrain, 181
balance, 338
balancing act, 334
Balfour Declaration, 166
Baltexit, 144
Baltic states, 143
bankruptcy, 152
baseline, 80, 281, 319
beliefs, 135
benchmarks, 319
BeReal, 24
Berne Convention, 256
bias, 86, 199
big data, 241
bilateral, 181
bilateral meetings, 178
biodiversity, 9–10, 15
biotechnologies, 51
black box, 28
Black Elephants, 115
Black Jellyfish, 114
Black Swans, 115
blind spots, 15, 84, 340
blockchain, 204
blue-sky thinking, 80
board governance, 213
Boeing, 300
borders, 52, 260
bottlenecks, 350
boundary, 77
boundary conditions, 73
boundary setting, 69, 80, 275
boundary spanners, 289
boundary spanning skills, 14, 140
BRAC, 345
brain, 261
brainstorming, 77, 284
Brazil, 323, 330
breakdown, 306
broker, 184
budget deficits, 167
budget planning, 66
building bridges, 177
bureaucratic, 63
business ecosystem, v
business or commercial diplomacy, 185
Butterfly Effect, 115
buy-in, 277

C

Cambodia, 81, 336, 340
Canada, 71, 259
capacity, 110, 238
capacity-building, 15, 353
carbon footprint, 47
caretakers, 83
Caribbean, 346
cascading, 131
catastrophe, 64
catastrophe response, 348, 355
causal layered analysis, 78, 337

causal mapping, 94
Central America, 346
CEPA, 185
certainty, 107
challenge, 64
challenge assumptions, ix, xi, 16, 288
Challenger Space Shuttle, 60
challenge their assumptions, 11
change agents, 278
chaotic, 80
charting a responsible future, 9
ChatGPT, 26, 204, 217, 362
child, 9
children, 14, 53, 264
China, 26, 44, 47–48, 303, 336
choice, 105
Cisco, 178
cities, 194
citizen journalism, 4
citizens, 339
citizenship, 53, 148, 166
civil servants, 304
civil unrest, 167, 169
clarity, 134
climate bank, 340
climate change, xi, 42, 204
cloud computing, 221, 225, 233
cloud platforms, 225
co-creation, 140, 372
cognitive, 104
cognitive agility, 119
cognitive biases, 268
coherence, 134
collaboration, 52, 94
collaborative partnership, 353
collective behaviors, 117
collective defense, 172
collective effort, 63
collective experiences, 20
collective good, 172
collective intelligence, xi, 8, 141
collectivism, 165
collectivist governance mechanism, 171
colonialism, 149, 166
colonial treaties, 174
Columbia, 97
co-managing, 140
command and control, 64
common good, 121
common purpose, 372
communication networks, 61
communications, 138
communitarian thinking, 130
communities, ix
competition, 6
complementary objectives, 76
complex, 80, 107
complex decision-making, 288
complexity, 50, 104, 106–107
complexity of the past, 7
complex phenomena, 94
complex systems, 67
compliance, 34
compound parameters, 106
confidentiality, 206
conflict, 86, 346
conflict of interest, 309
Congressional Research Service (CRS), 59
consensus, 9, 16
constitution, 161
context, 71
contingency, 45
contingency plans, 44
continuous improvement, 44
continuous monitoring, 198
control, 94
cooperation, 52
copyright, 247
corridors of connections, 165
cost–benefit, 312
coup, 170
courage, 36

creatively, 271
creativity, 29
credibility, 139
crises, 9, 21, 77
crisis management, xii, 351
criteria, 332
critical infrastructure, 212
Critical Systems Heuristics (CSH), 86
critical thinking, 112
cross-sector collaboration, 342
crowdsourcing, 140
cultural diplomacy, 186
cultural identity, 143
culture, 44
curiosity, 36, 65
currency devaluation, 167
current protocols, 61
cutting-edge, 212
cybercrime, 208
cyber defense, 212
cyber ecosystem, 13
cyber incidents, 211
cyber inequity, 211
cyber insecurity, 204
cyber-resilient, 203
cybersecurity, 113, 203
cyberspace, 206
cyber threats, 204

D

data, 21, 197
data acquisition, 249
data analytics, 46
data center, 5, 313
data collection, 252
data colonialism, 247
datafication, 237
data flows, 221, 247
data free flow with trust, 254
data owners, 249
data points, 78, 285
datasets, 221, 247
debate, 95
decentralized, 244
decision-makers, 34
decision-making, 22, 105
de-escalate risks, 14
de jure existence, 144
delay, 64
democracy, 157
democratic governance, 251
democratic principles, 157
Department of Homeland Security, 51
deregulate, 33
design, 65
design thinking, v
detect, 211
dialectical, 95
dialogue, 8, 361
dialogue space, 76
diffusion models, 257
diffusion of technology, 139
digital age, 205
digital copies, 256
digital economy, 213
digital feedback, 98
digital infrastructure, 47, 210
digital innovation, 46
digitalization, 16
digital natives, 35
digital networks, 206
digital security, 205
digital transformation (DT), 204, 235, 238
digital twins, 14
dignity, 355
dilemma, 64
diplomacy, 9, 165, 184
diplomatic mission, 182
diplomatic policy, 48
diplomats, 177, 187
disaggregation, 6

disaster, 345
disaster management, 64
discriminatory, 199
disinformation, 9, 139
displacement, 346
disruption, vi, 21, 51, 303
disruptive, 9
disruptive technologies, 51
diversity, 199
diversity of experiences, 3
diversity of thought, 73
diwan, 173
diwaniya, 173
DNA of the organization, 65
documentation, 199
documenter, 338
domain knowledge, 17, 200
double governance, 162
DRC, 346
dreamers, 53
drivers, 339
drones, 195
dual-purpose research, 372
Dubai, 9
dynamic capabilities, 44
dynamic environments, 93
dynamic problems, 17
dynamics of change, 267

E

early adopters, 196
early childhood research, 262
early warning signals, 8, 14, 69
early warning systems, 165
Earth Orbit, 301
Eastern Europe, 146
echo chambers, 341
economic dependency, 150
economic diplomacy, 185
economic growth, 47
economic instability, 204
economic recessions, 43
education, xi, 46–47
education diplomacy, 185
education disruption, 270
efficiency, 84
efficient analysis, 197
e-governance, 47
e-government services, 240
Egypt, 166
emergency, 52, 119, 330
emergency response, 347
Emergency Task Forces, 349
emergent agility, 118
emerging economies, 272
Emirates Airlines, 355
employability, 4
employment, 244, 272
empowerment, 355
empower people, 138
encryption, 216
endogenous, 77
energy, 44
energy grid, 207
enforceability, 257
engagement, 24
enlightenment, 146
environmental crises, 42
environmental sustainability, 47
errors, 175
Estonia, 34, 47, 143
ethical frameworks, 200
ethics, xi, 193
Europe, 4
European Union (EU), 3, 162
evaluation, 319
events, 288
evidence, 285
evidence-based policy, 371
existential, 105
existential risk, 112, 119
exogenous, 77
experience, 186
experiment, 196

experimentation, 104, 372
experts, 87
explainability, 199
explainable AI (XAI), 199
exponential, 104, 193
exponential change, xi, 6, 9
exponential growth, 19
exponential information, 35
exponential risks, 195
exponential technological change, 22
exponential times, 72

F

Facebook, 25–26
facial recognition, 198
facilitators, 271
failure, 14, 320
failure of agility, 63
fairness, 199
fair use, 255
family, 143
famines, 306
FDI, 179
feasibility, 73, 279
feasible options, 10
federation, 171
feedback loops, 92, 200
financial crises, 54
financial diplomacy, 185
financial support, 66
financial sustainability, 46
Finland, 34, 46
fit for purpose, vi, 237
flexibility, 80
focal issue, 89
Folk songs, 147–148
food, 44
food crisis, 208
foreign currencies, 150
foresight, v, ix, 3
foresight planning, 40
forward-looking, 43
forward-thinking, 40, 134
forward-thinking policy, 348
Fourth Industrial Revolution, 36
fragmentation, 137, 333
frameworks, 34, 305
framing problems, 221
France, 71, 144, 254
freedom of information, 309
French Revolution, 146
frontier knowledge, 75, 278
frontier leadership, 135
future, 6
future challenges, 67
future children, 261
future generations, 46, 261
future governments, vi
future horizon, 69
future impact, 71
future of work, 14
future opportunities, ix
future-proof, 15, 34, 340
future reality, 267
future shaping, xi
future shocks, 224
futures intelligence, 113
future skills, 140, 270
futures thinking, 15, 108, 336
future trajectories, 69
future visions, 70
futurist, 266

G

G7, 253
gamified education, 263
gaming, 263
gaps in knowledge, 65
gatekeepers, 371
Gavi, 345
GDPR, 250
GenAI, 26
generational effect, 32
generative AI, 4, 16, 215, 225, 247

generative artificial intelligence, 204
genetics, 269
geo-intelligence, 297
geo-political, v, 4, 44
geopolitical instability, 35
Germany, 71, 98
Gigamapping, 96
global AI governance, 252
global citizenship, 4
global context, 12
global corridors, 187
global fund, 345
globalization, 4
global policies, 210
global priorities, 337
global public good, 201
global risks, 122
global rules-based order, vi
global South, vi
good governance, 34
Google, 5
governance, vii, 236
governance architecture, ix, 205
governance mindsets, 57
governments, v, 22
government shaping, 83
GPS, 294
grassroots initiatives, 134
Gray Rhino, 114
Greater Arab Free Trade Area (GAFTA), 180
Great Leap Forward, 306
green technologies, 47
group-level decision-making, 265
guardrails, 14, 121, 271
Gulf Cooperation Council (GCC), 181

H

Hanseatic League, 146
hard stops, 284
hard systems, 91
healthcare, xi, 44, 47
healthcare emergencies, 44
healthcare system, 44, 346
health crises, 44
health logistics, 345
healthy societies, 51
Helsinki Accords, 152
hesitancy, 341
hidden agenda, 150
hierarchical rules, 172
high-tech sectors, ix
hindsight, 107, 372
Hiroshima AI Process Comprehensive Policy Framework, 253
history, 66
hubris, 69
human brain, 262
human capital, xi, 337
human-centered, 81
human-created works, 257
human expertise, 200
human ingenuity, 206
humanitarian, 169, 345
humanitarian crises, 346
humanitarian diplomacy, 186
humanity, v, 267
human oversight, 199
human rights, 157
Hurricane Katrina, 60

I

IBM, 223
Iceland, 162
ICTs, 240
identity, 56, 147, 276
ignorance, 116
imagination, 3, 36, 69, 274
IMF, 4, 6
immigrant, 52, 154
immigration, 52
impact, 69, 274, 356
impact measurement, 14, 305

imperialism, 149
implications, 65
implicit, 136
implicit information, 278
implicit knowledge, 139
impossible, 154
incentivization, 6
inclusive policies, 86
incremental, 192
incremental changes, 174
incremental thinking, 54
independence, 144, 155
India, 185, 309
indigenous, 146
Indonesia, 336
industrial policy, 301
industrial revolution, 192
inequity, 203
inert, 63
inflection point, vi
influence, 24
information, 19, 175
informational abundance, 32
informed decision-making, 41
infrastructure, 47, 346
infringement, 248, 250
innovation, 21, 200, 297
innovation management, 140
insecurity, 21
insights, 67
in silico regulations, 12, 191
inspiration, 134
instability, 108
institutional habits, 49
institutional knowledge, 35, 139
institutional memory, 64
integration, 134
Intel, 20, 178
intellectual capacity, 67
intellectual laziness, 50
intelligence, 124, 176, 266
intelligence management, xii
interactive planning, 99
interconnectedness, 17
interdependencies, 111
interdisciplinary integration, 56
intergenerational, 71, 138
intergenerational impact, 3
intergenerational inclusive benefit, v
intergenerational public, xi
intergenerational public value, 4
international business, 20
international collaboration, 258
international governments, 260
international humanitarian, 15
International Humanitarian City (IHC), 9, 345
international landscape, 21
international law, 144, 161
International Space Station, 296
internet, 21, 112
Internet of Things, 46
interrelationships, 97
intersecting, 104
intervention, 134
intuition, 74, 175
investigations, 63
involvement, 134
Iran, 169
Iraq, 167–168, 182
Ireland, 250
irreversible decisions, 112
Israel, 166
Israel–Hamas war, 44
iteration, 286
iterative, 58

J

Japan, 44, 71, 253
job, 5, 244, 272
Jordan, 166
jurisdiction, 255
justice system, 151

K
Kazakhstan, 336
Kingdom of Saudi, 181
kinship politics, 174
knowledge-based economy, 46
knowledge needs of policymakers, 56
knowledge sharing, 372
knowledge transfer, 354
knowledge translation, 361
Known Knowns, 114
Known Unknowns, 115
KPIs, 319
K-pop, 48
Kuwait, 181

L
lack of leadership, 64
large language models (LLM), vi, 263
Latvia, 143
launching, 131
law enforcement, 52
leadership, vi
leading from the back, 139
League of Nations, 166
LEAPFROG, 283
Lebanon, 166
legacy, 166
legislation, 53, 263
legitimacy, 50, 139
liaisons, 371
Libya, 167
life event, 32
likteņupe, 153
linear, 81
linear process, 94
LinkedIn, 24
listen, 3, 187
litany, 79, 281
litany of mistakes, 63
Lithuania, 143
lobby, 187
lobbying, 187, 362
Lockheed Martin, 300
logically, 271
logistics, 347
longer-term strategy, 104
longevity, 270
longitudinal research, 261
long-term impact, 59
long-term planning, 47
long-term thinking, 288
low-hanging fruits, 239
low-income countries, 272
lure diplomacy, 12, 143, 158

M
Maghreb, 171
majlis, 173
malicious, 260
Malta, 186
malware, 215, 252
management, 44, 138
managing change, xi
man-made, 57
man-made disasters, 61
marginalized communities, 199
Mars, 294
Mashreq, 171
MECE thinking, 23
MENA, 165
messy problems, 94
meta, 23, 25, 250
meta-governance, 77
meta-leaders, 19, 36
metaphor, 70, 80, 281
metaverse, 204
metrics, 286
Microsoft, 5, 132
Middle East, 4, 166
migration, 51, 346
military, 53
military conflicts, 44
military–industrial complex, 301

military satellites, 297
military strategist, 184
millennials, 32
miniaturization, 293
Ministry of Possibilities, 35
misinformation, 4, 139
mission, 125
mission-critical, 66
mission drift, 286
mission-oriented innovation, 75
misuse, 200
mitigation, 42
mitigation strategies, 200, 313
Mongolia, 336
monitoring, 319
Moon, 302
moral, 95
Morocco, 181
multidisciplinary expertise, 49
multigenerational, xi
multi-governance, 237
multilateral, 15, 141
Multilateral Development Banks (MDBs), 342
multilateralism, ix, 9, 301
multilayered, 165
multiple futures, 23
multiple perspectives, 86–87
multi-sectoral response, 353
multistakeholder, 216
Myanmar, 26

N

nanotechnology, 334
narratives, 8, 117
NASA, 295
national awakening, 147
national awareness, 143, 145
national competitiveness, 77
national consciousness, 143
national data policies, 252
national security, 213
national strategy, 121
nation-building, 9, 143
NATO, 162
natural disasters, 42, 346
natural environment, 270
navigable pathway, 86, 88
navigate complexity, 48
negotiator, 184
network diagram, 94
network effects, 31
networks, 140
network theory, 27
neural plasticity, 261
New Public Management, 235
NewSpace, 14, 293
New York Times, 248
New Zealand, 97
next-order implications, 103
NGOs, 154
nightmare scenario, 64
non-human, 260
non-human actors, 14
non-human elements, 88
nonprofit, 238
non-violence, 143
norms, 76
Northern Arabs, 170
Northrop Grumman, 300
Norway, 46
nuclear, 117
nudge, 194

O

OECD, 22, 233
OldSpace, 14, 293
Oman, 181
OpenAI, 26, 248
open-source, 198
operational intelligence, 209
opportunities, 187
organizational agility, 49
organizational biases, 49

organizational culture, 85
organizational purpose, 124
organizational readiness, 61
outcomes, 197
outer space, 302
outlier, 176
outsourcing, 4
oversight, 199
Overton Window, 263

P

Palestine, 166, 352
pandemic, vii, 3, 57
panic-driven decisions, 59
participation, 200
participatory process, 75, 278
past precedent, 19
paths of navigation, 99
pathway, 85
pattern library, 28
pattern mapping, 10
patterns, 19, 73, 84
peace, 4
peace diplomacy, 186
peaceful protest, 155
Pension Fund, 46
people diplomacy, 185
people-focused, 140
perception, 74, 265, 281
perestroika, 153
perfect storm, 21
Permacrisis, 108
permission, 256
personal futures, 82
personalized education, 14
personalized regulation, 198
personhood, 97
perspectives, 65, 88
PESTLE, 77
phenomena, 117
Philippines, 297
phishing, 215
phytosanitary, 326
planning, 94
plant health policy, 15, 323
platform, 24
plausibility, 70, 72, 279, 314
plausible, 271
Polanyi's Paradox, 30
polarization, 137
policies, 41
policy adaptation, 285
policy analysis, 15, 56
policy debates, 54
policy decisions, 41
policy design, 59
policy development, 59
policy domain, 77
policy entrepreneurship skills, 140
policy exhaustion, 66
policy focus, 57
policy futures, 75
policy gaps, 371
policy incoherence, 9
policy instrument, 83
policy lapses, 198
policymaker, v
policymaking, 23
policy panic, 54
policy problems, 50, 56, 241
policy research, 50
policy spillovers, 74
policy standoffs, 53
political connections, 280
political financing, 309
political orders, 51
political power, 150
political rifts, 57
political tensions, 169
political will, 11, 174
poly-crisis, vii
polycrisis, 123
poor coordination, 64
possibilities, 72, 276

post-colonization, 9
potential consequences, 103
potential outcomes, 111
poverty, 54
power imbalances, 194
power of networks, 35
power outage, 212
power structures, 95, 135, 159
power struggles, 146
predictability, 106
prediction, 117
predictive analytics, 243
predictive power, 198
preferred future, 69, 70, 103, 284
preparation, 63, 117
preparedness, 49
pre-positioning, 351
present horizon, 69
principles, 134
prioritization, 332
prioritized, 284
privacy, 198
private sector, 3
privatization, 4
proactive, 40
proactive decision-making, 235
probability, 65, 72, 314
problem-solving, 118, 271
process, 176
prototypes, 78, 192, 281
public administration, 236
public affairs, 51
public budgets, 293
public challenges, 57
public engagement, 200
public failures, 57, 59
public good, 6, 51, 123
public governance, 236
public leadership, 135
public management theories, 16
public mandate, 130
public mobilizations, 362
public opinion, 139, 362
public perceptions, 75
public policy, 40
public-private partnerships, 140, 345
public problems, 57
public procurement, 309
public purpose, 121
public relations, 362
public revelations, 66
public sector, v–vi, 130
public servants, 156
public service, 47, 67
public value, xii, 4, 69, 138, 260
public workforce, 232
purpose, 3, 74, 273
push-and-pull, 69, 273

Q

Qatar, 181
quality control, 326
quality of life, 47
quantum computing, 212, 221
quantum networks, 233
quantum readiness, 218
quantum risk, 218
quantum-secure, 218
quarantine pests, 325

R

RAND, 117
R&D, 280, 297
react, 177
readiness, 15
reality check, 73
real time, 175
real-time monitoring, 313
reason why, 132
recalibrate, 51
recycled ideas, 54
referendum, 161
reform management, 15
reforms, 10, 46, 333, 336

refugee, 52
refugee migration, xi
refugees, 166, 352
regional conflicts, 35
regional security, 168
regulation, 249
regulator, 259
regulatory oversight, 191
regulatory principles, 286
regulatory sandboxes, 191
reimagine the future, 17
reimaging, 50
reinvent the wheel, 342
relevance, 371
reliable, 175
religious diplomacy, 186
remedial policies, 50
Republic of Korea, 254
reputation enhancement, xii
research funding, 44
resilience, vi, 8, 15, 47
resources, 66
resource sharing, 172
response times, 15
responsible development, 200
responsible future, v, 9
responsible usage, 26
responsiveness, 237
retirement, 46
reversible, 112
rights, 51
Ripple Effects, 115
risk assessment, 200
risk mitigation, 306
risks, vi, 44
road map, 73
roadmap, 47
Role of Family, 270
root causes, 49
root factors, 57
rule of law, 51
rules, 137
Rumsfeld Matrix, 28
Russia, 112
Russia–Ukraine war, 44

S

safeguards, 200
sandboxing, 9
satellite, 295
scarcity of attention, 32
scenario analysis, 14
scenarios, 39
science advocacy, 372
science and technology diplomacy, 185
scientific rigor, 30
scope, 200
scoping, 69, 274, 276
screen time, 262
securing borders, 52
security, 198
security and privacy risks, 270
security by design, 13, 222
security ecosystem, 203
security-first mindset, 222
seismic shift, xi
self-regulation, 26, 191
self-reliance, 139
sensemaking, xii, 8, 80
sensors, 251
serendipity, 163
service delivery, 47
shape regulation, 201
shaping a responsible future, vi
shaping the future, ix
shared collective, 84
shared prosperity, ix
shared responsibility, 353
sharing of learnings, 285
Shell Company, 314
shield, 211
shift, 21, 72
shifting frames, 69

shocks, 49, 111, 224
short-term success, 59
shuttle diplomacy, 177
signal, 8, 28, 50
silos, 344
simulation, 99, 200
Singapore, 34, 46
Singing Revolution, 155
Sitra, 34
Six Pillars method, 78
skills, v
skills development, 266
SMACIT, 240
Smart Nation, 46
social capital, 237
Social, Ethical, and Moral Guidelines, 270
social media, 4, 23
societal challenges, 57
societal problem, 81
society, 193
socio-political, 77, 174
soft power, 186
soft systems, 91
soft systems methodology, 86
software, 193
solidarity, 159
South Africa, 178
Southeast Asian, 48
Southern Arabs, 170
South Korea, 36, 47, 263
South Sudan, 346
Soviet Union, 143
space, 51, 293
space budgets, 300
space economy, 298
space strategy, 14
space technology, 297
space tourism, 297
Space Treaties, 301
SpaceX, 296
spillover, 73, 191
sports diplomacy, 186
stability, 98
stability AI, 248
stakeholder, 80, 244, 320
stamina, 138
Starlink, 296
state responsibility, 157
status, 341
stockpiling, 44
strategic advisory groups, 35
strategic agility, 118
strategic alliances, 348
strategic change, 20
strategic consequences, vi
strategic foresight, 22, 27, 205
strategic inflection, 19
strategic inflection points, 20
strategic intelligence, 209
strategic location, 352
strategic options development and analysis (SODA), 94
strategic planning, 14, 108
strategic resilience, 112
strategic scenarios, 70
strategy, 125, 271
stress test, 248
subjectivity, 92
subtle diplomacy, 177
sum of its parts, 87
supply chain, 116, 204
surveillance, 242
sustainable development, 47
sustainable development goals (SDGs), 88, 317
sustainable economy, ix
sustainable environment, 47
sustainable prosperity, 43
Sweden, 71
SWFs, 185
Sykes–Picot, 166
synergy, 219
synthesis, 87

synthetic biology, 15, 361
synthetic biology governance, 361
synthetic data, 198
Syria, 166–167, 352
systemic, 4, 281
systemic change, 105
systemic collaboration, 211
systemic perspective, 79
systemic process, 8
system of systems, xi, 8, 99
systems, 63
systems analysis, 92
systems dynamics (SD), 86, 92
systems engineering, 92
systems thinking skills, 288
systems thinking (ST), 84–85

T

tacit, 64
talent, ix, 223
tangible, 134
tangible value, 96
teacher, 54
technological change, vi
technological disruptions, 43, 204
technological skills, 66
technology as a tool, 3
technology turns, 191
tectonic shift, 261
telecommunication, 297
tensions, 52
terrorist, 66, 243
Thalès, 300
The Futures Triangle, 78
the Philippines, 336
thinking out of the box, 71
Threat actors, 206
time horizons, 104
timeliness, 51
time-sensitive, 15
Timor-Leste, 336
tipping point, 32, 174
tolerance, 84
too-big-to-fail, 16
top-down ownership, 11
total shareholder return (TSR), 127
toxic optimism, 341
trade, ix
trade-offs, 4, 76, 274, 276
trade wars, 44
traditional leadership, 137
training, 247
trajectory, 273, 284
transformational change, 19
transformational skills, 140
transformations, 339
transformative approach, 45
transition, 143, 157
translate, 362
transparency, 6, 199, 223
treaties, 180
trial and error, 118
tribes, 165
trust, 4, 8, 120
Tunisia, 24
turbulence, vi
turning point, 241, 261

U

UAE, 9, 35, 181
UK, 88
Ukraine, 112, 212
unanticipated events, 49
unanticipated outcomes, 26
uncertainty, vi, 104
unchartered, 136
UNESCO, 266
unexpected consequences, 103
UNHCR, 166
unintended consequences, 51
unintended effects, 14
unintended outcomes, xii
United Arab Emirates, 47
United Kingdom, 194

unknowability, 106
unknown, 58, 65
unknown futures, 114
Unknown Unknowns, 115
UN Partition Plan, 166
unprecedented, 108
UN Refugee Agency, 166
UNRWA, 166
urban challenges, 46
urbanization, 47
USA, 9, 25, 51, 162
US government, 27
USSR, 151
utility, 56
Uzbekistan, 186, 336

V
validate, 73
values, 3, 76, 371
vectors, 203
viability, 65
Viable Systems Model (VSM), 86, 92
Vietnam, 336
violence, 159
virtual ministry, 35
vision, 47, 125, 271
vision clarity, 71
vision prompts, 276
visualization, 75, 199
visualize, 273
voice, 139
volatility, 104
volatility, uncertainty, complexity, and ambiguity (VUCA), 19, 28, 104
vulnerability, 219, 341

W
war, 4, 57, 352
warning, 64
water scarcity, 4
weak signals, xii, 65
weather, 57
WEF, 6, 36
weights of the past, 77
well-being, 262
West, vi, 165
Western Europe, 145
WHO, 108
whole, 87
whole of government, xi
wicked problems, xi, 72
Wi-Fi, 297
workforce, 46
World Bank, 6
World Economic Forum, 122, 204
World Governments Summit, 137
world politics, 144
worldview, 80, 87, 281
World War, 145
World Wide Web, 21

X
X, 23
X-Road, 47

Y
Yemen, 167, 346

Z
zero-sum game, 203
Zimbabwe, 186

www.ingramcontent.com/pod-product-compliance
Lightning Source LLC
LaVergne TN
LVHW011659200926
848484LV00004B/1004